C1

ADVANCED

FORMULA

FOR EXAM SUCCESS

COURSEBOOK

without key

and **Interactive eBook**

CONTENTS

LISTENING	READING AND USE OF ENGLISH – GRAMMAR	SPEAKING	WRITING
Part 1 Multiple choice p9 **Skill focus:** Understanding attitude and opinion **Topic:** Fake news	**Part 2 Open cloze** p10 **Language focus:** Perfect and continuous tenses **Topic:** Identity **Grammar file:** Perfect and continuous tenses pp98–99 **Pronunciation:** Stress	**Part 1 Interview** p11 **Skill focus:** Answering personal questions **Topic:** First conversations	**Part 1 Essay** pp12–13 **Skill focus:** Structuring an essay **Topic:** Pet hates **Writing file:** Essay p130
p29	p5	p37	p19
Part 2 Sentence completion p19 **Skill focus:** Identifying cues **Topic:** Second place	**Part 4 Key word transformations** p20 **Language focus:** Passive forms **Topic:** Life on two wheels **Grammar file:** Passive forms pp100–101 **Pronunciation:** Phonemes	**Part 2 Individual long turn** p21 **Skill focus:** Comparing **Topic:** Doppelgangers	**Writing Part 2 Review** pp22–23 **Skill focus:** Using descriptive and dramatic language **Topic:** Sequels **Writing file:** Review p135
p31	p9	p39	p29
Part 3 Multiple choice p31 **Skill focus:** Identifying agreement and disagreement **Topic:** The third place	**Part 2 Open cloze** p32 **Language focus:** Conjunctions **Topic:** The Brontës **Grammar file:** Conjunctions pp102–103 **Pronunciation:** Pauses and intonation	**Part 3 Collaborative task** p33 **Skill focus:** Interacting in a two-way conversation **Topic:** Three cheers!	**Part 2 Email or letter** pp33–35 **Skill focus:** Using correct register **Topic:** Triathlons **Writing file:** Email or letter pp131–132
p33	p5	p41	p23
Part 4 Multiple matching p41 **Skill focus:** Understanding the main point **Topic:** Sense of direction	**Part 4 Key word transformation** p42 **Language focus:** Reported speech **Topic:** The fourth dimension **Grammar file:** Reported speech pp104–105 **Pronunciation:** Stress and intonation	**Part 4 Discussion** p43 **Skill focus:** Justifying your opinions **Topic:** 24-hour charity challenges	**Part 2 Proposal** pp44–45 **Skill focus:** Writing an effective proposal **Topic:** National celebrations **Writing file:** Proposal p133
p35	p9	p43	p25
Part 1 Multiple choice p53 **Skill focus:** Identifying purpose and function **Topic:** The work week	**Part 2 Open cloze** p54 **Language focus:** Conditional forms **Topic:** The superfood myth **Grammar file:** Conditional forms pp106–107 **Pronunciation:** Schwa /ə/	**Part 2 Individual long turn** p55 **Skill focus:** Speculating **Topic:** Coins	**Part 2 Report** pp56–57 **Skill focus:** Structuring a report **Topic:** Hotels **Writing file:** Report p134
p29	p5	p39	p27
Part 2 Sentence completion p63 **Skill focus:** Understanding specific information and stated opinion **Topic:** Route 66	**Part 4 Key word transformation** p64 **Language focus:** Verb and noun phrases **Topic:** Hexagons **Grammar file:** Verb and noun phrases pp108–109 **Pronunciation:** Word stress	**Part 3 Collaborative task** p65 **Skill focus:** Evaluating, referring, reassessing **Topic:** Being organised	**Part 1 Essay** pp66–67 **Skill focus:** Complex sentences **Topic:** Historical dates **Writing file:** Essay p130
p31	p9	p41	p25
Part 3 Multiple choice p75 **Skill focus:** Understanding feeling **Topic:** Overpopulation	**Part 2 Open cloze** p76 **Language focus:** Future tenses **Topic:** Sustainability **Grammar file:** Future tenses pp110–111 **Pronunciation:** Silent 'h'	**Part 4 Discussion** p77 **Skill focus:** Developing the discussion **Topic:** '7 Up'	**Part 2 Review** pp78–79 **Skill focus:** Engaging the reader **Topic:** Espionage **Writing file:** Review p135
p33	p5	p43	p29
Part 4 Multiple matching p85 **Skill focus:** Understanding gist **Topic:** Sleep	**Part 4 Key word transformation** p86 **Language focus:** Clause patterns **Topic:** Clouds **Grammar file:** Passive forms pp112–113 **Pronunciation:** Rising and falling intonation	**Part 2 Individual long turn** p87 **Skill focus:** Structuring a long turn **Topic:** Music	**Part 2 Email or letter** pp88–89 **Skill focus:** Writing a formal email or letter **Topic:** Coming of age **Writing file:** Email or letter pp131–132
p35	p9	p39	p23

EXAM FILE REFERENCE: pp2–17 Reading and Use of English Parts 1–7 | pp18–27 Writing Parts 1 and 2 | pp28–35 Listening Parts 1–4
pp36–43 Speaking Parts 1–4 | p44 Exam overview

Pearson Education Limited
KAO Two
KAO Park
Hockham Way
Harlow, Essex
CM17 9SR
England
and Associated Companies throughout the world.

https://english.com/portal

Written by Helen Chilton and Lynda Edwards

The right of Ashley Lodge to be identified as author of the mindfulness section of this work has been asserted by him in accordance with the Copyright, Designs and Patents Act 1988

First published 2021
Third impression 2022

ISBN: 978-1-292-39149-6

Set in Avenir Next LT Pro
Print and bound in Italy, by L.E.G.O. S.p.A.

Acknowledgements

The publishers are very grateful to the following advisers and teachers who contributed to the initial research and commented on earlier versions of this material:

Jacky Newbrook

Celine De Almeida, Joe Bonfiglioli, Charlotte Gérard, Michael Grew, Astrid Starrevelt

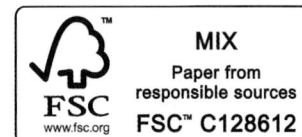

MIX
Paper from responsible sources
FSC™ C128612
www.fsc.org

VOCABULARY: Phrasal verbs

"" **That's one small step** for man, **one giant leap** for mankind. ""

1. Why do you think this line from the first Moon landing is so famous? What do you know about the first Moon landing?

2. 🎧 1.1 Listen to an extract from a news report. What does the reporter say about Armstrong's words after the first Moon landing?

3. How has space travel affected life on Earth since the first Moon landing?

4. 🎧 1.2 Listen to the rest of the news report. How many of your ideas from Ex 3 does the reporter mention? What else does he mention?

5. 🎧 1.3 Complete the phrasal verbs from the recordings with the correct preposition. Then listen again and check.

| forward   into   on (x2)   to   up   with (x2) |

1	come out	_____
2	associate	_____
3	move	_____
4	devote yourself	_____
5	throw yourself	_____
6	catch	_____
7	put	_____
8	spring	_____

6. Complete the text about creativity in space with the correct form of phrasal verbs from Ex 5. There are two which you do not need to use.

While many have [1]_____ into protecting our planet and making the way we live more sustainable, some scientists say it's inevitable that one day far in the future, we'll have to move to another planet.

We've [2]_____ from wondering about how to build structures and keep ourselves alive in space, to thinking about actual life in space. How would things like creative pursuits work without gravity?

The Space Exploration Initiative [3]_____ the idea of zero-gravity experiments to see how we'd cope with the challenges. So far, the programme has recruited people who work in fields not traditionally [4]_____ space, including lab scientists, chefs and artists. One designer who's already taken part was fascinated by how weightlessness affects not only the art itself but the artist, too. While creating a 3D 'drawing' in the air using a hot glue gun, she realised that creative people will always find a way to express themselves, and will [5]_____ the invention of new materials and techniques.

New cultures and ways of doing things would undoubtedly start [6]_____ if we lived in a weightless environment. Things like 'Space Art' perhaps!

7. Work in pairs. If you could be the first person to do something, what would it be?

1 Complete the travel survey. Then discuss your answers.

WHEN PLANNING YOUR HOLIDAY, HOW IMPORTANT IS

- the weather of the destination?
- having the opportunity to relax?
- it to consider the environment?
- the choice of travel company?

2 🎧 1.4 Listen to one person's response to one of the questions in the survey and answer the questions below.

1 Which different types of holiday does the speaker mention?

2 What reasons does she give for going on different holidays with different people?

3 Do you agree with her final comment?

3 Read a comment on a travel site. Why was the trip a disaster?

Weeks of planning and anticipation and then what happens? The dream road trip with a college friend proves to be a step too far for friendship and ends up with the two of us travelling in utter silence. It wasn't as though we didn't know each other well, but he certainly showed a different side of his character on the trip. He disagreed with every suggestion I made. If I bought croissants for a makeshift breakfast after a night in the tent, he'd go out to a pricey café. We didn't quite come to blows but it was close – and I couldn't wait for him to drop me off at home. I really wished I'd gone on my own!

EXAM FOCUS

Understanding inference and implication

A writer will often not say things directly in a text but will make implications. We might need to use synonyms, paraphrasing, exemplification and logic to interpret underlying meaning.

Text: The kitchen hygiene was quite disgusting and would never have passed any type of inspection.

Implication: Customers risked getting ill after eating there.

Text: Unfortunately, I disregarded the negative customer comments; I assumed the writers had it in for the hotel.

Implication: It was my own fault that we'd chosen a hotel that had a lot wrong with it.

4 Read the Exam focus. Choose which statements A–G are implied in the comment in Ex 3.

A The writer had doubts about travelling with their friend before the trip.

B An experience like this tests the strength of a relationship.

C The trip was decided at the last minute.

D The travellers had different opinions and didn't compromise.

E The writer thought their friend's attitude was unreasonable.

F The travellers used camp sites rather than hotels.

G The writer regrets their decision to go on this road trip.

EXAM BOOST p10

> Complete Exam file SECTION A on page 10.

5 You are going to read an article about a solo traveller. Why did the writer end up travelling solo and how did the trip go?

EXAM TASK

6 Read the article again. For questions 1–6, choose the answer (A, B, C or D) which you think fits best according to the text.

1 How did the writer feel about her friends' decision about their planned holiday?
- **A** reluctant to go without her friends
- **B** annoyed by their change in attitude
- **C** dismissive of their concerns about the proposed holiday
- **D** appreciative of their honesty

2 What contributed to the writer's determination to travel alone?
- **A** a certainty that she had the courage to face the challenge
- **B** a fear of missing out on a great opportunity
- **C** a desire to prove her friends wrong
- **D** a previous experience of a similar holiday

3 The writer views the online advice given as
- **A** useful information when considering solo travelling.
- **B** necessary advice for members of a group tour.
- **C** particularly valuable for people visiting China.
- **D** optional reading for the inexperienced traveller.

4 In paragraph 3 we learn that the writer
- **A** had an ingrained fear of flying.
- **B** had regrets about her decision to go on this trip.
- **C** was concerned about some of the other passengers.
- **D** caught the wrong connection at one airport.

5 The writer uses the example of being 'stung by taxis' to
- **A** warn people against travelling solo in certain countries.
- **B** describe an unavoidable occurrence when travelling.
- **C** show how she has profited from experience.
- **D** indicate why people should speak other languages.

6 What point is the writer making in the final paragraphs?
- **A** Solo travellers need to be aware of their vulnerability.
- **B** Travelling solo is more rewarding than in organised groups.
- **C** More unusual travel experiences are the most exciting.
- **D** Attitudes to solo travellers have changed for the better.

Speaking or writing

7 Discuss the questions.

1 What does the blog tell us about how the writer's attitude to solo travelling changed?

2 What would you say are the main advantages and disadvantages of doing other things alone?

8 Write the itinerary for a solo travel experience of seven days to your country or area. Give:

- reasons for your choice of accommodation, visits, transport, etc.
- advice about what to avoid.

GO ON. GO SOLO.

It was bravado at first, born of a desire to put my friends' backs up. In retrospect, I don't believe there was any real intention of following through on my decision, but there again, perhaps it was my subconscious talking when I announced that I would do the trip solo. I was feeling let down. A lot of time and energy had gone into discussing how best to profit from our hard-earned holiday, and I'd thought it was settled. The three of us had been back and forth over the destination, the timing, and of course the cost, and all that remained was to make the booking. At which point my two travelling companions got cold feet. Walking the Great Wall of China had sounded a fun challenge while it was still a dream, but when faced with the reality they backed down and opted instead for a beach package on a Greek island. I couldn't believe it. My reaction was a grumpy 'Well, I'll go on my own!' And I did.

I can't say that I didn't have second thoughts. Yes, I was apprehensive and the 'what-ifs' crowded in the more I thought about it. However, my friends' conviction that I would back down and a weird sense of elation combined to boost my determination to see it through. And determined I was, although lacking the confidence to organise the whole trip myself. I booked on a group tour for solos, relying on the travel company to organise accommodation, meals, guides and any transfers necessary. All I had to do was get myself to the starting point of the trip and dutifully read up on all the advice about preparation. Like, wearing in new walking boots beforehand and not packing them in hold baggage, in case it all got lost; everything being replaceable apart from those boots! The website I found was littered with similarly useful little tips that a potential adventurous solo traveller might hoard away for future reference. My excitement grew.

And then, at the airport, reality hit, and the apprehension took over. I'd never travelled long-haul before or experienced that panic of possibly missing a connection. Struggling to find the right queue in a heaving, noisy sea of passengers was daunting, and the second, third and fourth thoughts were coming thick and fast. Even when successfully boarded on the final leg of the journey, the apprehension didn't subside. I scanned the other passengers, wondering who might be in my group. Would we get along? Was I going to regret the whole thing? The happy truth is that I had the time of my life. Walking the Great Wall was as fascinating as I could possibly have imagined. And I made friends. I came back from that trip with promises to keep in touch with a host of lovely, interesting people. I savoured my achievement.

I had ventured out of my comfort zone and survived.

With that confidence I never looked back. It was empowering to realise that I was no longer dependent on the availability or preferences of friends, and I became ever more adventurous. Inevitably there have been the mistakes; getting stung by taxi drivers when I didn't know the language well; having to ditch half my clothes because I couldn't carry my backpack and more ... But I've learnt from them. About staying safe, about reading people and knowing who to trust. And knowing that the only person you can **totally** rely on is yourself. There isn't always someone there to lift your luggage! And yes, there might be a few lonely times and no one there to relive the memories with you on your return. But pitch all this against the freedom and the independence, and there's no contest!

I am now a seasoned solo traveller. The stigma that used to be attached to people travelling alone has gone. We are no longer seen as people with no friends, or easy targets for the unscrupulous. And although the more adventurous might choose to organise their own trips in far-flung places, there are many other options out there; travel operators are addressing this growing trend and offer a wide range of holidays for the individual traveller, from group camping tours in the Arctic to group luxury sunshine breaks in the Caribbean.

I am very glad that my show of bravado didn't end up being just a 'show'. It not only opened my eyes to learning more about the world, but also to learning more about myself and I hope that some of you reading this might be encouraged to do the same.

EXAM TRAINER | p24 p25 Ex 1

VOCABULARY: Fixed phrases

1 What does the expression 'one-hit wonder' mean? What reasons do you think contribute to only having one hit?

2 🎧 1.5 Listen to someone who became an overnight success by winning a TV talent show. What happened in the year following her win? Why didn't she go on to have a successful singing career?

3 🎧 1.6 Listen again and complete the sentences containing fixed phrases.

1 I wasn't convinced my singing would _____ the public's attention.

2 It was the live final and I smashed it! I definitely _____ my expectations!

3 I was **definitely** _____ **to** my new lifestyle!

4 I really felt like I'd made it, _____ of the fact that …

5 I was _____ of doing anything about it.

6 I'm _____ to think that shows like that are more about creating short-term celebrities.

7 All things _____ , my fifteen minutes of fame was an incredible experience.

8 Not many people get to _____ an ambition so young!

4 Match the fixed phrases 1–8 in Ex 3 to their definitions a–h.

a achieve something that you were hoping to achieve

b not able to do something

c when you weigh up all the parts or events of a situation

d hold a particular opinion, but not very strongly

e make someone feel very interested in something

f without being affected or influenced by something

g be acceptable or convenient for a particular person or in a particular situation

h do better than you hope to do

EXAM BOOST p2

▶ Complete Exam file SECTION A on page 2.

EXAM TASK

5 For questions 1–8, read the text below and decide which answer (A, B, C or D) best fits each gap. There is an example at the beginning (0).

One-novel wonders

First-time novelists are often one-time novelists. They **(0)** __B__ everyone's attention with a best-selling debut and shoot to literary fame – take *The Great Gatsby* by F. Scott Fitzgerald, for example. Having **(1)** _____ their expectations, many are either boosted by their success or struck by writer's block, **(2)** _____ that the public are expecting a follow-up to hit the shelves almost immediately. This perceived pressure can result in writers feeling **(3)** _____ of repeating their success, sometimes leaving fans waiting decades for their next book.

But there are also writers who have no intention of putting pen to paper – or fingers to keyboard – ever again after **(4)** _____ their ambition to become a published author. **(5)** _____ of their success, these writers are often happy enough to have got their 'own' story out there but do not **(6)** _____ to spending their lives writing. And then there are writers who just **(7)** _____ to produce something that **(8)** _____ with a new trend or philosophy. Timing can be everything, but one thing's for certain: the reasons for having a one-hit wonder are as individual as the stories – and writers – themselves.

0	A fascinate	B capture	C excite	D seize
1	A excelled	B beaten	C exceeded	D bettered
2	A persuaded	B convinced	C determined	D minded
3	A helpless	B unable	C lacking	D incapable
4	A attaining	B realising	C succeeding	D performing
5	A Albeit	B Nonetheless	C Regardless	D Notwithstanding
6	A desire	B aspire	C inspire	D require
7	A result	B fancy	C arise	D happen
8	A coincides	B occurs	C equals	D coordinates

Speaking or writing

▶ Go to page 92 for these exercises.

EXAM TRAINER | p7
p8 Exs 1–2

LISTENING - Part 1 Multiple choice

1 The photo shows the kind of thing that might happen on 1 April. What do you know about this day? Do you find this kind of joke funny?

2 🎧 **1.7** Listen to a psychologist talking about laughter and jokes. What role do they play in our lives?

EXAM FOCUS

Understanding attitude and opinion

Speakers don't always indicate that they're about to offer an opinion by using phrases like 'In my opinion' or 'I think'. You may therefore have to listen for the gist of their argument, and work out what the speaker thinks from the whole of what they say. Listen out for synonyms and paraphrasing. The following parts of speech can signal attitude and opinion.

Adverbs

Interestingly, …

Perhaps …

Adjectives

It can be very embarrassing …

Modal verbs

We shouldn't pretend …

3 Read the Exam focus then match the sentences 1–6 with their paraphrases a–f.

1 They intended it as a light-hearted joke.
2 It provides an outlet for stress.
3 It would fall short of expectations.
4 Within reason, of course!
5 This poses a real threat.
6 I'd be pretty red-faced at being taken in.

a It could cause serious problems.
b It won't be as good as you thought.
c As long as it's fair.
d It was supposed to be amusing.
e It would be embarrassing to be fooled.
f It helps you deal with pressure.

EXAM BOOST p28

▶ Complete Exam file SECTION A on page 28.

EXAM TASK

4 🎧 **1.8** You will hear three different extracts. For questions 1–6, choose the answer (A, B or C) which fits best according to what you hear. There are two questions for each extract.

Extract One

You hear two friends talking about April Fools' Day jokes.

1 According to the woman, the spaghetti on trees story shown on TV
  A made people who believed the story look silly.
  B was not well received by some viewers.
  C should have been shown on a different programme.

2 The man thinks that April Fool's Day
  A helps us deal with unreleased energy.
  B reminds us to be cautious about the kind of joke we play.
  C provides us the opportunity to get revenge on others.

Extract Two

You hear two journalists talking about fake news.

3 What does the woman say about fake news?
  A It does less damage than people believe.
  B It can be divided into distinct categories.
  C Its concept is a relatively recent one.

4 How does the man feel about it?
  A fortunate not to have been deceived by it
  B embarrassed to have repeated incorrect information
  C surprised so many people are convinced it is trustworthy

Extract Three

You hear two financial experts talking about avoiding being a victim of fraud.

5 What is the man doing?
  A describing some of the latest cons
  B highlighting the importance of internet security
  C pointing out the challenge of recognising cons

6 The woman suggests that listeners
  A pause before taking action.
  B learn from previous mistakes.
  C seek advice from recognised institutions.

Speaking or writing

5 Discuss the questions.

- How sceptical are you about what you read online?
- Have you ever been taken in by fake news items? How did that make you feel?

6 Some people think fake news is harmful but others see it as a joke. What do you think? Write your opinion, giving reasons, and then compare your ideas with a partner.

EXAM FILE p5

GRAMMAR FILE pp98–99

GRAMMAR: Perfect and continuous tenses

1 We're all 'one of a kind', they say. But, what makes each of us unique?

2 🎧 1.9 Listen to a scientist talking about fingerprints. What, in his opinion, is the most likely reason that we have them?

3 🎧 1.10 Listen again and answer the questions.

1 Why have scientists dismissed the idea that fingerprints help us grip things?

2 What happens as our fingerprints glide over surfaces?

3 What does this do?

4 Why doesn't it matter how we hold something?

4 Complete the sentences from the talk with the correct form of the verbs in brackets.

1 This is a question that scientists **have** long _____ (ponder).

2 But scientists **have** _____ (dismiss) this theory.

3 Although it was something that **had** _____ (puzzle) scientists for a long time …

4 Scientists who **were** _____ (work) in Paris conducted an experiment …

5 They **had** _____ (work) on their experiment for a while when they finally discovered that …

6 This helps us to sense what we**'re** _____ (hold).

5 Complete the sentences about unusual animals and their unique characteristics. Use an appropriate form of the verbs in brackets. There may be more than one correct answer.

1 Manx cats, which _____ (live) on the Isle of Man for at least 200 years, have little or no tail due to a naturally occurring genetic mutation.

2 As we _____ (peer) into the depths of the ocean, we noticed the natural 'headlights' of the pinecone fish, which lights up its prey with its jaw when hunting.

3 I _____ (film) in the mountains of Central Asia for weeks before I finally spotted a snow leopard – unlike other large cats, they can't roar, so you'd never hear one approaching!

4 Leafy sea dragon fish _____ (evade) capture by predators for centuries with their camouflaged form that looks just like seaweed.

5 Fran _____ (just, finish) photographing a horned lizard when it suddenly squirted at her from its eyes – one of the stranger traits of this particular animal!

6 Is that a mimic octopus? What _____ (it, disguise) itself as? I know it can mimic a lot of other sea creatures as a defence mechanism but I've no idea what that is!

🟦 **EXAM BOOST** p4

> Complete Exam file SECTION A on page 4.

EXAM TASK

6 For questions 1–8, read the text below and think of the word which best fits each gap. Use only one word in each gap. There is an example at the beginning (0).

How ears (or stripes) can identify individuals

Humans are **(0)** _____NOT_____ the only mammals to have features that uniquely identify individuals. Other primates also have finger and toe prints, no two of which are the same. Scientists **(1)** _____ recently discovered that koalas have fingerprints, too, which are just **(2)** _____ individual. And now, the stripes and spots of animals such as cattle and zebra, which zoologists of the past **(3)** _____ , until recently, only ever thought of as camouflage, are being used in conservation projects to track the movements of individuals.

Perhaps humans will be tracked in future, too. Our faces, heartbeats and even the shape of our ears are also unique, and these features could have wider biometric applications. **(4)** _____ you're anything like most people, you've probably **(5)** _____ using the same passwords for the last few years, and **(6)** _____ now becoming concerned that someone will eventually crack your 'code' and steal your identity. But biometric authentication is likely **(7)** _____ be at the forefront of rapid advances in IT security, and rely on unique personal data to confirm identity **(8)** _____ the use of touchscreens or other recognition devices.

Speaking or writing

> Go to page 92 for these exercises.

EXAM TRAINER | p11 p12 Ex 1

1. What impression do you think you might make on someone who meets you for the first time? Is this a true reading of your personality? Why? / Why not?

2. Do the quiz and compare your answers with your partner. If you choose 'it depends', explain on what.

3. 🎧 1.11 Listen to two candidates in the speaking test answering a question from Part 1. Which is the more appropriate answer, A or B? Why?

4. Read the Exam focus and check your ideas.

EXAM FOCUS

Answering personal questions

Avoid short, abrupt answers by extending your responses in different ways.

- Explain your reasons: I sometimes get stuck for words …
- Give an interesting example: Like at a social event and we both know the host …
- Give a contrasting idea to show balance: … at other times, like at a work interview …
- Use linkers to clarify what you're saying: Whereas …

/// EXAM BOOST p36

▶ Complete the Exam file exercises on page 36.

5. 🎧 1.12 Work in pairs. Read the Part 1 questions and listen to two candidate responses to questions 1 and 2. Discuss how the candidates could have extended their answers.

1. Would you say that you lead a healthy lifestyle? (Why? / Why not?)
2. Do you feel that your week includes as much free time as you'd like? (Why? / Why not?)
3. What childhood memory still makes you smile? (Why?)
4. What has been your most interesting holiday experience? (Why?)
5. Where would be your ideal place to live? (Why?)
6. What do you see yourself doing in five years' time?
7. If you could learn another language, what would it be? (Why?)
8. Which of your plans for the next few weeks do you think will prove to be most interesting? (Why?)

EXAM FILE p37

FIRST CONVERSATIONS

1. **Do you often strike up conversations with strangers, for example when travelling?**
   a) Yes, I think it's a great way to pass the time.
   b) No, I like to keep myself to myself because I'm a bit shy.
   c) It depends.

2. **When you're introduced to someone for the first time, do you find it easy to maintain a conversation?**
   a) Very easy. I'm never lost for words!
   b) Not really. It's OK if I find some common ground between us.
   c) It depends.

3. **Would you say that you tend to dominate conversations in general?**
   a) Perhaps. Once you get me started on something, it's sometimes hard to get me to stop!
   b) It's probably the opposite. It takes a while for me to come out of my shell – I think I come over as uninterested in people from time to time.
   c) It depends.

4. **Do you use humour to break the ice when talking to someone for the first time?**
   a) Yes, I do. If you can make someone laugh, it makes them feel more relaxed.
   b) Wow, no! I can never remember jokes. And if you don't know someone well, the jokes could fall flat!
   c) It depends.

5. **In a first conversation with someone, are there any topics you would steer clear of?**
   a) I think most topics are fair game for a first conversation. I can read people pretty well and usually know what to avoid.
   b) I'd avoid anything controversial – like politics, or very personal areas, like relationships.
   c) It depends.

6. Read the full set of questions in Ex 5 again. Which questions ask about these topics?

   past experience   plans for the future   routine

7. In pairs, think of another question that could be asked about each of these topics. Exchange your questions with another pair and answer them. Then share your questions with the class and find the most interesting question.

EXAM TASK

8. Work in pairs and take turns to ask and answer the remaining Part 1 questions in Ex 5. Remember to expand your answers using information from the Exam focus box.

EXAM TRAINER | pp88–90

1 What do you think is happening in the picture? Which person would you be in this situation?

2 🎧 1.13 Listen to a teacher explaining a game called Room 101. What does the game involve?

3 Work in pairs. Why might people want to put these things in Room 101? Which would you choose?

> cold callers   computer viruses   English grammar
> homework   plastic packaging   queues   rudeness
> social media   winter

4 Write down three more things people might want to put in. Swap with another pair. Choose one item from the list and one of you talk for a minute saying why it should go in. Your partner should talk for a minute about why it shouldn't go in.

5 Read the essay task and discuss what you might include in it.

Your class has had a discussion about aspects of working life today that concern many people. You have made the notes below:

> **Things that concern many people about working life today:**
> - constant connectivity
> - commuting
> - hot desking
>
> Some opinions expressed in the discussion:
> 'You can never get away from work these days.'
> 'Sitting in traffic jams is so frustrating.'
> 'Never knowing where you'll be working is really off-putting.'

Write an essay discussing **two** of the concerns in your notes. You should **explain which concern is the most serious**, giving **reasons** in support of your answer.

You may, if you wish, make use of the opinions expressed in the discussion, but you should use your own words as far as possible.

EXAM FILE p19
VOCABULARY FILE pp114-115
WRITING FILE p130

6 Read the body of a student's essay and compare your ideas.

INTRODUCTION
....

MAIN PARAGRAPH 1
Let's consider constant connectivity. Whether people work regular or flexible office hours, constant connectivity means that they are potentially always available and unable to completely switch off. Work can intrude on free time and personal lives. While the ability to get immediate feedback or answers to questions can be important, people also need space to develop a good work–life balance, which in turn makes workers more productive in the long term.

MAIN PARAGRAPH 2
Another concern is the frustration caused by the daily commute. With increased pressure on both road and public transport systems, delays and traffic jams are inevitable. Driving to work risks encountering hold-ups due to road works or increasingly heavy traffic. And taking trains leaves passengers vulnerable to delays caused by signal failures or weather-related problems.

CONCLUSION
....

EXAM FOCUS

Structuring an essay

Structure your essay clearly so that the target reader is taken logically through your ideas. Think about:

Introduction: This should engage the reader and outline or give background to the issues you will be dealing with, but not go into details of what you will include in the main paragraphs, or your final decision.

Main paragraphs: These should develop the outline in the introduction and deal with separate points, including your reasons for an opinion, with examples where possible.

Conclusion: This should review or summarise the main points you have made, but not repeat the same examples or use the same words. It should be balanced, but still clarify your point of view, giving a reason for your final decision.

WRITING - Part 1 Essay

1

7 Read the Exam focus and choose which would be a better introduction (A or B) and conclusion (C or D) for the essay.

Introductions

A A lot of people are not happy with aspects of their working lives. This is because of things like constant connectivity – always being at the end of a phone – and commuting to work, with all the delays there are today. I think both these things are concerning today, but the worst, in my opinion, is constant connectivity.

B Working life has changed significantly over the last few decades. Advanced communications technology has improved efficiency at work and faster transport systems have allowed people to move out of cities and towns and commute to work, giving them a greater choice of where to make their home. But what about the downsides?

Conclusions

C For me, the more serious concern is the intrusion of constant connectivity on people's work–life balance. Whereas commuting can be seriously frustrating, systems can be improved with investment, and journey times can be staggered to spread the congestion. Constant connectivity, on the other hand, seems to have become widely accepted as part and parcel of the working day and needs to be addressed and limited by those in authority before it dominates people's lives completely.

D So, to conclude, I think constant connectivity is the worst issue because people can't switch off and this means they don't have a good work–life balance, which is very important. Commuting to work every day can be frustrating, too, and wastes a lot of time, but overall, it's constant connectivity that is most concerning.

EXAM BOOST p18

> Complete Exam file SECTION A on page 18.

EXAM TASK

8 Read the essay task and choose which two points to write about. Note down ideas to include for the different paragraphs. Compare your choice and ideas with your partner's.

You have listened to a radio discussion about factors that people think are important for a happy life.

What is important for a happy life:
- close friends
- good level of health and fitness
- money

Some opinions expressed in the discussion:

'Friends are there to support you whenever you need them.'

'You feel good in yourself if you're fit and healthy.'

'If you haven't got enough money, you worry all the time.'

Write an essay discussing **two** of the factors in your notes. You should **explain which factor is the most important**, giving **reasons** in support of your answer.

You may, if you wish, make use of the opinions expressed in the discussion, but you should use your own words as far as possible.

9 Write your essay in 220-260 words, remembering the advice from the Exam focus.

EXAM TRAINER | pp52–53 p54 Exs 6–7

13

PRACTICE TASKS

READING AND USE OF ENGLISH – PART 1

1 Read the text below and decide which answer (A, B, C or D) best fits each gap.

BUILDING ON MARS

If NASA's proposed 2030s mission to Mars becomes a reality, astronauts will **(0)** __A__ need a base. All things **(1)** _____ , transporting building materials 225 million kilometres across space would not only be impractical, but phenomenally expensive, too. So, how could living spaces feasibly be created on the Red Planet?

For those who may be **(2)** _____ of the idea, it isn't actually as much of a **(3)** _____ into science fiction as it sounds. Mars has an abundance of regolith, a layer of crushed rock found throughout the solar system. It's certainly useable, but scientists have **(4)** _____ difficulties in developing technology that can bind it together successfully. Doing so would make it more **(5)** _____ to 3-D printing, the proposed building technique that would be carried out by robots.

What also **(6)** _____ a challenge is creating a material that allows structures to stand the test of time. The most likely contender is a concrete-like substance, similar to conventional construction materials used on Earth. Though the **(7)** _____ hasn't occurred yet, scientists are on their way to creating such materials, and life on Mars may not actually **(8)** _____ too far ahead.

	A	B	C	D
0	A undoubtedly	B nevertheless	C indeed	D utterly
1	A examined	B considered	C decided	D evaluated
2	A pessimistic	B dubious	C sceptical	D hesitant
3	A leap	B spring	C fall	D skip
4	A come round to	B come down with	C come up against	D come out in
5	A proper	B suited	C capable	D accepted
6	A describes	B exhibits	C displays	D presents
7	A breakthrough	B discovery	C outcome	D progress
8	A rest	B lay	C sit	D lie

READING AND USE OF ENGLISH – PART 2

2 Read the text below and think of the word which best fits each gap. Use only one word in each gap.

HOW TO MAKE THE MOST OF YOUR 'STAYCATION'

If you are **(0)** ___NOT___ travelling this summer, you might want to consider a staycation instead: a week or two staying at home **(1)** _____ no contact from work or college. It might sound boring but if you follow our tips, it'll be far **(2)** _____ it. You can have a 'real' holiday in your own home and don't need to spend a penny **(3)** _____ you want to.

The most crucial aspect of any holiday is getting some quality rest and relaxation. You can't completely switch off when your phone's pinging every ten seconds, **(4)** _____ why not unplug and unwind? Catch up on those novels that have kept **(5)** _____ put to one side, or start that craft project you've been planning but never quite got round to.

Once refreshed, go out and about. Expose **(6)** _____ to things you haven't done before: find a new walking route or discover a new place to hang out. Have a break from anyone who gets **(7)** _____ your nerves and seek out those **(8)** _____ company you enjoy. You may never leave home again!

2 | TWO

VOCABULARY: Nouns from phrasal verbs

1 How many famous mountains can you name in a minute?

2 🎧 2.1 How do you think the mountain K2 got its name? Listen and check.

3 Add the correct preposition to the verbs in brackets to form nouns used in the talk. Complete each sentence with the correct form of the noun.

1 The _____ from experienced mountaineers has resulted in more accessible routes to the summit. (PUT)

2 Everything had been planned to the last detail, but from the _____ the expedition seemed doomed to failure. (SET)

3 The interview to select climbers to join the expedition was far from a _____ also wanted evidence of our experience and put us through a gruelling 3-day climb to see how we coped.

4 The ascent was halted due to an _____ of a nasty virus in the team. (BREAK)

5 You should never attempt a difficult climb without the _____ of a good team. (BACK)

6 _____ in technology have made mountain expeditions safer, although they will never be risk-free. (BREAK)

7 Having reached the halfway point, the climbers experienced some _____ and had to return to base camp. (SET)

8 They're discussing whether to halt plans for a winter ascent of the mountain at this very moment, but as yet we have no idea what the _____ will be. (COME)

4 Complete the statements with nouns from Ex 3. Then say whether the statements are true for you. Compare your answers with a partner and give reasons or examples.

1 If there's an _____ of flu at college, it's inevitable that I'll catch it. I catch everything going.

2 I'm convinced that there'll be a _____ in how to tackle climate change in the near future.

3 I'm interested in the _____ of any international talks about penalties for illegal deforestation.

4 If I have a _____ in the early stages of a project, it can really demotivate me.

5 I think all local people should have some _____ into decisions that could significantly affect their neighbourhood.

6 I have a good friend who I can always depend on for _____ if I'm having an argument with someone.

5 Work in pairs. Take turns to give your partner one of the nouns from Ex 3. As quickly as possible, your partner should suggest an associated situation when it could be used.

A: setback

B: career plans

15

1 Work in pairs. Discuss the questions.

1 What decisions do you remember making today?

2 What's the biggest decision you have made this week?

3 Do you find you make better decisions at different times of the day?

4 How difficult do you find it to make decisions about these things?

> buying clothes   what to eat   what to post on social media   when to exercise
> when to message or call friends   when to spend and when to save

2 🎧 **2.2** Listen to three people discussing a question on a TV panel show. Which question from Ex 1 did the presenter ask? Which two speakers agree? Why?

EXAM FOCUS

Identifying contrasting opinions

When identifying how writers' opinions differ in texts, we need to:

Identify the section of each text that contains the relevant information: scan texts to find references to the topic you need to compare.

Consider use of contrasting linkers, or phrases: While I'm appreciative of the importance of … I feel that …

Consider different ways opinions can be expressed:

- verbs of opinion: I don't believe that … / … for me, it's not worth considering
- statements that illustrate an opinion rather than give it directly: Instead of I think the new design is terrible use I'm appalled at the new design for … , etc.

3 Read the Exam focus and answer the question.

Read the posts and decide which writer has a different opinion from the others about the value of seeking help when needing to make an important decision. Highlight the phrases that informed your answer.

A There are those crossroads we come to at various points when a decision can be life-changing. On those occasions I would definitely advise running options past someone, or some people, whose opinions you respect. Two heads are often better than one and although you may not necessarily eventually follow what they suggest, it can sometimes give you a new way of looking at the situation.

B Some people turn to others when they have to make an important decision; they might ask a family member, a friend or even a teacher for advice. While I'm appreciative of other's support when deciding something big, I feel that in the end, it is down to us as individuals, and we shouldn't let ourselves be swayed by others' points of view, however well-meaning they might be. We need to trust our own judgement.

C I was recently offered promotion at work, which entailed working abroad for six months of the year. I spent ages chasing the pros and cons around in my head, wanting to take the responsibility for making the decision myself. Eventually I opened up to a really good friend, who talked the whole thing through with me. I truly believe that people who know you well, with no agenda of their own, can help you look at things from different perspectives, and, while not making the decision for you, help you to decide what's in your best interests.

EXAM BOOST p12

⟩ Complete Exam file SECTION A on page 12.

4 What do you think 'decision fatigue' means? Read the texts on p17 and check your ideas.

EXAM TASK

5 You are going to read four reviews of a documentary about decision fatigue. For questions 1–4, choose from the reviews A–D. The reviews may be chosen more than once.

Which reviewer

has a different opinion from the others about the way the documentary was structured?

1 [ ]

shares C's attitude to the credibility of the research for the documentary?

2 [ ]

has a different view to B regarding the impact on viewers' habits?

3 [ ]

expresses a different opinion to D regarding their anticipation of a subsequent programme?

4 [ ]

Speaking or writing

6 Discuss in pairs.

1 Do you agree that people are unlikely to change their approach to making decisions because of a documentary like this? Why / Why not?

2 Are there any important decisions you will have to make in the coming months? What will you need to consider? What might be the potential consequences?

7 Write a comment for the website about how decision fatigue affects or doesn't affect you. Give examples.

IN TWO MINDS?

A Decision-making is something everyone has to do, every hour, every day of their lives, so a programme that explains what can affect our ability to do this was both educational and potentially helpful for those who watched it. The idea that our brains only have a limited amount of energy to use on decisions was well-explained through a carefully planned and well-filmed sequence of interviews and podcasts from the general public, although I have to say that some of the claims weren't really backed up by any real evidence. It was neither too serious nor too light, and I am sure it will be of help to many people, who, like myself, sometimes leave things like essay writing until late in the evening and then sit looking at a blank screen for ages! I know full well that if I leave it until the next day, the same task will take a fraction of the time. I shall definitely try to alter my work pattern.

B It had been billed as a documentary that could change the whole way we approach decision making, and was produced by an excellent team. As a result, I was expecting something rather special and I have to admit that it didn't disappoint. The attention to detail was impeccable. I followed up some of their survey sources online and they were totally accurate, which cannot be said of all documentaries! As a writer, my whole day is spent making decisions of varying complexity and importance, and I know that late in the day I can struggle to come up with ideas.
The documentary underlined very clearly, through a series of well-linked and logical stages, why this happens and I, personally, shall definitely take on board many of the suggestions. It will be interesting to hear what else they mention in the next programmes. However, I would say that most people are so settled in their own ways that although they may initially profess interest in the ideas put forward, they will eventually fall back into old routines.

C I'd heard about decision fatigue before watching the documentary, possibly because it had come up on a news programme at some point, and I found the idea intriguing. However, I don't think the programme told us anything that was very new, and certainly not life-changing for anyone. In my opinion, the fact that our brains get worse at making decisions as the day goes on, seems to me pretty logical. On the other hand, I was impressed by the way the documentary was put together, and I think the producers got the basic ideas across very well with some pretty sound statistics to back up their theories, in an entertaining way. The lack of an original approach has, unfortunately, put me off watching the rest of the series, although I can understand why other viewers might think differently.

D It's quite incredible that we take so many things that our brains do for granted. Last night's excellent documentary on decision fatigue was a case in point, and I am definitely looking forward to the next instalment. It appears that after a lengthy period of making choices our ability to weigh up pros and cons wanes and we end up taking the easiest and often most reckless options. Apparently, when the mental energy required to make decisions is depleted, so too are our self-control and our willpower.
So, that's why we shouldn't make important decisions or go online shopping late at night – note to self! Great documentary, in spite of all the very technical bits, which I think should have come at the end, rather than the beginning.

VOCABULARY: Prefixes

1 What things usually come in twos? Think about:

> everyday objects   food   people   things you wear

2 🎧 **2.3** Listen to part of a radio phone-in about losing things. How does the caller feel about losing things? What does the memory expert say about why this happens? What does the expert suggest the caller do?

3 🎧 **2.4** Add the following prefixes to the words in the box to make words from the recording: dis-, il-, im-, in-, inter-, ir-, mis-, re- and un-. Then match the prefixed words with the definitions below. Listen again and check.

> act   consider   logical   miss   noticed   placing
> possibly   regular   significant

1   not sensible or reasonable
2   too small or unimportant to consider or worry about
3   refuse to consider an idea because you think it isn't serious, true or important
4   have an effect on each other
5   not happening at times that are an equal distance from each other
6   lose something for a short time by putting it in the wrong place
7   without being seen
8   extremely
9   think again about a decision or opinion and decide if you want to change it

4 Look at the root words in the box. Form new words with the prefixes and add them to the table. You may need to change the form of the root word, too, e.g.
able ➜ ability ➜ inability.

> able   act   comfort   deny   doubt   law   lay
> lead   organise   person   respond   sane

dis-	il-	im-	in-	inter-	ir-	mis-	re-	un-
			inability					

EXAM BOOST p6

> Complete Exam file SECTION A on page 6.

EXAM TASK

5 For questions 1–8, read the text below. Use the word given in capitals at the end of some of the lines to form a word that fits in the gap in the same line. There is an example at the beginning (0).

Why **socks** don't come out of the **wash in pairs**

(0) __MISPLACES__ 1.3 socks every month. We believe our socks disappear in the wash, yet it seems somewhat **(1)** _____ that having put them all into the machine, some still come out without their partner.	**PLACE** **LOGIC**
It may appear to be an **(2)** _____ problem, but intrigued scientists have come up with a formula to predict the likelihood of socks going missing: (L (p x f) + C (t x s)) - (P x A).*	**SIGNIFY**
How attentive we are during our **(3)** _____ with clothes and machine, and how positive we feel about doing the washing, has an effect on how successful it is. Washing at **(4)** _____ intervals rather than a specified time each week could result in sock loss which goes **(5)** _____ , with them straying under beds or radiators in the meantime. And the bigger and more complex the load (the combination of darks, whites and fabric types), the more likely it is we'll **(6)** _____ the fact that some socks were already missing when we loaded the washer.	**ACT** **REGULAR** **NOTICE** **LOOK**
Washing isn't an **(7)** _____ difficult task, but perhaps we all too often **(8)** _____ the impact of abandoning our socks where we take them off, leading to them 'vanishing'!	**POSSIBLE** **ESTIMATE**

*(Laundry size (number of people in household x frequency of washes in a week) + washing complexity (types of wash, e.g. darks and whites x number of socks washed in a week)) – (positivity towards doing the laundry x degree of attention to the task)

Speaking or writing

> Go to page 92 for these exercises.

EXAM TRAINER | p16 p17 Exs 1–2

1 Look at the statements and decide the extent to which you agree or disagree with them. Then discuss your ideas with a partner.

1 It's better to win silver than bronze.

2 Second is nowhere.

3 Coming second makes people try harder next time.

4 No one remembers who came second.

2 🎧 **2.5** Listen to a young woman called Chloe talking about winning a silver award for business. How did she feel about this? How will this affect her business?

EXAM FOCUS

Identifying cues

When listening to a long monologue and completing the sentences, it's important to ensure you're focusing on the relevant section of the recording. The information you complete is in the same order as you hear it. There are cues on the question paper which help you follow the recording and identify the word or short phrase you need in order to complete the sentences. This information could come before and/or after the gap, and may use a combination of the words you hear, and paraphrases:

What you hear: ... the aim of the awards ... / ... first and foremost in our company's approach ...

What you read: the main objective of the awards / principal business goal

3 Read the Exam focus and look at the sentences which summarise Chloe's talk in Ex 2. Highlight the words and phrases which you think would help you follow the recording. What kind of word(s) might be missing in each case?

Chloe explains that the main objective of the awards is to boost the **(1)** _____ of family companies.

Chloe says that **(2)** _____ is their principal business goal, which won her company its award.

Chloe advertises her company's dishes as **(3)** '_____'.

Chloe hopes her business will be involved in **(4)** _____ in the future.

4 🎧 **2.6** Listen again and complete the sentences in Ex 3.

5 Match the paraphrases (1–5) from the sentences in Ex 3 with words and phrases (A–E) from Chloe's talk.

1 boost
2 which won her company
3 advertises
4 hopes to be involved in
5 in the future

A 'written on our promotional material'
B 'is on our radar'
C 'going forwards'
D 'what we were recognised for'
E 'raise'

EXAM BOOST p30

▶ Complete Exam file SECTION A on page 30.

EXAM TASK

6 🎧 **2.7** You will hear a sports psychologist called Oscar Wainwright talking on a podcast about the benefits of finishing second in sports events. For questions 1–8, complete the sentences with a word or short phrase.

THE BENEFITS

OF FINISHING
SECOND

Oscar says that the person who wins has to deal with **(1)** _____ from the public.

Oscar says runners-up do not miss out on **(2)** _____ from colleagues about their accomplishments.

Research indicates that those who come second do better in terms of **(3)** _____ as well as higher earnings after retirement.

Though physically similar, those desperate to come first tend to suffer poorer **(4)** _____ .

Second-finishers can feel more **(5)** _____ about not coming first than those who often win.

Oscar says that young people in particular face many **(6)** _____ in life and being the best is important.

Oscar has observed that **(7)** _____ is important for athletes still aiming to reach the top.

Oscar uses the word **(8)** '_____' to describe sportspeople who are influential but have never won.

Speaking or writing

7 Tell your partner about a time when you came first, second or last in something, such as a sports event or competition. How did you react? How do you feel about finishing somewhere in the middle?

8 Oscar says that there are many demands placed on young people to be the best these days. What do you think?

EXAM FILE p9

GRAMMAR FILE pp100–101

GRAMMAR: Passive forms

1   What does the phrase 'it's like riding a bicycle' mean?

2   Turn to page 94 and read the article about the history of the bicycle. Which bicycle(s)

1   is thought to have been created by a famous painter?

2   has been in use for around 40 years?

3   inspired others to develop it further?

4   was first to be produced on a large scale?

5   is considered the forerunner of modern bicycles?

3   Look at the passive forms in bold in the text on page 94. Do they refer to the past, present or future?

4   🎧 **2.8** Listen to a woman called Maddie, who works in a bike shop. What is unusual about the bike shop? Name three things that Maddie mentions which are unusual.

1   _____

2   _____

3   _____

5   Rewrite the summary sentences about Maddie's bike shop in an appropriate passive form.

1   Maddie prices her second-hand bikes for any budget.

2   We have donated hundreds of bikes to overseas communities.

3   No one had ever given these communities access to bikes before.

4   You can have a coffee while someone is fixing your bike.

5   Hopefully people will still be saying the bike shop is the best in the area in another ten years.

6   Maddie heard about a tandem bike ride someone was organising.

7   Sponsors helped participants raise a lot of money for the charity.

8   People have been holding campaigns around the country to make cycling proficiency part of the curriculum.

/// **EXAM BOOST** p8

> Complete Exam file SECTION A on page 8.

EXAM TASK

6   For questions 1–6, complete the second sentence so that it has a similar meaning to the first sentence, using the word given. Do not change the word given. You must use between three and six words, including the word given. Here is an example (0).

0   I didn't learn to drive because I couldn't afford it.

AFFORDED

If I could have AFFORDED IT, I WOULD HAVE LEARNED to drive.

1   I think it's a mistake when schools don't include individual sports in their curriculum.

NOT

In my opinion, it is a mistake when individual sports _____ in school curricula.

2   When people have built exercise into their daily routine, they tend to stick with it.

IT

People tend to stick with exercise when _____ their daily routine.

3   I went and did a bit of shopping in town while the mechanic fixed my moped.

BEING

While my moped _____ the mechanic, I went and did a bit of shopping in town.

4   The bike shop owner will fire Josefina if she makes any more costly mistakes.

DISMISSED

Josefina _____ the bike shop by the owner if she makes any more costly mistakes.

5   People will be talking about the findings of that sports psychology research for years to come.

BE

The findings of that sports psychology research _____ about for years to come.

6   Johanna probably wouldn't be a tennis champion today if she hadn't grown up next to a tennis club.

BROUGHT

If Johanna _____ next to a tennis club, she probably wouldn't be a tennis champion today.

Speaking or writing

> Go to page 92 for these exercises.

EXAM TRAINER | p20 / p21 Ex 1

1 Work in pairs and discuss your answers to the questions.

1 How would you feel if you found someone on social media who
   a) had exactly the same name as you?
   b) looked very similar to you?
   Has this ever happened to you? What did / would you do?

2 Do you believe that each of us has a doppelganger, someone who is a mirror copy of ourselves?

3 Why do you think some people are so interested in finding their doppelganger that they go on special websites to find them?

2 🎧 **2.9 How likely do you think it is to find an exact doppelganger?** Listen to an expert on facial recognition on a radio programme talking about doppelgangers, and check your answer.

3 Look at two pictures of pairs of people who have a similar appearance and read the question. Discuss in pairs what points you might include when answering the question. Your pictures show people who look similar to each other for different reasons. Compare the pictures and say what the relationships between these pairs of people might be like and how the people might be feeling.

4 🎧 **2.10 Listen to a student answering the question** and compare the points you discussed.

5 🎧 **2.11 Read the Exam focus.** Then listen again and discuss whether the student followed the advice in the Exam focus.

EXAM FOCUS

Comparing

When comparing pictures, mention both what is similar and what differences there are between the pictures.

Balance your answer with references to both pictures, rather than talking about them one after the other.

Where possible, try to extend the comparisons through your answers to the specific questions asked, in order to make your long turn not appear disjointed.

Useful phrases

Similarities	Differences
Similarly, …	Having said that …
The main focus of both pictures is …	A major/significant difference between the photos is …
What both pictures have in common is …	The pictures differ quite significantly in that …
	On the face of it … but …
	… but, looking more closely
	While …

EXAM BOOST p38

▶ Complete Exam file SECTION A on page 38.

EXAM TASK

6 Work in pairs. Student A, turn to page 96 and do the task for Unit 2. Student B, listen and answer the question below the pictures. Then go to page 97 and change roles.

EXAM FILE p27
VOCABULARY FILE pp116–117
WRITING FILE p135

1 Describe a famous film sequel to your partner. Can they guess the film and name the original?

2 How many film sequels can you name in one minute? Compare with the class.

3 🎧 2.12 Listen to two podcasts about film sequels. Which comment do you most agree with? Why? Give examples.

4 Are you ever swayed by film reviews to see/avoid a film? Why? Which of the following would you expect to find in a film review of a sequel which is no longer than 260 words?

1 brief information about the film, e.g. actors, storyline, without spoiler

2 short reference to original

3 detailed description of plot and locations

4 a summary of positive or negative points about the film, or a balance

5 some behind the scenes gossip

6 discussion of further planned follow-ups and how the characters might develop

7 the writer's clear opinion of the film, with examples

8 indication of potential box office success and future award nominations for film

9 a recommendation to see or avoid

5 Read a review of *Blade Runner 2049* and highlight examples of the relevant points from Ex 4. Would you be persuaded to see the film? Why? / Why not?

BLADE RUNNER 2049

Have you ever been totally blown away by a film that you'd been expecting to be a letdown? Well, that happened to me recently. I'd loved the original *Blade Runner*, completely getting why it became such a cult classic, and was convinced that no follow-up could ever match it. So, last weekend I settled down to a possibly entertaining, but not mind-blowing, couple of hours watching *Blade Runner 2049*. How wrong was I?

The film is stunning. Not only does it maintain the underlying menace of the first film with the dark, futuristic city drenched by relentless rain or sleet, but it moves the viewer on 30 years with a storyline that both extends from the original and also stands on its own. The action is generally slow-moving, allowing focus on great performances by Ryan Gosling and Harrison Ford among many others, and includes jaw-dropping visual sequences, created with clever use of colour. The orange landscape of a future LA and the pure whiteness of the snowy final scene are particularly memorable.

The original film explored questions related to developing AI. *2049* takes this interrogation further, dealing with the role and authenticity of memory and what actually makes us human. But what drives the film is a truly compelling story.

Blade Runner 2049, for me, is the perfect film sequel, which I am sure will also become a classic, in its own right. I would encourage both fans of the first *Blade Runner* and those who are new to the concept to watch it, and I defy anyone not to be mesmerised.

6 Read the Exam focus and find additional examples of the devices 1–6 in the review in Ex 5.

EXAM FOCUS

Using descriptive and dramatic language

When writing a review, it is important to give the reader a good impression of the subject under review. This will include conveying the writer's reactions as effectively as possible within the word limit.

Descriptive and emphatic devices

1 **Use a variety of adjectives to describe different aspects of the film and your reaction:** The films are **addictive** viewing. There are some **electrifying** moments.

2 **Use synonyms to avoid repetition:** the expanses of wasteland looked **desolate** / we return to this **bleak** scene again and again.

3 **Use compounds to provide variety:** a **spine-tingling** drama / a **tear-jerking** scene

4 **Use a variety of verbs to add drama:** the waves **pour** into the vessel, nearly **crushing** him

5 **Use adverbs to modify adjectives for emphasis:** I was **completely** engrossed for two hours.

6 **Use different sentence lengths to give emphasis:** It is pure escapism. The viewer is transported to a futuristic world, where even the most far-fetched technological inventions seem completely possible. Brilliantly written.

7 Complete the sentences with the correct adjectives.

> complex dreadful exceptional
> high-speed hilarious riveting

1 This actor has _____ talent, and I really admire his work.

2 However, his attempt at a Scottish accent is appalling. His voice coach must have been _____ .

3 The story line is enthralling. The way the plot unfolds is quite _____ .

4 The action is fast-moving. It's very well-paced and the _____ chases are particularly exciting to watch.

5 The script is great – very amusing, and some of the scenes are _____ and will have you laughing out loud.

6 I found the film rather complicated and some of the sub-plots really _____ and hard to follow.

8 Read the exam task. Think about what the review should include. Has the writer of the review in Ex 5 covered what is asked for in the task?

You see the following announcement on an international student website.

HOW GOOD IS THE **SEQUEL**?

We're putting together a list of must-see or must-avoid sequels. Send us a review of a film sequel you've seen, recently or in the past, to put on the website.

How did the sequel relate to the original? Did it live up to expectations or was it even better? Would you watch it again?

9 In pairs complete an exam task for a review. Think of three things you want the reviewers to include.

ALBUM REVIEWS WANTED!

We're looking for reviews of favourite albums albums to put on our website. Send us ....

EXAM BOOST p26

> Complete Exam file SECTION A on page 26.

EXAM TASK

10 Read the exam task in Ex 8 again. Write a plan for your review. Make notes about what to include in each section of the review. Refer back to Ex 4 and the Exam focus. Think about:

> the structure   the content   the language

11 Write your review in 220–260 words. Check your review against the advice in Exam focus and Exam boost.

12 Share your reviews with the class. Which review would most encourage you to see the film? Why?

REVIEW | UNITS 1-2

READING AND USE OF ENGLISH – PART 1

1 Read the text below and decide which answer (A, B, C or D) best fits each gap.

Why we shouldn't regret decisions

They say it's better to regret things we've done than things we haven't. While you may be in two **(0)** ___A___ about that, there are arguments in support of the idea that we shouldn't regret decisions we've made at all. This may be in our **(1)** _____ interests, as regret is an emotion which can cause a great deal of unpleasant psychological **(2)** _____ . This mental torment can prevent us from **(3)** _____ with our lives, as we get caught in the 'if only' trap.

At certain points in our lives, we seem to be **(4)** _____ of deciding what to do for the best. **(5)** _____ as we may to come to the 'right' conclusion, the truth is there's no way of knowing the **(6)** _____ of an option until we try it. This is where we should be kinder to ourselves: we make choices based on information available at the time, and that's why we shouldn't regret decisions, **(7)** _____ of how things turn out. Releasing ourselves from regret is perhaps one of the most **(8)** _____ things we can do for ourselves.

0	A minds	B heads	C thoughts	D opinions
1	A highest	B first	C biggest	D best
2	A discomfort	B disadvantage	C disorder	D disability
3	A going about	B moving on	C coming along	D getting up
4	A unable	B ineffective	C incapable	D unfit
5	A Exert	B Urge	C Pursue	D Strive
6	A outcome	B finding	C product	D conclusion
7	A notwithstanding	B otherwise	C regardless	D nonetheless
8	A persuasive	B empowering	C forceful	D convincing

READING AND USE OF ENGLISH – PART 2

2 Read the text below and think of the word which best fits each gap. Use only one word in each gap.

Double acts

What **(0)** ___HAVE___ Laurel and Hardy, French and Saunders and Ant and Dec got in common? Even **(1)** _____ you haven't the faintest idea who they are, the clue lies **(2)** _____ the pairing of names: they are – or were – 'double acts'.

A double act **(3)** _____ also known as a comedy duo, a form of comedy performance traditional in the UK and USA. Two artists perform **(4)** _____ one, either on stage or on screen. Many **(5)** _____ so for their entire working lives, forming a close bond with each other and establishing themselves as a mainstay of TV entertainment. Traditionally, one of the performers is the 'straight' man – or woman – who sets up the jokes for the 'comic', but there are other variations **(6)** _____ less defined roles.

Why has this perhaps odd-sounding form of comedy long **(7)** _____ such a success? Maybe because we see two good mates having a laugh together, and it reminds us of our own friendships. **(8)** _____ the reason, the double act, it seems, is here to stay.

READING AND USE OF ENGLISH – PART 3

3 Read the text below. Use the word given in capitals at the end of some of the lines to form a word that fits in the gap in the same line.

The secret languages of twins

Secret languages have **(0)** UNDENIABLY been around for as long as secrets themselves, with some speakers deliberately playing on the **(1)** _____ of others to communicate with their confidante. Secret languages between twins are different, developing early in childhood. From their first **(2)** _____ , many twins begin to develop what later becomes a language that only they understand.

It may seem **(3)** _____ that toddlers communicate in a language different from the **(4)** _____ they're receiving. It isn't the result of an **(5)** _____ to reproduce their mother tongue, although a not **(6)** _____ number of twin languages begin with a mispronunciation of the language(s) they hear. It's a natural consequence of them developing psychologically and linguistically at the same rate.

There is no deliberate attempt to **(7)** _____ caregivers as twins grow up, either. But because twins understand each other when their parents don't, errors can be reinforced. Without intervention, this can cause **(8)** _____ in language development, though the vast majority of twins have no difficulty in acquiring their mother tongue while continuing to use their secret language between themselves, occasionally even into adulthood!

DENY

IGNORE

UTTER

LOGIC

PUT
ABLE
SIGNIFY

LEAD

SET

READING AND USE OF ENGLISH – PART 4

4 Complete the second sentence so that it has a similar meaning to the first, using the word given. Do not change the word given. You must use between three and six words, including the word given.

0 The workings of the brain were puzzling for scientists for a long time until research helped them understand it.

HAD

How THE BRAIN WORKED HAD PUZZLED scientists for a long time until research helped them understand it.

1 We really need to determine the cause of this leaking tap!

BOTTOM

We really must get to _____ causing this tap to leak.

2 We discussed at length how to approach the problem of things being mislaid in the office.

DISCUSSION

We _____ how to approach the problem of things being mislaid in the office.

3 Our parents appreciated the time and effort that we put into organising their party.

OF

Our parents _____ the time and effort that we put into organising their party.

4 We hope that customers' enjoyment of our products will continue for many years to come.

STILL

We hope that our products _____ by our customers for many years to come.

5 There was some misinformation surrounding the rescheduling of the event.

ABOUT

We _____ rescheduled.

6 I did far better than I expected in my exams this year!

MY

I _____ in my exams this year!

READING AND USE OF ENGLISH – PART 1

5 Read the text below and decide which answer (A, B, C or D) best fits each gap.

Is second-hand fashion the future?

Consumers are on the **(0)** ___A___ for clothing which has little environmental impact, though many remain reluctant to **(1)** _____ up their fashionable look.

(2) _____ online retailers have cottoned on to this trend for sustainability, they also have to accept that most shoppers still want originality and won't wear garments that can be bought off the **(3)** _____ . So looking back seems to signpost the way forward, and vintage appears to be the answer. Clever marketing has brought about a **(4)** _____ in the second-hand clothing sector.

Nevertheless, there are potential **(5)** _____ for those who go this route. People's body shapes have changed over the decades, so garment sizing may be inaccurate. Fifty-year old fabrics probably display signs of wear and **(6)** _____ . Consumers are happy to pay for something that's truly vintage, but how can they **(7)** _____ the difference between that and something simply pre-owned? There are few guidelines, though to be classed as vintage a garment should somehow appear iconic.

So for the fashion-conscious, the **(8)** _____ of the game now is recycling. Could throwaway fashion be soon consigned to history?

0	A lookout	B pushover	C lookalike	D outcome
1	A get	B make	C do	D give
2	A Additionally	B Conversely	C While	D Moreover
3	A hook	B peg	C hanger	D handle
4	A breakthrough	B breakup	C breakdown	D breakoff
5	A onsets	B setups	C setbacks	D outsets
6	A split	B rip	C slash	D tear
7	A pick	B tell	C allow	D give
8	A title	B word	C name	D heading

READING AND USE OF ENGLISH – PART 2

6 Read the text below and think of the word which best fits each gap. Use only one word in each gap.

The 'step of two'

Ask someone what they know about ballet and they might say 'doesn't it have a pas de deux'? This 'step of two' has **(0)** _____BEEN_____ part of the art form since the 18th century, but often just acted as an opener for longer performances.

In its original form, two dancers **(1)** _____ mirror each other, performing separate moves and only touching occasionally. Over time this developed into something more complex, involving closer interaction between **(2)** _____ . However, the man's role **(3)** _____ considered secondary; he presented the ballerina to the audience, supporting her **(4)** _____ every sense of the word.

Moving forward to the late 19th century, something closer to **(5)** _____ today's ballet audiences might recognise made its appearance. And by the mid 20th century the 'step of two' had become a spectacle in its **(6)** _____ right, intended to front the skills of both dancers **(7)** _____ than just the woman.

Today, it's a key element of any narrative ballet. **(8)** _____ longer predictable and formulaic, it is impressive, involving spectacular lifts and movements for two equal dancers.

VOCABULARY: Phrasal verbs

1 How useful is it to be able to communicate your precise location to others at any given time?

2 🎧 **3.1** Listen to two friends talking about the what3words app. What uses of the app do the speakers mention?

3 🎧 **3.2** Complete the paraphrased sentences from the recording with the phrasal verbs in the box. You may need to change the form of the verb. Then listen again and check your answers.

> come about   do away with   get (sb) out   go into
> mess about with   refer to   set (sb) back   stem from

1 Three words _____ your exact location, and you can give these to emergency services.

2 They can then _____ you _____ of there really quickly.

3 How did it all _____ , then?

4 It all _____ one guy getting lost!

5 Going to the wrong place can really _____ you _____ when it comes to reputation.

6 A lot of work must have _____ it.

7 By using what3words, businesses have no need to _____ giving directions to visitors.

8 I think eventually we might _____ stuff like road maps altogether.

4 Rewrite these sentences using a phrasal verb from Ex 3. You may need to rephrase other words, too.

1 I think they're going to **get rid of** printed tickets soon – we'll only use electronic ones.

2 I **waste a lot of time** chasing that little blue dot on my mobile when I'm lost!

3 The blue dot is meant to **relate to** your location, but it isn't always completely accurate.

4 My lateness **is a result of** my reliance on map apps. I should look up the route first instead.

5 I **spend a lot of time and effort in** planning cycling routes.

6 A lot of technological progress **has been made** in recent years.

7 My journeys **take so much longer than they should** because I don't plan them in advance.

8 Let's **escape from** this boring dinner and do something more exciting instead!

5 Answer these questions and compare your answers with a partner.

- How often do you rely on navigation apps? Why?
- Do you think people have become too dependent on using apps?

6 What three words describe …

- where you were last night?
- your closest friend?
- your favourite place?
- your greatest ambition?

1 Some people say that 'Good things come in threes.' In pairs, discuss how true you think this is and give examples.

2 🎧 3.3 Listen to the beginning of a talk. The speaker uses sets of three ideas to exemplify what she talks about. What are they?

> Complete Exam file SECTION A on page 14.

4 Read the article about the Rule of Three, ignoring the gaps, and discuss what might be included in the missing paragraphs.

EXAM FOCUS

Using content clues

There will be content and language links between different sentences and paragraphs to establish coherence and guide the reader through a text.

1 Reference devices link back or forward to another sentence or paragraph. Specific items or clauses can be referred to or substituted: them / it / this / this one, etc.

2 Linkers, discourse markers or comment adverbs can help sequence sentences or paragraphs: As a result, / Logically, / Finally, …

3 Words or clauses can be paraphrased in following sentences or paragraphs to avoid repetition: an effective presentation = a talk which achieves its aim

4 Ideas can be expanded or exemplified in following sentences or paragraphs: knowledge is key = read up about a topic and check out as many sources as you can so that you can deal with any queries with confidence.

3 Read the Exam focus and look at the highlighted sections in paragraph B below. Find the words and/or phrases these sections relate to in paragraph A.

A It is vital for public speakers to be aware that the effectiveness of the message they are conveying in their talk is not restricted to their words alone, but in their use of the space available, their stance and their gestures. A listener will soon lose interest if a speaker looks uncomfortable, doesn't vary their intonation, stands in the same position and looks down all the time.

B In contrast, one who makes eye contact with their audience and uses notes as a guide and not a reading text will be far more engaging, and body language should be utilised to maximum effect. Facial expressions, open arm movements and a refusal to remain rooted to one spot all help exude confidence and support the words that are uttered. Attention also needs to be paid to vocal delivery. Who wants to be lectured to in a monotone? That is surely one of the quickest ways to bore an audience.

EXAM TASK

5 Read the article again. Six paragraphs have been removed from the article. Choose from the paragraphs A–G the one which fits each gap (1–6). There is one extra paragraph which you do not need to use.

A Public speakers like this can take advantage of the Rule of Three in several ways. I recently had to give a presentation to my colleagues and, heeding advice, I focused on three main messages only, with three supporting points for each. It worked. Not a glazed look in the room!

B Going beyond this, with an additional fourth or fifth element could (according to those in the know) mean that such messages would be forgotten or ignored. Our brains have to work harder to remember more than three items and if there's no real need, they won't! Of course, if we have to process longer lists, we can, but it takes a lot of concentration.

C Apparently, there is an extremely good reason for this and it's down to the way we group words, sentences or ideas into sets of three. This can have a powerful impact on multiple aspects of our lives including how we approach persuasion, how we react to storytelling and how we interact with others on a daily basis.

D An example was when I was recently talking about the introduction of closed-door offices. I phrased it thus: 'These mean that employees benefit from increased privacy, better conditions for concentration and [pause for effect] the opportunity to shout as long and loudly at their PCs as they wish.' I got my laughs and kept my audience's attention!

E With this in mind, I decided to note down sets of three in advertising slogans that I encountered during my morning commute. In just one hour, I was exposed to a whole range of subtle techniques – on TV, on social media and on public transport. And without thinking, I've just done that very thing myself.

F It also affects drama. What is a traditional theatre play made up of? Three acts. In children's fiction the hero often has to face three challenges or meets three animals and so on. Once you start looking you can find the power of three nearly everywhere.

G Thankfully without the same possible repercussions, going beyond three elements can also affect everyday conversations. People will listen to a list of events, and even anticipate a third component to complete the pattern. However, if we add more items, they are likely to interrupt. Or their eyes go vacant.

THREE RULES OK?

'Stop, look and listen.' It's the age-old mantra about crossing roads taught to generations of children by parents, teachers and safety campaigners around the world. Imagine instead, if you will, that the mantra was 'Stop, look, listen, think and cross.' Would it be such a successful phrase? Would it stick in young minds? Probably not, but why?

1 [   ]

If you look at the structure of my last sentence, you'll see an example of what is called 'The Rule of Three', and it's related to the way our brains instinctively search for patterns, three being the smallest number necessary to form one. It's a combination of brevity and rhythm, and as the Latin phrase 'omne trium perfectum' says – anything in a set of three is perfect. Our short-term memories can process and retain chunks of three easily, and this can be used to influence our buying decisions.

2 [   ]

Viewing them all through my new 'rule of three' mind frame it became clear that the product claims were grouped cleverly, to achieve maximum persuasive effect. This cereal bar will tickle your taste buds, keep your energy boosted and can be eaten on the go! Have one on the train, as a snack at work or add to your packed lunch. Three promises, three situations, three linguistic bullets to the brain and it's in our memory.

3 [   ]

Another interesting reason that our brains shy away from too much information goes back a long way, to when our ancestors had to make life or death choices in dangerous situations. Their survival was dependent on making the right choice, but an overload of options could have resulted in decision paralysis. Three choices was the maximum our brains could deal with. And so the pattern developed.

4 [   ]

How often have you seen a similar reaction on the faces of audiences at talks? An awareness of the 'rule of three' is vital for a successful speechmaker to maintain interest. Politicians are masters. A prime minister once said to emphasise a point: 'Education! Education! Education!'. People sat up and took notice. It was a powerful message which would have been diluted had he reduced his 'Educations' by one or added a fourth!

5 [   ]

Something else I also use in talks is humour, and oddly this also often follows the 'rule of three'. Comedians traditionally set up a punch line by using two elements to build expectation and then thwart this expectation with a twist. If presenters do the same and then deliver something surprising as the third element, they'll get a reaction, and the message will be remembered.

6 [   ]

Three is definitely the magic number and its effect is felt from the cradle. Can you imagine a fairytale where the hero was granted two wishes, and not three? It just wouldn't sit right, would it? Now, we know why.

Speaking or writing

6 Answer the questions.

1 Discuss the questions in pairs. Would the prospect of giving a talk to a large group concern you? Why? / Why not? How would you prepare?

2 Choose a topic you've discussed in class or at work recently. Plan a short presentation on the topic, using the advice on structure and using the rule of three. Using your notes, give your talk to your partner or in small groups.

7 Write an email to a friend who is worried about giving a presentation in class or at work. Tell him or her about the article you have just read and give some advice about planning the presentation.

EXAM TRAINER | pp38–39 p40 Ex 3

VOCABULARY: Collocations

1 What do we mean when we refer to the 'third rock from the sun'?

2 What do you think can be seen on Earth from space?

3 🎧 3.4 Listen to part of a radio programme about the things that can be seen on Earth from space. Check your answers to Ex 2. What does the presenter think listeners will be surprised by?

4 🎧 3.5 Match 1–8 with a–h to make collocations used in the talk in Ex 3. Then listen again and check.

1	exceptionally	a	symmetrical
2	highly	b	knowledge
3	distinctive	c	matters
4	remarkably	d	difficult
5	deepen	e	mysteries
6	complicate	f	features
7	unsolved	g	beautiful
8	accumulate	h	understanding

5 Complete the short texts with the collocations from Ex 4. You may need to change the form of some of the words.

MYSTERIES OF NATURE

The Bermuda Triangle is no longer an
[1] _____ . Meteorologists, who have
[2] _____ their _____ of the area,
believe that air pockets which appear there contain
winds strong enough to sink ships.

Crop circles – flattened areas of crops such as
cereals – regularly appeared on British farmland
in the 1990s, in often [3] _____ patterns.
Although it was often suggested that the
[4] _____ form of the circles could not have
been achieved by humans, they were eventually
proven to be an elaborate hoax.

Light pillars are a rather [5] _____ in
darkening skies. Vertical beams of light appear
to shoot up from light sources, but this is not an
[6] _____ 'mystery' to solve: they're simply
created by light reflecting from ice crystals in the air.

Folklore can sometimes [7]_____ when
scientists are trying to prove scientific explanations
for unusual phenomena. For example, as they
[8] _____ of 'sprites'– curiously spikey
lights in the sky – they had to convince people that
they were not alien spaceships but a distant relative
of lightning!

EXAM BOOST p2

➤ Complete Exam file SECTION B on page 2.

EXAM TASK

6 For questions 1–8, read the text below and decide which answer (A, B, C or D) best fits each gap. There is an example at the beginning (0).

THE RICHAT STRUCTURE:
THE 'EYE' OF THE
SAHARA

The Richat Structure is a distinctive **(0)** ___B___ in the desert landscape of Mauritania, Africa. **(1)** _____ symmetrical in shape, this circular structure, formed in the rock and 50 kilometres in diameter, is easily visible from space, and, as its nickname suggests, resembles an eye peering out of the desert.

The **(2)** _____ beautiful structure was originally believed to have been caused by the impact of an asteroid, or the result of a volcanic eruption. Both hypotheses have since been **(3)** _____ as geologists have **(4)** _____ their understanding of the area in which the structure lies. They now believe the structure is an eroded 'geological dome': uplifted rock sculpted by erosion.

However, they are finding it exceptionally difficult to **(5)** _____ the structure's exact origins, and what complicates **(6)** _____ is the fact that the 'eye' is so perfectly circular in shape, when most similar geological structures are not. As they continue to **(7)** _____ knowledge on our planet's past, however, they remain hopeful that answers will be found for this as yet **(8)** _____ mystery.

	A	B	C	D
0	A element	B feature	C quality	D aspect
1	A Deeply	B Highly	C Vastly	D Closely
2	A remarkably	B comprehensively	C intensively	D substantially
3	A denied	B released	C discharged	D abandoned
4	A promoted	B raised	C deepened	D grown
5	A distinguish	B determine	C diagnose	D detect
6	A events	B concerns	C points	D matters
7	A reserve	B assemble	C accumulate	D maintain
8	A unsolved	B unsettled	C undecided	D unconfirmed

Speaking or writing

➤ Go to page 92 for these exercises.

1 If home is the 'first place', and the place of work or education is the 'second place', what do you think is the 'third place'?

2 🎧 **3.6** Listen to part of a radio chat show about 'the third place'. Check your answers to Ex 1 and answer the question below.

How does the presenter say she initially felt about the café she goes to?

EXAM FOCUS

Identifying agreement and disagreement

When listening to a long discussion, you may need to decide what the participants agree or disagree about. Both speakers discuss the same point in turn, so you have to keep in mind what the first speaker says in order to decide whether or not the second speaker agrees with what the first speaker says.

Example of agreement

W: I do feel rather claustrophobic in the city at times.

M: It's almost as though the high-rises are closing in on you, isn't it?

Example of disagreement

M: The benefits of moving to a new place are endless – people to meet, places to go. It's like setting out on an adventure.

W: Well, there is homesickness to contend with and feelings of isolation.

3 Read the Exam focus then read Ex 2 and answer the question.

The speakers agree that the woman visits the café because she

A enjoys the light-hearted atmosphere there.

B did not have an established friendship group.

C wanted to step outside of her comfort zone.

D feels the need to seek out company.

Read audioscript 3.6 on page 142 and highlight the parts of the text which show the agreement.

4 🎧 **3.7** Listen to three extracts from another conversation about third places. What do the speakers agree (or disagree) about in each case?

/// EXAM BOOST p32

> Complete Exam file SECTION A on page 32.

EXAM TASK

5 🎧 **3.8** You will hear a radio programme in which two sociologists called Julia Bernardi and Adam Spright are discussing third places. For questions 1–6, choose the answer (A, B, C or D) which fits best according to what you hear.

1 What does Adam think is the most important shared characteristic of third places?

A their diversity

B their open-mindedness

C their sense of escapism

D their dissimilarity to first and second places

2 What does Julia say about third places?

A People who share them are often unaware of their significance.

B There is no way of determining which places will be popular.

C It can be difficult to define exactly what the term means.

D The concept is sometimes misunderstood.

3 Julia and Adam agree that the most important function of third places is to

A allow people to acquire new areas of expertise.

B help people gain an understanding of others.

C be encouraged to reconsider our world view.

D have a sense of belonging to a unique community.

4 When talking about third places on company premises, Julia and Adam both think that the places

A are more likely to be adopted by larger businesses.

B enable businesses to make the progress they desire.

C are less helpful to people than those outside work.

D give staff much-needed breaks from work.

5 How does Adam feel about social media as a third place?

A He is of the opinion that it does not qualify as a genuine third place.

B He mistrusts the friendships people form on virtual platforms.

C He thinks it can be beneficial for users who are geographically isolated.

D He believes online communities are completely distinct from physical ones.

6 What do Julia and Adam say about the possibility of a fourth place?

A They are keen to carry out research on the theme.

B They do not think it will be of relevance to most people.

C They are not completely sure it is a valid proposition.

D They find it difficult to understand the reasoning behind it.

Speaking or writing

6 Do you have a favourite 'third place'? Talk about:

- what's so distinctive/special about it.
- how you feel while you're there / after you've been there.

7 How do you think people's third places might change over their lifetimes? Write a paragraph offering your suggestions. Then compare ideas with a partner.

EXAM FILE p5

GRAMMAR FILE pp102–103

GRAMMAR: Conjunctions

1 What famous brothers and sisters can you think of? What are they known for?

2 🎧 3.9 You will hear a student giving a presentation about the three famous Brontë sisters. Listen and answer the question below.

What is the student doing? Choose A, B or C.

A comparing the sisters' work

B providing a history of the sisters' lives

C explaining which of the sisters' work she prefers

3 Read the sentences from the talk and look at the conjunctions in bold. Match the conjunctions in sentences 1–6 with their usage or synonym, a–f.

1 **While** the eldest sister, Charlotte, wrote four novels … only three were published during her lifetime.

2 **Not only** did the sisters write books now considered classics, **but** they were **also** held in high regard for their poetry.

3 **Since** she's an admirable and straightforward character, readers cannot help but identify with her.

4 **Whatever** your preference for the characters of Jane or Cathy, you'll certainly find plenty of people who agree with you.

5 **Either** readers are touched by Jane Eyre's honesty, dignity and triumph over adversity, **or** they prefer Cathy's darker, more passionate and complicated character.

6 For much of *Jane Eyre*, it's **as though** the character is talking to her audience.

a used to give a choice between two things

b used to say more than one thing is true

c regardless of

d as, because

e despite the fact that

f like

4 Choose the correct conjunctions to complete the sentences.

1 The three sisters initially felt it was important to use male 'pen names' **nor** / **or** they would not be taken seriously as writers.

2 **While** / **Since** Charlotte believed Anne's novel, *The Tenant of Wildfell Hall*, to be a mistake, it achieved immediate success due to its shocking nature.

3 **Whatever** / **However** much the sisters published as adults, they actually wrote more words as children.

4 **Either** / **Since** Charlotte didn't become a painter as she had hoped because her writing career took off, or she abandoned her artistic ambitions for another, unknown, reason.

5 **While** / **Since** Charlotte spent some of her earnings from *Jane Eyre* on dentistry, it is thought she was embarrassed by the poor condition of her teeth.

6 Because it seemed to Emily **as though** / **but** publishers had no interest in *Wuthering Heights*, she paid £50 to have it published.

EXAM BOOST p4

> Complete Exam file SECTION B on page 4.

EXAM TASK

5 For questions 1–8, read the text below and think of the word which best fits each gap. Use only one word in each gap. There is an example at the beginning (0).

How the BRONTËS continue to influence artists

It may **(0)** _____BE_____ almost two centuries since the Brontës' work was first published, but it still inspires artists in every domain. Musicians, writers and filmmakers have produced memorable songs, poems, books and movies taking inspiration **(1)** _____ the powerful imagery and heartfelt emotion in the novels. It's almost as **(2)** _____ the sisters are modern-day celebrities!

The Brontës' influence extended not only as **(3)** _____ as Kate Bush and her hugely famous Wuthering Heights song, **(4)** _____ Margaret Atwood, author of the critically acclaimed *The Testaments*, is a fan, too. Kate Mosse, who wrote, **(5)** _____ other things, *Labyrinth* and *Sepulchre*, also took inspiration from their work, and many actors, including Tom Hardy, have been keen to play the Brontë anti-hero, Heathcliff.

(6) _____ such artists have achieved themselves, they must still have been intrigued by the Brontë trio who succeeded at a time when women weren't taken seriously in the literary world. And **(7)** _____ the Brontës' work was excellent in itself, **(8)** _____ is undoubtedly the sisters' determination and fearlessness that got the work published in the first place.

Speaking or writing

> Go to page 92 for these exercises.

EXAM TRAINER | p12 Exs 2–3

1 Work in pairs and discuss the questions.

1 When was the last time you cheered to celebrate a success?

2 What sort of celebrations might get 'three cheers'?

3 Are there any traditional phrases/chants/gestures used to celebrate success in your country? Give examples.

2 How important is it to celebrate success at work or at school? In pairs, note down as many different ways a company might celebrate success with its employees as you can in two minutes. Share your ideas with the class. Vote on the most creative.

3 Read a blog extract about celebrating an achievement. Would you have enjoyed this or not? Why?

Three cheers!

Brilliant day! Very proud of ourselves at work after the really successful launch of the new soft drinks marketing campaign. Excellent feedback from all quarters and rumour has it that the whole team will be taken off for a weekend in Paris, compliments of the management! Now, that's what I call a celebration. Can't wait!

4 What factors might have contributed to the achievement in the blog? Think about:

motivation   dedication   time

5 🎧 3.10 Listen to two exam candidates discussing two of the factors that might have contributed to a success of this sort. Did the students interact well? Give examples.

6 🎧 3.11 Read the Exam focus. Listen to the discussion again and check which points are covered and which phrases the candidates use.

EXAM FOCUS

Interacting in a two-way conversation

Ensure a balanced discussion. Each participant should contribute about 50 percent, and a discussion involves interaction, not a series of long turns.

Ask for and give opinions	Refer to your partner's points
Don't you agree that?	I couldn't agree more.
… don't you think?	I don't entirely agree with you there, how about … ?
My view is that …	That's a great way of putting it.
Personally, I'd say that …	That's true, but on the other hand …
	Very nicely put!
So, how do you feel about … ?	When you say … , do you mean … ?
	You're right, but …
	You've got a point, but …

EXAM BOOST p40

> Complete Exam file SECTION A on page 40.

EXAM TASK

7 Work in pairs and read the task.

Here are some things people sometimes strive to achieve and a question for you to discuss. First you have some time to look at the task.

Now, talk to each other about the factors that might have contributed to achieving these different things.

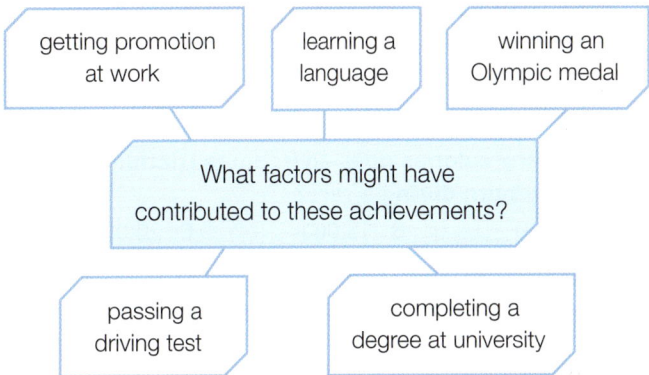

getting promotion at work

learning a language

winning an Olympic medal

What factors might have contributed to these achievements?

passing a driving test

completing a degree at university

Now you have about a minute to decide which of these achievements might affect a person's life the most.

8 Compare your decision with another pair and explain your reasons.

Speaking or writing

9 Work in pairs and discuss the questions.

1 How important do you think it is to celebrate minor achievements as well as big ones? Why?

2 Some people say that a person's upbringing and education play the greatest role in their future success. How far do you agree?

10 You see this notice on a website. Write your entry.

We're compiling a series of articles about personal success entitled: 'Three cheers for me!'

What personal achievement in your life so far are you most proud of and why? Send us your entry and we'll include the most interesting in the series.

EXAM TRAINER | p98
p99 Exs 1–4

EXAM FILE p21
VOCABULARY FILE pp118–119
WRITING FILE pp131–132

1 What do you know about these sports? Tell your partner.

> biathlon decathlon heptathlon
> pentathlon triathlon

2 🎧 3.12 Do the quiz with a partner. Listen to an extract from a question and answer radio session with a triathlete, and check your answers.

TRI, TRI, TRI AGAIN!

1 Which sports are featured in a triathlon? In which order?

A running   **D** archery
B show jumping   **E** swimming
C cycling   **F** fencing

2 How many calories does an Ironman triathlete typically burn during a race?

A 10,000   **B** 15,000   **C** 20,000

3 What was the age of the oldest person to complete the Ironman challenge?

A 75   **B** 85   **C** 90

4 When was the first official Triathlon?

A 1959   **B** 1966   **C** 1974

5 Which language does the word 'triathlon' come from?

A Latin   **B** Greek   **C** German

6 Where is the annual Ironman World Championships held?

A Japan   **B** Mexico   **C** Hawaii

EXAM FOCUS

Using correct register

Depending on your target reader you will need to write in the correct register. For the email/letter task this will be formal/semi-formal/informal.

An informal email will or may:

- use abbreviations: e.g. I'm / we didn't
- use idioms, phrasal verbs and colloquial language, e.g. I came up with / it's on the cards that / cool!
- use friendly opening and closing formats, e.g. Hi Katie / loads of love
- have a less rigid structure and include incomplete sentences, e.g. good to see you / Can't wait / And it's raining

3 Read the Exam focus and answer the question.

Read two extracts, giving advice to triathletes. Where might you find these extracts?

A So, the big day is coming up! Take it from me, it's going to be shattering. Need some final tips? Well, here's what I try to do before the event gets underway. Remember that the most important night's sleep is two nights before – so no late night or partying. Chill and get an early night. And it goes without saying – watch your food. Cut down on the fibre and sugary stuff the day before and give your body plenty of time to digest your pre-race-day dinner – a good twelve hours!

B When your race day is approaching, ensure that you pay attention to your nutrition. You should reduce your intake of fibre and foods with a high sugar content during the previous 24 hours. In addition to this, it is important to allow sufficient time, a minimum of 12 hours, for digestion of your pre-race-day evening meal. Bear in mind that a good night's sleep for the preceding two nights is extremely valuable. Therefore, avoid going to bed too late.

4 In pairs, discuss the differences between the extracts. Then underline examples of the points in the Exam focus in extract A. Find the more formal equivalents in extract B.

EXAM BOOST p20

> Complete Exam file SECTION A on page 20.

5 Read the exam task and a candidate's answer. Has the candidate answered the task well and followed the advice in the Exam focus? How could you improve on it?

You have received an email from an English-speaking friend.

> **From:** Maggie
>
> So looking forward to staying with you next month! As you know, I've entered the South East Triathlon this year and I'm well into training – but I've got to keep it up. While I'm with you, is there easy access to open water swimming, and some hilly bike riding? And do you know of a local club that could maybe help me with my training? Maybe you'd like to train with me?
>
> Thanks,
>
> Maggie

Write your email in reply. Write your answer in 220–260 words.

> **From:** Jocelyn
>
> Hi Maggie,
>
> Good to hear from you and can't wait for your visit. I've got a load of things for us to do. Seems ages since you were last here. We really mustn't leave it so long next time.
>
> Yes, I remember you saying you'd become a triathlete! The training must take it out of you. I can hardly run around the park without getting breathless! I would offer to keep you company while you train, but I'd only hold you back.
>
> About swimming – yes, we're quite near a lake and there's easy access – you could cycle there in five minutes. The water's relatively warm at this time of the year, and there's a 50-metre pool in the city, too, if the weather gets too bad. We have some steep hills in this area, too! You can either go through a maze of country lanes, or keep to the main roads if you prefer. My sister, Daisy, is really into cycling at the moment, so she might come with you, unless you'd prefer to go by yourself.
>
> Will you be bringing your bike on the train? If so, Jack can pick you up in his four-by-four and the bike can go on the rack.
>
> Really looking forward to seeing you!
>
> Love,
>
> Jocelyn

6 Read a reply to an alternative task on the same topic. What has the candidate been asked to do? In pairs discuss how the reply differs from the email in Ex 5.

> **From:** Evelyn Walker
>
> Dear Mr Turner
>
> I shall be staying at your hotel next month for a week. I am currently in training for the South East triathlon and I would like to continue my training during my stay with you. I would be grateful if you could let me know whether there is easy access to open water swimming close to your location. Is your hotel close to some steep hills for cycling training and are there any local sports facilities I could use? I understand that your hotel has a spa and treatment rooms. Is access to this free for guests?
>
> Yours
>
> Evelyn Walker.

7 In pairs write an email question. Write a short email from an English friend asking about a traditional sport or game in the other person's country for a project that he/she is doing. Think of three questions to include in the email.

8 In pairs, read the exam task below and discuss what you might include, and how to structure the email.

EXAM TASK

9 You have received an email from an English friend.

> **From:** Sammy
>
> I'm really feeling unfit at the moment! I know you're into sports so could you recommend something I could take up that I could do a couple of times a week, and that wouldn't cost a fortune in equipment or lessons? It would probably help my motivation if I could do it with other people, too!
>
> Thanks,
>
> Sammy

Write your email in reply. Write your answer in 220–260 words.

10 Exchange emails with your partner and comment on the structure, content and style.

PRACTICE TASKS

READING AND USE OF ENGLISH – PART 3

1 Read the text below. Use the word given in capitals at the end of some of the lines to form a word that fits in the gap in the same line.

Cold, isn't it?

The British weather, and the British people's
(0) ___APPARENT___ obsession with   APPEAR
discussing it has bemused and amused
other **(1)** _____ for a very long   NATION
time. Much research has gone into trying
to gain **(2)** _____ into why more   SIGHT
than 94 percent of Brits admit to having
discussed some aspect of the weather in
the previous six hours and nearly 40 percent
within the last hour.

There are actually some valid reasons for
this, one being the **(3)** _____   GEOGRAPHY
location of the UK which makes the
weather extremely **(4)** _____ ,   PREDICT
and therefore unreliable. If you have
(5) _____ of a hot, dry summer   EXPECT
holiday in the UK, let them go. One
(6) _____ August day might see   SEASON
people shivering in thick jumpers whereas
a November one could see them sporting
T-shirts. Little wonder the topic engages the
population.

However, discussing the weather also
serves another purpose according to
psychologists; as an icebreaker it can
help **(7)** _____ social inhibitions   COME
and as a conversation filler it can ease
(8) _____ . A mutual grumble can   ACT
also encourage bonding. Cold, isn't it?

READING AND USE OF ENGLISH – PART 4

2 Complete the second sentence so that it has a similar meaning to the first sentence, using the word given. Do not change the word given. You must use between three and six words, including the word given.

0 The workings of the brain were puzzling for scientists for a long time until research helped them understand it.

HAD

How THE BRAIN WORKED HAD PUZZLED scientists for a long time until research helped them understand it.

1 It was difficult to pronounce the new words, but they were easy to spell.

WHEREAS

It was easy to spell the new words
_____ very difficult.

2 'Who will be giving the presentation?' the teacher asked us.

QUERIED

The teacher _____
giving the presentation.

3 They say that the company was on the brink of collapse last month.

ALLEGED

The company _____
on the brink of collapse last month.

4 The committee members are discussing the issue of funding at this very moment.

DISCUSSED

The issue of funding
_____ the
committee members at this very moment.

5 So far no one has identified the person in the photograph.

AS

The person in the photograph
_____ yet.

6 'I'm really sorry we didn't inform you about the changes in arrangements,' the receptionist told us.

HAVING

The receptionist
_____ about the
room changes.

VOCABULARY: Phrasal verbs

1 The image shows a British afternoon tea. What time do you think this is traditionally enjoyed?

2 🎧 **4.1** Listen to an extract from a radio phone-in programme and answer the questions.

1 What is afternoon tea in the UK, and how did it develop?
2 What is the French equivalent, and how does it differ?
3 What unusual meals do the last two speakers mention and what reason do they give for having them?

3 🎧 **4.2** Listen again and complete the phrasal verbs in the sentences with the correct prepositions.

1 The presenter staves _____ his hunger pangs with biscuits.
2 He washes the biscuits _____ with a mug of tea.
3 The custom of afternoon tea dates _____ to when the Duchess of Bedford got hungry mid-afternoon.
4 She needed some food and drink to tide her _____ until dinner.
5 An afternoon tea at a good hotel can set you _____ a lot of money.
6 French schoolchildren work _____ an appetite for le goûter during the day.
7 The presenter's friend often plied him _____ thick bread with butter and cocoa powder mid-afternoon.
8 Jason passed _____ the second breakfast because he didn't realise lunch would be so late.
9 Some food is laid _____ especially for college students who are studying late.
10 The presenter used to rustle _____ an easy meal while he was studying.

4 Replace the words or phrases in bold with the correct form of phrasal verbs from Ex 3 and answer the questions.

1 Can you name a food custom in your country that **originated at** a particular time?
2 What do you usually snack on to **keep you going** until the next meal?
3 What meal can you **make quickly** in less than fifteen minutes?
4 Does your family **host** a special meal at any point during the year?
5 How much could a meal at the best restaurant in your area **cost you**?
6 When did you last **refuse** an offer of a free meal? Why?

5 Take it in turns to give a sentence, or the first part of a sentence, using one of the phrasal verbs from Ex 4. Your partner must add another sentence or complete the sentence you started.

A: The school laid on a special lunch for the students because …
B: … they wanted to celebrate the end of term.

37

1 How is the year divided into seasons in your part of the world? Have you noticed any natural events recently that do not seem to follow normal seasonal behaviour?

2 🎧 4.3 Listen to an environmental reporter talking on a documentary podcast about changes in seasons, and answer the questions.

1 What does the speaker say about traditional seasons in different parts of the world?

2 What examples does she give about humans' dependence on seasons?

3 What are some scientists saying about the seasons?

EXAM FOCUS

Identifying paraphrase

Information in a text is not always phrased in the way we expect. When reading the questions, look out for:

Synonyms

Different verbs/phrases/nouns/ adjectives to express a similar idea

believed – was of the opinion that

an extreme weather event – torrential rain that completely flooded the fields

Functional verbs to reflect the underlying meaning

I don't know whether to believe what he said or not.

He questions the truth of the statement.

A change in voice, order or word class

Scientists recorded the results and put them up on the website.

Findings were documented and posted online.

A summary or combination of ideas from different sentences

Let me show you what I mean. We put in a claim for damages in early May. However, we received no payment for six months, which was ridiculous.

He cites the example of late settlement by the insurance company.

3 Read the Exam focus and answer the questions.

Read the extracts (a) from the documentary in Ex 2. Highlight the changes to the phrases in bold in the paraphrases (b).

1 a Some experts are now **talking in terms of** two main seasons.
 b The reporter refers to changes in the way scientists describe the seasons.

2 a It's down to us – humans have really **messed up**.
 b The speaker blames people for creating the current problems.

3 a It is now becoming clear to us all. **We've all seen** unseasonable activity.
 b The speaker points out how personal experience is bringing the issues home to us.

4 a The whole **delicate balance maintained in nature** is controlled by the seasons and any changes can have far-reaching consequences.
 b The speaker warns of the extensive impact if seasonal shift disrupts natural cycles.

⫸⫸⫸ EXAM BOOST p16

> Complete Exam file SECTION A on page 16.

4 A website has asked for online contributions in relation to the way the seasons are changing. Scan the text on page 39 and say which TWO contributors do NOT mention solutions to the problem.

EXAM TASK

5 You are going to read the contributions to an online magazine. For questions 1–10, choose from the contributors (A–D). The contributors may be chosen more than once.

Which contributor

explains how economic reasons have enforced certain changes?	1
rephrases terminology readers may not understand?	2
suggests that the public are unaware of the full extent of a problem?	3
describes a potential solution to a global problem?	4
refers to terminology which is no longer appropriate?	5
indicates that nature has helped reduce the rate of climate change?	6
mentions an unwanted positive effect of climate change on certain wildlife?	7
exemplifies a phrase by giving a measurement?	8
points out how current research methods aid learning?	9
refers to information only recently acquired?	10

Speaking or writing

6 Work in pairs. Should our focus be on halting, reversing or accepting and coping with the effects of climate change? Why?

7 Discuss with your partner how climate change is affecting your area or country. Then write a short report for an international student website.

SEASONS COME AND SEASONS GO

... OR DO THEY?

Four readers give us their views on seasonal shift.

A It's a sad news story; groups of cows stranded on small islands of grass during floods; hundreds of sheep drowned. But it's even sadder to realise that this is only the most obvious and well-known indication of the hardship that farmers, both agricultural and dairy, have been facing for decades because of increasingly unpredictable seasons. Think about it. Farmers depend on the seasons to know when to plant, when to harvest, when to let livestock graze and when to bring them in. In parts of Rwanda, for example, farmers used to be guided by the names of the months which were taken from the weather; the name for March meaning hot and dry, for example. Now sadly, that correlation is gone. In many countries we're getting longer and wetter, and longer and hotter periods, with extreme rainfall and drought. The knock-on effect is crystal clear. You don't have to be a former farmer like myself to understand that you can't plant when it's too wet, and that droughts mean smaller crops, ravaged by increased numbers of pests and weeds that thrive in the hot conditions. Animals have less grass to graze on and need to be fed – and that costs money!

B OK, so which biome on Earth (that is – a large region on the planet with its own range of living things) has no really distinct seasons at all? Well done everyone who said the marine biome. You're much better informed than I was before starting a project last month. Of course, conditions do change throughout the year in the oceans as a result of changing weather in different locations, but for the living organisms in this biome it is the wider global climate change that is having an enormous impact. I wasn't aware that the oceans have been taking in extremely high amounts of carbon dioxide, which is a result of human industrial activity, and this has, in effect, slowed down global warming for us. However, it's reaching a limit and salt water on the earth is now showing a 25 percent rise in acidity. This, combined with warmer waters and the more commonly discussed rise in sea levels, is affecting practically all sea creatures. Coral reefs are dying, fish are moving towards the poles and coastal wetlands are being 'drowned'. We are on the brink of marine disaster, and it isn't showing up in seasonal shifts.

C So, what do kids know about the causes of the changing seasons? Actually, quite a lot! The environment has been an important topic for us in education for a long time now. Classroom walls have been decorated with posters about recycling, surveys have been conducted, trees have been planted. Now, with movements such as that spearheaded by climate activist Greta Thunberg, the urgency for action is touching young people all over the world. In my opinion, how teachers address the topic of climate change is all about balance. It's vital to give information but without instilling fear, instead showing how scientists are trying to find ways through the problems – such as Dr Leslie Field's research into sprinkling a particular type of sand over the Arctic ice to prevent the shrinking. The idea of using sand to reflect the sun links ideally to basic physics lessons, too – a real life-changing application of scientific theory! Knowing that there are people actively working on solutions may even encourage some children into scientific research careers themselves. And that will help us all.

D OK, my livelihood is at stake, so I can't be objective here, but believe me, the impact of climate change and seasonal shift on the tourist industry will be devastating. I'm a ski instructor and I'm seeing the results first hand. Snowfall used to be predictable, particularly at 'snow-reliable' resorts. To those not in the know, these are resorts providing a continuous 100-day ski season with at least 30 centimetres of snow on the slopes. But predictions now indicate that the Alps could lose up to 50 percent of these resorts by the 2070s and for some lower-altitude ski resorts it is already a thing of the past. Shorter seasons and the need to 'top-up' with artificial snow obviously involves higher costs, and smaller resorts have had to close; the business is just no longer viable. Those that remain open are looking to raise prices which will make winter sports holidays even more exclusive. Having said that, it's not all doom and gloom. Some resorts have refocused and are promoting activities less dependent on reliable snowfall such as hiking, mountain biking and snow shoeing. I guess I'll maybe have to refocus, too!

EXAM FILE p7

VOCABULARY: Suffixes

1 Look at the items below. Do you think they are considered to be lucky or unlucky in the UK? What things are lucky or unlucky in your culture?

- breaking a mirror
- crossing your fingers
- Friday 13th
- the number seven
- a black cat crossing your path
- finding a four-leaved clover
- opening an umbrella indoors
- walking under a ladder

2 🎧 4.4 Listen to a student talking about four-leaved clovers and answer these questions.

1 What did she research?

2 How have four-leaved clovers been used over time?

3 Why does she think the beliefs around four-leaved clovers have endured over time?

3 🎧 4.5 Match the words to the correct suffixes. Then listen again and check.

> common   depend   discover   distinct
> heal   prosper   ration   thank

> -al   -ent   -ful   -ing   -ity   -ive   -ly   -y

4 Complete the text about whether luck really exists. Add a suffix from the box to the end of each of the words. There is one suffix that you need to use twice.

> -ent   -ful   -ity   -ive   -less   -ly   -ness

Does luck **really** exist?

Some people seem to have been born lucky, whereas others seem never to get any luck at all. But is luck a real thing or ¹non-exist_____ ? Surely winning a prize draw is lucky but being struck by lightning is not. Or is luck ²subject_____ ? If something matters to you and it doesn't go as planned, ³doubt_____ that would be considered unlucky, whereas if you weren't bothered about the outcome, luck wouldn't even come into it.

Say you're playing football, and you score a brilliant goal. Depending on your ⁴mental_____ , you will either say it was luck or skill. But unless you can do it ⁵count_____ times you were probably lucky. ⁶Similar_____ , you'd be unlucky to be struck by lightning more than once! In our ⁷eager_____ to explain why good and bad things happen, we overlook the fact that if something occurs on a regular basis, then it's nothing to do with luck, and it's therefore ⁸unhelp_____ to suggest that some people are lucky and others aren't.

EXAM BOOST p6

> Complete Exam file SECTION B on page 6.

EXAM TASK

5 For questions 1–8, read the text below. Use the word given in capitals at the end of some of the lines to form a word that fits in the gap in the same line. There is an example at the beginning (0).

Why athletes have LUCKY CHARMS

If you've ever watched athletes preparing for a race, you'll have **(0)** UNDOUBTEDLY noticed some of them performing unusual-looking rituals. They might touch an item of clothing **(1)** _____ or say some mantra over and over as if their very life was **(2)** _____ on it.

Although these 'twitches' may look odd to spectators, they don't feel strange to athletes. To their mind, failing to observe these **(3)** _____ rituals could result in losing the race.

This may seem an **(4)** _____ view to take, but there are compelling reasons for the behaviour. An athlete who achieves success in an event will, in all **(5)** _____ , look back on their last-minute preparations and attribute their successes in part to these, rather than congratulate themselves purely on the fact they're so **(6)** _____ in their chosen endeavour. This preparation **(7)** _____ includes things like eating particular foods or wearing certain kit.

(8) _____ , the athletes may not be far wrong: research indicates that recreating rituals before every event may have an impact on success because of the boost in confidence it provides.

DOUBT	
REPEAT	
DEPEND	
DISTINCT	
RATION	
PROBABLE	
SKILL	
COMMON	
ULTIMATE	

Speaking or writing

> Go to page 92 for these exercises.

EXAM TRAINER | p17 Exs 3–5 | p18 Exs 6–9

EXAM FILE p35

1 How important is it to have a good sense of direction? Why? Tell your partner.

2 🎧 **4.6** Listen to two friends talking about why some people have a good or bad sense of direction and answer the questions.

1 Does the man have a good or bad sense of direction?

2 What reason does the woman give for how good someone's sense of direction is?

EXAM FOCUS

Understanding the main point

When you listen to each speaker, you have to decide what is the main point of what they are saying, so you can choose the correct option. The options you choose from summarise the whole of what the speaker says, rather than reflecting a single detail.

3 🎧 **4.7** Read the Exam focus. Then listen again and answer the question below.

What is the woman doing?

A adding support to an explanation

B gauging her friend's intelligence

C highlighting the benefits of technology

4 🎧 **4.8** Listen to the woman explaining people's sense of direction further. What is her main point?

Some people

A take a lot of notice of minor details.

B are less aware of their abilities than others.

C have a natural aptitude for direction.

EXAM BOOST p34

> Complete Exam file SECTION A on page 34.

EXAM TASK

5 🎧 **4.9** You will hear five short extracts in which people are talking about getting lost.

TASK ONE

For questions 1–5, choose from the list (A–H) what the unexpected benefit was for each speaker of getting lost.

A gaining employment

B establishing a new relationship

C acquiring a better understanding of a place

D having time for reflection

E being reminded of something in the past

F practising a new skill

G gaining a sense of pride

H resolving a frequent worry

Speaker 1 **1** [ ]
Speaker 2 **2** [ ]
Speaker 3 **3** [ ]
Speaker 4 **4** [ ]
Speaker 5 **5** [ ]

TASK TWO

For questions 6–10, choose from the list (A–H) how each speaker says they avoid getting lost now.

A I use nature to navigate.

B I plan overseas travel well in advance.

C I never go out unaccompanied.

D I ensure I receive detailed descriptions of routes.

E I never take shortcuts.

F I memorise man-made landmarks.

G I ask people for directions.

H I make sure I have necessary tools.

Speaker 1 **6** [ ]
Speaker 2 **7** [ ]
Speaker 3 **8** [ ]
Speaker 4 **9** [ ]
Speaker 5 **10** [ ]

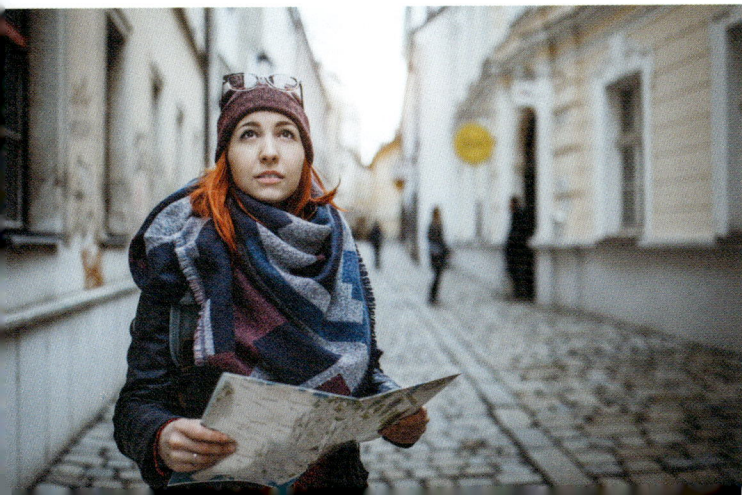

Speaking or writing

6 Do you generally have a good sense of direction or a poor one? Tell your partner an anecdote about a time you got lost, how you resolved the situation, and what the consequences were, if any.

7 Write directions for a friend or classmate to your home from the nearest transport link. Include natural or man-made landmarks rather than road names.

GRAMMAR: Reported speech

1 What is the fourth dimension?

2 🎧 4.10 Listen to a physicist explaining the fourth dimension and check your ideas. What examples does the speaker give of 1-D, 2-D, 3-D and 4-D?

3 Complete the summary sentences with the correct form of appropriate reporting verbs from the box. Choose two possible verbs for each sentence.

> acknowledge   admit   clarify
> concede   encourage   point out
> recognise   prompt

1 'A dimension is just a direction in which you can go.'
The physicist _____ that a dimension was just a direction in which you can go.

2 'I'm sure you'll be very familiar with the concept of 3-D.'
He _____ the fact that we would be very familiar with the concept of 3-D.

3 'Let's think about what 4-D means.'
The speaker _____ us to think about the meaning of 4-D.

4 'It's difficult to visualise because we can only see things in 3-D.'
He _____ that it might be difficult to visualise 4-D in our 3-D world.

4 Match the sentences with the reporting verbs in the box. What does each verb mean?

> assert   compliment   contradict
> exaggerate   query   reassure

1 'Of course it's important to teach geometry at school! I don't know why you think it isn't!'

2 'You've got such a fascinating way of viewing the world. It's very refreshing.'

3 'It's true! Our belongings really are moving! They're travelling through time with us!'

4 'This report's like, a million pages long, and I can't understand a single word of it.'

5 'As long as you keep learning in tiny increments, you'll understand the bigger picture in the end.'

6 'Let me get this straight. You're saying that X always equals Y?'

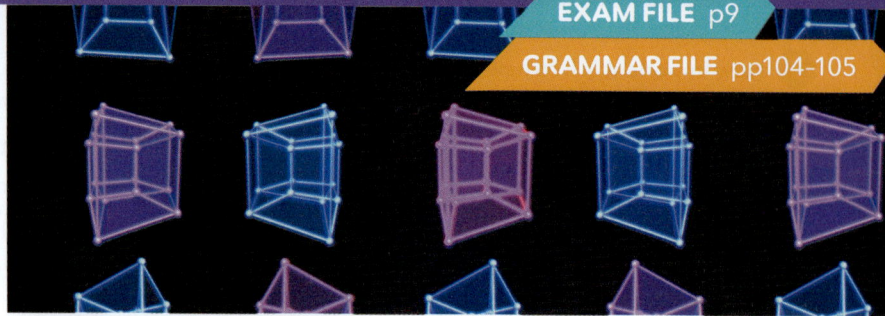

EXAM FILE p9
GRAMMAR FILE pp104–105

EXAM BOOST p8

> Complete Exam file SECTION B on page 8.

EXAM TASK

5 For questions 1–6, complete the second sentence so that it has a similar meaning to the first sentence, using the word given. Do not change the word given. You must use between three and six words, including the word given. Here is an example (0).

0 'Well, it's true that tesseracts are not easy to visualise,' the teacher said.
CONCEDED
The teacher CONCEDED THAT TESSERACTS WERE NOT easy to visualise.

1 'Do you think time travel will ever be a possibility?' said Tim.
WONDERED
Tim _____ to travel through time at any point in the future.

2 'Why can't we travel backwards and forwards through time?' asked Florence.
UNABLE
Florence wanted to _____ travel backwards and forwards through time.

3 'So, the report says that the drug is safe to use,' the pharmacist said.
CONCLUDED
The pharmacist told us that the report had _____ safe.

4 'It really isn't as difficult as it sounds!' our maths teacher told us.
REASSURED
Our maths teacher _____ as difficult as it sounded.

5 'Can I just ask why you're setting the experiment up in that way?' the professor asked us.
QUERIED
The professor _____ setting up the experiment.

6 'You've produced a sound hypothesis – well done,' he said to her.
COMPLIMENTED
He _____ up with a sound hypothesis.

Speaking and writing

> Go to page 92 for these exercises.

EXAM TRAINER | p21 Ex 2

1 Do the online survey for a charity website. Discuss your choices with a partner and give your reasons. Which challenge do you think might be most popular and raise the most money for the charity?

(24) **Twenty-four-hour charity challenges: tick those that you would accept!**

Add three more ideas.

Spending twenty-four hours …

1 in the gym.
2 offline.
3 going vegan.
4 producing zero waste.
5 dancing.
6 silent.
7 saying 'yes' to everything.
8 _____ .
9 _____ .
10 _____ .

2 🎧 **4.11** Listen to a reporter talking about a recent challenge undertaken by a TV presenter. How many jobs can you remember? Why did she take on the challenge?

3 Think about the last twenty-four hours in your life. In pairs, discuss the amount of time you spent:

> doing a sport or hobby
> on your phone or tablet   studying
> with your family   with your friends   working

4 Work in pairs and discuss the question.

How difficult would you say it is to get a good work-life balance for students or workers these days? Think about these things:

> ambition   constant connectivity   deadlines
> home pressures   money   relationships

5 🎧 **4.12** Read the Exam focus and listen to three responses to the question. Decide which answer (A–C) is the best and discuss why.

Some people say that we focus too much on getting a good study or work-life balance these days. What's your opinion?

EXAM FOCUS

Justifying your opinions

Always justify your opinion and add details, including examples and short anecdotes where appropriate, to extend your answers.

Justifying

The thinking behind this is / the reason I say this is …

Giving examples

Let's say for instance / a perfect example of this would be … / you've only got to look at …

Adding anecdotes or personal experience

Speaking from experience / I once saw … / There was this time when …

EXAM BOOST p42

> Complete Exam file SECTION A on page 42.

EXAM TASK

6 Work in pairs. Take turns to answer the first 4 questions individually. Discuss questions 5–7 together.

1 Do you think that these days we are too pressured into filling each day with activities and we don't have enough time to simply relax? Why?

2 What is the busiest twenty-four hours you can remember recently? What was the experience like?

3 Do you think it's necessary for people to put in a lot of hours in order to become successful at something? Why? / Why not?

4 How important is it for schools or colleges to enforce regular breaks during the day? Why?

5 Do you think that people will work longer or shorter hours in the future? Why?

6 Some people say that children shouldn't have to do a lot of homework in the evenings. How far do you agree? Why?

7 Do you think it's important for people to spend part of the day completely on their own? Why? / Why not?

7 What examples, anecdotes or personal experiences did your partner mention during the task? Share with the class.

Speaking or writing

8 Work in pairs. Describe a typical day in the life of someone famous, without giving the name. How long before your partner guesses?

9 Write a paragraph describing a memorable 24 hours in your life.

EXAM FILE p23
VOCABULARY FILE pp120–121
WRITING FILE p133

1 🎧 **4.13** What national celebration do you think the picture on page 45 relates to? How much do you know about it? Listen to a podcast about attending a celebration and check.

2 🎧 **4.14** Listen again and list the different things the speaker experienced.

3 In pairs, do the quiz about annual celebrations in different countries.

WHERE IN THE W🌐RLD?

Match the festivals and countries.

Canada   Finland   Hong Kong   Russia   South Korea   Spain

1 The mud festival in July celebrates the properties of mud, and people slop about in a huge mud pool!

2 The bun festival in early May remembers food shortages and has great towers of buns in the streets that people climb.

3 The Air Guitar World Championships festival in August claims to promote peace and celebrates great rock music.

4 The Scarlet Sails event during the White Nights festival in early summer celebrates the end of the school year.

5 The Flour Fight Festival on 28 December is filled with craziness and finishes with a fun and messy battle with flour and eggs.

6 The International Hair Freezing Contest happens annually when the air and water is cold enough to freeze hair into fantastic shapes.

4 Tell your partner about a national celebration or festival you know about – either from your country or another. Talk for a minute and include:

- the name of the occasion.
- the reason for the occasion.
- the manner of the celebration.
- your own experience or participation.

5 Discuss in pairs.

1 Do you find big public celebrations enjoyable? Why? / Why not?

2 How important do you think it is for a region to maintain its traditions? Why?

6 Read the task and discuss what could be proposed.

Your college for international students is celebrating 50 years since it opened and wants to celebrate the day with an open-air summer event for students and local people. The students have been asked to offer suggestions as to what the theme for the event should be with possible activities, giving reasons and outlining the benefits of such an event.

1 Activities

_____

2 Reasons

_____

3 Benefits

_____

7 Read the proposal and check if your ideas have been included. Do you think the college will agree? Why?

Introduction

The aim of this proposal is to suggest how the college's 50-year anniversary could be celebrated. The proposal will describe a possible theme for the day and outline activities that could be included.

Theme

As the college is proud to welcome students from countries all over the world, it would be appropriate to hold a multicultural event that could involve students from several nationalities. As well as giving current students the opportunity to showcase various aspects of their culture according to their abilities, it would also be educational for other students and the local people who attend the event. Promoting knowledge of other cultures has been one of the college's main focuses over the last half century.

Activities

The event would be held in the college grounds and include a garden party with stalls where visitors can taste samples of dishes prepared by the students. There would be live performances of traditional music and dancing displays throughout the day. In the evening there would be a party for the guests and students with night-time lights and lanterns designed by the students, typical of those used in festivals in their own countries. The event would finish off with a fireworks display.

Conclusion

I would urge you to consider this proposal favourably as it would be both a fitting celebration for the college and promote cultural understanding. The preparation would involve a cost to the college, but I am convinced this would be worth it because of the goodwill and enthusiasm the event would create.

8 If you were a student at the college, what would you contribute in terms of ideas for food or performances from your country?

9 Read the Exam focus. In pairs, discuss how well the writer of the model proposal has followed the points.

EXAM FOCUS

Writing an effective proposal

A proposal is written to offer suggestions to solve a problem or for a project, and the desired outcome is for the proposal to be accepted by the target reader.

To achieve this:

Use appropriate language depending on the reader, usually formal or semi-formal.

It would be great if you could see your way to agreeing … = We would appreciate your considering the proposal …

Follow a clear structure that clearly lays out the relevant points for the reader.

1 Start with an introduction that sets out your proposal.
2 Divide it into clear sections and use headings.
3 Finish with a summary or conclusion.

Use persuasive language

I would urge you to consider …

It would be of great benefit to all involved.

I am convinced that these plans would be successful in …

We would be extremely grateful if you could agree to …

EXAM BOOST p22

> Complete the Exam file exercises on page 22.

10 Read the Exam task and discuss in pairs what points you might include.

EXAM TASK

Your local council has decided to fund the organisation of a day of activities in your town to celebrate a national festival. It has asked local people for proposals for activities on the day, which would benefit inhabitants and attract visitors to the town.

Write a proposal outlining activities you think would be popular, giving your reasons for your choice and mentioning the benefits for the area.

11 Plan and write your proposal in 220–260 words.

12 Share your proposal with the class. Whose proposal is the most interesting? Which might the council choose and why?

REVIEW | UNITS 1-4

READING AND USE OF ENGLISH – PART 1

1 Read the text below and decide which answer (A, B, C or D) best fits each gap.

The wonder belt

Do you despair that you have absolutely no **(0)** ___A___ of direction whatsoever? You are not alone. It appears that a significant number of us find **(1)** _____ problematic, even when we're not completely off the beaten **(2)** _____ . Whereas some of us might not be overly concerned about the issue and use sat-navs or smartphone apps, **(3)** _____ to maps or simply ask for directions, others find it so **(4)** _____ that they actually avoid going to unfamiliar locations.

The answer might be an intriguing new type of belt which **(5)** _____ a compass and Bluetooth connection and can be linked to smartphones. The belt, when worn, vibrates to indicate to the wearer which direction is north. The **(6)** _____ of this innovation is considerable. **(7)** _____ with such a device, getting about could be much more **(8)** _____ . It could relieve the demands on the eyes and ears of a sightseer or a cyclist by taking people's focus off their phone or map and guide them through vibrations around their waists!

0	A sense	B feeling	C indication	D sign
1	A locating	B navigating	C directing	D pinpointing
2	A road	B path	C way	D track
3	A look	B refer	C exploit	D employ
4	A unrelenting	B irrational	C intimidating	D illogical
5	A brings	B amasses	C unites	D incorporates
6	A potential	B expectation	C availability	D breadth
7	A Enabled	B Acquired	C Attached	D Armed
8	A straightforward	B immediate	C plausible	D viable

READING AND USE OF ENGLISH – PART 2

2 Read the text below and think of the word which best fits each gap. Use only one word in each gap.

Cheers!

A decade or so **(0)** ___AGO___ , cheerleading was generally associated with entertainment at American sporting events. It had come **(1)** _____ originally as a form of encouragement for the sports teams involved and cheerleaders performed smart, synchronised dance routines with catchy chants, echoed by the crowds. Today, however, cheerleading **(2)** _____ acquired different associations. Its popularity **(3)** _____ a sport in its own right is rapidly increasing, and clubs are springing up everywhere with national and international competition entries at an all-time high.

Cheerleading has **(4)** _____ own distinctive style and is a unique combination of group gymnastics, acrobatics and a touch of glamour. It's **(5)** _____ sport that demands a combination of strength and coordination in **(6)** _____ to solid teamwork. Participants point out **(7)** _____ the benefits of getting involved in cheerleading include improved fitness and a sense of great camaraderie. Safety measures are also considered paramount in a sport which is thought **(8)** _____ be one of the riskiest sports around, so do bear this in mind if you're thinking about joining a squad.

READING AND USE OF ENGLISH – PART 3

3 Read the text below. Use the word given in capitals at the end of some of the lines to form a word that fits in the gap in the same line.

Hot desking? No way.

With a large number of **(0)** __EMPLOYEES__ opting to accept their company's offer of flexible working hours in order to beat the rush hour traffic or spend quality time with their families, it would not be **(1)** _____ of those companies to impose a hot-desk policy. Indeed, there are **(2)** _____ reasons for such a move, not least that of maximising the **(3)** _____ of office equipment.

The practice has been in place for many years at some **(4)** _____ but its popularity is questionable. The need for a dedicated office space that is one's own and contains that person's **(5)** _____ is deeply rooted in many people and is linked to an almost **(6)** _____ fear of being unsettled, rather like a wanderer or traveller who has no base. There is a sense that not being given a personal space implies that the employee is **(7)** _____ . For others, however, the very lack of dedicated office space brings a **(8)** _____ element of freedom.

EMPLOY

REASON
COMPEL

AVAILABLE

ESTABLISH

BELONG

PRIME

VALUE

DEFINE

READING AND USE OF ENGLISH – PART 4

4 Complete the second sentence so that it has a similar meaning to the first sentence, using the word given. Do not change the word given. You must use between three and six words, including the word given.

0 The workings of the brain were puzzling for scientists for a long time until research helped them understand it.

HAD

How THE BRAIN WORKED HAD PUZZLED scientists for a long time until research helped them understand it.

1 In addition to loving rock bands, he was also a fan of classical music.

LOVE

Not _____ rock bands, but he was also a fan of classical music.

2 'You're right, I underestimated the seriousness of the problem,' the director said.

CONCEDED

The director _____ the seriousness of the problem.

3 From his appearance I thought he'd had a sleepless night.

THOUGH

He looked _____ all night.

4 People think that settlers brought this type of vegetable here centuries ago.

TO

This type of vegetable is _____ here by settlers centuries ago.

5 You've made a lot of careless errors in the report,' my manager said.

POINTED

My manager _____ a lot of careless errors in the report.

6 After completing three questions I realised that I was looking at the wrong section.

BEFORE

I _____ that I was looking at the wrong section.

READING AND USE OF ENGLISH – PART 3

5 Read the text below. Use the word given in capitals at the end of some of the lines to form a word that fits in the gap in the same line.

The four humours

Five hundred years ago people's understanding of medical issues was **(0)** UNDOUBTEDLY far more primitive than it is today. In fact, it was believed that everything in the body revolved around just four **(1)** _____ fluids, known as humours. Each of these, namely blood, yellow and black bile and phlegm, played their part in an individual's emotional life, appearance and **(2)** _____ . If someone became unwell, it was believed that these humours had become **(3)** _____ .

However, the origins of these four humours are rather vague and **(4)** _____ . They were linked to physical organs, the four elements of fire, water, earth and air and even to the galaxy. This was probably a **(5)** _____ of how people at the time believed that everything was intertwined and people were merely part of this pattern.

Maybe it also exposed the rather **(6)** _____ nature of superstition, and beliefs people held about the stable and **(7)** _____ nature of the world. Shakespeare mentioned the humours in his plays, so learning about them makes his work more **(8)** _____ to modern audiences.

DOUBT
BODY
PERSON
BALANCE
MYSTERY
REFLECT
RATION
CHANGE
ACCESS

READING AND USE OF ENGLISH – PART 4

6 Complete the second sentence so that it has a similar meaning to the first sentence, using the word given. Do not change the word given. You must use between three and six words, including the word given.

0 The workings of the brain were puzzling for scientists for a long time until research helped them understand it.

HAD

How THE BRAIN WORKED HAD PUZZLED scientists for a long time until research helped them understand it.

1 I don't think theatres will produce paper tickets in future - they'll just send out e-tickets.

RID

In future I _____ paper tickets and just send out e-tickets.

2 'You did very well in your project Clara,' said the teacher.

COMPLIMENTED

The teacher _____ in her project.

3 I'll finish class early today unless anyone objects.

LONG

I'll finish class early today _____ objections.

4 The singer was one of his favourites, so Jack enjoyed the show just as much as he'd expected.

UP

The show _____ because the singer was one of Jack's favourites.

5 If you're not looking directly at people in an interview, you won't be very successful.

EYE

You won't be very successful if you don't _____ during an interview.

6 Sometimes in winter there's so much snow that we can't leave our house.

IMPOSSIBLE

Sometimes the amount of snow in winter _____ leave our house.

VOCABULARY: Body idioms

1 What does the 'high five' in the picture represent? When might people do this? Do you ever do this? When? Who with?

2 How many of the emojis do you recognise? Work in pairs. You have two minutes to decide what they all mean!

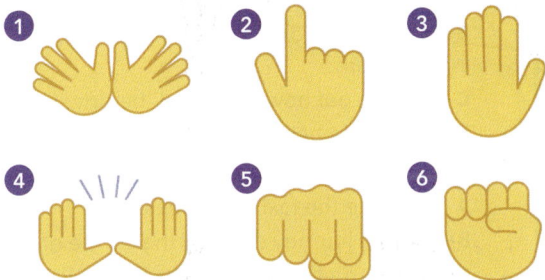

3 What gestures are used in your culture to:

• greet someone you know well / are meeting for the first time?

• congratulate someone?

• say goodbye to someone you know well / have just met for the first time?

4 🎧 5.1 Listen to a linguistics student talking about why we use gestures when talking to other people. What overall reason does she give?

5 🎧 5.2 The speaker uses three idioms which include parts of the body. Listen again and identify them. What do the idioms mean?

6 Complete the body idioms and match them to their meanings.

> eye (x2)   face (x2)   head   neck

1 take at _____ value

2 turn a blind _____

3 lose your _____

4 keep an _____ out for someone/something

5 be a pain in the _____

6 _____ the music

a be annoying

b accept something without thinking about it

c stop being calm in a difficult situation

d accept punishment / criticism for something you know you did wrong

e choose to ignore something you know is wrong

f watch carefully to see if they / it appears

7 Work in pairs and discuss these questions.

• Would you like to be in the public eye? Why? / Why not?

• What everyday things do you find a pain in the neck?

• What might make you lose your head?

• Do you think it's ever OK to turn a blind eye to something?

• How important do you think it is to face the music?

EXAM FILE p11

1 Discuss what you know about a big city in your country, or one in a different country. Think about:

> buildings   culture   history   parks   shopping

2 Using the same points, discuss what you know about Paris.

3 🎧 5.3 Listen to a teacher talking about how the districts of Paris were numbered and answer the questions.

1 How are the arrondissements arranged?

2 What's the history behind this?

3 What does the teacher say about the fifth arrondissement?

EXAM FOCUS

Understanding purpose and attitude

Purpose of text, words and phrases

Identify the target reader: students, tourists, website users?

Ask yourself how a reader would feel at the end of the text: informed, encouraged to do something, impressed by something, etc. This can help work out the writer's intention.

Do not ignore single words or phrases which can give us additional meaning: "I thought that might happen," he said smugly. Think why the writer used the word 'smugly'.

Understanding attitude and tone

At times we need to understand the writer's attitude or opinion when it is not clearly stated. Look for synonyms, paraphrases, words, actions and examples that show their feelings: It's a fascinating area. = 'The writer is interested and curious about the area.'

4 Read the Exam focus and the extract. Answer the questions.

1 What is the writer's attitude to the bookstore?

   A We don't know because the writing is impersonal.

   B He admires the previous owner.

   C He thinks the ethos of the place is outdated.

2 What is the purpose of the paragraph?

3 Why does the writer use the word 'refuge' in line 10?

The name is misleading. You'd be forgiven for thinking it could be a shop found in Stratford-upon-Avon in England, or the name of a theatre group. Shakespeare & Company is, in fact, a remarkable bookstore in the Latin Quarter of Paris. This, one of the most famous bookstores in the world, looks quite ordinary. But Shakespeare's, since it first opened in 1919, has had the reputation of being rebellious. It was the first bookstore to publish James Joyce's controversial 'Ulysses' in its full form. In 1951, another bookstore within sight of Notre Dame took on the name (the original having closed in the 1940s). The owner George Whitman was legendary

10 for his eccentricity, allowing the shop to become a **refuge** for wandering writers. Anyone who turned up could stay, sleeping on one of the tiny beds stored between the stacks of books. Their payment was to work two hours a day, read a book and write a one-page autobiography on the shop's special blue paper. Whitman may no longer be with us but the store is still open and attracting visitors.

EXAM BOOST p10

> Complete Exam file SECTION B on page 10.

5 You are going to read an article about a visit to Paris. Read the definition and the article and say why you think the article was given the title.

EXAM TASK

6 Read the article again. For questions 1–6, choose the answer (A, B, C or D) which you think fits best according to the text.

1 When talking about memory in paragraph 1, the writer is

   A sure that individual memories fade too quickly.

   B confused about its unreliability.

   C concerned that some events disappear forever.

   D aware that he remembers what he's seen rather than heard.

2 What does the writer say about his reaction to the taxi driver outside the station?

   A He was conscious of reacting uncharacteristically.

   B He was surprised to learn about the difficult transport situation.

   C He resented the man's assumption that he was rich.

   D He was reluctant to consider taking a taxi.

3 Why does the writer mention the 'cases' in line 30?

   A to emphasise how much luggage they had

   B to illustrate how he was trying to get a lower fare

   C to point out how unhelpful the driver was

   D to indicate how the weather was changing

4 What does 'that' refer to in line 37?

   A the route the taxi driver takes

   B a return journey through the centre of Paris

   C the reason he had brought Ellie to Paris

   D a potentially difficult experience

5 The writer mentions a bookstore to show that

   A buildings reflect the people who have used them.

   B his memory had sadly failed him again.

   C the essence of the area was the atmosphere.

   D places like this had to move on and not live in the past.

6 In the final paragraph the writer suggests the scaffolding

   A hid the worst of the structural damage

   B was an ugly reminder of the power of fire

   C was the sign of a hopefully positive outcome

   D provided an interesting subject for photography

THE PERFECT FIFTH.*

It was snowing. Nothing unusual there, really – snow in Paris in February. It was simply that in my memory Paris had always been bathed in a spring sunshine that dappled the waters of the Seine and warmed the neck of my guitar. I've recently found myself reflecting a fair amount on the nature of memory. Why, for instance, do our memories usually hold on to the best images, idealising events and scenes, and push the darker ones into the shadows, where they lie, undeleted and only ready for scrutiny should we wish to go there? My mental image bank of Paris didn't quite go so far as to completely idealise my student year in the city, but it got close.

The cold and the icy rain met us head on as we exited the Gare du Nord station. One Paris illusion gone. Not an inch of blue sky.

'Are we getting the Métro?' Ellie asked, her voice rising above the noise of the surging crowd.

'Métro on strike – all day. Here, over here!' a loud voice insisted, and a blue gloved hand grabbed Ellie's arm, another lifted her bag. I would normally have reacted to this unwanted contact, but wrongfooted by the weather and wiped out by the journey from the UK, I followed the taxi driver and Ellie to his small car, its windows hardly visible through the settling snowflakes.

My first sight of Paris had been from a taxi. The driver had dropped me at my lodgings in the fifth arrondissement after taking me on a 'Paris by night' sightseeing tour, entertaining me all the while with anecdotes and information about the various sights; he'd wanted to show off the city he loved. Might this driver do the same for Ellie, on this her first visit? No. We ended up having a tremendous argument about his proposed
30 inflated fare, in the road, in the snow, with our **cases** lifted in and out of the boot as the negotiations progressed. Another memory compromised.

A crawl through the heart of the city to the beat of car horns and the steady swish of wipers on the windscreen, and then we were crossing the Seine and onto the Boulevard Saint-Michel.

I purposely kept my eyes straight ahead, not quite yet ready to see the damage. **That** would 37 be faced later. In the meantime, my spirits lifted; we were on familiar territory, the fifth arrondissement. My breath caught, and neither the snow nor the taxi driver could stop the smile I felt creep onto my face. We offloaded our luggage at the hotel and I practically dragged Ellie around the corner and into the evening world of the Quartier Latin.

Time had passed since I'd last been here, and familiar landmarks had been replaced; my favourite musty old bookstore, where chemistry books used to rub shoulders with books of poetry, was now a souvenir shop selling mini Eiffel Towers and bright T-shirts. But nothing can erase an atmosphere, and the narrow lanes were still buzzing with an underlying edge of nonconformity.

Before, the sound of different accents used to come from the competing invitations of waiters outside the many small restaurants. Now, it came from the tourists who shared the streets with locals and students. The various intonations created an exciting soundtrack to a whole new language. Great artistic and literary rebels had talked controversy in these cafés and streets. A sense of anarchy and chaos still echoed, and I imagine always will at some level. It's at the heart of the quartier. My memory hadn't cheated me on that.

Then it was time, and as we rounded the last corner to bring us back onto the banks of the Seine, I looked up at the Notre Dame Cathedral, blackened from the terrible fire in 2019. However well you prepare, the initial shock of seeing scaffolding rising over the roof and partially obscuring the dark eyes of windows is sharp. I'd photographed the glorious building in the spring sunshine all those years ago. Today I raised my camera to record another view. I'd expected my heart to be heavy, as it had been when the first news images of the fire raced round the world, but what I actually felt was a strange relief. The scaffolding wasn't symbolic of destruction, but it held a promise that the cathedral would recover. I was glad I had returned. My memories may have been dented a little, but not irreparably. The fifth was still the most fascinating arrondissement in Paris for me. Not perfect, but nearly.

*The perfect fifth is a musical term describing an interval and is often believed to be the basis of harmony.

Speaking or writing

7 Work in pairs and discuss the questions.

1 Talk for a minute about a landmark or building in a city you know or have heard of. Would you recommend visiting it to a tourist? Why? / Why not?

2 Discuss your current location and the advantages and disadvantages of living there.

8 Think of something in the area you live in that could be improved. Write a short proposal to the relevant authority saying what needs to be done. Share your proposals with the group. Which is the most likely to be accepted?

EXAM TRAINER | p25 Ex 2 pp26–31

VOCABULARY: Phrasal verbs

1 What do the five rings of the Olympic flag represent? What else do you associate with the Olympics and Paralympics?

2 🎧 5.4 Listen to a short talk about how Olympic sports are chosen. How are they chosen? Make notes and compare with a partner.

3 🎧 5.5 Choose a preposition or particle to complete the phrasal verbs in the sentences below which summarise the talk. Then listen again and check.

1 Now, around 30 or so sports are usually lined **on / in / up** for inclusion in the Games each time.

2 They certainly can't rush **to / into / onto** making decision.

3 Once an activity has been put **forward / through / over** by a sports organisation for consideration, …

4 … the committee takes **in / on / to** the job of making sure it's recognised internationally as a sport.

5 The sport must thereby comply with all rules drawn **around / up / under** in the Olympic Charter.

6 Another rule forbids sports which come **under / over / beneath** the heading of 'mind sports'.

7 The opportunity for a new sport to be admitted to the Games only comes **over / up / through** when the decision to drop something else that year is made.

8 It's also important that the sport fits **in / by / on** with the Games' values.

9 The IOC is keen to cater **for / around / towards** young people in the sports it selects.

10 Events that come **up / in / off** well will likely be included next time round.

4 Turn to page 94 and read the text about the benefits for a country of hosting the Olympic Games. Complete the text using some of the phrasal verbs from Ex 3. You may need to change the tense of the verb.

//// **EXAM BOOST** p2

▶ Complete Exam file SECTION C on page 2.

EXAM TASK

5 For questions 1–8, read the text below and decide which answer (A, B, C or D) best fits each gap. There is an example at the beginning (0).

A HISTORY OF THE OLYMPIC MASCOT

In recent times, many Olympic Games have been represented by a mascot, a cultural figure, often in the form of an animal or cartoon character, which often **(0)** __B__ on event merchandise.

While Schuss, a cartoon skier, wasn't **(1)** _____ to as a mascot when he first appeared on souvenirs for the 1968 Winter Games in France, he was the first character used to **(2)** _____ interest in merchandise sold at Olympic events.

In 1969, the Organising Committee for the 1972 Games attended a party, where they were invited to come up with a concept for an official mascot. One attendee **(3)** _____ the idea of Waldi the dachshund, and the cute little dog was elected to represent the Games. This **(4)** _____ well, and Olympic committees have never **(5)** _____ .

Since Waldi, mascots have included everything from squirrels to superheroes. Not only do they help sell souvenirs, but they often **(6)** _____ an appearance at events, rousing the crowd and **(7)** _____ spectators who want a memorable selfie by **(8)** _____ a pose.

0	A	covers up	B	pops up	C	looks up	D	stores up
1	A	attended	B	related	C	cited	D	referred
2	A	introduce	B	build	C	catch	D	tempt
3	A	put forward	B	put together	C	put back	D	put about
4	A	came up	B	came under	C	came off	D	came around
5	A	bounced back	B	looked back	C	come back	D	got back
6	A	make	B	turn	C	put	D	take
7	A	drawing on	B	lining up	C	holding on	D	catering for
8	A	bumping	B	hitting	C	striking	D	coming

Speaking or writing

▶ Go to page 93 for these exercises.

1 Do people in your country work or study 'nine to five'? Do they do a five-day week? How productive do you think the typical hours worked in your country are?

2 🎧 5.6 Read the Exam focus and then listen to part of a radio programme about productivity. What is the woman doing?

EXAM FOCUS

Identifying purpose and function

In this part of the exam you may have to identify the purpose or function of what the speakers say. You need to listen to the whole text before choosing your answer.

Example function question

1 What is the speaker doing?
  A **advising** workers to …
  B **warning** people against …
  C **recommending** that employees …

Example purpose questions

1 Why does the speaker mention …?
  A to **persuade** managers that …
  B to **suggest** that managers …
  C to **encourage** managers to …
2 The speaker talks about … in order to …
  A **exemplify** a possible cause of …
  B **define** the concept of …
  C **acknowledge** the idea of …

EXAM BOOST p28

> Complete Exam file SECTION B on page 28.

EXAM TASK

3 🎧 5.7 You will hear three different extracts. For questions 1–6, choose the answer (A, B or C) which fits best according to what you hear. There are two questions for each extract.

Extract One

You hear two colleagues discussing the number of hours in the working week.

1 What is the man doing?
  A promoting a concept he has recently come across
  B reflecting on changes that have occurred at his workplace
  C praising an action that appeared to achieve success
2 What is the woman doing?
  A highlighting the drawback of a plan the man mentions
  B explaining how an idea would work in practice
  C acknowledging the difficulty in establishing the best hours

Extract Two

You hear two programmers talking about a new computer game they're working on.

3 Why does the woman mention a previous version of the game?
  A to encourage the man to learn from its errors
  B to convey her feelings about the latest edition
  C to complain about how challenging it was to work on
4 What is the man doing?
  A explaining his reasons for asking to work on the game
  B describing the features he would like to see included
  C clarifying what he thinks makes the game so special

Extract Three

You hear two friends talking about Mondays.

5 Why does the man mention birthdays?
  A to make a comparison with his least favourite day
  B to point out the reason for people's feelings about Mondays
  C to explain why people seem to enjoy them so much
6 Why does the woman mention the seminar she attended?
  A to suggest an alternative to having set days of work and leisure
  B to recommend a way in which people could approach work
  C to support an argument the man has made

Speaking or writing

4 Look at the jobs. What are the most and least positive aspects of them? Discuss your ideas with a partner.

app designer   emergency doctor   make-up artist politician   professional athlete

5 Are you as productive as you could be? Think about work, study or chores. Write down areas in which you could improve. Exchange ideas and write some advice for your partner which would help them increase their productivity.

EXAM FILE p5

GRAMMAR FILE pp106-107

GRAMMAR: Conditional forms

1 How often do you eat your 'five a day'? Are there any recommendations in your country for how much fruit and veg to eat each day?

2 🎧 5.8 Listen to a nutritionist explaining the benefits of 'going vegan'. What benefits does she mention?

3 🎧 5.9 Complete the sentences from the recording. Then listen again and check.

1 If you _____ yet embraced a plant-based diet, perhaps you'll _____ come round to the idea by the end of this brief talk.

2 If we _____ all to go vegan, the environment _____ be better off.

3 If you _____ one of the people who believes vegans don't get enough calcium or protein, you _____ want to think again.

4 Should you stick to a vegan diet for long enough, your risk of getting diabetes, heart disease or other serious conditions _____ drop.

5 'If you _____ only been fed vegan food from birth, you might even _____ healthier now.

6 If we all _____ to a plant-based diet, we _____ smell better, too.

7 If you should _____ to see a vegan dish on the menu one day, _____ it a go.

4 Complete the text by choosing the best conditional form in bold.

Q: How do I know if I ¹**would / could** like being vegan?

A: Well, you'll never know if you ²**don't / won't** try it! Make sure you get yourself a good recipe book, or you ³**would / will** probably keep trying to make the same style of dishes you've been used to – and that might not work out.

Q: If I have to go out and buy all this new food, ⁴**won't / shouldn't** that cost a fortune?

A: If you didn't have a budget for food shopping, you ⁵**might / would** be a very lucky person! Fortunately, many vegetables are inexpensive. Whole grains, potatoes and beans are all really affordable, so if I ⁶**were / weren't** you, I'd start with those.

Q: ⁷**Won't / May** I miss out on essential vitamins only found in meat if I go vegan?

A: You ⁸**had / should** better get this on your shopping list or you might suffer: buy a vitamin B12 supplement! That's one of the few nutrients you can't get from many plants and you need it for brain health.

EXAM BOOST p4

▶ Complete Exam file SECTION C on page 4.

EXAM TASK

5 For questions 1–8, read the text below and think of the word which best fits each gap. Use only one word in each gap. There is an example at the beginning (0).

THE **SUPERFOOD** MYTH

We're so used to hearing it that we don't even question it anymore: some foods are superfoods. Even **(0)** _____IF_____ you rarely eat blueberries, spinach or kale, you will certainly know that they're *really* good for us: better, they say, than everything else.

But **(1)** _____ you be thinking of switching to a superfood diet, you **(2)** _____ want to think again. Scientists say that 'superfoods' don't have their own food group. If it **(3)** _____ down to them, they wouldn't use the word at all **(4)** _____ connection with this small number of foods widely believed to be so good for us.

It isn't that the foods don't have health benefits: they do. But if **(5)** _____ wasn't for marketing, the term would not exist. Scientists believe that it is simply a marketing tool, and that **(6)** _____ there are studies out there which prove otherwise, there is **(7)** _____ to say this particular set of foods does anything more 'super' than other healthy ones. If **(8)** _____ we'd known that before filling our shopping carts with expensive superfood items!

Speaking or writing

▶ Go to page 93 for these exercises.

EXAM TRAINER | p12 Ex 4

1 **Work in pairs. Discuss the questions.**

1 Without looking, what information or visuals can you find on a coin, either British or from your own country?

2 What different coins are used in your country? Do you know what coins are used in the UK?

3 What is a commemorative coin? Do you know of any that have been produced in your country?

2 🎧 5.10 **Listen to a podcast by a coin collector. Which two British coins does he mention? What differences are there between them?**

EXAM FOCUS

Speculating

There will usually be a need for speculation when comparing the pictures and dealing with the questions. You may need to speculate about:

- **what is shown in the pictures**: they look as if …
- **what might have happened before**: they may well have …
- **what might happen later**: it's a possibility that they could …
- **reasons for an activity**: my guess would be that they're doing this as a result of …
- **the people's emotions, feelings and opinions**: they're looking expectant, as though they're hoping for …

3 🎧 5.11 **Read the Exam focus. Listen to a student comparing these two pictures and complete the sentences (1–6).**

Why are coins being used in these situations? How might the people be feeling?

1 I _____ imagine he's been busking.

2 In all _____ the guy has an official space.

3 It _____ well be that his time is up.

4 There's no _____ that is payment of any kind.

5 I would _____ that they're about to toss the coin.

6 I _____ the children are feeling pretty excited and _____ hoping their side wins the toss.

EXAM FILE p39

EXAM BOOST p38

> Complete Exam file SECTION B on page 38.

EXAM TASK

4 Work in pairs. Student A, turn to page 96 and do the task for Unit 5. Student B, listen and answer the question below the pictures. Then go to page 97 and change roles.

Speaking or writing

5 Work in small groups. Take a random coin and imagine where it has been and what it has been used for. Take turns to hold the coin and tell the coin's story. Compare your group's story with other groups. Which coin had the most interesting journey?

A: I was first given to a shop to be used as change …

6 Discuss: How would life change if all cash was replaced by digital payments? Who might benefit or lose out as the result of such a change?

7 Prepare a plan and then write a for and against essay entitled: Should cash be kept in circulation?

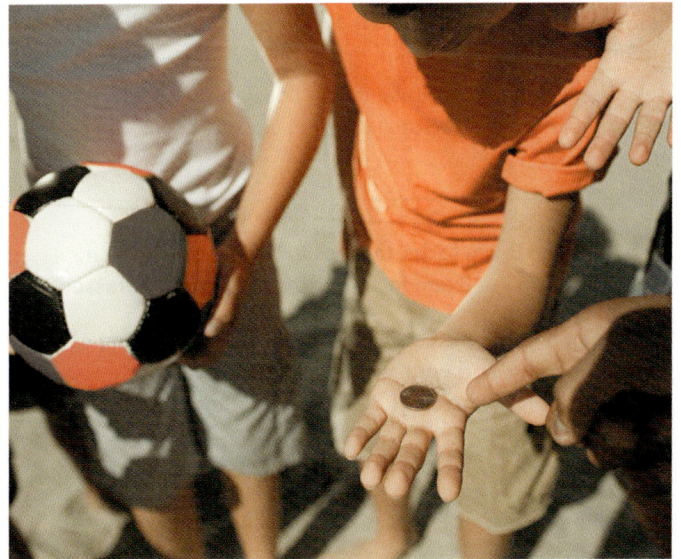

1 Do you usually leave an online review when prompted after a purchase or using a service? Why? / Why not? What would make you leave a five-star review?

2 🎧 5.12 Listen to a marketing expert talking about the current trend in rating. What does he think about the importance of rating? Do you agree?

3 Look at the two extracts. Which is from a review and which is from a report? How do you know?

> **A** If the opportunity presents itself, grab it and you won't be disappointed. The fish specialities are to die for. But I'd advise against going on a Saturday evening. Understaffing was a bit of a problem and although the service was good and friendly, it took a long time to get served.

> **B** The food is locally sourced, well cooked and presented by clearly talented kitchen staff. However, delays in service were significant and this needs to be addressed before the star rating can be given. See my recommendations below regarding other aspects in need of improvement.

EXAM FOCUS

Structuring a report

A report is usually written in response to a request from someone in authority.

Remember to use formal or semi-formal language: … problems need to be addressed …

Use headings to divide your report neatly and clearly for the reader to follow your reasoning: Introduction / Facilities / Recommendations / Conclusion

Clearly state the purpose of the report at the beginning: The aim of this report is to evaluate …

Make clear recommendations: It would benefit those involved if …

Summarise your opinion in the final section: Overall, the experience was beneficial in that it …

Be objective and impersonal throughout, although you may be referring to personal experience: The décor was impressive.

4 Read the Exam focus, the task and the report. Which point(s) in the Exam focus has the writer not addressed?

A hotel chain has commissioned you to stay at one of their hotels and write a report about your experience, without the hotel staff being aware of the purpose of your stay.

Your report should describe your stay at the hotel, outline any problems and make recommendations for improvements.

EXAM FILE p25
VOCABULARY FILE pp122-123
WRITING FILE p134

★★★★☆

Report on Beech Hotel

Introduction

The purpose of this report is to give an overview of the facilities and services provided by the Beech Hotel, from a guest's perspective, outlining any areas in need of improvement.

Staff

At the start of my overnight stay I was greeted warmly by the receptionist and checked in quickly and efficiently. I was given full information about the various services offered and personally shown to my room. Unfortunately, other members of staff were not so accommodating. When querying the lack of options for a vegetarian in the restaurant, I was treated abruptly. And on checking out the following morning there was a long delay while a different receptionist struggled with tech issues, giving no apology or explanation. My room was clean, well equipped with basic necessities, and tastefully designed and furnished. What was unacceptable was the fact that the windows would not completely close and it was freezing. I was unable to change rooms as the hotel was full. The room information folder was also outdated.

Facilities

The indoor pool was closed for repairs and some parasols in the gardens were broken. However, the gardens themselves were well tended and I loved the guest lounge.

Recommendations

There needs to be more attention to detail, such as updating room information and carrying out general repairs systematically in order to maintain a good standard. From my conversations with the staff it appears that there is a high turnover, for whatever reason. More should be done to retain staff, with additional training being offered.

Conclusion

The hotel runs well and offers good accommodation, grounds and facilities. If the issues outlined above are addressed, there is no reason why the Beech Hotel should not regain its status as one of the popular hotels in the locality.

5 Quickly read the report below and answer the questions.

1 Who requested the report?

2 What is its purpose?

3 What rating (out of five) do you think the writer would give?

6 Complete the gaps 1–5 in the report with the correct sentences A–E.

Report on local parks

Introduction

As requested by the council I am submitting this report on the state of our local parks from a local resident's point of view. I have considered how well they are maintained and include recommendations for any aspects that require improvement. ¹_____

Plants and trees

The parks have been well designed and the choice of flowers, trees and shrubs in these areas is generally good. ²_____ It also appears that trees that had come down in the gales last winter have not yet been completely removed or replaced. Branches still block a few park paths. The amount of park space given to grass is satisfactory, in my opinion.

Maintenance

In general park maintenance seems to be appropriate and efficient. ³_____ I noticed that the fence bordering the river in Laine's Gardens is falling into disrepair and this could possibly present a danger to children playing close to it.

Recommendations

It would be appreciated if more brightly coloured flowers could be planted to keep parks colourful throughout the year. ⁴_____ The riverside fence must be repaired as a matter of urgency because of the potential danger it presents.

Conclusion

Overall, the current state of the parks and gardens in the area is impressive.

⁵_____

A If the above recommendations are implemented, it will ensure that the public can continue to profit from the relaxing open spaces offered.

B However, I was somewhat concerned about the lack of colour in the south of Kennett park.

C Grass is cut regularly, and litter collected and cleared every day.

D Fallen branches should be removed and replaced as soon as possible to unblock the paths.

E It is based on interviews conducted with members of the public who use the parks on a regular basis.

EXAM BOOST p24

> Complete the Exam file exercises on page 24.

7 Read the Exam task in Ex 8 then look at the ratings below. In pairs, discuss what things could be mentioned in each of the categories and what the details might be in relation to the ratings.

1 Location and amenities: ★☆☆☆☆

2 Basic services: ★★★★☆

3 Décor and furnishings: ★★★★★

EXAM TASK

8 A company that rents out city accommodation for short breaks has asked you to stay in one of their apartments for a few days and to write a report on your experience. The owner will not know the reason for your stay.

Your report should describe your stay at the property, outline if and when it fails to meet expectations and suggest any improvements that could be made.

Write your report in 220–260 words.

9 Exchange your reports with another pair and compare the points you commented on in Ex 7. Do the reports follow the points in the Exam focus?

PRACTICE TASKS

READING AND USE OF ENGLISH – PART 1

1 Read the text below and decide which answer (A, B, C or D) best fits each gap.

Small town living

The small town often gets overlooked in the debate about whether city living or country life is better. But they are by no **(0)** __A__ second best, and in fact, there are some excellent advantages to living in one.

On the **(1)** _____ of affordability, for example, small towns can be relatively cheap to live in. As a **(2)** _____ of thumb, shopping and accommodation are significantly cheaper than **(3)** _____ city prices. This means your salary, especially if you earn it in a nearby city, goes a lot further.

It **(4)** _____ to reason that there's a slower pace of life in smaller places, too, with shorter rush hours and lower pollution levels. There's often a reduced crime rate, and there are other **(5)** _____ , too: you'll rarely be competing for a table at a restaurant or seat at the cinema.

But if you're **(6)** _____ to think small-town life sounds boring, think again. Smaller towns often have an increased sense of community, friendships are **(7)** _____ easily, and there's often a **(8)** _____ social life.

0	A means	B accounts	C ways	D times
1	A field	B concern	C detail	D subject
2	A rule	B test	C case	D point
3	A expanded	B heightened	C inflated	D extended
4	A comes	B stands	C makes	D gives
5	A perks	B additions	C premiums	D assets
6	A decided	B persuaded	C convinced	D inclined
7	A brought up	B struck up	C caught up	D drawn up
8	A living	B succeeding	C thriving	D profiting

READING AND USE OF ENGLISH – PART 2

2 Read the text below and think of the word which best fits each gap. Use only one word in each gap.

The paleo diet

The paleo diet is what we believe our ancient ancestors ate. If it hadn't **(0)** __BEEN__ for agricultural progress, we might still be eating this way today. Many think that if we **(1)** _____ to follow it ourselves, we'd be less likely to develop certain health conditions.

So, what does the diet consist of and **(2)** _____ we better adopt it in order to keep ourselves healthy? It **(3)** _____ assumed that before farming, people only ate what they **(4)** _____ hunt, fish or gather. This would **(5)** _____ included meat, fish, poultry, eggs, vegetables, fruits, berries and nuts. Dairy, sugar, salt and grains weren't consumed.

It sounds good, but **(6)** _____ you be thinking the paleo diet must be better for us since it includes no processed foods, you'd only be partly right. It can have detrimental effects, warn nutritionists. Without dairy, for example, it can be difficult to get enough calcium, and **(7)** _____ you ate more meat to replace pasta, say, you might unwittingly **(8)** _____ consuming more 'bad' fats. The bottom line? Balanced diets rule.

VOCABULARY: Fixed phrases

1 What are the attractions of playing traditional games as opposed to playing popular computer games? Describe a traditional game from your country without giving the name, for your partner to guess. Think about pieces, board, instructions, etc.

2 🎧 6.1 You are going to hear a researcher of traditional games on a podcast about dominoes. What might you expect him to mention? Listen and compare your ideas. Which information was new for you?

3 In what context does the speaker use the following words and phrases?

> all accounts   first glance   loose end   my element
> no means   no time   stretch

4 Complete the sentences with the correct prepositions.

1 She looked everywhere on the hard drive _____ **vain** for the assignment and had to start again from scratch.

2 I posted a comment about the new game and _____ **no time** it went viral.

3 _____ **no means** can I come to the gaming convention _____ **such short notice**.

4 The word game asks the players to solve a clue which _____ **turn** leads on to the next.

5 David reached the final of the competition _____ **default** because his opponent in the semis was ill and pulled out.

6 My dad is _____ **his element** when we get out board games. He usually wins and never lets us forget it!

5 In pairs, complete the B sentences by choosing the correct alternative. Then write a possible A sentence for each pair.

1 A I try to fit in at least half an hour's aerobic exercise every day.
  B In **theory** / **theme** it's really good for your health, but it takes a lot of dedication!

2 A _____
  B At a **length** / **stretch** I can keep going for about 30 minutes!

3 A _____
  B At first **look** / **glance** it looked easy, but it certainly wasn't.

4 A _____
  B I usually do that when I'm at a(n) **loose** / **extra** end.

5 A _____
  B I would really love to see him in **action** / **movement**!

6 A _____
  B I wish I'd seen it. By all **summaries** / **accounts** it was excellent.

6 Do you think computer games will outlive traditional games like dominoes? Why? / Why not?

EXAM FILE p13

1 Work in pairs. Discuss the question. Then share your ideas with the class.

Some people believe that humans have a sixth sense. How many examples of what is sometimes considered to be a sixth sense can you think of?

2 🎧 6.2 Listen to extracts from listeners to a radio programme inviting comments about a sixth sense. Were any of your ideas from Ex 1 mentioned?

EXAM FOCUS

Identifying similar opinions

It may not be immediately clear whether one writer agrees with another's opinion.

1 Look for synonyms for different words: hunch = intuition
2 Check for paraphrasing of verb phrases: The argument was difficult to follow = I was confused about the writer's opinions
3 Read beyond one sentence
   a to look at exemplification which clarifies an opinion.
   b to see whether the writer backtracks (returns to a previous point) to change an opinion.

3 Read the Exam focus and answer the question.

Do the writers of these comments agree about intuition? Highlight synonyms and paraphrases that support your answer.

A As far as having a 'gut feeling' about something implying that some sort of sixth sense is concerned, I have my reservations. While I would go along with the possibility that we can pick up clues from people's behaviour about how they're feeling and maybe what they're going to do, I wouldn't go so far as to say this is something extraordinary.

B People talk about having hunches or being intuitive, and I don't want to disagree completely. There may be something in the idea that body language or voice inflections can subconsciously alert us to certain things but for me, this is something quite natural and I can't see it being linked to the idea of a sixth sense.

EXAM BOOST p12

> Complete Exam file SECTION B on page 12.

4 Read the definitions for empathy and sympathy. In pairs, think of an example situation for both words. Share your ideas with the class.

sympathy
is when you understand and care about the feelings of another

empathy
is when you understand the feelings and can imagine yourself in the same situation.

EXAM TASK

5 You are going to read four reviews of a book about how empathy might be considered a sixth sense. For questions 1–4, choose from the reviews A–D. The reviews may be chosen more than once.

Which reviewer

holds a different view from the others regarding whether empathy may be considered a sixth sense?

1 [ ]

disagrees with reviewer C about how the book develops?

2 [ ]

has a similar view to reviewer D about the proof offered in the book for the theories stated?

3 [ ]

has a similar view to reviewer C about the book reflecting current public interest?

4 [ ]

EMPATHY – our SIXTH SENSE?

A The belief that humans possess a sense in addition to the five we are aware of is by no means new or revolutionary. Far from it. The proponents of a 'Sixth Sense' have a conviction that since scientists cannot yet understand the function of a significant part of our brains, that there must be a sixth sense hiding in there somewhere. In this, they are rather similar to those who insist that because the universe is so vast, there simply has to be life beyond Earth. In her book 'Empathy – sixth sense?' Anna Dawlish deals with the possibility that the ways human beings understand and identify with others' emotions may potentially hold the answer to the question of that extra sense. In that, I applaud her thinking. However, for me the research was not sound, and I found myself confused by a sea of anecdotal evidence. Her link between intuition and empathy could have been better made, and the logical structure of the book seemed flawed to me. I remained unconvinced that reading the book had been a good investment of my time.

B My immediate reaction to reading 'Empathy – sixth sense?' was one of relief. It appears that there might be a specific reason for what people have labelled 'my extreme sensitivity'. I've long mocked my own tendency to cry easily, described my discomfort in crowds and preference for solitude as phobic, and considered my physical reactions to others' injuries as squeamish and a weakness. Dawlish has allowed me to reconsider this self-assessment by maintaining that we all have a threshold for empathising with others, and that some, like yours truly, have a low one – basically, I identify with others' feelings, etc. more than most people do. It is good to read about a topic that people actually haven't considered before, and the book is well-constructed and easy to follow, but I do wonder however whether she goes too far (certainly out on a limb as far as other psychologists are concerned) when she speculates that this characteristic is in some way linked to a sixth sense. It seems to me that although offering some convincing evidence for her claims that this is something slightly more than a personality trait, to give extreme empathy this title is awarding it too much significance.

C There seems to be a fashion these days to attribute certain behaviour to our genetic make-up and while I admit that there are some conditions that warrant this, for the most part, giving scientifically official sounding names to things that are simply elements of people's characters irritates me considerably. 'Empathy – sixth sense?' by Anna Dawlish is an example of one such trend in my estimation. We all know the meaning of empathy but to suggest that it could be considered a sixth sense is simply, in my view, a clear-cut attempt to get a book on the best-sellers list. I would perhaps be less irritated if Ms Dawlish had written a book that clearly presented her ideas, with a logical progression. Instead, her writing takes the reader off on tangents and, in particular, her chapter on hunches seems disconnected from the main thrust of her arguments. In spite of my being an overly sensitive person, there is no way I could consider myself to have a sixth sense. The idea is, unfortunately, laughable.

D 'Empathy – sixth sense?' takes us through some fascinating interviews with people who have a high level of empathy, and who, according to the writer, are ultra-sensitive to the feelings and intentions of others. This publication is just the most recent in a long line of many on the popular topic of empathy, but differs from the rest in terms of its central premise that extreme empathy can be considered a sixth sense. While I can understand that empathy can explain in psychological terms the idea of hunches and intuition and removes the psychic element, the book has been compiled without any proper scientific studies and as such cannot be seen as adding anything relevant to that search for a sixth sense which intrigues so many of us. While doing little to satisfy this quest, I found the book engaging which was mainly due to the colourful characters whose experiences are documented.

Speaking or writing

6 Work in pairs. Have you ever had a hunch or a feeling about people or situations?

7 Write a post for the website detailing your opinions about whether, in your opinion, humans have a sixth sense, and what it is, or not, giving your reasons.

VOCABULARY: Internal word changes

1 What do you know about the six-dot braille system? Tell your partner. What other means of communication are there for those with visual or hearing impairments?

2 Turn to page 95 and read the text about the modern applications of braille. What are they?

3 Look at the words in bold in the text on page 95. What are their root words? What changes have taken place to create the new word?

Word	Root word
0 invaluable	_value_

Remove the 'e' and add the suffix -able

1	variation	_____
2	simplify	_____
3	inability	_____
4	undeniable	_____
5	visible	_____
6	comparable	_____
7	assurance	_____
8	reliably	_____

4 🎧 6.3 Listen to two people talking about using braille. Then complete the sentences.

Speaker 1

1 Blind people don't have a better sense of touch or better hearing than _____ (sight) people.

2 We have to work hard at braille … and use the same _____ (memory) techniques.

3 Braille has a huge _____ (signify) for me.

4 Unfortunately, braille _____ (literate) is on the decline, as younger blind people have a high _____ (depend) on note-takers and mobiles to get by.

Speaker 2

5 When people who know little about being blind see me holding one of my _____ (technology) gadgets, they _____ (vary) want to know how it works.

6 I don't mind their _____ (curious).

7 It's the perfect opportunity to educate people about what life's like for blind or _____ (vision) impaired people, and that promotes understanding and _____ (tolerate).

8 New technology's currently in development … so that people like me can read _____ (continue) with a stationary finger.

EXAM BOOST p6

> Complete Exam file SECTION C on page 6.

EXAM TASK

5 For questions 1–8, read the text below. Use the word given in capitals at the end of some of the lines to form a word that fits in the gap in the same line. There is an example at the beginning (0).

URBAN ART:
graffiti for the blind

Although he is **(0)** ___SIGHTED___ himself,	**SIGHT**
the graffiti artist known as 'The Blind' produces urban street art in braille for people with	
(1) _____ impairments.	**VISION**
Using oversized braille letters created from plaster, The Blind's tactile art can be found on public walls everywhere from his home town of Nantes, France, to Saint Petersburg in Russia.	
His **(2)** _____ appeal both to those	**INSCRIBE**
who can see and those who can't. They are also	
(3) _____ amusing: 'Do not touch'	**DENY**
reads one **(4)** _____ .	**COMPOSE**
Since graffiti is prohibited in many public spaces, The Blind's graffiti is actually **(5)** _____ .	**LAW**
It all started after he was thrown out of a museum in an **(6)** _____ manner after touching	**DIGNITY**
an exhibit which he thought had a fascinating-looking texture. A favourite anecdote of his is the time he told police he was carrying out an	
(7) _____ for blind people by making	**INITIATE**
public signs for them. They thought it was a great idea and left him alone.	
Nowadays, The Blind makes a living from his braille graffiti and is considering his most	
(8) _____ work yet: a graffito on the	**PROVOKE**
Great Wall of China.	

Speaking or writing

> Go to page 93 for these exercises.

1 What do you know about Route 66? What other famous routes or roads do you know of? Are there any famous routes people travel in your country?

2 🎧 6.4 Listen to a tour guide talking about Route 66 and answer these questions:

- Why did the road become popular?
- What contributed to its decline?
- What is happening to the road now?

EXAM FOCUS

Understanding specific information and stated opinion

In this part of the exam, you need to process and understand specific information and the speaker's stated opinion in order to complete the gaps with the right word(s).

Here are some examples of sentences which express the speaker's opinion:

- Victor uses the word 'overwhelmed' to describe how he felt on arrival at his destination.
- Victor thought that the history behind the road was especially fascinating.

Here are some examples of sentences which state specific (factual) information:

- Victor was invited to attend a car auction at his first stop on the route.
- Victor's sole companion on the boat talked about his work as a lighting technician.

3 Read the Exam focus. Now look at some information from the recording in Ex 2. Which sentences are factual (F)? Which include opinion (O)?

1 Route 66 was established on November 11th, 1926.
2 Road signs weren't erected until the following year.
3 The road served as the main – and what's more, crucial – route for migrants to the west during the 1930s.
4 The highway became increasingly popular and, understandably, businesses sprang up along it to cater for travellers.
5 Numerous roadside attractions were built, such as museums, animal farms and drive-in movie theatres.
6 Although many sections of the new roads followed alongside the old route, it was eventually replaced in its entirety.
7 It ultimately fell into disrepair, and sadly, multiple business died with it.
8 The road was officially decommissioned from the U.S. Highways System in 1985.
9 Those who wanted to travel the old Route 66 for nostalgic reasons found it frustratingly difficult to navigate.
10 Now people can drive parts of the Historic Route 66, and there is a route for bicycles, too.

EXAM FILE p31

EXAM BOOST p30

> Complete Exam file SECTION B on page 30.

EXAM TASK

4 🎧 6.5 You will hear a woman called Nadine talking on a radio programme about her experiences of travelling Route 66 in the USA. For questions 1–8, complete the sentences with a word or short phrase.

Travelling Route 66

Nadine and her friend did a lot of research before travelling in case of any **(1)** _____ they took.

Nadine enjoyed trying some **(2)** _____ at their first stop at a diner.

Nadine describes her experience of staying the night in a motel as a(n) **(3)** '_____' one, due to its historic past.

At the Hall of Fame Museum, Route 66 **(4)** _____ caught Nadine's attention.

Nadine took some great shots of what she and her friend called the **(5)** _____ when they got lost one day.

Nadine thinks some listeners will be interested by a stretch of road known most commonly as the **(6)** _____ .

Nadine particularly enjoyed seeing the **(7)** _____ as they drove through varied landscapes.

Nadine uses the word **(8)** '_____' to describe the way their journey had sometimes been.

Speaking or writing

5 You're going to circumnavigate the world! What planning would you need to do in advance? Discuss ideas with your partner.

6 Write about a memorable or 'epic' journey you've made. Include key points, such as the mode of transport, what you ate and saw, who you met or where you stayed. Then tell your partner about it.

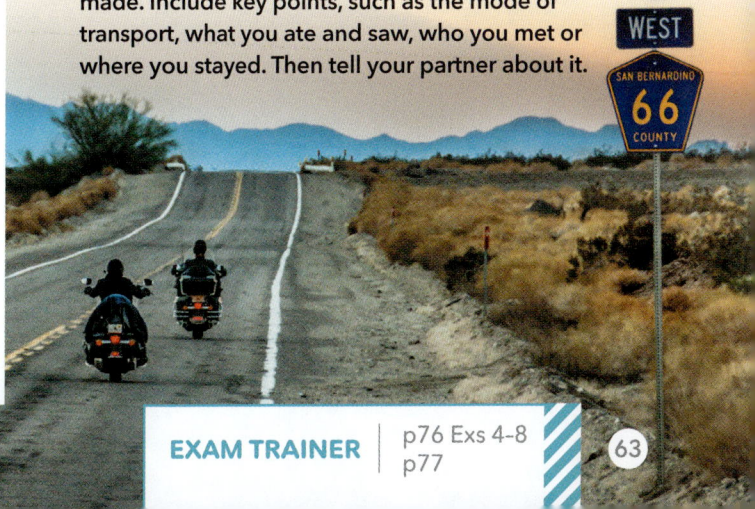

EXAM TRAINER | p76 Exs 4-8 p77

EXAM FILE p9
GRAMMAR FILE pp108–109
EXAM BOOST p8

GRAMMAR: Verb and noun phrases

1 Snowflakes naturally have six points. Can you think of any other examples of six-sided shapes in nature?

2 🎧 6.6 Listen to a science student giving a talk about six-sided shapes in nature. What six-sided things does she mention?

3 Look at the sentences from the talk in Ex 2. Replace the words in bold with a noun (n) or verb phrase (v) to complete the second sentence.

1 Honeycomb provides **storage** for honey.
Honey _____ (v) in honeycomb.

2 Honeycomb hexagons soften into **interlocking** shapes.
Honeycomb hexagons soften and _____ (v + adj in different form) in different shapes.

3 Dragonflies **experience** colour in a far superior way to any other known creature.
The _____ (n) dragonflies have of colour is far superior to any other known creature.

4 It is in inorganic structures that we might **expect** to find hexagons more frequently.
There is _____ (n) that we will find hexagons more frequently in inorganic structures.

5 Water molecules **form** hexagons when they are arranged just right.
The _____ (n) hexagons takes place when water molecules are arranged just right.

6 This hexagon is an **unchanging** feature of that planet.
This hexagonal feature of the planet does _____ (v).

4 Turn to page 95 and read the text about the use of hexagons in everyday life. Transform the phrases in bold in the text using the words given in capital letters below and any other necessary words. You will need to change the form of the word in capital letters, using the part of speech shown in brackets.

0 CIRCLE (n) If nuts and bolts were <u>formed as circles</u>, it would be hard for tools to grip them.

1 TIGHT (v) When nuts and bolts are screwed together, they _____ as a result.

2 PREVAIL (n) The _____ of the shape of nuts and bolts throughout the centuries is due to this.

3 DENSE (adv) Individual pieces can _____ together.

4 CREATE (n) The _____ takes place when they are stitched together.

5 PREVENT (v) The pencil's hexagonal shape _____ rolling.

6 MANUFACTURE (v) While they _____ , they can be stacked together without wasting space.

EXAM TASK

5 For questions 1–6, complete the second sentence so that it has a similar meaning to the first sentence, using the word given. Do not change the word given. You must use between three and six words, including the word given. Here is an example (0).

0 Circles cannot be packed as densely together as hexagons.
COMPARISON
Circles have a low packing <u>DENSITY IN COMPARISON WITH</u> hexagons.

1 It is the rigidity of triangles that makes them one of the strongest shapes.
ARE
Triangles _____ what makes them one of the strongest shapes.

2 The square is not a particularly strong shape as it can easily be flexed into a rhombus.
DEAL
There is not a great _____ the square as it can easily be flexed into a rhombus.

3 Circles are measured by circumference, diameter and radius.
OF
The _____ consist of its circumference, diameter and radius.

4 Triangles aren't commonly used in home construction – imagine walking through a triangular door!
COMMON
It isn't _____ using triangles – imagine walking through a triangular door!

5 The majority of man-made diamonds are used for industrial purposes.
USAGE
The _____ man-made diamonds is industrial.

6 In maths, symmetry can have a very precise definition.
BE
Symmetry can _____ in mathematics.

Speaking or writing

> Go to page 93 for these exercises.

EXAM TRAINER | p22 Exs 5–6

1 Look at the picture and discuss what it might tell us about the character of the person whose workspace this is. If we say that this person is 'at sixes and sevens', what do you think the phrase might mean?

2 🎧 **6.7** Listen to an exchange on a radio programme about organisation between the owner of the workspace in the picture below and a psychologist and answer the questions.

1 What examples of disorganisation does the speaker give?

2 What reassurance does the psychologist give him?

3 Answer the survey questions and compare your answers with a partner, giving examples. How similar are you?

Do you
(or someone you know …)

1 usually write 'to-do' lists? If so, do you tend to do the things on the lists or not?

2 have a special place for everything?

3 ever double-book yourself, or forget appointments?

4 usually plan things or leave them to the last minute?

5 make a daily schedule for when you're on holiday?

6 usually arrive on time, well before time, or late for arranged meetings?

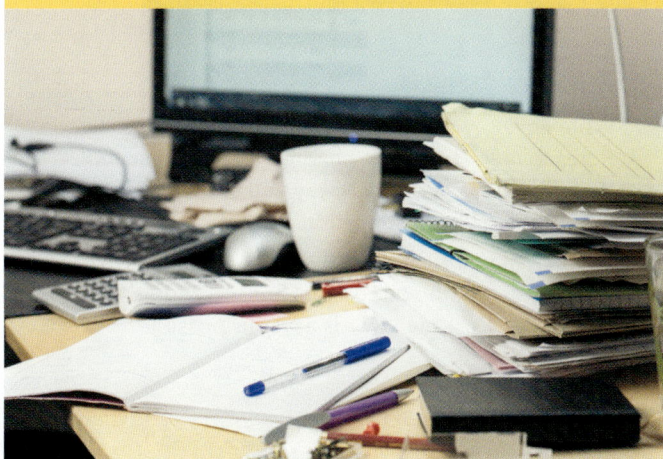

4 In pairs, write down some problems there might be when living with a very disorganised person. Swap with another pair and discuss the different problems.

5 🎧 **6.8** Listen to two candidates discussing which of several problems about living with a disorganised person might be most difficult to deal with. Which problems do they mention?

6 🎧 **6.9** Read the Exam focus. Listen again to the discussion from Ex 5. Which phrases from the Exam focus did they use?

EXAM FOCUS

Evaluating, referring, reassessing

After a Part 3 discussion task you will be asked a decision question related to your discussion. When discussing this question, you will need to revisit the points you discussed, evaluate them, perhaps reassess and work towards a decision or choice.

So, looking again at these …

Taking everything that we said into consideration, I'd go for …

I know we talked about these two points as being important, but if we have to choose the most … which would you go for?

I appreciate that we said that … but … on reflection

OK, to summarise – if I remember rightly, we agreed that these two points were … because …

EXAM BOOST p40

> Complete Exam file SECTION B on page 40.

EXAM TASK

7 Here are some aspects of our lives where we need to be organised to some extent, and a question for you to discuss. First you have some time to look at the task.

Now, talk to each other about how important it is to be organised in these aspects of our lives.

at work or at college	in our personal spaces	with food and health routines

How important is it to be organised in these aspects of our lives?

when socialising	with financial matters

Now you have about a minute to decide which aspect of our lives is most important to be organised.

Speaking or writing

8 Do you think multitasking or dealing with one task at a time is the more efficient way of working? Why?

9 A friend has emailed you complaining about their lack of organisation and asking you for your advice on how to become better organised. Reply to their email, either sympathising with them, explaining that you have similar problems, or giving them some tips.

EXAM FILE p19

VOCABULARY FILE pp124–125

WRITING FILE p130

1 Write down as many important dates from history as you can remember in one minute. Compare with your partner and see if they know what happened on the dates you've written. Do you think it's important to learn dates in school history lessons? Why? / Why not?

2 Match the important dates in world history with the events.

HOW'S YOUR WORLD HISTORY?

MATCH THE YEARS TO THE HISTORICAL EVENTS.

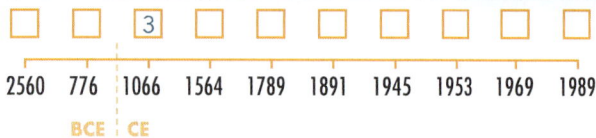

☐	☐	3	☐	☐	☐	☐	☐	☐	☐
2560	776	1066	1564	1789	1891	1945	1953	1969	1989

BCE : CE

1 Invention of World Wide Web
2 First man walked on the moon
3 Norman invasion of Britain
4 French Revolution began
5 Great Pyramid of Giza completed
6 Discovery of DNA structure
7 First Olympiad
8 United Nations formed
9 Shakespeare was born
10 Invention of basketball

3a Read the essay title in Ex 4 and discuss what points you might include and related opinions. Complete the notes below in Ex 4, using your own ideas.

3b 🎧 **6.10** Now listen to a podcast from a writer talking about history lessons. Does he mention any of your points or opinions?

4 Your class has watched a TV discussion about the best ways to teach history to children at primary school. You have made the notes below:

> **What's the best way to teach history to children at primary school?**
> _____
> _____
> _____

> Some opinions expressed in the discussion:
> _____
> _____
> _____

Write an essay discussing **two** of the best ways in your notes to teach history to children at primary school. You should **explain which way you think is the more important**, giving **justifications** for your answer.

You may, if you wish, make use of the opinions expressed in the discussion, but you should use your own words as far as possible.

EXAM FOCUS

Complex sentences

Creating complex sentences and guiding the reader through the essay.

1   Use linking devices and reference phrases:
    Attempts have been made to rectify the problem **and yet** there are still issues.
    For a similar reason, it has proved difficult to implement the second policy.

2   Focus attention on a point by using wh- clefts: **What is interesting is that** this idea was first proposed about ten years ago.
    What is equally important is that we learn from the past …

3   Use words and phrases to sequence your points: As a start / Firstly / To conclude / Another important point is …

5   Read the Exam focus then the example essay for the essay title in Ex 4. Does it include different points or opinions to those you included in your essay? Highlight examples of words and phrases the writer has used to create more complex sentences.

Generations of young children have been put off studying history because of its seeming irrelevance to the present, and yet its importance as part of a general education is undeniable. In light of this, teachers today need to find ways to engage their students so that history becomes intriguing as opposed to a chore.

Firstly, while it is true that children are eager to learn new things, their interest can fade if their imaginations are not captured quickly and held. A way to do this with history lessons is to not isolate history from other subjects. One example could be bringing history and cooking together, engaging the children in a physical activity and creating a memorable experience. Making meals that people used to eat could be more meaningful than reading or hearing about it. Likewise, comparing building plans from houses in the past with houses of today can help children learn about how people lived in past times.

What is also engaging for young children is to learn about a subject through story-telling. History is full of dramatic stories and what child is not interested when there is humour involved? There are some wonderful history storybooks today that bring historical characters to life through comedy. Some of these have even been made into TV series and using them in class can definitely make history come alive.

To conclude, I would add that what is equally important as these examples of how to interest children is the enthusiasm of the teacher. Together with the points described above, a committed history teacher can inspire children to learn about the past in ways that textbooks alone cannot manage.

EXAM BOOST p18

> Complete Exam file SECTION B on page 18.

6   In pairs, read the essay question in the exam task. Discuss which two points you would write about and think of some examples.

EXAM TASK

7   Your class has listened to a radio discussion about the reasons why it is important for students to study world history at school. You have made the notes below:

> **What reasons are there for studying world history at school or college?**
>
> - understand our present world
> - learn from mistakes made in the past
> - become culturally aware

> Some opinions expressed in the discussion:
>
> 'Perhaps understanding other countries' history can help us understand those people's viewpoints today.'
>
> 'Surely we need to know why our world is like it is today?'
>
> 'I don't think we ever learn from our mistakes in the past – unfortunately!'

Write an essay discussing **two** of the reasons in your notes for the importance of studying world history at school or college. You should **explain which reason you think is the more important**, giving **justifications** for your answer.

You may, if you wish, make use of the opinions expressed in the discussion, but you should use your own words as far as possible.

8   Exchange essays with your partner and compare the complexity of the sentences and your use of cohesive devices.

EXAM TRAINER p54 Exs 8–9
p55

REVIEW | UNITS 1-6

READING AND USE OF ENGLISH – PART 1

1 Read the text below and decide which answer (A, B, C or D) best fits each gap.

Can there really only be six degrees of separation?

The six degrees of separation theory **(0)** ___A___ out the possibility that we can all connect with each other through just six other people. At first **(1)** _____ it seems crazy, right?

It was originally proposed in 1930 by the Hungarian writer Frigyes Karinthy, when the whole idea of online social media was **(2)** _____ . His premise was that the number of people connected to a single person increases exponentially. So for **(3)** _____ let's take an individual called Sam. Sam knows 100 people, each of whom knows a different 100, so the people Sam could potentially have access to increases to 10,000, and so on. All he'd need to make contact is one meeting. At a **(4)** _____ he could hypothetically reach millions.

It's a great theory, but how useful is it in practice? Well, networking and establishing contacts is what turns the **(5)** _____ of much of the business world. Given that, it follows that **(6)** _____ your position in a company, you should file away details of every new person you come **(7)** _____ for reference later. Your future success may **(8)** _____ not from what you know, but who.

0	A	sets	B	gives	C	carries	D	works
1	A	view	B	glance	C	stare	D	gaze
2	A	undeniable	B	invisible	C	unreliable	D	unimaginable
3	A	instance	B	clarification	C	illustration	D	case
4	A	distance	B	length	C	stretch	D	space
5	A	wheels	B	engines	C	motors	D	generators
6	A	however	B	whatever	C	whenever	D	wherever
7	A	about	B	among	C	with	D	across
8	A	leap	B	jump	C	spring	D	bound

READING AND USE OF ENGLISH – PART 2

2 Read the text below and think of the word which best fits each gap. Use only one word in each gap.

Board games aren't boring!

At the board games café there are some chess players as usual, but two opponents are engrossed in a different board game. They're trying to outdo each **(0)** ___OTHER___ by placing the highest-scoring word they **(1)** _____ on the board in turns.

One player starts to place a letter tile on the board, then decides to reconsider his move instead. He frowns **(2)** _____ concentration, as though this **(3)** _____ not a conventional word game but instead an exceptionally complex game of chess. Attentive to his every move, his opponent waits for him to finish his turn.

He is clearly uncomfortable with the scrutiny and appears to **(4)** _____ in, all but throwing the word he **(5)** _____ chosen onto the board. With that, his opponent triumphantly places her own word on the board, and **(6)** _____ a quick tally of the scores, declares herself the winner. The man sighs in undeniable annoyance, then breaks out into a broad grin and shakes the victor's hand. There was **(7)** _____ any real rivalry between the two opponents – they've clearly enjoyed this novel outlet for their stress and now the game **(8)** _____ over, they relax into easy chat.

READING AND USE OF ENGLISH – PART 3

3 Read the text below. Use the word given in capitals at the end of some of the lines to form a word that fits in the gap in the same line.

Driving round Iceland

The land of fire and ice has plenty to entertain the road tripper, no matter which **(0)** _____LENGTH_____ of road you find yourself driving along. Stunning landscapes are a given, and there'll always be natural **(1)** _____ that are definitely worth making a **(2)** _____ for: glaciers, hot springs and volcanoes abound. It isn't **(3)** _____ of for visitors to extend their stay in order to take in more of the incredible sights.

Iceland is by no means a huge country and no matter how far into the wilderness you think you've gone, comfortable **(4)** _____ where you can rest your head for the night are never far away. Its small size means circumnavigating the whole island in just a few days is far from **(5)** _____ , and pretty much anyone with a vehicle and the inclination to do it, can. Even if you aren't a **(6)** _____ road traveller, you'll find many of the relatively empty routes away from the capital both highly **(7)** _____ and gloriously beautiful, providing the sense that you're away from it all yet never too far from civilisation. Wherever your Icelandic road trip takes you, you'll be **(8)** _____ you took the plunge!

LONG

ATTRACT
DIVERT

HEAR

LODGE

MANAGE

SEASON

ACCESS

THANK

READING AND USE OF ENGLISH – PART 4

4 Complete the second sentence so that it has a similar meaning to the first sentence, using the word given. Do not change the word given. You must use between three and six words, including the word given.

0 The workings of the brain were puzzling for scientists for a long time until research helped them understand it.

HAD

How THE BRAIN WORKED HAD PUZZLED scientists for a long time until research helped them understand it.

1 People called the first bikes velocipedes and rode them in the early 19th century.

AS

The first bikes were _____ ridden in the early 19th century.

2 You published a book and won a prize for it, too!

YOU

Not only _____ you won a prize for it, too!

3 Bella told me she loved the shoes I'd chosen for the occasion.

COMPLIMENTED

Bella _____ of shoes for the occasion.

4 One student has suggested that we do fewer but longer days at college.

FORWARD

One student has _____ that we do fewer but longer days at college.

5 If we all ate fewer meat and dairy products, we'd improve our health and the planet's, too.

WERE

We'd improve our health and the planet's, too, _____ eat less meat and dairy.

6 We have a commitment to preventing fake news from spreading.

THE

We are _____ of the spread of fake news.

69

READING AND USE OF ENGLISH – PART 3

5 Read the text below. Use the word given in capitals at the end of some of the lines to form a word that fits in the gap in the same line.

How we think of music

Most people would probably name around six categories into which they place their music, including classical, rock, pop, folk, blues and soul, but could this breakdown be **(0)** _____DIVISIVE_____ , **DIVIDE**
even elitist? Could music be labelled more
(1) _____ ? One suggestion would be **INCLUDE**
to consider its purpose and impact rather than its genre.

To test the **(2)** _____ of this, consider **FEASIBLE**
the kind of music people find **(3)** _____ . **LIFT**
Most would accept that singing creates a feeling of well-being, but the actual music that's sung
seems to be **(4)** _____ . It may straddle **RELEVANT**
more than one traditional category but its effect is
(5) _____ the same. **DENY**

Now take the need for **(6)** _____ . **ASSURE**
Everyone hums soothing melodies to crying babies, or plays nostalgic tunes at times of emotional turmoil. Yet one person's musical choice in such
situations may be **(7)** _____ to others. **COMPREHEND**

It follows that we shouldn't pigeonhole ourselves as classical or rock fans, but how we use music and what it does for us. Although some may find this provocative, they might actually be surprised at the
(8) _____ of their own playlists! **DIVERSE**

READING AND USE OF ENGLISH – PART 4

6 Complete the second sentence so that it has a similar meaning to the first sentence, using the word given. Do not change the word given. You must use between three and six words, including the word given.

0 The workings of the brain were puzzling for scientists for a long time until research helped them understand it.

HAD

How ___THE BRAIN WORKED HAD____
____PUZZLED____ scientists for a long time until research helped them understand it.

1 Students have misplaced a significant number of ID cards.

BY

The number of ID cards that have

_____

insignificant.

2 They wouldn't have printed your article if they didn't like it.

MUST

They _____
they wouldn't have printed it.

3 'You should definitely enter the marathon – you'll manage it easily,' my aunt said.

ENCOURAGED

My aunt _____
part in the marathon and said I'd easily manage it.

4 I recently accepted the task of clearing up after the school sports day.

TAKEN

I _____ the
task of clearing up after our school sports day.

5 There would be huge benefits for the Earth should we all go vegan.

WENT

The Earth would benefit

_____ vegan.

6 Many things are hexagon-shaped in nature.

NATURALLY

Many things have

_____ shape.

VOCABULARY: Phrasal verbs

1 How much do you know about nitrogen (atomic number 7)? Complete the fact file about nitrogen using the words in the box.

air anaesthetic buildings colour computers liquid poisonous

NITROGEN FACT FILE

1 Nitrogen has no _____ , taste or smell.

2 Nitrogen is _____ in its purest form.

3 A form of nitrogen is used to demolish old _____ .

4 Nitrogen makes up around 88 percent of the _____ around us.

5 Nitrogen is used in _____ to cool them down.

6 Nitrous oxide is used as a(n) _____ .

7 Nitrogen is a(n) _____ at very low temperatures.

2 7.1 Listen to a university lecturer talking about the uses of nitrogen and answer the following question.

How is nitrogen used in the following industries?
- medicine
- electronics
- food
- motorsports

3 7.2 Complete each sentence with the correct form of a phrasal verb from the box. Then listen again and check.

dispose of draw on go into keep from kick in make up

1 Although nitrogen forms part of us and it _____ most of the air we breathe, it can have a devastating effect on the body in certain circumstances.

2 The rapidly changing pressure of water releases nitrogen bubbles into the body and decompression sickness _____ .

3 A lot of effort _____ conserving blood and other biological specimens and in its liquid state, nitrogen is perfectly suited to do this.

4 Although nitrogen itself can be a pollutant, it is also used to control worse pollutants, by _____ toxic liquids and vapours from industrial tools.

5 Nitrogen's used in packaging to ensure a stable atmosphere within it. This _____ the food _____ oxidising, which would lead to it going off.

6 Motorsports engineers also _____ nitrogen's properties.

4 Match the phrasal verbs in Ex 3 with the words and phrases below.

a use information or knowledge
b form
c spend creating or doing
d get rid of, throw away
e start to happen
f prevent

5 Which of the uses of nitrogen do you think is the most valuable or interesting?

1 In pairs, discuss the question.

What are the ingredients of a good story?

2 🎧 **7.3** It is said that there are seven basic plots and every story will use one of these. What might they be? Listen and check your ideas. Do your examples from Ex 1 fit these categories?

1 What are the seven basic plots?

2 What is the speaker's opinion of the book?

3 Read three paragraphs from an article about professional story-tellers and put them into the correct order. What helped you decide?

A This ability involves a honing of a natural skill, requiring a talent for giving a voice to individual characters, almost personifying the story with gestures, expressions and movement to enrapture the audience, whether that is a child in a hospital bed or adults on a ghost walk.

B I would hazard a guess that when most people think of 'story-telling' they imagine a parent reading a bedtime story to a child. The idea that people can earn a living from telling stories professionally might be quite alien. However, the job is becoming ever more popular and is clearly fulfilling a need in our society today.

C The story-teller taps into our inborn desire to escape into a different world for a while. There is something magical about being told a story, seeing the characters brought to life by someone who is expert at engaging with the listener.

4 Read the Exam focus and summarise the focus of each paragraph in Ex 3 in your own words.

EXAM FOCUS

Understanding the structure of a text

A text is written following a logical structure that leads the reader from one point through expansion, comment, opinion and example, to another.

- Look for ways in which a paragraph develops from ideas mentioned in the first.
- Check tenses to help follow the track of a developing account or narrative.
- Sometimes a paragraph may return to a previous idea, but there will always be references.
- Make a mental summary of what each paragraph is about, or its purpose, to identify where a paragraph fits in a text.

EXAM BOOST p14

> Complete Exam file SECTION B on page 14.

EXAM TASK

5 You are going to read an extract from a magazine article. Six paragraphs have been removed from the extract. Choose from the paragraphs A–G the one which fits each gap (1–6). There is one extra paragraph which you do not need to use.

A In addition to this, she thought she would be doing something that would genuinely add to the town's mix. 'When I moved there, shops were closing down in the recession. I felt it was a way to combine my passion and bring other artists together as well as to do something useful for the community. Which it did.'

B With a couple of hours to kill before her evening performance of ghost stories, she leads me over to the infinitely more convivial surroundings of the Hungry Elephant Café tent where Brand continues to explain how she reached this point in her life.

C 'I've always loved stories and story-telling ever since I was a little girl,' she recalls. 'I remember I always wanted to be the one who read out the story, to the point where my mother said to me, 'Isn't it time you just wrote your own?' I grew up in Bombay, and in India there's always some cultural festival taking place and there's always a story behind it.'

D Afterwards we troop into the darkness. From the conversations outside, it's apparent that many of those in the tent have returned for the second night running, many people went thinking they'd just go to one event but found themselves attending several. Why? 'That's just about the simple pleasure of listening to a good yarn.'

E Part of that meandering took her back to India and to Southeast Asia, touring with a show based partly on her own upbringing in India, and which she staged successfully again in Settle soon after relocating there. To the surprise of many local people though, the Settle festival's first incarnation was pitched mainly at an adult audience.

F As an example, she points out that many of the classic stories told today have evolved over many ages and through countless retellings, in many lands. 'Take Cinderella,' she says. 'There's a Vietnamese version and various North African versions, a North American version, a European one …' She smiles. 'I like that.'

G Bombay to Yorkshire might seem an unlikely path to tread but for Brand – with an English mother and a South Indian father – it is the fulfilment of a dream. Her introduction to Yorkshire came about ten years ago on a trip to look up old family friends, 'I just fell in love with the place; I thought, this is where I want to live,' she says.

TELL ME A STORY!

Sita Brand is recounting the tale of how story-telling came to be in her blood, and as one might expect of a professional story-teller, she is doing a pretty good job of it.

1

It's a dismally wet and chilly evening at the arts and music festival in North Yorkshire, where I first find Brand. She has been booked to tell rounds of stories – children's fairytales during the afternoons and some darker, more ghostly recountings after dusk – but has suffered some unexpected nocturnal goings-on herself, her tent having filled up with rainwater the previous night. Yet, in keeping with the festival mood, she seems stoical as we squelch through a custard-like mud swamp.

2

She has lived and worked in several parts of England but most recently in Settle, the Yorkshire town beloved of walkers and railway enthusiasts but not hitherto known for its story-telling scene. In the four years since moving there, however, she has worked energetically to change that, establishing her own business, as well as founding an annual story-telling festival. But why here?

3

Not that her yearning came entirely without precedent. 'The most exciting thing,' she says, 'is that I recently discovered that my mother's side of the family came from this area. So, deep down inside I was always a Yorkshirewoman!' She laughs. Having worked on and off as a story-teller for several years, Brand conceived the idea for the Settle Storytelling Festival as a way of establishing herself professionally in the area.

4

Before settling there she'd found work with Common Lore, a company of story-tellers and musicians. Later, she branched out and worked variously as an actor, writer, director and producer. She's travelled a lot doing different things, but she admits, 'In my heart, I've always loved stories and storytelling.'

5

This was a deliberate move on Brand's part to get across her conviction that story-telling should not just be aimed at children. 'When you look at books of traditional stories, they're called folk tales,' she says, raising her voice above the thudding jazz-rock bass emanating from beyond the tent. 'They're literally tales for the folk. That's all of us.' This year she says there will be more events specifically laid on for kids, 'but the emphasis is very much on the oral tradition, about stories being passed down from generation to generation.'

6

Brand says many of her own stories were themselves passed on from family members, that she has then changed and reworked. 'The way I tell it today might be different to the way I tell it tomorrow or the day after.' Through that process, like a Chinese whisper, she says a story is refined and shaped in different directions.

Speaking or writing

6 If you were given the job of being a professional story-teller for a day, what would you find interesting or difficult about it? Why?

7 Work in pairs and tell each other a story you enjoyed being read when you were a child. Try to act it out with voice, expressions and gestures. Find out who is the best story-teller in the class.

8 On a blank piece of paper, write an opening paragraph to a story. Rotate the papers and continue the stories one paragraph at a time.

EXAM FILE p3

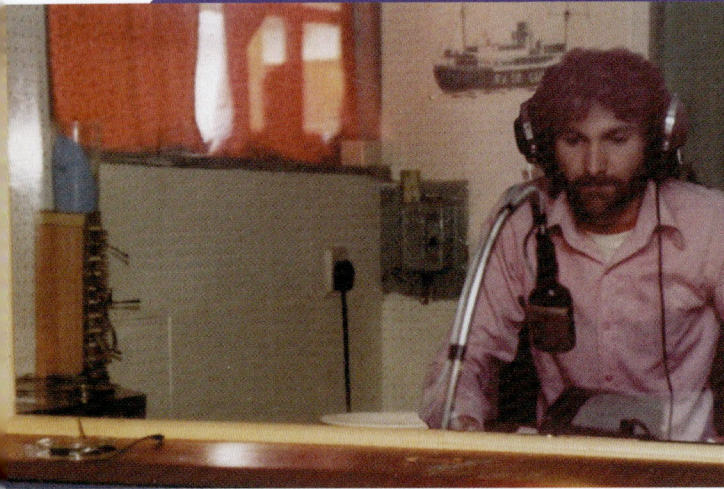

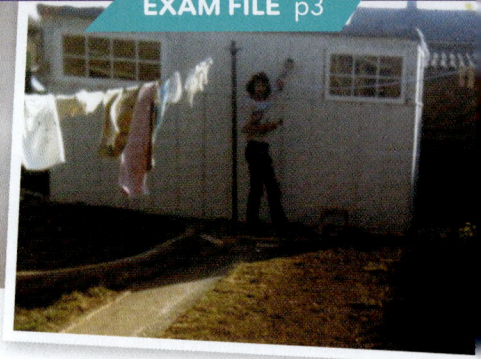

VOCABULARY: Easily confused words

1 What do you think the man in the photos is doing? Where is he? What do you think his ambitions are?

2 🎧 7.4 Listen to a short news programme about how one man's lifelong dream became a reality. What happened?

3 Choose the correct word in each of the summary sentences about Deke Duncan and Radio 77.

1 Deke was under no **illusion** / **allusion** that he would ever become a professional DJ.

2 Radio 77 ran **continually** / **continuously** on weekend days from dawn until midnight.

3 Deke **implied** / **inferred** that when his wife popped out, his whole audience had switched off.

4 The BBC's tweet worked to great **affect** / **effect**, prompting a local radio station to track Deke down.

5 Deke was **assured** / **ensured** he would get the chance to play his favourite tunes on air for a whole hour.

6 Deke thought it was a huge **complement** / **compliment** to be offered the chance of a lifetime.

4 What dreams or ambitions did you have when you were younger? Have you fulfilled any of them? How have your dreams/ambitions changed since then?

5 Turn to page 95 and read the text about the world's first vlog. Complete it with words from the box below. Do not use any word more than once. There are six words you do not need to use.

account   composed   comprised   farther
further   historic   historical   peruse   pursue
principal   principle   recount

EXAM BOOST p2
Complete Exam file SECTION D on page 2.

EXAM TASK

6 For questions 1–8, read the text below and decide which answer (A, B, C or D) best fits each gap. There is an example at the beginning (0).

THE FUTURE OF broadcasting

Reports often **(0)** __B__ to the 'fact' that TV is dying. On the contrary, it's evolving rapidly and, in order to stay current, it's had to adapt. The most **(1)** _____ change is that audiences who watch programmes on an actual TV set are on the **(2)** _____ , and many people rely solely on digital devices to access the news, weather and other programmes. You'd be right to **(3)** _____ from this that broadcasters have had to, and will have to, keep **(4)** _____ their strategies to remain relevant.

Many broadcasters, for example, now use what are known as 'over-the-top' (OTT) delivery systems. Viewers don't need to **(5)** _____ to use the service – which is delivered over the internet – as they would for traditional cable or satellite services. But to keep today's tech-dependent viewers engaged, broadcasters will need to **(6)** _____ update the way they do things.

Experts say that in future, TV companies will **(7)** _____ their broadcasts through augmented intelligence, new and interactive delivery technologies, big data and more powerful smartphones for consumers, to **(8)** _____ they maintain their core values: to educate and inform.

0	A suggest	B allude	C indicate	D elude
1	A noticed	B famous	C distinguished	D notable
2	A decline	B downturn	C decrease	D descent
3	A reason	B infer	C imply	D hint
4	A adjusting	B correcting	C amending	D converting
5	A ascribe	B prescribe	C subscribe	D proscribe
6	A restlessly	B eternally	C interminably	D continually
7	A air	B express	C convey	D move
8	A insure	B assure	C ensure	D secure

Speaking or writing

Go to page 93 for these exercises.

EXAM TRAINER | p9 Ex 6

1 The world's population has recently passed 7.7 billion. What are the challenges created by a low/high population in a country or region? What might be the reasons for population decline or growth?

2 🎧 **7.5** Listen to two geography students talking about the concept of overpopulation. What causes of overpopulation has the boy read about?

3 🎧 **7.6** Now listen to the girl talking about the suggested effects of overpopulation. What effects does she mention?

EXAM FOCUS

Understanding feeling

In this part of the exam, you need to understand how people feel about something. This may be stated directly or indirectly.

Direct statement of feeling, e.g.

Sounds like a weak argument to me. Forgive me for being sceptical.

I feel thoroughly ashamed of what humanity has done to our beautiful planet.

Indirect statement of feeling, e.g.

The idea that people don't understand the impact of overpopulation is totally patronising! I wish people didn't say that sort of stuff. (annoyed)

I find it incredibly difficult to understand why, with the current climate emergency, people still keep travelling by plane. (frustrated)

4 Read the Exam focus. How do you feel about what the girl said? Choose a feeling or feelings from the box and explain why, without using the adjectives themselves.

The idea that there could be conflicts over lack of water in the future bothers me.

> ambivalent devastated disgusted
> frustrated helpless inspired privileged
> troubled uncomfortable

EXAM BOOST p32

> Complete Exam file SECTION B on page 32.

EXAM TASK

5 🎧 **7.7** You will hear part of a discussion with two scientists about global population. For questions 1–6, choose the answer (A, B, C or D) which fits best according to what you hear.

1 How does Hugo feel about being asked to talk about overpopulation?
  A resigned to the fact that his arguments will attract criticism
  B frustrated that people refuse to try to understand his ideas
  C annoyed that he cannot resist getting into an argument about it
  D regretful that he doesn't always manage to get his point across

2 When Hugo is asked about overpopulation being a problem, he says that humans
  A can modify their needs to suit their environment.
  B are quickly able to adapt to changing environments.
  C have always been innovative within their environment.
  D could rely more heavily on the natural environment.

3 When talking about the extinction of species,
  A Hugo chooses not to counter Bethany's argument.
  B Bethany and Hugo are unable to find any common ground.
  C Bethany is prepared to back down on one particular point.
  D Bethany and Hugo express annoyance at each other's viewpoint.

4 How does Bethany feel about overcrowding?
  A alarmed at the rapid rate of development in cities
  B appalled by the conditions in which many people live
  C upset by the thought that little can be done about it
  D guilty about the impact she has personally had on things

5 When asked about food and hunger, Hugo says he
  A is in disagreement with the ideas put forward by some people.
  B feels upset that we have not yet worked out how to feed everyone.
  C is exasperated by the current slow rate of technological progress.
  D has concerns that there may not enough space for agriculture in future.

6 When discussing the subject of becoming vegan, Bethany and Hugo agree that
  A eating a plant-based diet is the best way forward.
  B having a wider variety of food would be healthier for us.
  C developing new sources of food would be beneficial.
  D nature is affected negatively by our present actions.

Speaking or writing

6 What possible solutions could there be to deal with issues that may arise from overpopulation? Discuss your ideas in small groups.

7 Write a paragraph about the pros and cons for small or falling populations in a region or country. Then tell your partner.

EXAM TRAINER | p80 Exs 5–6 p81

EXAM FILE p5
GRAMMAR FILE pp110-111

GRAMMAR: Future tenses

1 Work in pairs and discuss the following questions.

- How sustainable do you think your lifestyle is?
- How different do you think the future will be in seven generations' time?

2 🎧 7.8 Listen to a sustainability studies student talking about a company called Seventh Generation. What are the company's plans for the future?

3 🎧 7.9 Complete the summary sentences with a future verb form. Then listen again and check.

1 They will be _____ (do) a lot of things to achieve their goal of becoming a zero-waste company,

2 These things _____ (include) reducing the amounts of products and packaging that end up in landfill.

3 By 2025, 100 percent of their products and ingredients _____ (be) bio-based.

4 By then, the company will also have _____ (work) hard to reduce the amount of palm oil they use, and will _____ (replace) 30 percent of it with bio-based oil.

5 In addition, they are _____ (ensure) that all their packaging will be reusable, reused, recyclable, recycled and biodegradable.

6 They are _____ (not leave) rubbish for other people to deal with.

7 I wonder how many other companies will _____ (follow) in Seventh Generation's footsteps by 2025?

4 Read about two young people and their plans to live even more sustainable lives in the future. Complete each gap with an appropriate auxiliary verb. There may be more than one correct answer.

EXAM BOOST p4

> Complete Exam file SECTION D on page 4.

Karla 'I've been experimenting with making my own make-up using all-natural ingredients – soaps and shampoo, too. I ¹_____ start selling them to friends and family soon, and if that takes off, I ²_____ think about setting up my own business.

Raffi Tomorrow I ³_____ celebrating the fact that I haven't bought anything that wasn't absolutely necessary for six months. By the same time next year, I ⁴_____ doing that for 18 months, and I hope to continue that way for the rest of my life! I get second-hand clothes, and cycle to work. People think that one person's actions ⁵_____ make any difference to the planet, but if we all join in, they absolutely will.

EXAM TASK

5 For questions 1-8, read the text below and think of the word which best fits each gap. Use only one word in each gap. There is an example at the beginning (0).

SUSTAINABILITY IN THE 2020s

Experts have **(0)** ___BEEN___ considering the sustainability trends of the 2020s. One of the first things that we will **(1)** _____ to make more effort with is dealing with plastic pollution. They say that **(2)** _____ there is currently much anti-plastic sentiment, it isn't yet leading to enough action.

They also predict that by 2050 there will have been a huge increase **(3)** _____ the number of people displaced by climate issues, reaching an all-time high of one billion people. And in the 2020s, half the world will **(4)** _____ online. Reports state that we are **(5)** _____ to have to speed up our energy revolution and work out how to share information on a wider scale.

Another trend **(6)** _____ that citizens are becoming more involved in acting against climate change and governments will have to start being more proactive in dealing with issues. Businesses simply **(7)** _____ face today's challenges head on, and find solutions that will enhance our environment.

Hopefully, by the time 2050 comes round, we will be living in a far **(8)** _____ sustainable world than we are now.

Speaking or writing

> Go to page 93 for these exercises.

EXAM TRAINER | p13 Exs 5–6

1 **Read the quote and discuss what you think it means.**

> Give me a child until he's seven and I will give you the man.

2 **Read a blog about a TV programme called '7 Up' and answer the questions.**

1 Summarise the content of the blog in two sentences.

2 Do you agree that our life is mapped out for us by the age of seven? Why? / Why not?

3 Would you like to have taken part in such a series? Why? / Why not?

How would YOU like to have your life watched and filmed at the age of seven, and then discussed and broadcast to the nation? This is what happened to a group of seven-year-olds back in 1964. In what has since been described as the first true reality TV show, the lives of 14 children from a range of different socio-economic backgrounds were filmed, initially as a one-off documentary to show how strong class structure is in the UK and how people's future lives can be determined by the age of seven. As it turned out, the documentary proved so interesting that another documentary has been filmed with the same people every seven years since, the most recent being '56 Up!'. It has been fascinating to see how the lives of these people have developed; a reality TV show in the real sense of the word 'reality'. In most cases, the original premise that people are defined by their social background has been upheld: those from more privileged backgrounds becoming more successful than those from less privileged families. However, over the intervening years the series has become much more of a human-interest story. I, personally, would love to see another series that follows seven-year-olds from today into their futures, to see what, if anything, has changed for those born in the 21st century.

3 **Work in pairs and discuss how these people and things can have an influence on young children's development and assess their relative importance.**

books   family and friends   games and computers
social media   teachers   local community

4 🎧 **7.10 Listen to two friends discussing a Part 4 question in the Speaking exam and answer the questions.**

1 What is the examiner's question?

2 Is the discussion smooth or not? Why?

5 🎧 **7.11 Read the Exam focus and listen to two different candidates discussing the same question. Is their discussion smoother than that in Ex 4 or not? Why?**

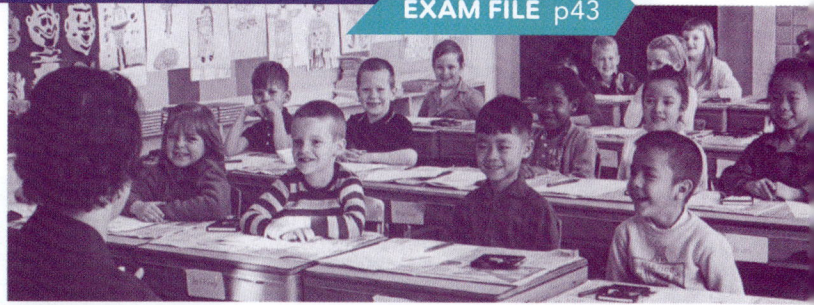

EXAM FOCUS

Developing the discussion

To develop the discussion in Parts 3 and 4 you may need to do the following:

Interrupt politely

If I could just come in here …

Excuse me, but I'd like to say that …

Sorry, that's really interesting, but …

Before you go on I'd like to …

Add your opinion to another student's answer

This is something I've also thought about quite a bit …

I would completely agree with … In my experience, I've found …

What an interesting idea. You've made some great points.

Can I expand on that a little? I once …

Ask for clarification

OK, so when you say … , do you mean that … ?

What are you thinking of? / Could you give an example perhaps?

I'm sorry, I don't think I follow what you're saying.

EXAM BOOST p42

> Complete Exam file SECTION B on page 42.

EXAM TASK

6 **Work in pairs. Take turns to answer the first 4 questions individually. Discuss questions 5 and 6 together.**

1 Who did you most look up to in your childhood? Why?

2 Would you say that genetics plays a large part in determining our personality? Why? / Why not?

3 Do you think people have similar opinions at the age of 70 as they did at the age of 17? Why?

4 How early in their lives do you think a child's personality begins to show?

5 Some people say that the social background a person is born into determines their future. How true do you think that is? Why?

6 Celebrities are increasingly becoming significant role models for young people today. Would you say that this is a good thing? Why? / Why not?

EXAM FILE p27
VOCABULARY FILE pp126-127
WRITING FILE p135

1a Which numbers do you associate with spies and spy films?

1b In pairs, discuss what qualities are needed to become a good spy. How might the life of a real spy and a fictional spy differ? Why?

2 Complete the titles of the famous spy films. Have you seen any of them? In pairs, discuss what you know about one or more of the films.

Complete the titles of some FAMOUS SPY FILMS!

1 'Quantum of _____ ' (2008)
2 '_____ of Spies' (2015)
3 'Mission _____ : Fallout' (2018)
4 'Tinker, Tailor, _____ , Spy' (2011)
5 'The _____ Legacy' (2012)
6 'Kingsman: The _____ Circle' (2017)

3 🎧 7.12 Listen to an extract from a podcast by a university lecturer talking about espionage and its history, and answer the questions.

1 What does the speaker say about the public's knowledge of espionage today?
2 What do we learn about some famous writers of the 20th century?
3 What do you think the purpose of the podcast is?

4 Read a review of a spy novel.

1 What is the focus of each paragraph?
2 What is unusual about the book?
3 How does the writer indicate whether he enjoyed the book or not?
4 Do you think people might be encouraged to read the book after reading the review? Why?

A Perfect Spy – The Perfect Read

If you're looking for a classy piece of spy fiction that doesn't simply move at breakneck speed from one chase to another, but focuses completely on the spy himself, then 'A Perfect Spy' by John Le Carré has got to provide the 'perfect' answer.

The book, published in 1986, has been described as one of the best English novels of the 20th century, and I can absolutely see why it has received such an accolade. We are taken through the life of Sir Magnus Pym, a British agent. Magnus is in a secret location, having deserted both his wife and lifelong friends and colleagues, writing his memoirs. From the beginning it is unclear whether he has been a loyal agent, or a duplicitous one, for his entire working life.

The brilliance of 'A Perfect Spy' lies in the style and reach of the recollections. As the book progresses, we learn about the complex relationship Magnus had with his own father, a lovable but completely immoral rogue. It also gradually becomes clear that he is questioning his own personality; who is the real Magnus, where were his true loyalties? Is this what made him the Perfect Spy? The narration doesn't move in a direct timeline, but leaps forward and back, and the story is passed from one narrator to another, even giving a voice to the different aspects of Pym's own personality.

While this complex book requires high levels of concentration, it is worth the time and effort. Not only does it unpick the detailed life of an intriguing individual, it also encourages us to question who WE truly are and why.

Skyfall, 2012

5 Read the Exam focus and highlight words and phrases in the review that illustrate the points mentioned.

EXAM FOCUS

Engaging the reader

Engage the reader's attention from the outset

Ensure the first sentence has impact, e.g. outline a situation.

Delay mentioning the subject of the review immediately.

Use direct or rhetorical questions.

Keep the reader's attention throughout

Don't give long, complex explanations or lengthy descriptions.

Use semi-formal language, which is more lively.

Use humour where possible.

Leave the reader with something to think about.

EXAM BOOST p26

> Complete Exam file SECTION B on page 26.

6 Think about how you might recommend a book by an author from your country to an English friend. Consider these things:

> plot   language   style   length   cultural background

7 Choose a book and complete the sentences.

1   You'd love reading this because _____ .

2   What excites me about this book is _____ .

3   The popularity of this book is down to _____ .

8 Check back on what to include in a review in Unit 2.

EXAM TASK

9 You see the following notice on a book club website.

> # WE NEED YOUR REVIEWS!
>
> Have you read a really fascinating book recently? Write a review for our members saying why the book was compulsive reading and compare it to one or more other popular books of the same genre.

Write your review in 220–260 words.

10 Share your reviews with the class. Which of the books reviewed might you like to read? Why?

11 Would you say that you are more influenced by professionally written book reviews or by friends' recommendations? Why?

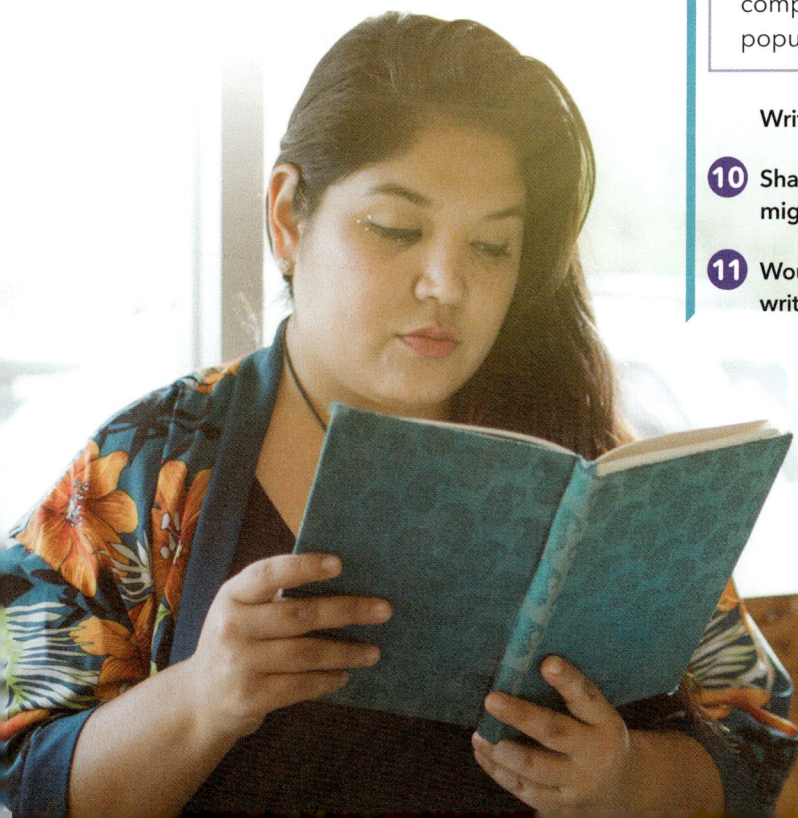

PRACTICE TASKS

READING AND USE OF ENGLISH – PART 3

1 Read the text below. Use the word given in capitals at the end of some of the lines to form a word that fits in the gap in the same line.

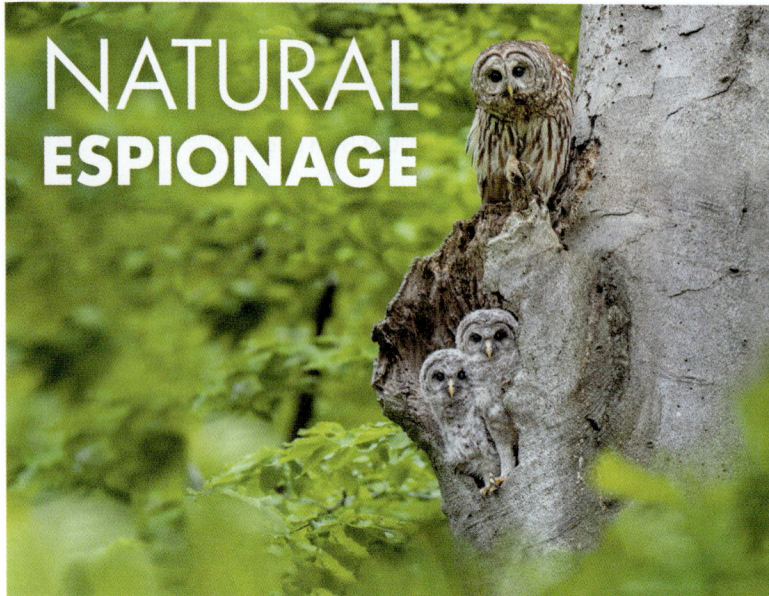

NATURAL ESPIONAGE

A well-made nature documentary is always popular viewing and there seems to be no limit to the **(0)** ___INNOVATIVE___ approaches used today. — **INNOVATE**

One intriguing series films the natural world from an unusual **(1)** _____ . — **POINT**
Entitled 'Spy in the wild', tiny cameras are built into artificial animals that look and act like one of the species being filmed, giving them **(2)** _____ arms, — **ROBOT**
legs and heads. This is a quite remarkable **(3)** _____ technique, as the real — **FILTRATE**
animals seem completely undisturbed by their presence.

The **(4)** _____ of the robots is — **SOHPISTICATED**
amazing. Developers have built in specific animal calls and animal scents, and they only become **(5)** _____ on very — **DETECT**
close inspection. Having a 'spy' at the centre of the natural action allows the film-makers to reveal **(6)** _____ environmental — **LIE**
issues that we might otherwise be totally unaware of. It is also **(7)** _____ — **FINITE**
preferable to having a human attempting to film certain scenes, although the little 'spies' do have some **(8)** _____ ; they — **SHORT**
can be squashed or even knocked off cliffs!

READING AND USE OF ENGLISH – PART 4

2 Complete the second sentence so that it has a similar meaning to the first sentence, using the word given. Do not change the word given. You must use between three and six words, including the word given.

0 The workings of the brain were puzzling for scientists for a long time until research helped them understand it.

HAD

How THE BRAIN WORKED HAD PUZZLED scientists for a long time until research helped them understand it.

1 All these late nights are beginning to affect me.

FEEL

I'm starting

_____ of all these late nights.

2 We'll finish decorating before you arrive.

SHALL

By the _____ finished the decorating.

3 Immediately after finishing dinner, Alice started playing a computer game.

HAD

No _____ she started playing a computer game.

4 'Yes, I shall definitely be performing at the music festival,' the singer said.

CONFIRMED

The singer _____ at the music festival.

5 Freddie doesn't know his exam results yet and it's very frustrating for him.

WELL

Not _____ in the exam is very frustrating for Freddie.

6 Although the airline increased its fares, it continued to attract a lot of passengers.

ITS

The airline continued to attract a lot of passengers

_____ fares.

VOCABULARY: Collocations

1 Work in pairs. Can you name any films, songs or paintings which feature umbrellas or umbrella-carrying characters? What is the use of the umbrellas? Share your ideas and identify the most famous.

2 🎧 **8.1** Listen to an extract from a series of podcasts by unusual collectors and answer the questions.

1 Why does he have a passion for umbrellas?

2 Summarise what we learn about the history of umbrellas.

3 What interesting facts does he include in his podcast?

3 🎧 **8.2** Listen again and say what the speaker is referring to when he uses the following collocations.

1 universally known

2 endlessly versatile

3 strikingly similar

4 widely believed

5 exclusively used

6 infinitely preferable

7 fiercely competitive

8 notoriously difficult

4 Complete the questions with the correct collocations from Ex 3. Then discuss them with a partner.

1 Name a product that is _____ by a name other than its original.

2 What aspect of learning English is _____ ?

3 Do you know someone who is _____ ?

4 What did you find _____ to doing homework as a child?

5 Do you know of something that is _____ but is untrue?

6 Can you name an object in this room that is _____ ?

5 Work in pairs and discuss the questions.

1 Are there any times or places when people should NOT use umbrellas? Why?

2 Are there any modern things we use where you feel the original design might have been better? Why?

3 What features could you add to an umbrella to make it more modern and useful?

6 Work in pairs. What other equipment designed to deal with weather conditions has more than one use? Share your ideas with the class.

1 Work in pairs and discuss the questions.

1 What would you say are the most common phobias that people have?

2 Do you know of any unusual phobias?

3 What might cause phobias such as those you've outlined?

2 🎧 8.3 **Why do you think some people might have a phobia about the number 8? Listen to a vlog about phobias and check your ideas.**

3 Scan the two posts on the website quickly to find which phobias the people have. Which do you find the strangest? Why?

Nadia

My phobia is the weirdest I've heard of – bambakomallophobia – a fear of cotton wool. That fluffy, harmless, useful commodity is guaranteed to bring me out in a sweat should I see it, accidentally touch it or even hear the word spoken. It's something I rarely admit. I mean there are people out there with solid, well-known fears of heights or small spaces and they might go slightly pink if it's mentioned, but me – I go brick red – it's such a ridiculous thing to admit to. Most people can trace their phobias back to an event or something, but there's nothing in my past to explain it. No cotton wool fights as a child, no joke sandwiches filled with cotton wool, just this sudden aversion. In spite of suggestions to get therapy I haven't summoned up the courage yet. I'm scared that the cure may be worse than the phobia.

Ken

I hear that I'm in good company. Steve Jobs, the former top Apple guy, supposedly shared my phobia for – of all things – buttons! Since childhood I've been unable to touch the things. I'm like my mother in this. She worries that she passed her phobia onto me, but I don't necessarily agree. I mean I don't remember her freaking out wildly when doing up my coat as a toddler, although I guess these things can run in families. After some hesitation about getting some help, I'm glad I finally did, and I'd honestly recommend it. My fear has become much more controllable now. Unlike before, when I couldn't watch someone buttoning up their coat, I'm OK now, a bit shaky admittedly – but progress is progress!

4 Read the Exam focus. Read the posts in Ex 3 in more detail and use the information to answer questions 1–3.

Which person

1 uses a comparison to emphasise embarrassment about a phobia?

2 encourages seeking help for a phobia?

3 refers to a possible cause for his particular phobia?

EXAM FOCUS

Avoiding distraction

Avoid being misled by distraction in both the questions and the sections of text.

Underline the key words in the questions that you need to use.

Compare references to the key information that may be present in two or more of the sections.

Check that the information you find in a section gives a full answer to the question.

Remember that you may need to read across more than one sentence to find the answer.

EXAM BOOST p16

> Complete Exam file SECTION B on page 16.

EXAM TASK

5 **You are going to read an article about phobias. For questions 1–10, choose from the sections (A–D). The sections may be chosen more than once.**

In which section does the writer

refer to a general coping strategy employed by many phobic people? **1** ☐

mention different types of phobias when pointing out their possible impacts? **2** ☐

describe how the results of giving in to a fear has been minimised? **3** ☐

use a personal example to preface a theory? **4** ☐

detail some common physical symptoms of phobias? **5** ☐

express an admiration for a particular solution to overcoming phobias? **6** ☐

wonder whether some phobias might subconsciously be copied from others? **7** ☐

suggest that our mental development has not kept up with the changes in the world around us? **8** ☐

explain that having a phobia is not as inexplicable as we tend to think? **9** ☐

exemplify an extreme effect of a particular phobia? **10** ☐

Many of our phobias are an
EVOLUTIONARY HANGOVER
from ancient survival instincts

A It sounds like a dream: you're in a theatre and you're the star of the show. Except that it's an operating theatre, you're the patient, and you're still awake, but you can't speak. Now it's a nightmare! A surprising number of people have a phobia about being conscious under anaesthetic. But where does this fear come from? Surely not from experience! Phobias can be crippling in the effect they have on people, whether it's a fear of something that others view as innocent – like ants or clouds – or perceived dangers that can be potentially serious such as heights or, as above – anaesthetics. And scientists have long been intrigued by where these often deep-seated and long-held fears come from. Do we take on our parents' fears or are we perhaps influenced by films or stories we encounter as children? Maybe some fears are reactions to personal experiences.

B In fact, the more we learn about our supposedly irrational fears, the more rational they seem to become. Phobias are a persistent feature of the human psyche – and many of the most common ones are thought to serve a survival purpose. For the past week, I have been making detours in my garden to get to my rubbish bins, so as not to disturb the enormous spider's web stretching between the bins and the hedge. This is cowardice rather than respect for the spider's skill at engineering; the idea of seeing the occupant as I dispose of the rubbish inspires an uncontrollable shiver. Arachnophobia, which is one of the 10 most common phobias listed on anxiety websites, is among those suspected of having an evolutionary origin.

C The argument goes like this: as we evolved, the humans who enjoyed the best chance of survival were those who were most aware of threats. Poisonous spiders and snakes represented real dangers – only those who dodged them survived to pass on their genes. Our fearful ancestors thus won the battle for survival – and we inherited their brain patterns. Our environments, meanwhile, have changed far faster than the pace of evolution can keep up with: even though these natural threats have largely disappeared, our neurological circuits remain pretty much prehistoric. And so, to this day, certain objects or situations – spiders, snakes, the dark, strangers – continue to stir a terror in the soul. That terror triggers physiological changes, such as sweating and an increased heart rate. We continue this tradition of fearfulness when we become parents. I have yet to meet a parent who didn't peer anxiously into the cot at night to establish that the baby was still alive. A doctor friend even used to use a feather to help detect breathing, to keep her nocturnal investigations brief.

D So, what, if anything, can be done to help those sufferers of phobias whose symptoms prove life-changing? A simple avoidance method used by many works when there is an alternative, such as using stairs instead of the lift, or keeping a fair distance from the windows of high buildings – maybe forgoing the opportunity to get to the top of the Eiffel Tower. But these techniques do not get to the heart of the problem and for those with serious phobias it doesn't work at all; avoidance for an agoraphobe would be never to leave their house. Therapists encourage people to confront their phobias, but this can prove too distressing for some to continue. However, there is a glimmer of hope, which lies in the use of VR. With avatars, patients can confront their fears in the virtual world and some results have been spectacular. In one trial, all arachnophobes who participated found themselves later able to approach spiders in the real world with up to 68 percent reduced levels of fear. There is hope that in future VR units with apps for different scenarios will be available to buy and people will be able to treat themselves. I gain a lot of satisfaction from the thought that there is a very modern answer to a possibly very old problem! However, until this effective form of treatment becomes more widely available, I shall bravely continue to put the rubbish out, defying the enemy that has taken up residence outside my house.

Speaking or writing

6 How far do you agree with the theories put forward in the article about the causes of phobias and the treatment? Why?

7 Work in pairs and look at some unusual phobias. Discuss why people might have these phobias, imagine how they might impact the people's lives and suggest coping strategies or cures. Then choose one to write a post about for the website.

fear of beards   fear of cheese   fear of clowns
fear of the colour yellow   fear of rain   fear of trees

EXAM FILE p7

VOCABULARY: Compounding

1 What does the shape in the picture represent? How would you explain this to someone who doesn't know what it is?

2 🎧 8.4 Listen to a teacher talking about the concept of infinity. Which fields of study and applications does she mention?

3 There are two compound nouns in the recording, 'overview' and 'viewpoint'. Complete each sentence with one of the words, then match them with the definitions, a or b.

1 In mathematics there are three kinds of infinity – I won't go into that now as it's pretty complex, so I'll just give you a brief _____ of infinity in other fields.

2 While the universe itself is thought to be finite, the _____ of some astrophysicists is that there may even be an infinite number of universes.
   a a way of thinking about a situation
   b a short description of a subject or situation that gives the main ideas

4 Match a word in column 1 with a word in column 2 to create compound words. Then match each word with its definition.

1 break down draw mean over out short up

2 back beat coming down look come side time

definitions

a the negative part or disadvantage of something
b fault/weakness making something less successful than it should be
c in the period of time between now and the future, or two past events
d suddenly have too much of a feeling
e positive and making you feel that good things will happen
f failure of a relationship or system
g likely future situation
h disadvantage of a system, situation, product etc.

5 Turn to page 95 and read the text. Complete the text with compound words from the box below.

lifetimes never-ending outlook overcome shortcomings troublesome

EXAM BOOST p6

> Complete Exam file SECTION D on page 6.

EXAM TASK

6 For questions 1–8, read the text below. Use the word given in capitals at the end of some of the lines to form a word that fits in the gap in the same line. There is an example at the beginning (0).

Why positive thinking **doesn't** work

We're told we can do anything if we put our minds to it. If you have a positive **(0)** ___OUTLOOK___ , they say, there are no limits to what you can achieve. **LOOK**

(1) _____ , it can sometimes be **DOUBT**
helpful to try to remain **(2)** _____ **BEAT**
when things are difficult, but it's virtually impossible to do so all the time.

The **(3)** _____ of willing ourselves **DOWN**
to be positive is that we can end up feeling more anxious – obviously a huge
(4) _____ . Trying to eliminate **BACK**
negative thoughts is unrealistic say the experts: research shows that 80 percent of our thoughts are negative!

What <u>should</u> we do? Accept our feelings instead of trying to **(5)** _____ them, **PASS**
that's what. In one study, people about to give a speech were instructed to try to calm their nerves. Others were told to take
(6) _____ of their anxiety. The best **OWNER**
speeches were given by the second group. Suppressing negative feelings takes up brain power, and in the **(7)** _____ , **TIME**
we might miss out on helpful experiences and consequently **(8)** _____ the **FORE**
opportunity to change things for the better!

Speaking or writing

> Go to page 93 for these exercises.

EXAM TRAINER | p19 Exs 13–15 Exam task

1 Work in pairs and answer the questions.

- Do you get the recommended eight hours of sleep a night?
- What's the minimum number of hours' sleep you can get away with and still function normally?
- How do you feel when you:
a don't get enough sleep?
b have too much sleep?

2 🎧 8.5 Listen to a sleep specialist talking about why we need sleep. How many theories are mentioned? What are they?

EXAM FOCUS

Understanding gist

In this part of the exam, you may need to understand the gist of what the speakers are saying, that is, the general meaning. You will need to listen to the whole of what they say before choosing an option, rather than listening for specific details.

Detail comes from a small part of the text:

You can see this in big cats such as lions, for example, which don't move around much unless they are hunting for food. (detail: here, an example is given as part of the longer text)

Gist comes from across a larger chunk of text:

We all know that at a certain time of the evening our bodies start winding down for sleep. We also know that sleep is vital for our health and well-being. We certainly feel more alert after a few hours' shut-eye, with increased energy and better mood. Without enough rest, we can feel sleepy and down. (gist = sleep is good for our physical / mental well-being)

3 🎧 8.6 Read the Exam focus then listen again and summarise each theory in one sentence.

EXAM BOOST p34

> Complete Exam file SECTION B on page 34.

EXAM TASK

4 🎧 8.7 You will hear five extracts in which people are talking about sleep.

Task one

For questions 1–5, choose from the list (A–H) what each speaker says about their sleep.

A I have worried others when I'm asleep.

B I am only sometimes aware of a sleep habit.

C I am amused by what occurs when I sleep.

D I dread going to sleep because of what happens.

E I am unsure as to why I do something when I sleep.

F I have little understanding of others' sleep problems.

G I take inspiration from what happens when I'm asleep.

H I wonder about the effect of my sleep style on my body.

Speaker 1 **1**
Speaker 2 **2**
Speaker 3 **3**
Speaker 4 **4**
Speaker 5 **5**

Task two

For questions 6–10, choose from the list (A–H) what each speaker says has been the benefit of adopting a new sleep habit.

A knowing a future problem can be avoided

B suffering less from stress

C feeling more positive about life in general

D getting rid of a health problem

E understanding the benefits of sleep

F feeling more refreshed in the morning

G having a better memory

H completing tasks in a timely manner

Speaker 1 **6**
Speaker 2 **7**
Speaker 3 **8**
Speaker 4 **9**
Speaker 5 **10**

Speaking or writing

5 In the past, people used to have two sleeps: it was normal to be awake for a couple of hours in the night and talk, read or even visit neighbours! How would you pass the time if we still had two sleeps during the night?

6 Imagine that you have a sleep issue of some kind, for example, waking up in the night or having vivid dreams. Write an email asking for advice. Swap emails with a partner and write a response, offering solutions to the problem.

EXAM FILE p9

GRAMMAR: Clause patterns

1 What do you think these idioms mean?

- to have your head in the clouds
- every cloud has a silver lining
- be under a cloud

2 🎧 8.8 Listen to a weather forecaster talking about clouds and the oktas chart. What is it?

3 🎧 8.9 Listen again and complete the clauses using the words in brackets where applicable.

1 _____ (study) more closely, the clouds would tell us all kinds of things about the atmosphere.

2 Meteorologists do _____ (best) to interpret the approaching weather.

3 _____ (base) something known as the oktas chart, meteorologists can tell us what percentage of the sky is covered.

4 _____ (should) mist or fog around, then it is not possible to apply the scale.

5 _____ (have) a great understanding of weather as a youngster, I believed that the vapour trails left by planes were also a kind of cloud.

4 Complete the clauses in the text with the appropriate form of the words from Ex 3. You may also use appropriate alternatives.

CLOUD APPRECIATION

The Cloud Appreciation Society does exactly what it says on the tin: it appreciates clouds. Or rather, its members do. [1] _____ the information in its manifesto, they believe that clouds are particularly beautiful.

[2] _____ sign up to the society, however, you'll not only receive a 'cloud a day' picture (see one [3] _____ you definitely haven't seen them all) or an interesting piece of cloud science on a daily basis by email, but you'll help others, too. With members in 120 countries, the society is a business and donates membership fees, [4] _____ the best it can to help fund interesting projects. These include fog harvesting, whereby fog is collected via special nets or greenhouses and turned into much-needed fresh drinking water.

Lacking access to fresh drinking water at certain times of the year, one South American community is already benefiting from 35 fog nets erected in the mountains. These collect around 6,300 litres of water per day, which if [5] _____ , can be used during the dry months.

EXAM BOOST p8

> Complete Exam file SECTION D on page 8.

EXAM TASK

GRAMMAR FILE pp112–113

5 For questions 1–6, complete the second sentence so that it has a similar meaning to the first sentence, using the word given. Do not change the word given. You must use between three and six words, including the word given. Here is an example (0).

0 Being late for the star-gazing trip wasn't what I wanted, so I ran quickly to the meeting point.

BE

I ran quickly to the meeting point, _____NOT WANTING TO BE_____ late for the star-gazing trip.

1 In comparison with how thick a sheet of paper is, cloud droplets are about five times smaller.

TO

When _____ a sheet of paper, cloud droplets are about five times smaller.

2 I didn't know that 'mother-of-pearl' clouds were so rare and I wasted a lot of time looking for them.

HAD

I wouldn't have wasted so much time looking for 'mother-of-pearl' clouds _____ rare they were.

3 Regret is probable if you go to the Antarctic Indian Ocean – it's the cloudiest place on Earth.

PROBABLY

Go to the Antarctic Indian Ocean _____ regret it – it's the cloudiest place on Earth!

4 Some countries create clouds by injecting the atmosphere with carbon dioxide because they don't receive enough rain.

LED

Not _____ to some countries creating clouds by injecting the atmosphere with carbon dioxide.

5 NASA scientists continue to try to discover what they can about the red and green clouds at Saturn's north pole.

BEST

NASA scientists are _____ out more about the red and green clouds at Saturn's north pole.

6 Clouds can be seen to have a rainbow appearance in specific light conditions.

COLOURED

Clouds can sometimes _____ in specific light conditions.

Speaking or writing

> Go to page 93 for these exercises.

EXAM TRAINER | p22 Ex 7 p23

1 Work in pairs and discuss the questions.

1 Do you notice people's voices when you first meet them? Why? / Why not?

2 Do you think a person's voice can reflect their character in any way? Why? / Why not?

3 How many octaves do you think the average human voice has?

2 🎧 8.10 Listen to a voice trainer and check your ideas.

3 🎧 8.11 Answer the questions. Listen and check.

1 What's the average octave range for a normal singer?

2 What range has the music teacher got?

3 Why can't we hear the lowest note recorded?

4 What do we learn about a man who can imitate bird call?

4 Look at two pictures showing people using their voices for different reasons. Compare the pictures and say how the people are using their voices in these situations and what the effect on their audiences might be.

5 🎧 8.12 Listen to a student completing the Speaking task given in Ex 4 and compare the points you made.

6 🎧 8.13 Read the Exam focus and listen again to the student's answer. Which phrases did they use when speaking?

EXAM FOCUS

Structuring a long turn

Go through the questions as logically as you can: compare, deal with the first question, deal with the second question.

1 Guide the listener through your one-minute talk with linking words or phrases:
   I'd like to talk about pictures … and …
   Starting with a comparison, I have to say that …
   To begin with I think that …
   I'd like to start by pointing out that …
   Going back to the first picture …
   Moving on to the reasons for …
   As for/to how important …

2 Refer to the questions written above the pictures to remind you of what to include.

3 Continue the comparison while answering the questions.

4 At times look at the examiner and your partner to involve them in your talk.

EXAM BOOST p38

▶ Complete Exam file SECTION C on page 38.

EXAM TASK

7 Work in pairs. Student A, turn to page 96 and do the task for Unit 8. Student B, listen and answer the question below the pictures. Then go to page 97 and change roles.

Speaking or writing

8 Work in pairs and discuss the questions.

1 How valuable do you think it is for children to learn to play an instrument? Why?

2 If you had to reduce your playlist to eight songs only, what would your choice be? Why?

3 Some people say that everyone has the ability to sing and to dance. How far would you agree?

4 There is a saying 'Silence speaks louder than words.' What do you understand by this and do you agree?

EXAM FILE p21
VOCABULARY FILE pp128–129
WRITING FILE pp131–132

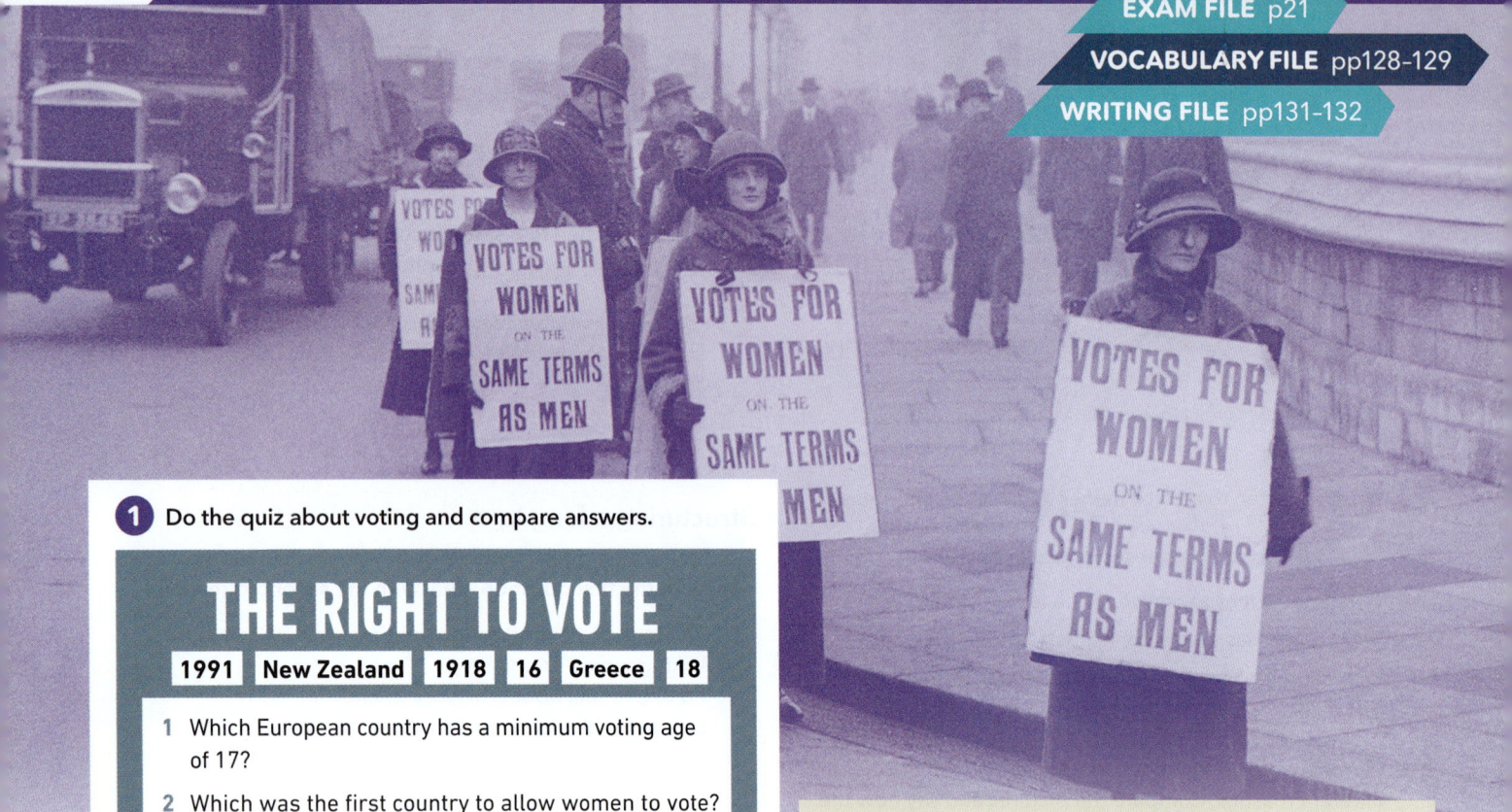

1 Do the quiz about voting and compare answers.

THE RIGHT TO VOTE

| 1991 | New Zealand | 1918 | 16 | Greece | 18 |

1 Which European country has a minimum voting age of 17?
2 Which was the first country to allow women to vote?
3 What is the minimum voting age in Austria?
4 When were all Swiss women given the vote?
5 What age did Japan lower the voting age to in 2016?
6 When were some women allowed to stand for election in the UK?

2 🎧 8.14 Listen to a recorded exhibition guide giving background information about the picture above, which is part of an exhibition about the suffragettes. Note down the key dates the guide mentions. Then use the dates to retell the story of the suffragette movement.

3 Work in pairs and discuss the question.

What are the ages for learning to drive and voting in your countries? Do you think these ages are appropriate or should they be raised or lowered? Why?

4 Read the writing task and the model. In pairs, discuss how well you think the writer has written the letter and what, if anything, could be improved.

You see this announcement in your local newspaper. Write your letter in 220–260 words.

> The current age to be allowed to drive a car in this country is 17, and a moped 16. Many people believe the ages for both should be raised to 18. We would like your letters on the topic, giving the reasons for your opinions. The most interesting letters will be published in the next edition.

Dear Sir,

I am writing in response to your request for opinions on the topic of raising the age to hold licences for both cars and mopeds to 18, and I've got to say from the outset that I believe it to be a backward and ill-thought-through proposition. I started driving a car at 17 and many of my peers did the same. It is an important step for teenagers in becoming independent and taking responsibility, and as far as I am concerned younger drivers are more careful on the roads than older ones, who can often become more careless over time and I also find the suggestion of raising the age for moped riders to be totally outrageous. Riding a moped allows an important degree of freedom and, once again, these riders are frequently far more road aware and safety conscious than older riders, and in my experience have, or cause, far fewer accidents.

I'd suggest that the age for holding a driving licence should in fact be lowered to be brought in line with moped licensing, making the age for both 16. Young people are becoming mature at an earlier age these days and this should be reflected in the age they acquire independence through riding and driving. If road safety concerns are at the heart of these proposals, I'd think that there are other measures that could be taken. For example, the current driving test could be made more stringent. In addition to this, I truly believe that all drivers should have to retake their test at regular intervals throughout their driving lives – something which doesn't happen now.

Yours,

Jermaine Barker

5 Read the Exam focus and check your ideas from Ex 4.

Writing a formal email or letter

1 Avoid abbreviations or idiomatic language.

2 Use complex sentences, but do not just add clause after clause.

3 Use formal phrases for different functions, for example:

Making references

With reference to your …

Regarding the suggestions put forward, I …

I am writing in response to …

Giving opinions

In my honest opinion, I would have to say that …

In the unlikely event that …

I would have to agree that …

Expressing concerns

I was alarmed to read that …

The proposition is extremely worrying …

EXAM BOOST p20

> Complete Exam file SECTION B on page 20.

6 Imagine that you disagree with the writer of the letter. Rewrite these extracts from the letter, giving a different opinion.

1 I believe it to be a backward and ill-thought-through proposition.

2 As far as I am concerned younger drivers are more careful on the roads than older ones, who can often become more careless over time.

3 Riding a moped allows an important degree of freedom and, once again, these riders are frequently far more road aware and safety conscious than older riders, and in my experience have, or cause, far fewer accidents.

4 I'd suggest that the age for holding a driving licence should in fact be lowered to be brought in line with moped licensing, making the age for both 16.

7 Work in pairs and discuss the questions.

1 What are the age restrictions for doing these things in your country?

2 Do you think they are fair? Or should they be changed? Why / Why not?

A using social media

B playing video games

C watching any film without an adult

D getting half price / reduced fare on transport

E leaving home

F leaving secondary school

G getting part time work

H flying a glider

8 Read the Exam task below and list points you might include. Group these into paragraphs.

9 You see this announcement on a local newspaper website.

> **Topic of the week**
>
> There is a movement to lower the voting age from 18 to 16 and we would like to publish letters from our readers indicating their opinions about this, giving reasons. If you have a strong opinion about the topic, please write in.

Write your letter. Write 220–260 words.

10 Share your letters with the class. What is the consensus of opinion?

11 Work in pairs. Choose one of the statements below and think of three reasons for and three reasons against it. Then join a class debate on the issue.

No one over the age of 85 should be allowed to hold a driving licence.

OR

Voting should be compulsory for all eligible voters.

REVIEW | UNITS 1-8

READING AND USE OF ENGLISH – PART 1

1 Read the text below and decide which answer (A, B, C or D) best fits each gap.

I know that voice!

Not all artists in the entertainment industry are
(0) __D__ recognisable. There are some whose faces would mean nothing to us, but whose voices would. The voice artist does many things, from **(1)** _____ stories to life in audio books to persuading us to buy products in radio adverts.

However, having acting ability and a **(2)** _____ voice is not all that is required to become **(3)** _____ after. Many actors **(4)** _____ the assumption that because they can act, they can 'voice' but this is not necessarily the case. It's true that an actor who is 'voicing' because she has some time to **(5)** _____ between engagements will be able to **(6)** _____ on experience, but she will also need to **(7)** _____ her vocal skills. A voice artist cannot use facial expressions or actions, so her voice must convey everything.

Some voicework projects, such as narrating a prime-time TV documentary, are **(8)** _____ competitive and for the right artist, the job can be extremely lucrative.

0	A directly	B widely	C fully	D instantly
1	A lending	B letting	C bringing	D making
2	A typical	B developed	C balanced	D distinctive
3	A looked	B sought	C pursued	D requested
4	A make	B take	C face	D think
5	A rest	B waste	C kill	D use
6	A draw	B extract	C perform	D profit
7	A ply	B focus	C trigger	D hone
8	A painstakingly	B drastically	C fiercely	D hopefully

READING AND USE OF ENGLISH – PART 2

2 Read the text below and think of the word which best fits each gap. Use only one word in each gap.

Skip breakfast for extra shut eye? Not a good idea.

We've **(0)** ____BEEN____ warned. Apparently, it isn't always so much about what we eat as when we eat that is important for our well-being. **(1)** _____ appears that too many of us are missing the most important meal of the day, either because we're watching our weight **(2)** _____ we have a tight daily schedule and prefer spending a few extra minutes in bed **(3)** _____ than using that precious time to eat.

(4) _____ to nutritionists and dieticians, missing breakfast encourages us to eat heavier meals at lunch and dinner, which can disrupt our sleep patterns, too. Starting the day on an empty stomach **(5)** _____ also claimed to have a negative effect on our ability to focus at work.

It can be a vicious circle. Eating more, later, is our body's way of making up **(6)** _____ not eating earlier in the day. This can result in a lack of appetite on waking, **(7)** _____ then leads to skipping breakfast and so on. So, follow the advice – eat breakfast and it will tide you over until later in the day. You **(8)** _____ feel the benefit!

READING AND USE OF ENGLISH – PART 3

3 Read the text below. Use the word given in capitals at the end of some of the lines to form a word that fits in the gap in the same line.

The spotlight effect

Do you ever have the **(0)** ___IMPRESSION___ that if you do
something embarrassing, the whole world is looking at
you? Apparently, this tendency to **(1)** _____
the importance to other people of how we look or what
we do has a name – 'The spotlight effect.' It relates to
a(n) **(2)** _____ belief that our actions are
more **(3)** _____ than they really are, and
this is because although we are the centre of our own
world, we're not the centre of everyone else's! We
sometimes get **(4)** _____ anxious about
a bad haircut or saying something silly. However, the
(5) _____ that others will remark on it is low
because they are also the centre of their own worlds,
and they too are busy thinking about themselves. That is,
unless they are extremely **(6)** _____ .

The label is also **(7)** _____ to when we do
positive things. We might say something that we think is
really clever or funny and assume that everyone picks up
on it. In reality, this is not the case either and we need to
overcome this **(8)** _____ !

IMPRESS

ESTIMATE

RATIONAL
NOTICE

NECESSARY

LIKELY

ATTEND
APPLY

TEND

READING AND USE OF ENGLISH – PART 4

4 Complete the second sentence so that it has a similar meaning to the first sentence, using the word given. Do not change the word given. You must use between three and six words, including the word given.

0 The workings of the brain were puzzling for scientists for a long time until research helped them understand it.

HAD

How ___THE BRAIN WORKED HAD PUZZLED___ scientists for a long time until research helped them understand it.

1 The test will be difficult, so please don't think otherwise.

ILLUSION

Please _____ test will be easy, because it won't.

2 Jake's food order will depend on how many guests are attending.

BASED

Jake will order an appropriate amount of _____ guests attending.

3 I didn't take Denny's advice and I had a problem with the wi-fi.

HAVE

Had I _____ avoided the problem with the wi-fi.

4 'I'm not sure that Katy researched the topic properly,' the teacher said.

WONDERED

The teacher _____ the topic properly.

5 The rain started while the man was cleaning the windows.

WHEN

The windows _____ to rain.

6 I have two laptops that I use for work, because one might have a problem.

CASE

I have two laptops that I use for work _____ a problem.

91

Unit 1

READING AND USE OF ENGLISH – PART 1
(page 8)

Speaking or writing

6 Can you think of any one-hit wonders? Tell your partner about them.

7 Have you ever done anything that you were really proud of that you've never achieved again? How bothered were you / would you be about that? Write a paragraph explaining your feelings.

READING AND USE OF ENGLISH – PART 2
(page 10)

Speaking or writing

7 What makes you individual? Tell your partner.

8 In what ways do you like to be the same as other people? In which ways are you happy to differ? Think about:
- opinions and beliefs.
- fashion sense.
- musical taste.

Unit 2

READING AND USE OF ENGLISH – PART 3
(page 18)

Speaking or writing

6 Tell your partner about a time when you misplaced something important. What were the consequences?

7 How can you avoid misplacing important or valuable things, such as your passport or items of jewellery? Write a list of suggestions and then share it with your partner.

READING AND USE OF ENGLISH – PART 4
(page 20)

Speaking or writing

7 Which activities do you think are generally more successful with two people? Why?

8 What are the pros and cons of playing sport with a partner as opposed to doing individual sports?

Unit 3

READING AND USE OF ENGLISH – PART 1
(page 30)

Speaking or writing

7 Answer the questions. Then tell your partner.
- What would you like to be exceptionally talented at?
- Is there anything you'd like to deepen your knowledge of?
- Do you think it's more important to accumulate knowledge or wealth?

8 What is the most incredible natural or urban landscape you've seen or would like to see? Explain what was so impressive about it, or why you would like to go there.

READING AND USE OF ENGLISH – PART 2
(page 32)

Speaking or writing

6 What would you like to be famous for, if anything? How important do you think it is to create a legacy – something people will remember you by?

7 The Brontës were very determined in getting important messages across in their novels. Do you think it is the place of artists such as singers or actors to draw attention to causes?

Write a short essay, offering your opinions.

Unit 4

READING AND USE OF ENGLISH – PART 3
(page 40)

Speaking or writing

6 Do you consider yourself a 'lucky' person? What lucky things have happened to you in your life? Discuss your experiences in small groups.

7 Do you think people can make their own luck, for example, by working hard and becoming successful?

Write a short article, giving some examples from your own life if possible.

READING AND USE OF ENGLISH – PART 4
(page 42)

Speaking or writing

6 The fourth dimension is also known as 'space-time'. What do you think this means? Explain the concept to your partner.

7 Write about a piece of advice you've been given at work or school.

- Who gave it to you?
- What did they say? (use reported speech)
- Did you think it was good advice? Why? / Why not?

Unit 5

READING AND USE OF ENGLISH – PART 1
(page 52)

Speaking or writing

6 How do you think sports events of any size or importance unite people who attend them? Tell your partner.

7 A small sports event is going to be held in your area. Makes notes about what the event would be, who would compete and how it might be funded and organised.

Then write a short proposal for the event.

READING AND USE OF ENGLISH – PART 2
(page 54)

Speaking or writing

6 Write a list of your ten favourite foods. If you had to give up five of them for health reasons, which could you manage to live without? Tell your partner.

7 'You are what you eat.' Discuss the extent to which you agree or disagree with this statement. Write a short article explaining your reasons.

Unit 6

READING AND USE OF ENGLISH – PART 3
(page 62)

Speaking or writing

6 How can different art forms be made more accessible for people who may not be able to experience them in conventional ways? Discuss your ideas in small groups.

7 Research either a) a street artist or b) an accessible arts project and write a short article about the work or how it has had an impact on others.

READING AND USE OF ENGLISH – PART 4
(page 64)

Speaking or writing

6 What kinds of patterns (e.g. spots, stripes, geometric, flowers, etc.) appeal to you a) for clothing or b) for decoration in the home? Do you think your preferences say anything about you as a person?

7 Scientists say there is harmony in symmetry, such as in buildings or art. To what extent do you agree? Write a paragraph giving your ideas.

Unit 7

READING AND USE OF ENGLISH – PART 1
(page 74)

Speaking or writing

7 Would you like a career in the media, perhaps as a TV presenter, radio DJ or even a social media influencer? What appeals to you about it, or what would make you shy away from doing something like that?

8 Work with a partner. Prepare a vlog about a topic you're interested in that you'd like to share information about. Think about how you can make it interesting and/or amusing.

READING AND USE OF ENGLISH – PART 2
(page 76)

Speaking or writing

6 What are you planning to do to become more sustainable in the future? Tell your partner.

7 How can governments and authorities help or encourage people to live more sustainably? Write a short paragraph explaining your ideas.

Unit 8

READING AND USE OF ENGLISH – PART 3
(page 84)

Speaking or writing

7 Do you think anything's possible if you try hard to achieve it? Why? / Why not? Tell your partner.

8 Are you an optimist, a pessimist or a realist? What do you think might be the benefits of each thinking style in one's professional and personal life? Which would you say is most beneficial on the whole? Write a short essay explaining your ideas.

READING AND USE OF ENGLISH – PART 4
(page 86)

Speaking or writing

6 Are you able to predict the weather by looking at the clouds? What other ways of predicting the weather are there? Tell your partner.

7 How conscious are you of the clouds? Do you do any 'cloud spotting'? What might people get out of it? Write a short text presenting your ideas.

Unit 2 (page 20)

Life on two wheels

Throughout its several-hundred-year history, the bicycle has undergone numerous transformations. The first documented bicycle design appeared in the early 16th century, and **was attributed** to one of Leonardo da Vinci's apprentices, Gian Giacomo Caprotti da Oreno. However, this **has never been confirmed** by experts, and a question mark still hangs over the document's authenticity.

The first bike to resemble those that **are ridden** today was Baron Karl von Drais' two-wheeled 'running machine', which materialised in 1817. Without pedals, its rider had to run along the ground to propel it forwards. Unfortunately, it caused several accidents, but its potential **had already been spotted** and many sought to make improvements. Subsequently, in 1839, the pedal-powered pushbike came into being, but the first mass-produced bike didn't put in an appearance until 1863. With no suspension it was uncomfortable to ride, and became known as the 'boneshaker'.

In the meantime, another kind of bike **was being developed** and in 1872, the Penny Farthing was first seen in the streets of Europe, with its huge front wheel and tiny rear one. This bicycle was not only notoriously difficult to climb up onto, but riding was limited to those with longer legs who were able to reach its pedals! Then, in 1885, along came the 'safety bicycle' which had a chain making it easier to ride, and tyres were later added, too. This was the bike which laid the foundation for the ones we know and love today.

However, this bike, too, was replaced by the 'roadster' in the early 1900s. On this bike, riders were forced into a more upright position, and had gears and brakes at their disposal. It was applauded for its durability and quickly became a favourite with those whose working lives were transformed by the relatively cheap method of transportation, including postal workers and police officers. Bicycles **have been being built** like this ever since.

By the 1980s, new kinds of bike were rapidly being built, most notably mountain bikes and BMXs, with their off-road and sporting capabilities. Nowadays, innovation in bicycle design has more or less come to a standstill, though technology continues to make bikes ever more refined and efficient. Who knows **what's being dreamt up** right now, or what we **will be riding** in a few years' time?!

Unit 5 (page 52)

Hosting the OLYMPIC GAMES

Every two years, cities around the world **(1)** _____ themselves _____ as potential hosts for future Olympic Games. Many countries that **(2)** _____ the Games _____ receive welcome rewards in terms of economic, social and cultural benefits. As the country's profile is raised in the lead-up to the Games, tourism increases and there is greater understanding of a nation and its people. The host country attracts business investment, and perception of the place often improves, boosting its reputation. If the whole thing **(3)** _____ without trouble, long-term investment may be secured. Individuals can benefit, too, as job opportunities **(4)** _____ when help is required for the Games.

However, deciding to make a bid for the Games isn't a decision to be **(5)** _____ . Once the host country's been selected, it must consider how it will **(6)** _____ the huge numbers of athletes and visitors who will descend on the country once the Games begin. Huge costs are involved in building or repurposing stadiums and accommodation for athletes, plans for improved infrastructure must be **(7)** _____ , and then there's security to pay for. This can result in huge costs and possible hikes in taxes post-event. However, the Games can improve the cities in which they're held and instil the residents there with an enormous sense of pride.

Unit 6 (page 62, page 64)

How braille system keeps up with the times

It might have been around for 200 years, but there's nothing antiquated about braille. Designers and artists are making sure this writing system, which is **invaluable** to those with little or no sight, is keeping up with modern life.

The system, invented by then 11-year-old Louis Braille in 1824, himself unable to see, was first developed as a **variation** on an existing military code. Louis thought it would be useful to **simplify** the code (which was used by Napoleon's soldiers for silent communication in the dark) to six dots instead of 12, and employ it as a means of communication for those with an **inability** to read and write in a conventional manner.

Louis' innovation was an **undeniable** success, and while virtually unchanged since the expanded 1905 version, the way in which braille is now applied differs significantly. Not only does it appear in novels and other printed materials, but it is punched into food and pharmaceutical packaging to make their contents **'visible'** to those who can't see them. There are also magazines, games instructions, sheet music – which can be used in conjunction with a braille e-reader. And blind children can learn to read and write at an early age with the help of braille bricks. **Comparable** to LEGO® in appearance but with one letter in raised dots per brick, blind children can combine them to make words, and this provides them with the **assurance** they need to communicate **reliably** with others. Today's braille applications open up whole new worlds to those who previously found certain aspects of life inaccessible.

Hexagons in everyday life

Hexagons are everywhere, not only in nature but in engineering, too. Take nuts and bolts. If they **⁰were circular in form**, it would be considerably harder for tools to grip them. What the hexagonal shape results in is **¹a greater tightening effect** when they're screwed together, and this is precisely why **²the shape has prevailed** throughout the centuries since its invention in the 1700s.

And if you look more closely at a football, you'll make the discovery that it's made up of a combination of hexagons and pentagons, stuck together. This allows for **³the dense packing together** of the individual pieces which make up the ball. When stitched together, they **⁴create the ball's – almost – spherical structure**.

The majority of pencils, too, are hexagonally shaped. This could be to do with **⁵the prevention of** rolling pencils falling off the edges of tables, but it could also be to do with grip. Additionally, they can be stacked together without wasting space during **⁶the manufacturing process**.

Unit 7 (page 74)

THE WORLD'S FIRST VLOG

At the beginning of the year 2000, ambitious twenty-something Adam Kontras decided to **(1)** _____ his dream of working in show business, and set off from his home in Ohio on a road trip to California in search of a job. He decided to **(2)** _____ tales of his journey along the way, and on 2nd January, 2000, he uploaded a video to accompany his blog in what was to become an **(3)** _____ moment: the first vlog was born.

Kontras' **(4)** _____ aim of 'The journey', as he named his videos, was simply to provide a short accompaniment to his written updates, but they constitute what is now known as a vlog. Although 'The journey' began its life as a means of informing his parents and friends of his trip to Hollywood, it eventually **(5)** _____ a series of commentaries on how he hoped to **(6)** _____ his career there. It continues to this day on YouTube, where Kontras still posts videos twice a week.

Unit 8 (page 84)

Why can't we imagine infinity?

We've all done that thing in our minds where we try to imagine space going on forever, with no end. And if there were a border, wouldn't there be something outside that border? It's rather ¹_____ for our minds to get round! So, too, is the idea that numbers are ²_____ . But why is it so difficult for us to understand?

We can understand the concept of infinity, but we can be ³_____ by the difficulties of imagining it in terms of space and time. This is doubtless because everything we see around us is finite in terms of space – we live in a town in a country in the world – and also because of the way we perceive time – in finite minutes, months or ⁴_____ !

At the other end of the scale, we find it equally as tricky to imagine nothing. As with infinity, we can grasp the concept, but not the reality. This is nothing (!) to do with our own ⁵_____ , though: science tells us there simply can't be nothing.

So, what's the ⁶_____ for our brains, then? It doesn't seem as though we're getting any nearer to coping with the ideas of infinity and nothingness. The best we can do, it seems, is find ways to talk about them.

Unit 2

Here are your pictures. They show pairs of people doing different activities together. Compare two of the pictures and say how the people depend on each other and what the challenges of doing these activities might be.

Which pair might get the most satisfaction from the experience? Why?

Unit 5

Your pictures show people with coins in different situations. Compare two of the pictures and say why the people might have these coins and how long they might keep them.

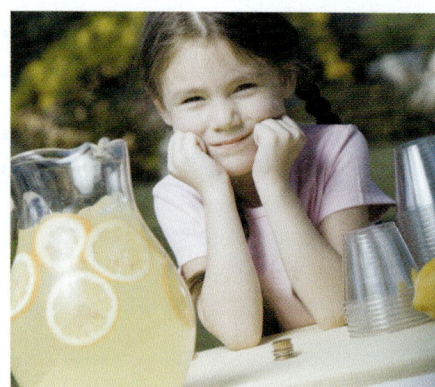

In which situation might the people most appreciate their coins? Why?

Unit 8

Your pictures show people playing instruments in different places. Compare two of the pictures and say why the people might be playing the instruments in these different places and how difficult the experience might be for them.

Who do you think is most enjoying the experience? Why?

Unit 2

Your pictures show people who are working with each other in different situations. Compare two of the pictures and say what the benefits of working together in these situations might be and how likely it is that the people will repeat the experience.

Which people do you think are most enjoying the situation they are in? Why?

Unit 5

Your pictures show people paying for things in different ways. Compare two of the pictures and say why they might have chosen to buy things in these different ways and whether they might do it differently another time.

Which form of payment might change most quickly in the near future? Why?

Unit 8

Your pictures show people listening to music in different places. Compare two of the pictures and say how the music might differ in each place and how memorable these moments might be.

In which situation do you think the sound quality is the best? Why?

UNIT 1 GRAMMAR FILE

REFERENCE

PERFECT AND CONTINUOUS TENSES

Simple aspect

The action is viewed as a fact. We use this for routine or regular repeated actions, habits and for permanent situations.

I **don't eat** meat.

I usually **got** the tram to work.

They will **live** in a side street off the Ramblas.

Continuous aspect

The action is continuous. We use the present continuous when we use dynamic (action) verbs to talk about:

actions happening at a particular moment.

A: Where's Terry?

B: She's in the kitchen – she**'s making** a cup of tea.

When Sam called, I **was eating.**

changing/developing situations.

Inma **was improving** her English.

temporary situations.

He **will be working** as a cleaner until he can find a better job.

annoying or surprising habits with **always**.

I**'m always forgetting** to charge my mobile.

present plans and arrangements for the future.

Are you **doing** anything next weekend?

PERFECT ASPECT

Simple

The action happened at some unknown time between then, the past, and now, the present time of speaking; a point before a time in the past; the present and a point of time in the future.

I **have eaten** a lot today.

I overslept because I **had forgotten** to set my alarm.

We**'ll have finished** eating by the time you get here.

We use the perfect simple:

to talk about states, single or repeated actions over a long period of time up to the present (often with **ever / never**, **often / always**).

I**'ve always dreamt** of visiting New York

It was only the second time I **had travelled** by plane.

He **will have missed** at least ten of the classes this term.

to talk about recent single actions with a present or past result (often with **just**, **already**, **yet**).

I**'ve already started** making spaghetti for dinner, so I don't want to go out.

I**'d just got back** from Australia so I was tired.

to talk about an unfinished period of time up to the present, past or future (often with **for / since**, **this week / month / year**).

Irene **has lived** in Abu Dhabi for just over a year.

They **had been married** since early that year.

We **won't have seen** him for a couple of months.

Continuous

We use the perfect continuous:

to talk about a recent activity when the effects of that activity can still be seen in the present or past.

A: Why are you crying?   **B:** I**'ve been chopping** onions.

to emphasise the length or repetition of an action.

I**'ve been trying** to get through to Max all morning, but he doesn't have his phone switched on.

In January **he'll have been working** there for six years.

I**'d been working on** the essay for over two weeks.

to suggest the short-term nature of an activity.

I**'ve been working** in advertising for the past ten years but now feel it's time for a change.

to suggest that an action is not complete.

I**'d been trying** to teach myself to play the piano but I'm still pretty terrible.

We tend to prefer the perfect simple for talking about more permanent situations.

She**'s lived** in Rome since she was a child.

We prefer to use the perfect continuous for more temporary situations.

She**'d been living** out of suitcase for months, so she was glad to get home.

STATIVE AND DYNAMIC VERBS

There are two categories for verbs in English: stative verbs and dynamic verbs.

Dynamic verbs can be used in simple and continuous aspects. Stative verbs cannot normally be used in the continuous.

Some verbs have both stative and dynamic meanings. We only use them in continuous forms with their dynamic meaning, but not with their stative meaning.

I was **feeling** a bit rundown. (dynamic; feel = experience a feeling or emotion)

I **feel** that the situation will improve in the near future. (stative; feel = have an opinion)

PRACTICE

PERFECT AND CONTINUOUS TENSES

1 Complete the sentences using the correct present form of the verbs in brackets.

1 I _____ a lot of headaches over the last couple of months. (get)

2 Karl _____ from home at the moment. (work)

3 Rafaella _____ in Sweden for six months next year because of her job. (live)

4 My neighbours cut down two tall trees last month because people _____ that they were dangerous. (always complain)

5 They _____ the results of the survey by the end of next week. (publish)

6 I _____ the strangest message from Karen about her plans for the summer. (just have)

7 Where _____ of travelling to next? (you / think)

8 I _____ revising but I still went out with my friends. (not finish)

2 Five of these sentences contain errors. Find the errors and correct them.

1 I'm loving living in London at the moment. It's great.

2 They're having three children: Hanna, Charlie and Aurora.

3 She denies having had anything to do with the robbery.

4 This soup tastes a bit strange.

5 He's not understanding anything about technology.

6 I have a break at the moment in the garden, so I'll get back to you a bit later.

7 We were thinking about whether to visit you while in London, but decided there wasn't enough time.

8 I'll believe it when I am seeing it!

3 Choose the correct alternatives.

Working freelance

Before going freelance, I ¹**was / 'd been travelling** to work for over a decade. I ²**was trying / 'd tried** doing the journey by train. There was a lot of staring out of windows and waiting because signals ³**had failed / been failing** or other trains ⁴**had broken down / been breaking down**. Once we ⁵**were waiting / waited** for the train to leave when the station announcer said, 'No trains at all ⁶**will be running / have run** for the next four hours!' Fury all round! But now, for at least the forseeable future, I ⁷**work / am working** from home. I ⁸**think / am thinking** that being alone, without distractions, ⁹**has benefitted / benefitted** me considerably over the last few weeks. I am more productive and I feel that friends and family respect the fact that I ¹⁰**have / am having** certain hours in the day when I am 'at work' so to speak, and they ¹¹**don't always ask / aren't always asking** me out. By the end of this week I ¹²**'ll have been working / 'll work** from home for two months and I'm guessing I¹³**'ll have got through / 'm getting through** 20 percent more work by then than I used to get through in the office. So, I ¹⁴**'m not returning / won't be returning** to the daily commute any time soon!

Pronunciation

4 Mark the three main stresses in each sentence.

1 What have you been doing since I last saw you?

2 How have you been feeling over the last few days?

3 Where had you been working before coming here?

4 How will you be commuting when the job hours change?

5 What's been the most important thing you've learnt today?

6 How much will you have earned by the end of the year?

5 🎧 1.1GF Listen and check. Then listen again and repeat the sentences.

6 Make questions from the prompts. Put the verbs in the correct forms.

1 What you / work on / when / the computer / crash?

2 How long / plane fly / before / they serve / dinner?

3 How much / report / you complete / by the time / you leave / later today?

4 How / you / commute / when / train strike / happen / next week?

5 How long / you / not sleep / well?

6 How many people / you / discuss / the problem with / last week / before / you / get a result?

7 Why / he / always complain / about the food in our canteen? It / usually be / fantastic.

99

UNIT 2 GRAMMAR FILE

REFERENCE

PASSIVE FORMS

We form the passive using the appropriate tense of the verb **be** + the past participle of the main verb.

The parliamentary debate **is being televised** right now. (present continuous)

Elderly people **are** regularly **scammed** by fraudsters on the phone. (present simple)

The company's main office **has been broken into** twice in the last three years. (present perfect simple)

Ahead of the storm, everyone **was advised** to stay indoors and away from the windows. (past simple)

The main course **was being served** when there was a power cut and the whole restaurant was plunged into darkness. (past continuous)

We**'d been offered** alternative accommodation but turned it down. (past perfect)

The incident **will be investigated** by experts in the department dealing with airport security. (future simple)

The matter of appropriate dress **is to be discussed** at next week's meeting. (to-infinitive)

The project **will have been completed** by the end of the week. (future perfect)

The flowers **must have been sent** by Jim. (modal verb)

The matter **must be dealt with** quickly and effectively. (modal verb)

NB: In theory, perfect continuous and modal continuous passives can be formed, but are very rarely used. We prefer to use the simple or active form instead.

It **has been being discussed** for the last hour. = It has been discussed for the last hour.

He **should be being interrogated** by the police right now. = The police should be interrogating him right now.

We use passive forms to talk about actions, events and processes when the action, event or process is considered more important than the agent (the person responsible for the action, event or process). Passive forms are frequently used in academic writing and in business reports.

We use the passive:

to focus on what happens to the subject of an action when the agent (the subject of an active verb) is unknown.

The original manuscripts **have been lost** over the years

unimportant.

The event **was staged** in the park.

assumed / common knowledge.

He **was fined** for speeding on the motorway.

I **was** first **taught** English at the age of five.

with a complex agent.

I was contacted **by a person with a strong northern accent**.

I'm being helped **by the clarity of the online reports**.

with an agent, when it is needed to complete the information.

The college rules were developed **by the first head teacher**.

with **it**, to front a sentence with reporting / thinking verbs when

we want to be tentative and avoid stating something as a fact such as **believe**, **claim**, **report**, **say** and **think** in impersonal passive structures in formal situations, when we don't know or don't wish to specify the subject.

It is thought that the two companies are negotiating a takeover.

It has been alleged that a senior officer leaked the information to the press.

It is said that we all need about eight hours' sleep a night.

we want to avoid giving more specific information about the agent, for example naming who made a certain decision.

It is felt that your work is below standard and you would benefit from further training.

It was decided that a pay rise will be put on hold for another year.

We can use an alternative impersonal passive structure:

The two companies **are thought to be** in negotiation for a takeover.

The two companies **are thought to have entered** into takeover negotiations last week.

She **is rumoured to be releasing** a new album next month.

An announcement **is considered to be** imminent.

PRACTICE

PASSIVE FORMS

1 Complete the sentences with the correct passive form of the verbs in brackets.

1 Large numbers of dolphins _____ (sight) in recent weeks off the north Cornwall coast.

2 All flights from Gatwick will continue _____ (delay) this afternoon by a strike involving all the baggage handlers at the airport.

3 The flood defences along the river _____ (breach) last night by rising water.

4 Several suspects _____ (currently / question) in connection with the riots last weekend.

5 The side effects of the new drugs _____ (shouldn't / underestimate) by those prescribing them.

6 My father complained to the hotel management that we _____ (not alert) to the possibility of noise from the nearby construction site.

2 Rewrite the sentences in the passive. Include the agent only where necessary.

1 The receptionist asked us to complete a questionnaire following our stay at the hotel.

2 Years of eating food with low nutritional value greatly increases the risk of illness.

3 The judge is sentencing the armed robbers later today and the cameramen will televise the ruling.

4 A drone delivered the parcel to a special point in the company car park and both staff and customers watched the unusual event.

5 Agatha Christie wrote the play and actors have performed it continuously in London for over 68 years.

3 Rewrite the sentences using impersonal passive structures.

1 It is alleged that several politicians submitted fraudulent expenses claims in the last financial year.
Several politicians _____ .

2 It is rumoured that a popular boy band will be breaking up later this year.
A popular boy band _____ .

3 It is guaranteed that people who have had problems will be compensated.
People who have had problems
_____ .

4 It is believed that taking vitamin supplements builds up our immune systems.
Taking vitamin supplements _____ .

5 It is thought that many of the poet's works were written while he was living in Rome.
Many of the poet's poems _____ .

4 Complete the second sentence so that it has a similar meaning to the first sentence, using the word given. Do not change the word given. Use between three and six words.

1 A news bulletin alerted me to possible train delays before I set off.
BEEN
Before _____ to possible train delays by a news bulletin.

2 I'm sure someone threw out those old books years ago.
MUST
Those old books _____ years ago.

3 If students arrive late, the teachers won't allow them into classes.
BE
Students not arriving on _____ into classes.

4 People say that Ada Lovelace developed the first computer programme in the nineteenth century.
TO
Ada Lovelace _____ the first computer programme in the nineteenth century.

5 The local surgery is reported to have bought scanners to help doctors in their diagnoses.
THAT
It _____ bought by the local surgery to help doctors in their diagnoses.

6 It's important that the directors consider the potential impact of this information.
SHOULD
The potential impact of _____ ignored by the directors.

Pronunciation

5 What additional phoneme do we use when linking the words in bold in the sentences?

1 Life spans are thought **to have** increased over the last century.

2 Most people are said **to have** had a salary increase in the past year.

3 Recent findings are believed **to encourage** people to change to a plant-based diet.

4 The company is reported **to have** laid off hundreds of workers this month.

5 A politician was claimed **to have** leaked the information, but it was later found to have been someone else.

6 Reports are claimed **to underestimate** the real impact of the government policy.

6 🎧 2.1GF Listen and repeat the sentences.

UNIT 3 GRAMMAR FILE

REFERENCE

CONJUNCTIONS

We use conjunctions to join ideas within a sentence. They may come at the beginning or in the middle of a sentence. They improve the cohesion of a text.

Conjunctions which are used to make a contrast include **although**, **while**, **whereas**, **yet**.

The task wasn't difficult, **yet** Tom found he couldn't complete it on time.

While / Although the task wasn't difficult, Tom found he couldn't complete it on time.

Tom found himself unable to complete the task on time, **whereas** Harry finished it quickly.

Conjunctions which are used to add information include **and** and **nor**.

He wasn't afraid of taking risks **and** he didn't worry about the potential consequences.

He wasn't afraid of taking risks **nor** did he worry about the potential consequences.

Conjunctions which are used to give a condition include **as long as**, **provided that**, **if**, **unless** and **if only**.

As long as / Provided (that) she earned enough money to cover her bills, she didn't care about becoming rich.

Unless he improves his performance, he won't be promoted.

If he doesn't improve his performance, he won't be promoted.

If only he would have a bit more confidence, he would do really well.

Conjunctions which are used to give a reason include **as**, **because**, **since** and **so**.

As he hadn't had time to study, he didn't do as well as he'd hoped in the exam.

If two main clauses are connected with **and** or **but**, we need to put **that** after the conjunction.

'I'll come, but I'll be late.' → He said that he would come **but that** he would be late.

If the subject is left out in the second clause, then we do not use **that**.

'I used to be a software designer and worked for myself.' → He said he used to be / had been a software designer and had worked for himself.

We can use a negative adverbial expression to link ideas in a sentence. For emphasis, we can put the negative adverbial at the beginning of the sentence and invert the auxiliary and the subject.

She **not only** wanted to study forensic science at university, **but** she **also** wanted to keep up her foreign languages.

Not only did she want to study forensic science at university **but** she **also** wanted to keep up her foreign languages.

Tommy decided to become an actor but **not until** he'd finished his degree.

Not until he'd finished his degree did Tommy decide to become an actor.

We **only** decided to cancel the booking **when** we heard about the bad storm.

Only when we heard about the bad storm did we decide to cancel the booking.

LINKING ADVERBIALS

We use linking adverbials to connect one sentence to another in a logical way. They usually appear at the beginning of a sentence and are followed by a comma. They help to make writing more cohesive.

Linking adverbials used to give extra information include **additionally**, **as well as**, **besides** (**this**), **furthermore**, **moreover**, **what's more**.

We decided there was little to be gained by waiting any longer. **Besides,** there was a storm coming.

Linking adverbials used to give a reason or result include **for this reason**, **consequently**, **as a result**, **in view of**, **given**.

We decided there was little to be gained by waiting any longer. **Consequently,** we managed to catch the last train home.

Linking adverbials used to make a contrast include **on the contrary**, **on the other hand**, **in contrast**, **alternatively**, **despite this**, **even so**.

We decided there was little to be gained by waiting any longer. **Despite this,** we ended up wasting another half an hour trying to agree what to do next.

PRACTICE

CONJUNCTIONS

1 Complete the sentences with the conjunctions in the box.

> as (x2)   if only   nor   provided that
> whereas   yet

1 I knew it would have changed a lot _____ I still longed to go back.

2 Simon always had his head in a book _____ his brother spent most of his time watching television.

3 She should be able to join us for dinner, _____ her plane arrives on time.

4 _____ the plumber still hasn't come, we won't be able to use the bathroom today.

5 _____ Jessica were here. She would know what to do.

6 Nigel loves hiking _____ does his girlfriend Georgia.

7 I don't eat meat. _____ does my partner.

2 Link the sentences using the words in brackets. This may result in one or two sentences.

1 He might be busy. He always finds time to help. (matter)

2 We increased the prices. The sales have fallen. (result)

3 The arts students have very few morning lectures. The science students have many. (contrast)

4 My parents like to holiday in the city. My grandparents prefer the beach. (while)

5 He got home. He immediately noticed the broken window. (sooner)

6 We had a lot of problems on the journey. It was a complete nightmare. (words)

3 Choose the correct linking adverbial.

1 Living abroad would be the adventure of a lifetime. **On the other hand / Besides**, it might be terribly lonely.

2 **As well as / As a result of** having to look after three young children, she also had to manage two part-time jobs.

3 Her parents gave her a car and threw a huge party for her 18th birthday. **What's more / Consequently**, she was given a lot of money for her gap year trip.

4 The restaurant was very overpriced and we had to wait ages for a table. **In view of this / Even so**, I'd still recommend it.

5 There's no point trying to persuade him to do the sensible thing; he won't listen. **For this reason / Despite this**, we've decided to let him make his own mistakes.

4 Complete the text with one word in each gap.

The Triangle

[1] _____ learning a musical instrument at primary school may not have been a pleasure for all of us, there was one instrument that didn't take much talent, and [2] _____ was the triangle. [3] _____ your musical ability, you could easily tap a metal triangle with what is called a 'beater' and produce a loud, clear sound that cut through everyone else's recorders, guitars or violins. What's [4] _____ , you could make your contribution and then continue daydreaming for the rest of the time! [5] _____ , the triangle is actually a well-respected instrument that is part of a full orchestra and can take a long time to master completely. This small triangle of metal dates back to the 10th century and was originally [6] _____ triangular [7] _____ gapped – as it is today, [8] _____ had four sides of continuous metal. It was popular in Turkey in the 18th century but [9] _____ when Franz List featured a triangle solo in one of his piano sonatas [10] _____ it really find a place in the professional orchestra. As a [11] _____ , more and more pieces were written for the humble triangle and it even features in modern popular music. [12] _____ instance, even the Foo Fighters have played triangle solos on some of their tours!

Pronunciation

5 Where would you pause slightly in these sentences and add a comma? Would the previous word generally carry an upward or downward intonation?

1 On the other hand not everyone really wants to learn an instrument.

2 In other words two heads are better than one.

3 As a result the triplets became famous throughout the world.

4 As yet no one has beaten her triathlon time.

5 However you feel about it you need to consider your future actions.

6 🎧 **3.1GF** Listen and check. Then repeat the sentences.

UNIT 4 GRAMMAR FILE

REFERENCE

REPORTED SPEECH

Verb tenses in reporting

We usually change the tense of the original verb so that it moves further back in the past. We also change time expressions and pronouns as necessary.

'**We spoke** to him **yesterday**,' they said. → They said that **they had spoken** to him **the day before**.

We do not change the tense if the situation we are reporting still exists and if the reporting verb is in the present tense.

'She**'s** currently **working** in London.' → He **says** she**'s** currently **working** in London.

Modal verbs in reporting

We usually change modal verbs in reported speech.

will → would; can → could; may → might; needn't → didn't have to; must → had to

We do not change modal verbs if the situation we are reporting still exists and if the reporting verb is in the present tense.

'We **need to** visit our cousin.' → She **says** we **need to** visit our cousin.

Modal verbs are often reported using other verbs (e.g. **must**, **should**, **ought to** → **advised**, **urged**; **let's** → **suggested**).

'You **should** ask for help.' → He **advised** me to ask for help.

REPORTED QUESTIONS

Reported Yes/No questions

When there is no question word in the direct speech question, we use if/whether. The word order is the same as in the statement. The verb tense and other changes are the same as for other types of reported speech.

'Could I borrow your notes?' she asked.
She asked / wondered / wanted to know **if / whether she could borrow** my notes.

Reported wh- questions

The **wh-** word is followed by normal word order (subject + verb). The verb tense and other changes are the same as for other types of reported speech.

'Why did you leave that job?' she asked him. She asked **him why he had left** that job.

VERB PATTERNS WITH REPORTING VERBS

NB: some verbs can follow more than one pattern.

verb + infinitive

examples: agree, claim, decide, hope, offer, promise, refuse, threaten

We **refused to go** to the meeting.

verb + object + infinitive

examples: advise, beg, encourage, invite, order, permit, persuade, remind, tell, warn

She **persuaded me to lend** her some money.

verb (+ that) + clause

examples: accept, admit, assert, claim, doubt, explain, promise, recommend, say, suggest

She **recommended (that) we should visit** the museum.

verb + object + (that) + clause

examples: promise, remind, tell, warn, reassure

He **warned us (that) he might be** late.

verb + -ing

examples: admit, deny, recommend, regret, suggest, mention

He **suggested visiting** the museum.

verb + preposition + -ing

examples: apologise for, insist on, object to, compliment on

She **apologised for forgetting** my name.

verb + object + preposition + -ing

examples: accuse sb of, blame sb for, congratulate sb on, discourage sb from, forgive sb for

She **discouraged him from going** to university.

verb + wh- word + infinitive

examples: describe, explain, know, wonder

She **explained where to find** the library.

verb + object + wh- word + infinitive

examples: ask, remind, tell

The manager **told us what to expect** in the interview.

NB: It's not always necessary to report statements word for word. The information can be summarised.

'I think it would be a really good idea for you to apply for the job in Paris,' said Emma's dad.

Emma's dad encouraged her to apply for the job in Paris.

IMPERSONAL REPORTING VERBS

Impersonal reporting verbs are used in formal written English to report general opinions. Verbs such as **believe, consider, expect, suggest** can be used.

It **is believed that** migration will increase substantially in the next ten years.

PRACTICE

REPORTED SPEECH

1 **Complete the second sentence so it has a similar meaning to the first.**

1 'Please don't forget to phone me as soon as you arrive,' said my mum.

My mum reminded

_____ .

2 'Have you taken my keys again?' my brother said.

My brother accused

_____ .

3 'It's Dan's fault that we missed the plane,' Kerry said.

Kerry blamed

_____ .

4 'I wish I'd never left my old job,' said Rob.

Rob regretted

_____ .

5 'Ella told me the party would be terrible, so I didn't go,' Amy said.

Ella discouraged

_____ .

6 'It's not fair that we have to work such long hours,' said Jon.

Jon objected _____ .

2 **Report each sentence in two different ways using the reporting verbs in the box. In both sentences, use the same reporting verb and begin with the word in brackets.**

> agree   apologise   complain   ~~confess~~
> deny   hope   insist   mention   promise

0 'I haven't done my homework.' (she)

She confessed that she hadn't done her homework.

She confessed to not having done her homework.

1 'I'll definitely help you.' (he)

2 'Yes, I'll come with you on Friday.' (she)

3 'You must attend the meeting.' (he)

4 'I hope I can get time off.' (he)

5 'No, I didn't tell him!' (she)

6 'We may go to see our grandparents this weekend.' (they)

7 'I've got far too much work to do.' (he)

8 'I'm sorry I won't be able to help this week.' (he)

3 **Use the information in the dialogue to complete Evan's story.**

Evan and his sister, Ella, are driving to Leeds, using motorways and not going through big cities.

Evan: Let's use the map.

Ella: No, we'll use the sat-nav. It's very reliable.

Evan: Look, I think we're going into the city centre. Have we taken the wrong road?

Ella: No. The sat-nav indicates that we're heading in the right direction.

Evan: We're in the middle of Birmingham. Turn round now!

Ella: OK. Maybe you're right.

Evan: Do you think you put in the wrong address?

Ella: No. I probably set it to shortest, instead of fastest route! OK, I was wrong and you were right!

We were on our way to Leeds and planned to take motorways all the way, avoiding big cities like Birmingham. I suggested ¹_____ but my sister insisted ²_____ because ³_____ . We followed the voice directions and after a while I pointed out ⁴_____ the centre of Birmingham, which on a Saturday lunchtime was NOT a good idea. I queried ⁵_____ the wrong road. Ella reassured ⁶_____ in the right direction. After another ten minutes of sitting in a traffic jam I told ⁷_____ because ⁸_____ in the middle of Birmingham. Ella conceded ⁹_____ , and turned round. I wondered ¹⁰_____ but she concluded ¹¹_____ the sat-nav to shortest rather than fastest route. Red-faced, she admitted ¹²_____ and ¹³_____ . I smiled.

Pronunciation

4 **Look at the verb forms in bold in the sentences. Do they take the same length of time to say, or different lengths of time?**

1 He **suggested** that they go to the theatre.

2 She **queried** the use of an apostrophe in the contraction.

3 The teacher **complimented** me on my pronunciation.

4 Her mother **encouraged** her to take up swimming.

5 He **exaggerated** his ability to play the violin.

6 She **acknowledged** her difficulty in speaking German.

5 🎧 **4.1GF Listen and check. Then repeat the sentences.**

6 **Now find other examples of reporting verbs in the text in Ex 3.**

UNIT 5 GRAMMAR FILE

REFERENCE

CONDITIONAL FORMS

Zero conditional

We use the zero conditional (**if** / **when** + present tense + present tense) for general truths or consequences.

If I **hunch** over my laptop for too long, my neck **aches**.

Alternatives to **if** include:

Unless they **are** under threat, cats **don't** usually **pounce** on people.

First conditional

We use the first conditional (**if** + present tense + future form or **might/could**, etc.) for the consequence of a possible future action/situation. We can also use words/phrases like **unless**, **in case** and **provided that** instead of **if**.

If we **cut down** that hedge, the blackbirds **will have** nowhere to build their nests.

The clamped car **will be removed** this afternoon **unless** you **pay** the fine immediately.

We can also use **if**, etc. + present continuous / present perfect + future or imperative in the main clause to talk about possibility or likelihood in the present/future.

If you**'re coming** to London this weekend, I **will be** able to show you all the sights.

Second conditional

We use the second conditional (**if** + past simple + **would/could/might** + infinitive) for hypothetical actions/situations in the present, and to give advice.

If I **were** you, I**'d transfer** your photos from your phone to your laptop.

Third conditional

We use the third conditional (**if** + past perfect + **would have** + past participle) for hypothetical actions/situations in the past.

If I **had known** you were heading to the music festival, I **would** definitely **have got hold of** a ticket.

Mixed conditionals

We use mixed conditionals:

to speculate about the possible result in the present of a hypothetical action/situation in the past (**if** + past perfect + **would** + infinitive).

If we **hadn't taken** the car, we**'d still be** stuck at the station waiting for the train to turn up.

to speculate about the past result of a hypothetical action/ situation in the present (**if** + past + **would have** + past participle).

If the book **were** more engaging, I**'d have suggested** we read it at our book club.

to speculate about the future result of a hypothetical action/ situation in the past (**if** + past perfect + **would** + infinitive).

If we **hadn't spent** so long at the arcade, we**'d be watching** that new film at the cinema now.

Alternative forms

We can use the following alternative conditional structures:

should instead of **if** with the first conditional (**should** + subject + infinitive + future simple). We use this structure in more formal situations, to be more polite.

Should you have any further questions, I**'ll be** online later today to answer them.

if + subject + **were to** + infinitive with the second conditional (**if** + **were to** + infinitive + **would** + infinitive) in less likely situations.

If the students **were to ask for** an extension on their loan repayment, **would** the bank **grant** it?

To increase formality, we can invert this form.

Were the students to ask for an extension on their loan repayment, **would** it **be** granted?

inversion with the third conditional (question form of past perfect + **would have** + past participle) in more formal and less likely situations.

Had Rob **requested** an interview, they probably **would have arranged** one for him.

Modal verbs in conditional sentences

Modal verbs (**can**, **could**, **might**, etc.) can be used in all types of conditional sentences.

If I **knew** how to go about it, I **could start** an online shop selling the jewellery I make.

If I **hadn't missed** the bus that day, I **might** never **have met** my husband!

if + (should) happen to

We use **if** + (**should**) **happen to** to suggest that something is more unlikely or just a chance possibility. **Should** and **happen** can be used together.

If you (**should**) **happen to see** Professor Wainwright, do give him my best wishes.

suppose / what if … ?

Suppose means **what if** … ? and can be used with different tenses.

Suppose Charlie **had found out** about the money. You'd have had to share it with him.

if + will/would

We use **if** + **will/would** to make requests more polite. In this case the auxiliary **will/would** means **be willing to**.

If you **will** just **bear** with me for a second, I'll see if the doctor's available.

PRACTICE

CONDITIONALS

1 **Complete the sentences with the correct form of the verbs in brackets.**

1 If you are an avid reader, you _____ (be) likely to have a better vocabulary than those who aren't.

2 If you _____ (use) a few gestures during your presentation, people will be more engaged with what you're saying.

3 I'd put forward the idea of a four-day school week if I _____ (think) our teachers would listen!

4 If I _____ (know) how many hours I'd end up working, I wouldn't _____ (go) self-employed!

5 Unless you drink water while you exercise, you _____ (become) dehydrated.

6 I'll _____ on the 1 p.m. train if it isn't delayed.

7 If I _____ (be) you, I _____ (apply) for that game tester job – you've got the experience.

8 I _____ (encourage) you to do a research degree if I'd known you might be interested.

2 **Write mixed conditionals about the situations. Start with 'if'.**

1 I didn't learn any foreign languages at school. I can't speak any now.

2 Filipe doesn't like curry. He didn't go out for a curry with his friends at the weekend.

3 I have a dentist's appointment this afternoon. I didn't eat onions at lunch!

4 Amy specialised in paediatrics. She's working at a top children's hospital now.

5 I didn't learn to drive when I was a teenager. Now I'm reliant on public transport.

6 I mislaid my car keys again yesterday. I'm looking for them now.

3 **Rewrite the sentences using the word given, so that the pairs of sentences are similar in meaning. Where the word has a capital letter, begin the sentence with that word.**

1 I'll go through that homework with you if you're having difficulty with it.

Should

_____

2 If Sara tried a plant-based diet, I'm certain her health problems would improve.

Were

_____

3 The food in the college canteen would be better if they'd found a better chef.

Had

_____

4 If you bump into dad while you're out, ask him to drop that book round.

happen

_____

5 If you hold for a second, I'll see if I can put you through to the manager.

will

_____

6 Imagine if you'd got that job at the hardware store. You'd have to work every weekend.

Suppose

_____

Pronunciation

4 **Look at the sentences. Underline the /ə/ (as in teach<u>er</u>) sounds in each sentence. There may be more than one /ə/ sound. One sentence does not contain the /ə/ sound.**

1 I wouldn't have told you about my placement abroad if you hadn't asked.

2 If I'd known you were going to dissuade me from getting a dog, I wouldn't have mentioned it!

3 Unless people wanted to tell me what was worrying them, I'd never pry.

4 Should you find a copy of today's newspaper, pick one up for me, please.

5 Had I discovered the old letters earlier, I would've given you them to read.

6 If I had worked during my summer break, I'd have quite a bit of money now.

7 I won't illustrate my points with slides this time as I haven't had time to prepare any.

8 Suppose you hadn't warned them about the train strike. They'd have never got here!

5 🎧 **5.1GF Listen and check.**

107

UNIT 6 GRAMMAR FILE

REFERENCE

VERB AND NOUN PHRASES

Verb and noun phrases allow us flexibility in the use of language, enabling speakers or writers to express the same actions, concepts and objects in different ways. This can help us to avoid repetition of grammatical structures, for example, or re-phrase to clarify meaning.

Verbs to nouns

Verbs can be changed to nouns in several ways:

by adding a suffix, e.g.

store (v) → stor**age** (n)

manufacture (v) → manufactur**ing** (n)

prevent (v) → prevent**ion** (n)

by adding an article, e.g.

a leap into the unknown

make **an** address

the appeal was successful

by adding a possessive, e.g.

His first **draft** of the report.

She prepared for **her** annual **hike.**

The newspaper**'s review** wasn't very complimentary.

Nouns to verbs

Nouns can be changed to verbs by:

adding a suffix, e.g.

class (n) → class**ify** (v)

character (n) → character**ise** (v)

strength (n) → strength**en** (v)

removing a suffix, e.g.

explan**ation** (n) → explain (v)

assign**ment** (n) → assign (v)

annoy**ance** (n) → annoy (v)

Verbs to adjectives

Verbs can be changed to adjectives in several ways:

by adding the gerund, e.g.

absorb → absorb**ing**

diminish → diminish**ing**

empower → empower**ing**

by forming the past participle, e.g.

frustrate → frustrat**ed**

divide → divid**ed**

exhaust → exhaust**ed**

by adding a prefix and/or suffix, e.g.

analyse → analy**tical**

stick → **un**stuck

comfort → **un**comfort**able**

Adjectives to verbs

Adjectives can be changed to verbs by adding a suffix, e.g.

captive → captiv**ate**

intense → intens**ify**

legal → legal**ise**

Nouns to adjectives

Nouns can be changed to adjectives by adding a suffix: **-able, -al, -ary, -ent, -ful, -ible, -ify, -ity, -ive, -less, -ly, -ous, -y**, e.g.

accident → accident**al**

custom → custom**ary**

athlete → athlet**ic**

Adjectives to nouns

Adjectives can be changed to nouns:

by removing a suffix, e.g.

respect**ful** → respect

moment**ary** → moment

trust**worthy** → trust

by changing the suffix, e.g.

attract**ive** → attract**ion**

diploma**tic** → diploma**cy**

archaeologi**cal** → archaeolog**ist**

Adverbs from verbs, nouns and adjectives

Adverbs are usually formed from other parts of speech by adding the prefixes **-ably, -ally, -ily, -ly**:

verb to adverb, e.g.

continue → continu**ally**

realise → realisti**cally**

remark → remark**ably**

noun to adverb, e.g.

principal → principal**ly**

hour → hour**ly**

public → public**ly**

adjective to adverb, e.g.

ready → read**ily**

comprehensive → comprehensive**ly**

dramatic → dramatic**ally**

PRACTICE

1 Complete the table with the correct forms. There may be more than one form for each box.

verb	noun	adjective	adverb
1 expect			
2 irritate			
3	creation		
4	consideration		
5		inclusive	
6		encouraging	
7			enthusiastically
8			continuously

2 Complete the second sentence so that it has a similar meaning to the first sentence, using the word given. Use between three and six words, including the word given.

1 It is commonly believed that teams that wear red often win football matches.

IS

There _____ that teams that wear red often win football matches.

2 You've offended everyone we've met today!

TO

You've _____ everyone we've met today!

3 No one explained what was going on.

WAS

No _____ to what was going on.

4 The team seemed somewhat reluctant to implement the new process.

SOME

There seemed _____ on the part of the team to implement the new process.

5 They say that travelling makes the mind broader.

IS

Travel _____ the mind.

6 My essay got a lot of criticism from the teacher and I didn't like it.

SO

I didn't like the way the teacher _____ much.

3 Five of these sentences contain incorrect word forms. Find the errors and correct them.

1 We've been incredibly well informed about what's going on during the building of the new offices.

2 Passing your driving test is a real cause for celebrating – well done!

3 I must respectfully decline your invitation but thank you most sincerely for asking our company to take part in the event.

4 Crime preventing in the poorest of inner-city areas ranks highly on the local council's agenda.

5 We'd like to welcome viewers to the broadcast of this most historical of occasions.

6 The new diet has been remarkably beneficial for the children's health.

7 The team were comrehendingly smashed by the opposition with a final score of 15-0.

Pronunciation

4 Underline the strongly stressed sounds in the word sets.

1 anticipate, anticipation, anticipatory

2 appeal, appeal, appealing, appealingly

3 science, scientist, scientific, scientifically

4 demonstrate, demonstration, demonstrative, demonstratively

5 discriminate, discrimination, discriminatory, discriminatingly

6 dismiss, dismissal, dismissive, dismissively

7 interpret, interpretation, misinterpret, misinterpretation

8 presume, presumption, presumably

5 🎧 6.1GF Listen and check.

UNIT 7 GRAMMAR FILE

REFERENCE

FUTURE TENSES

Future simple

We use the future simple for:

predictions and beliefs (often following **I think**, **I know**, **I'm sure**, etc.):

I **won't get** home till way after dinnertime, so don't make any for me.

I'm sure Debra **will forgive** you for not inviting her to your wedding!

facts.

The lights **will turn off** automatically after five minutes.

decisions made when speaking.

I'**ll get** a takeaway on my home if you like.

an assumption about the present.

Fernanda **will be** on her way to us at this very moment.

Future continuous

We use the future continuous for:

an activity that will be in progress at or around a point of time in the future.

Give me a ring later. I'**ll be decorating** the living room but I can stop for a chat.

This time next year I'**ll be studying** abroad in Japan.

an activity that is part of a normal or organised sequence of events.

Mum **will be going** to the pharmacy this afternoon, so she'll pick up some headache tablets then.

Future perfect simple and continuous

We use the future perfect simple for:

an assumption about the present:

The DIY store **will have shut** by now so I'll have to wait till tomorrow to get more nails.

an activity that will be completed before a point in the future.

The ship **will have sailed** by early evening.

We use the future perfect continuous for an activity that will have been in progress up to certain point in the future.

By the time you come to visit me, I'**ll have been living** in Paris for six months.

'going to'

We use **going to** for:

actions that are inevitable or unstoppable.

It'**s going to get** dark soon.

He'**s going to trip** up those steps.

intentions or plans made before the time of speaking.

They'**re going to deliver** the pizza so we don't have to go and collect it.

I'**m not going to lend** that game to Liza – I'll never get it back.

Present tenses

We use the present simple for timetabled, organised events.

The flight **leaves** at 2.45 p.m.

We use the present continuous for arrangements.

They'**re voting** on the policy tomorrow, so we'll see what happens then.

We use **be to** for official plans or obligation.

Nobody **is to start** packing up until I tell them to.

We use present tenses (including the present perfect) after time clauses (e.g. clauses with **when**, **before**, **as soon as**, **once**, **after**).

When / As soon as the money **comes** through, I'll make the transfer.

After / Once I'**ve finished** this bit of work, I'll help you make lunch.

We use an infinitive after **be due to**, **be about to**, **be bound to**, **be expected to** and **be hoped to**.

Aunt Jayne's **due to arrive** any minute.

We'**re about to go out** – I'll call you back later.

Javi'**s bound to miss** the bus again. He does it nearly every day.

The minister **is expected to make** a speech at around three o'clock this afternoon.

PRACTICE

1 Why is the future simple used in each sentence? Choose from the uses A-D.

A an assumption about the present

B decisions made when speaking

C facts

D predictions and beliefs

1 Joseph will be halfway round the world by now. _____

2 The sun will set at 17.42 this evening. _____

3 I'll put the kettle on and make us a coffee. _____

4 Dad will be in the shed, building something as usual! _____

5 I know Ken won't be back till late so don't bother waiting up for him. _____

6 The screensaver will kick in after ten minutes of inactivity. _____

7 I'll ring Sonya and see if she knows of a cool place to meet on Saturday. _____

8 I think João will help us put this furniture together. I've no idea how to do it. _____

2 Choose the correct tense: future continuous, future perfect simple or future perfect continuous.

1 By this time on Sunday, **we'll be relaxing / we're going to relax** in the sun in Greece!

2 Jon **will have been finishing / will have finished** work by by now so he'll probably come and join us at the café.

3 They**'ll have done / 'll have been doing** the building work for about a year by the time it's finally completed.

4 This time on Wednesday I**'ll have / 'll be having** my first driving lesson.

5 I think the bus **will have left / will have been leaving** by nine o'clock but you might just manage to catch it.

6 Ms White **will be holding / will have been holding** a dance lesson in the hall at lunchtime if anyone would like to attend.

7 Do you think the cinema **will be closing / will have closed** by now? I think I left my umbrella behind after the film.

8 **We're going to organise / We'll have been organising** a party for all school-leavers at the end of June.

9 The guys **are putting / will put** the tents up for us as we speak, so we won't have to do it when we get to the site.

10 Our college **breaks / is breaking** up for summer earlier than usual this year.

3 Complete the sentences with the phrases from the box. There may be more than one possible answer.

> about to   after (x3)   as soon as (x3)
> bound to   due to   once (x3)   when (x3)

1 I've promised to give my cousin a hand with his school project _____ I've finished my own homework.

2 Oh, hi, Becky! Thanks for calling but I'm _____ go for a jog. Can I call you back?

3 I think the train's _____ arrive any minute. Come on!

4 _____ this programme's over, I'm going to bed. It's been an exhausting day.

5 You're _____ drop all those things – they're balancing very precariously!

6 Will you show me how to do this calculation _____ you've got a minute?

7 I'm _____ get a cold when we're on holiday – I always get sick when I stop rushing around!

8 I am _____ start a new job this autumn but they haven't given me a start date yet.

Pronunciation

4 Which of the words in bold contain a silent 'h'?

1 I will **have** been studying Portuguese for about ten years when I finish my degree.

2 When you **have** finished what you're doing, would you mind giving me a **hand**?

3 I **have had** a terrible day and now I'm going to go and **have** a soak in the bath and chill out.

4 The theme park will **have** opened by now – why don't we **head** on over there for a while?

5 The dinner will **have** burnt by now. I shouldn't **have** spent so much time on the phone.

6 Don't call me before five because I'll be **having** my Zoom interview for most of the afternoon.

5 🎧 7.1GF Listen and check.

111

UNIT 8 GRAMMAR FILE

REFERENCE

CLAUSE PATTERNS – SUBORDINATE CLAUSES

Non-finite clause with '-ed' form

A non-finite subordinate clause with an **-ed** form before a main clause can be used to give focus, e.g.

Compared to previous reports, this one is particularly positive about the future of the company.

Non-finite clause with 'if' + past participle

There are some systems that, if implemented, would make us far more efficient as an organisation.

Non-finite clause introduced by 'Not' + '-ing'

A non-finite clause, introduced by **not + -ing**, can be used to give more information, e.g.

Not being familiar with the area, I sought out interesting things to see and do.

Imperative + 'and' conditional

An imperative can be used to introduce a condition followed by **and** to introduce a consequence of the condition, e.g.

Try our delicious paellas and you'll definitely be back for more!

CLAUSE PATTERNS – EMPHATIC STRUCTURES

Cleft sentences

'it' clefts ('it' + 'be' + phrase + defining relative clause)

We use **it** clefts to change the normal sentence structure in order to emphasise or focus on certain information.

It was after their reunion concert that the band actually decided to part ways forever.

The important information is directly after **it + be**. It can:

emphasise the subject of the defining relative clause.

It was me who caught the thief red-handed.

emphasise the object of the defining clause.

It was your phone that the police called last night.

emphasise the whole phrase.

It was last weekend that the noisy neighbours finally moved out.

Note: When the subject of the defining clause is plural, we still use **it + be** in the singular.

It was Angel's **sisters** who **were cheering** so loudly.

'wh-' clefts

We use **wh-** clefts to emphasise new or interesting information which usually follows the **wh-** clause.

What amazes me is how professional musicians play entire concerts without referring to the score.

We use:

what (as subject) + verb + **be** + emphasised word/phrase.

What's fascinating is how the director got the actors to work so well together.

what + clause + **be** + emphasised word/phrase.

What I'm thinking about doing is going to university to study engineering.

Note: We can also use phrases such as the reason why, the place where, the person who.

The place where they first settled in this area is just over there.

Inversion after adverbs/adverbial phrases with a negative meaning

We use inversion after adverbs or adverbial phrases to focus and give emphasis on what we're saying (adverb/adverbial phrase + modal auxiliary + subject):

No sooner had we arrived at the picnic spot than it started pouring down.

Little did I know who'd be waiting for me when I got home.

Not until we'd eaten the dish **did we find out** exactly what was in it.

In no way would I ask anyone to do something I wouldn't do myself as their manager.

Only when they saw what was inside the parcel **did they realise** what was going on.

Barely had I got in when the phone starting ringing.

Note: Using negative adverbs and phrases to front an inverted sentence is more often used in formal or written English. This is especially true of sentences using inversion after *so* and *such*.

So bumpy was the flight that we had to keep our seatbelts fastened the whole way.

'should'/'had'/'were' + subject + verb

Introducing a subordinate clause with inverted **should/had/were** + subject + verb can be used in formal contexts, e.g.

Should you require any assistance in filling out the form, do not hesitate to call the number provided.

COMPARING

Intensifying and modifying comparisons

Some words can intensity and modify comparative forms, e.g.

considerably / a great deal more/less surprising than

more and more challenging

a bit / slightly / a little broader

no worse than

just / quite / easily as fascinating as

not nearly / nowhere near as helpful as

PRACTICE

1 Complete the subordinate clauses in the sentences using the correct form of the verbs in the box.

> base   be   buy   compare
> design   have   require   know

1 _____ to last week's performance, today's concert was so much better.

2 The new building, _____ well, will give us more space and allow more light into the rooms.

3 Bring binoculars and you _____ a fantastic whale-watching expedition with us!

4 _____ interested in sport, I didn't accept the tickets for the basketball match.

5 _____ on the latest figures, sales are significantly up this quarter.

6 _____ the first in the series of 'collector' magazines and you'll want to get them all!

7 _____ that I was supposed to queue, I unwittingly annoyed other customers.

8 _____ , high seats for small children are available from the restaurant reception.

2 Five of these sentences contain incorrect forms. Find the errors and correct them.

1 No sooner we unpacked the car than we realised we'd arrived at the wrong place.

2 Never before had I seen such an incredibe landscape.

3 So unpleasant were the fumes from the factory that we had to keep all our windows closed.

4 You want to speak to a member of staff, please wait here until called.

5 It was Jennifer who first noticed that the alarm was going off at the end of the street.

6 I known you were thinking of applying for the course, I'd have given you some better information.

7 Not until we'd completed the walk along the cliffs we realised how risky it had been.

8 I'm considering at the moment is retraining to become a nurse.

3 Complete the sentences with the correct phrase from the box.

> did the best   harder and harder
> just as compelling   no worse
> not nearly as   nothing like as exhausting
> slightly taller   very much warmer

1 This series is _____ exciting as the previous one.

2 I _____ I could under difficult circumstances.

3 Wow! The sea temperature is _____ than it was a couple of weeks ago.

4 Dan might be _____ than his brother, but they're fairly similar in height.

5 This work gets _____ every day and I'm struggling to keep up.

6 Getting the bus for such a short journey is _____ than getting the train.

7 I think the sequel to the novel is _____ as the original.

8 The drive was _____ as I'd expected it to be.

Pronunciation

4 Mark rising and/or falling intonation at the end of the sentences. There is an example to help you.

0 Never before had we been to see such a fascinating kind of play.

1 This documentary's nowhere near as good as that other one, is it?

2 So, you're telling me that you think this flat's no worse than our old one?

3 Not knowing where I was going, I wasted a lot of time driving round in circles.

4 I'm sorry but this is the best I can do without having access to the right data.

5 Based on what you already know about the author, I'd like you to write a short introduction about him.

6 There's no way it was Imelda who broke the vase, surely?

7 Do you really believe this system is no faster than the old one?

8 Had I thought about it in advance, I'd have brought my laptop to show you my photos.

5 🎧 **8.1GF** Listen and check. Then repeat the sentences in the pauses.

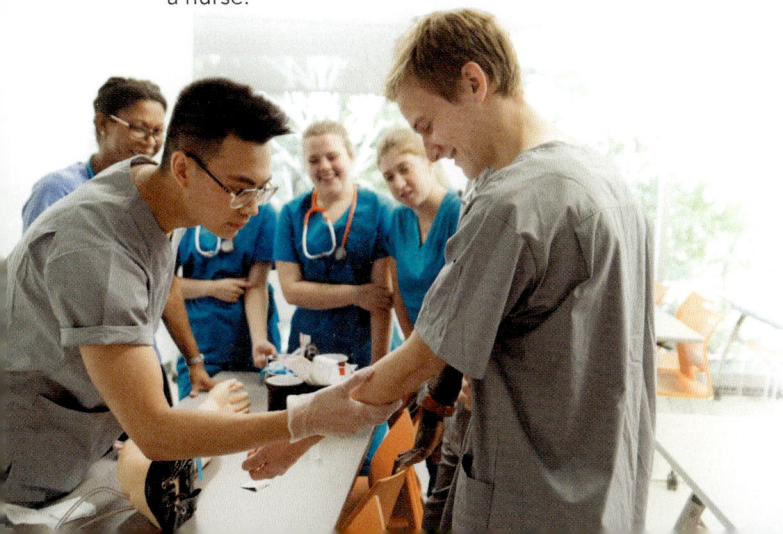

UNIT 1 VOCABULARY FILE

WORDLIST

Phrasal verbs	Nouns	Adjectives + prepositions	Fixed phrases
associated with	bravado	incapable of	a step too far
back down	camouflage	regardless of	all things considered
catch on	fingerprint	suited to	at the forefront
come out with	leap		be inclined to think
devote (yourself) to	outlet	**Verb + noun collocations**	capture the public's attention
fall for (nonsense)	practical joke	boost your determination	come to blows about
follow through on	primate	dismiss a theory	get cold feet
move on (with)	ridge	exceed (your) expectations	get stuck for words
pay someone back for	segment	play a joke on	get stung by
put (yourself) forward for	stigma	pose a threat to	in retrospect
put forward	(someone's) take on (something)	realise an ambition	in the same breath
read up on		release tension	let alone
spring up	**Adjectives**	seasoned traveller	out of your comfort zone
take (someone) in	apprehensive		play on ignorance
throw (yourself) into	credible		roll off the tongue
	daunting		while I'm on the subject
	empowering		
	makeshift		
	misleading		
	sceptical		
	unscrupulous		

PRACTICE

1 Complete the sentences with the correct form of verbs from the wordlist.

1 Suzie is _____ **with** her life now, after being off sick for a while.

2 I totally _____ **for** this ridiculous story my classmate told me and felt really silly!

3 I've been _____ **on** British history and it's really interesting.

4 Who put salt in my coffee?! I'll _____ you _____ **for** that when I find out!

5 I don't think the technology _____ **on** until it's more affordable.

6 Our brand is _____ **with** luxury.

7 Daniel _____ **with** this really funny joke the other day – we couldn't stop laughing.

8 Sam's thinking about _____ himself _____ **for** president of the chess club.

2 Replace the phrases in bold with the correct form of these phrasal verbs.

> back down   devote (yourself) to   follow through on
> put forward   spring up   take (someone) in   throw (yourself) into

1 I've really **put a lot of effort and energy into** my new job – I love it.

2 The team have **given a lot of time and attention to** the project and we've made great progress.

3 Zeke **suggested** the idea of holding a talent contest and everyone thought it would be a success.

4 New restaurants are **appearing** all over the town now it's becoming more prosperous.

5 It's OK making promises but you need to **carry them out**.

6 Jenny never **admits to being wrong** in an argument. It's really frustrating.

7 I was completely **deceived** by the guy's story and gave him my last few coins.

3 🎧 **1.1VF** Listen and decide what noun from the wordlist is being described by each person.

1 _____   4 _____   7 _____

2 _____   5 _____   8 _____

3 _____   6 _____

4 Match the adjectives in the wordlist with their definitions.

1 behaving in an unfair or dishonest way
2 deserving or able to be believed or trusted
3 worried or nervous about something you are going to do
4 made to be used for only a short time when nothing better is available
5 frightening in a way that makes you less confident
6 tending to disagree with what other people tell you
7 giving someone more control over their own life or situation
8 likely to make someone believe something that is not true

5 Complete the text with verb + noun collocations from the wordlist.

I'm not a particularly ¹ _____ , but I have been on a few holidays abroad with family and friends. Holidays are the perfect opportunity to relax, unwind and ² _____ that's built up over months of work or study. I'm not what you might call adventurous, and I tend to choose organised package holidays that don't ³ _____ to my confidence – travelling solo would be my worst nightmare! So, it may come as a bit of a surprise to you that I recently ⁴ _____ of mine without dragging anyone else along to accompany me. It involved joining a tour to base camp on Mount Everest. I actually ⁵ _____ my own _____ and not only managed to make the journey without too much of a struggle, but I made some great friends, too. It's really ⁶ _____ my _____ to do some other interesting trips in the future, too.

6 Complete the sentences with the correct form of useful phrases from the wordlist.

1 I'm having second thoughts about moving to the USA now. It's a bit scary and I've _____ .
2 Extreme sports are totally _____ ! I'd much rather do something safer indoors.
3 I just do not know what to say! I'm completely _____ !
4 That taxi driver charged me an absolute fortune. I've really _____ by him.
5 My flatmate and I _____ who should clean the dishes yesterday. We've made up now, though.
6 _____ , I should have studied tourism instead of history at university. It would've helped me get a job as a holiday rep more easily.

7 I know you like playing jokes on me, but throwing eggs at my windows is just _____ .
8 What a brilliant name for your company. It just _____ and is really memorable.

Pronunciation

7 🎧 1.2VF Match the word stress patterns to the words (o = weak, 0 = strong). Then listen and check.

Oo o0o 0oo oo0o o0oo ooo0o

0 ambition _o0o_   5 traveller _____
1 suited _____   6 tension _____
2 incapable _____   7 determination _____
3 regardless _____   8 theory _____
4 expectation _____

8 🎧 1.3VF Listen again and repeat the words, using the correct word stress. Then write one more word or phrase from the word list which has the same word stress as the patterns below.

1 0o _____   4 oo0o _____
2 o0o _____   5 o0oo _____
3 0oo _____   6 ooo0o _____

VOCABULARY BOOST

9 Complete the verbs with these prepositions. Which verbs + prepositions are separable?

at from on to

1 Residents of the town **objected** _____ the plans for a new motorway nearby.
2 I'm sorry but I've no idea what you're **hinting** _____ . Why don't you just tell me straight what it is you want?
3 Junior politicians should **abstain** _____ criticising the government.
4 We've **consented** _____ act as guarantors for our daughter, so that she can get a loan to set up her business.
5 I **pride** myself _____ meeting work deadlines, no matter how challenging it is to do so.
6 The council have **imposed** a ban _____ people riding bicycles through the park.
7 I've no idea how Nicola **inferred** all that _____ what I said. She's got the wrong end of the stick.
8 What are you **peering** _____ through the window? The neighbours will think you're spying on them!

115

UNIT 2 VOCABULARY FILE

WORDLIST

Nouns from phrasal verbs
backup (n)
breakthrough (n)
input (n)
outbreak (n)
outcome (n)
outset (n)
pushover (n)
setback (n)

Compound adjectives and nouns
a follow-up (n)
a spin-off (n)
blown-away (by) (adj)
far-fetched (adj)
jaw-dropping (adj)
mind-blowing (adj)
slow-moving (adj)
spine-tingling (adj)
tear-jerking (adj)

Competition
come second (phr)
come up with the goods (phr)
perk (n)
present a challenge (phr)
prove someone wrong (phr)
relish the opportunity (phr)
runner-up (n)
scrutiny (n)

Prefixes
discomfort (n)
illogical (adj)
inability (n)
insane (adj)
insignificant (adj)
interaction (n)
misleading (adj)
misplace (v)
reconsider (v)
reorganisation (n)
underestimate (v)
undoubtedly (adv)

Phrases with prepositions
be appreciative of
be attributed to
be down to
be prone to
fall back into
forge ahead with
keep track of
open up to

Adjectives
accessible
engrossed
enigmatic
lengthy
reckless
relentless
sensory
shortlisted
sound

Useful phrases
be in someone's best interests
be in two minds
come to a standstill
know full well (that)
raise someone's profile
take someone/something for granted
take something as read
to cut straight to the chase
to foil an attempt
to produce from scratch
to take (something/someone) seriously
two heads are better than one

PRACTICE

1 🎧 **2.1VF Complete each speaker's comments with a word from the wordlist.**

1 _____
2 _____
3 _____
4 _____
5 _____
6 _____
7 _____
8 _____

2 **Complete the sentences with the correct form of the words in brackets.**

1 There was a _____ delay before the company responded to our complaint. (length)

2 The _____ of the discussions will not be learnt until all the notes have been compiled. (come)

3 The majority of shops and restaurants in the High Street are now _____ to wheelchair users. (access)

4 The police have been _____ in their search for the perpetrators of a series of burglaries. (relent)

5 A _____ within the company has resulted in a different salary structure, too. (organise)

6 _____ , this new legislation will have a significant impact on the economy. (doubt)

3 Complete the sentences with the correct words from the box.

> appreciative   down   fall   forge   open   track

1 I'm very _____ of everyone's support during this difficult period at work.
2 I can't keep _____ of time while I'm reading a good book.
3 The council is going to _____ ahead with its plans to redevelop the factory site.
4 The success of this enterprise is _____ to everyone involved in the decision-making process.
5 As a child, I found it difficult to _____ up to people about how I was feeling.
6 Now you've established a new routine, you mustn't _____ back into your old habits.

4 Replace the words or phrases in bold with the correct form of items from the wordlist.

1 On behalf of the management I would like to thank you for your valuable **contributions** at the regular Monday meetings.
2 I **didn't think highly enough of** my sister's ability to deal with internet issues. She solved my problem in moments.
3 Micky gave me some **reliable** advice about how to invest my savings and I made a profit.
4 Sometimes when there is a lot of snow and ice in this area everything **stops**!
5 The information we received was **not completely correct** and we interpreted it wrongly.
6 **It's good to have someone else's help** when solving problems like these.
7 Lexi ran well and was **second** in the race.
8 I am still **undecided** about whether to sign up for another course or not.

5 Complete the definitions.

1 book or film with no pace, boring (*adj*): _____
2 something that stops progress, a problem (*n*): _____
3 forget where you have put something (*v*): _____
4 a film or book that makes you cry (*adj*): _____
5 fail to appreciate something (*phr*): _____
6 not taking care, possibly dangerous (*adj*): _____
7 fail to realise the real value of someone or something (*v*): _____
8 critical observation (*n*): _____

Pronunciation

6 Mark the syllable stress on the words in bold.

1 The TV series was a **spin-off** from the original film.
2 The task is a **pushover**.
3 The scene was **jaw-dropping**.
4 I spent an **insane** amount of time on the project.
5 The book was a **follow-up** to the one he wrote ten years ago.
6 I always keep a **backup** of my files.
7 I liked her company from the **outset**.
8 I tend to **misplace** things like keys and TV remotes.

7 2.2VF Listen and check your answers to Ex 6. Then listen again and repeat the words. What do you notice about the word stress?

VOCABULARY BOOST

8 Add a preposition to the verbs in brackets to create a word that completes each sentence. Which section of the wordlist do they fit into?

1 My grandfather's _____ was completely different to my mother's. (bringing)
2 When the government refused to change its policy on taxation there was a public _____ . (cry)
3 The recommended daily _____ of vitamin tablets is indicated on the bottle. (take)
4 There was a great _____ to welcome the cup-winning football team home after the tournament. (turn)
5 Although the initial _____ can be quite significant, you will earn back your money within two years. (lay)
6 The _____ following the dramatic election defeat has left the party needing to choose a new leader. (fall)
7 Experts predict a(n) _____ in the economy because of the failure to close large trade deals. (turn)
8 The weather _____ for the coming weeks appears to be good, with plenty of sun and relatively high temperatures. (look)

9 Choose six words from Ex 8 that you think will be most useful to you and write new sentences showing the use of each.

UNIT 3 VOCABULARY FILE

WORDLIST

Phrasal verbs
come about
come round to
do away with
get (somebody) out of
go into
mess about with
refer to
run (something) past
set back
shy away from
stem from

Collocations (verb + noun)
accumulate knowledge
boost energy
complicate matters
deepen understanding
determine the facts
draw on experience
establish a rapport
exude confidence
heed advice
meet the criteria
strike up a friendship
thwart expectations

Collocations (adverb/adjective/noun)
distinctive feature
exceptionally difficult
heartfelt emotion
highly symmetrical
highly thought of
relatively unsurprising
remarkably beautiful
stark contrast
unique combination
unsolved mystery

Adjectives
armed (with)
compatible (with)
diluted
intimidating
plausible
straightforward
undervalued

Nouns
adversity
brevity
chunk
cradle
mantra
protagonist
punch line
repercussions
stance
swirl
the naked eye

Useful phrases
a far cry from
can't string a sentence together
different walks of life
eyes go vacant
it's more a case of
keep someone in the loop
let me get this straight
on the go
rooted to the spot
take exception to
to and fro

PRACTICE

1 Match the phrasal verbs from the wordlist with their meanings.

1 get rid of or stop using
2 avoid doing because you aren't confident
3 develop as a result of something else
4 be spent or used to get, make or do something
5 delay progress of development
6 bother with unnecessarily
7 happen
8 change your opinion of something

2 Which collocation (verb + noun) from the wordlist is being described in the sentences below? There may be more than one correct answer.

1 Our plans have been ruined by the weather – it was going to be such a great picnic.
2 I've got all the right qualifications and experience for the job, so I should be a suitable candidate.
3 Reading is a great way to build on what you already know.
4 It's important to try to get on well with the people you work or study with as things go more smoothly that way.
5 Lyla just radiates positivity and self-belief – I wish I was more like her.
6 I got chatting to someone on the bus who designs apps like me and we've kept in touch ever since.
7 You really should listen to what people say because it might come in useful one day.
8 We really need to get to the bottom of who broke the shop window. Let's check the CCTV.

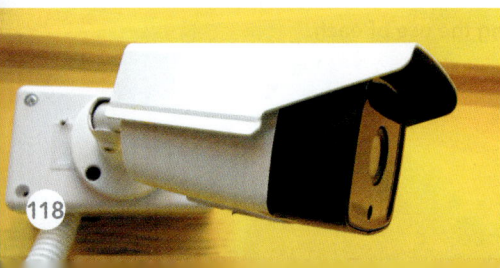

3 Complete the adverb/adjective/noun collocations with these words.

> atmosphere call complex kind
> reminder puzzle straightforward thanks

1 This is a highly _____ mathematical equation and I need to think carefully about how to solve it.

2 The penguin has a distinctive _____ which makes it sound like someone's playing an instrument badly!

3 The impact of the huge storm is a stark _____ that humans really can't control nature.

4 I must offer you my heartfelt _____ for helping me settle into the neighbourhood.

5 The directions were relatively _____ which meant we arrived early at the party.

6 The _____ remains unsolved. I just can't figure out what the missing word is.

7 There's a unique _____ in this library. Everyone's so respectful of its age and beauty.

8 It's exceptionally _____ of you to offer me a lift but I think I'd rather walk home.

4 Complete the sentences with adjectives from the wordlist.

1 My grandparents arrived back from holiday _____ with gifts for us all!

2 Could you give us a more _____ explanation of what the 'fourth place' is? It's too complicated for me.

3 Is the new software _____ with this laptop?

4 I thought the new college head was pretty _____ . She makes me feel nervous and a little scared!

5 Many workers feel _____ in their jobs and would like a pay rise in recognition of what they do.

6 There must be a _____ explanation as to why the books don't balance.

5 Complete the phrases using nouns from the wordlist. Then match them with their meanings.

1 to triumph over _____

2 _____ is beautiful

3 take a _____

4 repeat a _____

5 the _____ of civilisation

6 here comes the _____ of the joke

a where developed society is said to have emerged

b expressing things in a few words is better than using too many words

c keep saying a word or phrase representing a rule or principle, often annoying or boring

d do well, even though there are lots of problems

e here are the last few words of a joke or story that make it funny or surprising

f adopt a political or philosophical position

6 🎧 3.1VF Listen to five speakers. Which of the useful phrases from the wordlist are they talking about?

1 _____   4 _____

2 _____   5 _____

3 _____

Pronunciation

7 The final letter 's' can be pronounced in two ways, /s/ or /z/. Look at the words from the wordlist. How is the final 's' pronounced? Tick the correct column.

	/s/	/z/
chunks		
repercussions		
matters		
facts		
swirls		
protagonists		
loops		

8 🎧 3.2VF Listen and check. What rule can you deduce about how the final letter 's' is pronounced?

VOCABULARY BOOST

9 Match these technology verbs and prepositions with their definitions.

> boot up   go down   hack into   hook up
> key in   opt out   power up   scroll down

1 connect wires from machines to a power source or other machine

2 start running a computer system

3 switch on an electrical device, especially a computer

4 move down to the bottom of the text on screen

5 interrupt the flow of information to a computer

6 put information into a computer, or give it a particular instruction

7 enter a computer or network illegally

8 choose not to receive emails or advertising

10 Write sentences using the verbs and prepositions from Ex 9.

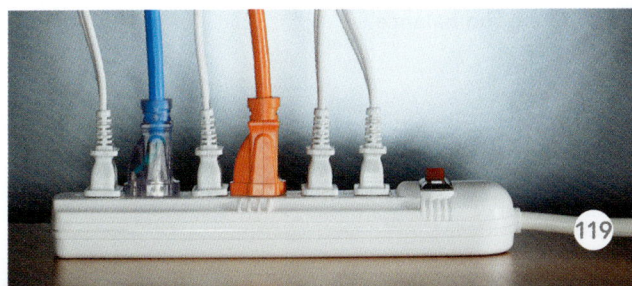

UNIT 4 VOCABULARY FILE

WORDLIST

Phrasal verbs	Nature and seasons	Suffixes Adjectives	Verbs
date back to	acidity (n)	attentive	acquire
elaborate on	biome (n)	compelling	concede
indulge in	correlation (n)	delicate	dictate
lay on (a meal)	cycle (n)	distinctive	navigate
mess up	graze (v)	far-reaching	resolve
pass on something	harvest (n/v)	geometrical	
ply someone with	latitude (n)	healing	**Useful phrases**
rustle up something	livelihood (n)	irrational	a bit of a thing
set someone back	livestock (n)	stranded	all doom and gloom
stave off	pest (n)	thankful	be at stake
stay over	ravage (v)	viable	dead to the world
switch off	seasonal shift (n)		follow a pattern
tide someone over	thrive (v)	**Nouns**	have the guts to
warm up	unseasonable (adj)	belongings	off the beaten track
wash something down with	wetland (n)	breadth	on the brink (of)
work up (an appetite)		dimension	strike a good balance
		endeavour	swallow your pride
		increment	talking in terms of
		insight	those in the know
		prosperity	understand the bigger picture
		ritual	

Practice

1 **Complete the sentences with the correct form of verbs from the wordlist.**

1 We completed a 10 km walk and really _____ **up** an appetite by the time we got home.

2 The main course was chicken but it was so dry that we had to _____ **it down** with a couple of glasses of water.

3 I'd really thought I was right but as it turned out I had to _____ **my pride** and admit that I'd been wrong.

4 My colleague's files got infected by a virus and it _____ **him back** a week.

5 The boss entrusted me with a difficult project but I really _____ **up** and I don't think he'll let me do anything like it again.

6 With all the pressure we get at school and work these days it's important to _____ **a good balance**.

7 I remember that my Spanish friend's family _____ **on** an incredible meal for my first evening at their home.

8 Don't worry about ordering in any more printer paper – we've got plenty to _____ **us over** until next week.

2 Complete the report with the correct form of words from the wordlist.

People whose ¹ _____ depend on the countryside have had to deal with the widespread effects of ² _____ weather over recent years. After last week's torrential rain, I went to interview a local farmer and while ³ _____ flooded roads noticed different ⁴ _____ who, because of unusually high water levels, were ⁵ _____ on the highest parts of the fields. The farmer later pointed out that people like himself had to cope with both reduced areas for these animals to ⁶ _____ on and a reduction in winter food stores because of poor or failed ⁷ _____ . Hotter summers meant an increase in ⁸ _____ and because of bans on certain insecticides, they were free to ⁹ _____ the crops. There will need to be dramatic changes in the farming industry if it is to ¹⁰ _____ in the future.

3 🎧 4.1VF Complete the topics each speaker is talking about with words from the wordlist.

1 _____ consequences
2 _____ shapes
3 a(n) _____ student
4 a(n) _____ decision
5 a(n) _____ voice
6 the _____ process
7 _____ evidence
8 a(n) _____ alternative

4 Complete the sentences with the correct phrases.

1 Scientists are **on** _____ developing a vaccine to protect cattle from the new strain of a deadly disease.

2 Recent news indicates that it's not **all** _____ when thinking about the global economy.

3 I know I should confront my issues regarding my phobia of spiders but I'm afraid I **don't have** _____ at the moment.

4 **Those** _____ say that we shall be dealing with severe weather conditions over the coming fortnight.

5 We need to consider this decision carefully because there's **a lot** _____ , and we could end up in a much worse position.

5 Complete the definitions of words from the wordlist.

1 a set of fixed actions, performed regularly, often to bring luck: _____

2 a person's possessions: _____

3 a deep and sometimes sudden understanding of a complicated problem: _____

4 a regularly repeated series of events: _____

5 an attempt to do something: _____

6 to gain possession of something: _____

Pronunciation

6 Look at the final consonant clusters in the words in bold. Identify 1) two words where a consonant is silent and 2) a word where a consonant is pronounced differently than normal.

1 My neighbours heard mice in their attic and had to call **pest** control.

2 Seasonal **shift** had wide implications for people living in certain latitudes.

3 The **breadth** of the research done by the company was quite amazing.

4 This year's **harvest** has been delayed by inclement weather.

5 Sometimes I used to get bored in class and I'd just **switch** off.

6 In my job, we get an annual **increment** in our salaries.

7 There are eggs and cheese in the fridge so I can easily **rustle** up an omelette.

8 Karen always wears a **distinctive** perfume, which I imagine is rather expensive.

7 🎧 4.2VF Listen and check. Repeat the sentences, paying attention to the correct pronunciation of the consonant clusters.

VOCABULARY BOOST

8 Replace the phrases in bold in the sentences with the correct form of these phrasal verbs.

gobble down   pick at   plump for   polish off   wean off

1 There was far too much food on the table and I couldn't eat any more, but my brother **ate** everything that was left.

2 My mother insists on telling everyone that I was a very fussy eater as a child and only ever **ate very little of** my food.

3 Doctors say we shouldn't **eat** food **quickly** but take our time eating as it's better for our digestion.

4 I've been told that I drink way too much coffee, and it isn't good for me. I can't give it up completely so I shall just have to try to **reduce my consumption** gradually!

5 If we're having a take-away, I will always **choose** a Chinese meal because I just love their noodles.

9 Choose four phrasal verbs from Ex 8 and write an example sentence for each which is true for you.

UNIT 5 VOCABULARY FILE

WORDLIST

Body idioms	Phrasal verbs	Nouns	Money
a rule of thumb	come off well (or badly)	boot	cash in (something) (v)
at face value	come together	brand loyalty	face value (n)
be a pain in the neck	come under (a heading)	eccentricity	go up in value (v)
be in the public eye	draw up	glitch	in circulation (phr)
face the music	fit in with	knock-on effect	inflated (fare) (adj)
go hand in hand	go against (instincts)	lodgings	loose change (n)
lose your head	hold up (evidence/	maze	toss a coin (v)
turn a blind eye	argument)	nerd	
	iron out	nonconformity	**Verbs**
Adjectives	line up	scaffolding	compromise
chunky	rush into	scrutiny	dapple
legendary	show off	soundtrack	offload
musty	step up	spiral	redesign
rebellious	take on	stack	
underlying	wind round	swish	**Useful phrases**
unheard of			bear in mind
widespread			it stands to reason
wiped out			on the subject of
			peaks and troughs
			rub shoulders with

PRACTICE

1 Complete the sentences with the correct form of body idioms from the wordlist.

1 I wouldn't like to _____ , having my every move scrutinised.
2 Language and culture _____ : you can't have language without culture or culture without language.
3 Would you _____ if you saw someone doing something illegal, or would you report them?
4 I made a silly mistake at work because I wasn't concentrating. Now I have to go and talk to my boss and _____ .
5 I admire Tom's patience – he never _____ , even when he's in a stressful situation.
6 We're such good friends now, my sister and I, though I used to think she was _____ when we were younger – she broke all my toys and I hated that!
7 As a general _____ , you need to water the plants in the garden each morning and night in the summer.
8 You shouldn't take everything you read online _____ because there's a lot of fake news around.

2 Complete the text with the correct form of phrasal verbs from the wordlist.

They say you should never go back to a place that holds lots of special memories in case it doesn't live up to expectations. I [1]_____ my instincts last year – the warning signals that said 'don't do it!' – and returned to the town I'd grown up in. It wasn't a snap decision that I [2]_____ : it was actually my childhood friend who first suggested going back to where we'd been raised and initially, I hesitated. What if things weren't the same? She managed to convince me, and in the end we [3]_____ a plan and hoped it would all [4]_____ nicely. We looked up old friends and arranged to meet, and [5]_____ some interesting things to do. These included some of our old haunts, such as the outdoor pool which we hoped would still be as much fun to visit as it had been when we were kids. Happily, it all [6]_____ well, and it turned out to be one of the best trips I've ever done.

3 Choose the correct alternatives.

1 I'm just **holding up / ironing out** a few inconsistencies in this report and then I'll email it over to you.

2 Jamie's really **stepped up / drawn up** his efforts and he's doing very well at college now.

3 I think I've **taken on / fitted in with** more work than I can handle.

4 The evidence presented at the trial didn't **hold up / come off** and the accused got off without being sentenced.

5 I'll **come together / fit in with** your plans on Saturday. I've nothing in particular to do that day so can be ready for the beach whenever you are.

4 Match adjectives from the wordlist with their definitions.

1 extremely tired

2 very famous and admired

3 existing or happening in many places or situations, or among many people

4 deliberately not obeying people in authority or rules of behaviour

5 thick, solid and heavy

5 Complete the sentences with these words and phrases. Then write a sentence of your own using the remaining word or phrase.

> cash in (something) (v)
> face value (n)   in circulation (phr)
> inflated (adj)   loose change (n)
> toss a coin (v)

1 I couldn't pay for parking because I had no _____ .

2 These old notes are no longer _____ I'm afraid, but you can pay them into your account.

3 The value of the shares is dropping. I think I'll _____ before they fall too much.

4 It's no wonder young people can't buy property in the city when the prices are so _____ .

5 Some of the coins they mint for special occasions can't be sold at their _____ , so you pay more for them than they're actually worth.

6 🎧 5.1VF Listen to four speakers. Which verb from the wordlist describes what they are talking about?

1 _____   3 _____

2 _____   4 _____

7 Complete the useful phrases with your own ideas.

1 On the subject of …

2 It stands to reason …

3 Bear in mind that, although …

4 Every business goes through its peaks and troughs, so …

5 Have you ever rubbed shoulders with …

Pronunciation

8 It can sometimes be difficult to know how to pronounce the letter 'c' in English. Look at these words. Are the 'c's pronounced /s/ or /k/ or are they part of another sound?

	/s/	/k/	other sound
stack			
scrutiny			
face			
nonconformity			
glitch			
march			

What about the different 'c' sounds in the following words?

knock-on effect   eccentricity

9 🎧 5.2VF Listen, check and repeat.

VOCABULARY BOOST

10 Complete the body idioms with these words. Then use each one in a sentence.

> back   blood   ears   hand   nose   throat   toe

Idiom	Definition
1 It's no skin off my _____	I don't care because it doesn't affect me.
2 My flesh and _____	someone who is part of my family
3 jump down someone's _____	suddenly speak angrily to someone
4 be all _____	be very keen to hear what someone's going to tell you
5 _____ the line	do what people in authority tell you, whether you agree or not
6 be an old _____	have a lot of experience of something
7 scratch someone's _____	do someone a favour, with the expectation that one will be done in return

UNIT 6 VOCABULARY FILE

WORDLIST

Fixed phrases	Internal word changes Adjectives	Nouns	Road trips
at a loose end	anecdotal	curiosity	bypass (v)
at a stretch	chronic	dependence on	cater for (v)
at first glance	clear-cut	dragonfly	decommissioned (adj)
at sixes and sevens	continuously	drought	drive the length of (phr)
by all accounts	conventional	empathy	fall into disrepair (phr)
by default	defeatist	honeycomb	go off track (phr)
by no means	flawed	hunch	gravel (n)
in action	gory	inflection	head for (v)
in conjunction with	inaccessible	initiative	make a diversion (phr)
in my element	invaluable	inscription	memorabilia (n)
in no time	laughable	proponent	spring up (v)
in turn	nostalgic	quest	stretch (n)
in vain	pharmaceutical	rivalry	trading post (n)
	provoking	threshold	
Useful phrases	sighted	tile	**Science**
at breakneck speed	squeamish	wax	circumference
beyond recovery	stationary		diameter
go out on a limb	tactile	**Verbs**	hexagon
have a gut feeling	undeniable	abound	miniscule
have a mental block	undignified	backtrack	radius
in its entirety	unmanageable	compile	rhombus
yours truly		outdo	symmetrical
		promote understanding	technological
		topple	

PRACTICE

1 Complete the descriptions with adjectives from the wordlist.

1 His argument isn't logical. It's _____ .
2 He doesn't like watching medical soap operas where they show operations. He's a bit _____ .
3 You can't trust the evidence because it's not actual proof, it's just what people think. It's _____ .
4 There's no way anyone can get through that fence onto the property. It's _____ .
5 She's never confident that people will accept her ideas. She's _____ .
6 Some people wear anything they like to work but I've always preferred a more _____ style of clothes.
7 There are no queries about the objective at all. It's _____ .

2 Label the diagram with the correct words.

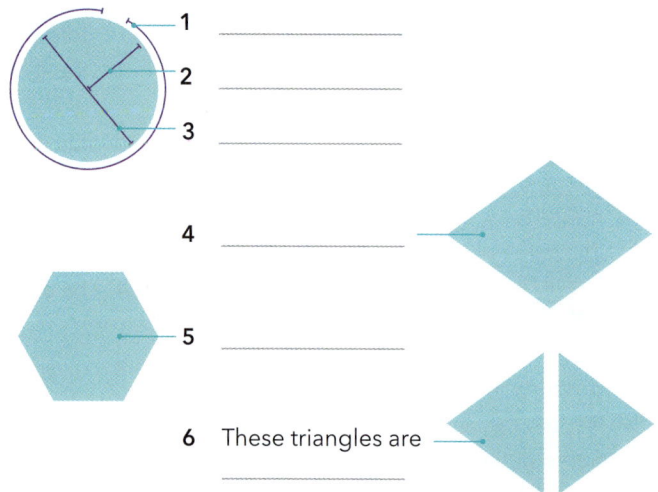

1 _____
2 _____
3 _____
4 _____
5 _____
6 These triangles are _____

124

3 🎧 **6.1VF** Listen to the speakers and complete the sentences with the correct form of prepositional phrases from the wordlist.

1 He's _____ .

2 When she's dancing she's _____ .

3 They did the project _____ another class.

4 He's been trying _____ to contact his friend.

5 _____ , the exam questions looked impossible.

6 This afternoon she's _____ .

4 Complete the blog with the correct words from the wordlist.

> Motorway driving can be a nightmare at times. On the one hand you can travel at high speeds and ¹ _____ busy towns, which saves a lot of time on a long journey. However, when the road surfaces fall into ² _____ , which can happen with some of the oldest ones, the sections of road closed for the necessary work can ³ _____ for miles, and motorists have to make ⁴ _____ , or risk being completely ⁵ _____ in traffic for ages. Another disadvantage of motorway driving is that if you're hungry and you ⁶ _____ for the nearest service station that ⁷ _____ for motorway users, you're likely to be charged way over the odds for a cup of coffee or a simple sandwich. It's undeniable that lack of competition accounts for these high prices. Interestingly, there are some strange people whose hobby is to drive the ⁸ _____ of a motorway, turn around and come back again! By all ⁹ _____ there is a friendly ¹⁰ _____ between these people, and they ¹¹ _____ reports of their journeys to share. Personally, I can't wait to get off a motorway as soon as possible.

5 Choose the correct alternatives.

1 I had a(n) **initiative** / **hunch** that you might be working late so I thought I'd come over.

2 Out of **empathy** / **curiosity**, could you tell me where you first heard the news about the school closures?

3 The film was made to **compile** / **promote** understanding about the different cultural groups who live in the area.

4 My cousin suffers from **gory** / **chronic** backache which doctors can't really do much about.

6 Replace the words in bold in sentences 1-4 with phrases A-D.

1 The man was driving **very fast** along the motorway when the police caught him.

2 I got a new book for my birthday which was so gripping that I read it **all** in one night!

3 My uncle **took a risk** and invested some money in a renewable energy company and he made a load of money within five years.

4 When it comes to remembering the names of politicians, I **just can't do it**! Not even famous prime ministers.

A have a mental block   C went out on a limb

B in its entirety   D at breakneck speed

Pronunciation

7 🎧 **6.2VF** Identify the silent consonants in five of the words. Which one does NOT have a silent letter? Listen and check.

1 honeycomb   4 limb

2 sighted   5 undignified

3 rhombus   6 drought

VOCABULARY BOOST

8 🎧 **6.3VF** Complete the phrases in the sentences with 'at', 'in', 'on', 'to' or 'out'. Listen and check.

1 The meeting was _____ **an uproar** when the government announcement to cut funding was made. Everyone started shouting at the same time.

2 I was going to book the taxi for 8.30 but _____ **second thoughts** that might be too late, so I'll book for 8.00.

3 After the accident in the town centre, the traffic was _____ **a standstill** for half an hour.

4 I wasn't intending to buy a new laptop, but the price was so good I bought it _____ **impulse**.

5 The boots in my size that I want to get are _____ **of stock**, so I'll have to check out some other stores.

6 My brother doesn't usually remember family birthdays but _____ **his credit** he did remember mine this year and got me a great present.

7 It's important to be _____ **good terms** with your neighbours as you can often help each other out when there are problems.

8 _____ **line with** government policy, there is going to be an increase in the number of CCTV cameras in city centres.

9 Choose four adjectives from the wordlist and add three nouns that could be described by each.

1 _____   3 _____

2 _____   4 _____

UNIT 7 VOCABULARY FILE

WORDLIST

Phrasal verbs
die out
dispose of
draw on
go into
keep from
kick in
make up
map out
smooth out
speed up
tap into
track down

Physics and chemistry
decompression sickness
element
fluctuations in pressure
high-voltage
oxidise
pharmacological
pollutant
specimen
stable atmosphere
vapour
ventilated

Books and stories
accolade
bring to life
enrapture
fatal flaw
narrative structure
personify
pitch at
recount
yarn

Easily confused words
Adjectives
applicable
classy
convivial
duplicitous
formative
harmonious
life-threatening
lifelong
near-perfect
patronising
sceptical
sought-after
speechless

Nouns
allusion
asphyxiation
categorisation
clarification
defection
displacement
diversity
espionage
ignorance
incarnation
infiltration
jingle
mortality
onslaught
premise
principal
principle
sentiment
sophistication
upbringing
wisdom

Verbs
adhere to
amend
ascribe
complement
deter
ensure
fulfil
hone
outrun
proscribe

Verb collocations
face head on
fall into a category
fulfil a need
hazard a guess
make an assumption
under no illusion

Useful phrases
be in operation
have time to kill
in pursuit of
in some circles
(second) night running

PRACTICE

1 Complete the sentences with the correct form of phrasal verbs from the wordlist.

1 Some people have their lives all _____ , but you can't plan for everything in life.

2 The air around us is _____ nitrogen, oxygen, water vapour, argon and carbon dioxide.

3 You will need to _____ several sources in order to build your essay's argument.

4 Used gloves must be _____ in the bins provided.

5 Clearly, a lot of work has _____ your report but there are one or two issues with it.

6 The headache tablet should _____ shortly and you'll feel a lot better.

7 I've been trying to _____ Jon for days but no one seems to know where he is.

8 The film really _____ our innermost fears as human beings.

2 🎧 **7.1VF** Listen to the speakers. Which word or phrase related to physics and chemistry are they explaining?

1 _____
2 _____
3 _____
4 _____
5 _____
6 _____
7 _____
8 _____

3 Complete the review with the correct form of words about books and stories from the wordlist.

Having recently read 'Navigation', I was pretty impressed by the writer's ability to ¹_____ what sea voyages were really like in times gone by. I'm not someone who's able to comment much on ²_____ or any other sort of literary device, but I do know it was a really good ³_____ that kept me hooked from start to finish. It's almost like a sailor from bygone times is ⁴_____ the tale himself. The language is ⁵_____ a level that's neither 'dumbed down' nor too complex for the average reader and it certainly deserves all the ⁶_____ it's received in the media.

4 Match nouns from the wordlist with their definitions.

1 strong criticism of someone
2 the activity of secretly finding out information and giving it to enemies
3 a statement or idea that you accept as true and use as a base for developing other ideas
4 something said or written that mentions a subject, person, etc. indirectly
5 when a group of people or animals are forced to leave the place where they usually live
6 the complexity of a machine, system or method that is very well designed and advanced, and often works in a complicated way

5 Match adjectives from the wordlist with their synonyms.

1 friendly _____
2 doubtful _____
3 wanted _____
4 stylish _____
5 deceitful _____
6 relevant _____
7 condescending _____
8 deadly _____

6 Complete the phrases with a verb from the wordlist. There may be more than one answer for each verb.

1 _____ a competitor
2 _____ an error
3 _____ a requirement
4 _____ a skill
5 _____ rules and regulations
6 _____ someone from doing something

7 Complete the sentences with useful phrases from the wordlist.

1 The play's being put on for the twentieth _____ . It must be really popular.
2 We might as well have a look around the shops. We've got _____ before the bus comes.
3 _____ , it just isn't acceptable to use rude language or criticise others.
4 I'm currently _____ of my dream to go to a top university and am working hard for my exams.
5 How long has this company been _____ ? The factory's been here for as long as I can remember.

Pronunciation

8 The schwa (/ə/) is a very common sound in English, and often represents unstressed sounds in words like *teach*<u>er</u> or <u>a</u>*bout*. Read the following words aloud and underline the letter or syllable which contains the /ə/ sound.

1 ignorance   5 principle
2 wisdom   6 principal
3 clarification   7 diversity
4 jingle   8 sentiment

9 🎧 7.2VF **Listen, check and repeat.**

VOCABULARY BOOST

10 Match a verb and preposition to make phrasal verbs which can be used when talking about science. Then match the phrasal verbs with their definitions.

about   at   down (x2)   for   into   off   on

1 account _____
2 arrive _____
3 be _____ to something
4 bring _____
5 boil _____ to
6 buy _____
7 give _____
8 narrow _____

a to reach a decision, solution, etc. after a lot of effort
b accept an idea is right and allow it to influence you
c have an idea/information likely to lead to an important discovery
d be the main point or cause
e produce a smell, heat, light, gas, etc.
f reduce the number of things included in a range
g give a satisfactory explanation of why something has happened
h make something happen

UNIT 8 VOCABULARY FILE

WORDLIST

Collocations
blissfully unaware
blisteringly hot
endlessly versatile
exclusively used
fiercely competitive
fully alert
infinitely preferable
instantly recognisable
intricately carved
notoriously difficult
painstakingly decorated
strikingly similar
universally known
widely believed

Phrasal verbs
button up
derive from
dispose of
freak out
keep up with
pass something on
stick to (a routine)
take on

Nouns
anaesthetic
aversion
circuit/circuitry
commodity
cotton wool
detour
loop
occupant
octave
pitch
suffrage
vapour

Compounding
doubtless (adj)
downside (n)
drawback (n)
forego (v)
meantime (n)
never-ending (adj)
outlook (n)
overcome (v)
overview (n)
ownership (n)
setback (n)
shortcoming (n)
troublesome (adj)
upbeat (adj)
viewpoint (n)

Adjectives
affectionate
crippling
detectable
distressing
eligible
evolutionary
exquisite
fluffy
heavy-duty
squeaky
stringent
underlying
unmanly

Verbs
defy
dodge
forgo
peer
trigger

Sleep
deprivation (n)
drop off (v)
hypersomnia (n)
nap (n/v)
nocturnal (adj)
restorative (adj)
shut-eye (n)
tuck someone up (v)
wind down (v)

Useful phrases
bark an order
be in good company
for the time being
glimmer of hope
it got me thinking
no takers?
on a practical note
run in families
spark an idea
summon up the courage
the heart of the problem

PRACTICE

1 🔊 **8.1VF** Listen to eight speakers and write the missing words or phrases.

> eligible never-ending ownership practical note sparked an idea
> strikingly similar summon up the courage upbeat

1 _____   3 _____   5 _____   7 _____
2 _____   4 _____   6 _____   8 _____

2 Complete the text with the correct form of words from the wordlist.

Experts say that it's often a good thing to have a quick
¹_____ during the day. Even just ten minutes of
²_____ can be good for us. If we do a lot of creative
work and sometimes struggle to ³_____ brain
fatigue, then this relaxation can be very ⁴_____ and
give us the energy to continue. However, for some people it's
not a great idea. For insomniacs it might mean that they have
trouble ⁵_____ off at night, which in turn can have a
⁶_____ effect on their work the following day. Advice on
how to relax properly before ⁷_____ yourself up for a
good night's sleep includes using meditation techniques, which as
most people would agree is ⁸_____ preferable to taking
medication. Of course, some of us do most of our creative thinking at
night and as such can be described as ⁹_____ . For these
people a short sleep during the day is not simply an option but an
absolute necessity, otherwise they will possibly suffer the effects of
sleep ¹⁰_____ .

3 Complete the definitions with words from the wordlist.

1 the person who lives in a house or flat: _____
2 what you are given before an operation: _____
3 when you look very carefully at something: _____
4 a strong dislike and wish not to do something: _____
5 when you refuse to obey: _____
6 your attitude towards something: _____

4 Complete the sentences with the correct adjectives from the wordlist.

1 The bowl is made of _____ plastic and will last for a very long time.
2 The examination will reveal any _____ problems you may not be aware of.
3 Children love _____ toys and often sleep with a favourite one.
4 You will need to show proof of employment to be _____ for this loan.
5 There are very _____ laws about new developments in town centres.
6 I was nervous about giving the speech and at the beginning my voice was rather _____ .
7 He gave his wife a(n) _____ ring which used to belong to his grandmother.
8 The news reports have been quite _____ and I hope the situation improves soon.

Pronunciation

5 🎧 8.2VF With adverb-adjective collocations there is usually one main syllable stress and one secondary syllable stress. Mark them on these collocations. Listen and check.

1 blissfully unaware
2 fully alert

6 🎧 8.3VF Rhythm is important in spoken English. Both collocations above take the same time to say, although they have a different number of syllables. This is because of stress and weak vowels. Listen and repeat.

1 blissfully unaware
2 fully alert
3 widely believed
4 blisteringly hot
5 exclusively used
6 instantly recognisable

VOCABULARY BOOST

7 Match adverbs and adjectives from Boxes A and B to form collocations.

A actively   deeply   painfully
readily   sorely   strictly
strongly   vaguely

B available   familiar   forbidden
involved   missed   offended
opposed   shy

8 Choose four of the collocations and write sentences to show their meanings.

1 _____
2 _____
3 _____
4 _____

9 Find vocabulary items on the wordlist that look similar to items in your own language but which have a very different or slightly different meaning.

WRITING FILE

Part 1 Essay

EXAMPLE QUESTION

▶ Unit 1 pp12-13, Unit 6 pp66-67

You have listened to a radio discussion on how to get communities more involved in environmental issues. You have made the notes below:

Ideas for making communities more aware of environmental issues

- easy recycling system
- 'clean-up' groups
- leaflets

> Read the task carefully. Be careful to include the correct number of points from the notes.

> Some opinions expressed in the discussion:
>
> 'The recycling system is so complicated at the moment. If the council could make it easier to follow, …'
>
> 'I think distributing advice leaflets to people's homes is the best system.'
>
> 'Surely, we need something active to appeal to young people like small groups in schools and colleges.'

Write an essay for your tutor discussing two of the ideas from your notes. You should **explain which idea would be more effective in making communities more aware of environmental issues**, giving **reasons** to support your opinion.

You may make use of the opinions expressed in the discussion, but you should use your own words as far as possible.

Write **220-260** words.

EXAMPLE ANSWER

Everyone is very concerned about the environment nowadays, but not everyone considers the environment on a daily basis. In fact, sometimes it is quite the opposite, so we need to look at how we can get everyone actively involved with environmental issues.

I think we can try and make it easier for people to contribute to helping improve their environment. Firstly, I believe it would be a good idea to create very straightforward leaflets with some clear and simple advice that everyone can follow. These could be dropped directly into people's homes. In this way, local residents will definitely see them and may even, for example, keep the leaflet in their kitchen as a checklist to follow.

Another immediate way to involve communities would be to set up 'clean-up' groups. These groups could not only do occasional cleaning of neglected areas such as parks but members could also train to become mentors who go into schools and make students aware of how they can help.

Overall, I would suggest that having clean-up groups may be the most effective route to involving people more widely in environmental issues because it is is very active and so likely to encourage young people's involvement. And these people will be the next generation who will be responsible for the environment, so to train them is vital.

> Use your introduction to explain what the essay will discuss in general terms.

> Remember to use topic sentences at the beginning of each paragraph.

> When you are explaining why your chosen idea is the most effective, remember not to repeat the same points you made about this idea in earlier paragraphs.

EXAM HELP

- Reword others' opinions if used as support.
- Add reasons to support your opinions and examples to justify your arguments.
- Use linking expressions to connect ideas within and across paragraphs.
- Try and make your conclusion persuasive.

OVER TO YOU

Now write your own answer to the task. Include everything required in the task and use the Exam help to check your work.

USEFUL LANGUAGE

Introduction

Many people today think …

Nowadays there is a problem with …

It could be said that …

Presenting an argument

For this reason, …	Although …
As a result, …	While …
This is due to …	Many people feel …
On the other hand, …	According to …
In contrast, …	

Conclusion

I am in favour of …	On the whole, …
It seems to me that …	Overall, …

Part 2 Informal email or letter

EXAMPLE QUESTION

▶ Unit 3 pp34-35

Read part of an email from a friend who is planning to visit your country.

> Of course, I'd really like to see as much as I can but with so little time (only a week) I wonder if that's feasible. Do you have any suggestions on where to go and what to do in your country?

Reply to the email offering your friend some advice.
Write your **email** in **220-260** words.

EXAMPLE ANSWER

Hi Sam,

I thought I'd better reply as quickly as possible since I see you're actually leaving next Monday. I'm so excited. I can't wait to see you.

> *Begin by telling your friend why you've decided to write.*

You're right that in such a short time it won't be possible to see everything. What I would do is to explore one area in depth. I have to say that Victoria, where I live, would be an excellent choice.

> *Expand upon the task input.*

You could start by spending a couple of days in Melbourne and then rent a car and head for the Great Ocean Road. It's a really spectacular road that follows the coastline and stretches for over 250 kilometres. If I were you, I'd plan to spend a couple of days driving along, stopping for the night in Lorne or Apollo Bay.

> *Divide your letter into paragraphs, each of which should cover a different element from the task input.*

You asked about things to do and I have to say it's hard to know where to begin. While you're in Melbourne, I'd definitely try to visit the National Gallery of Victoria and the South Bank complex which is nearby. There are some great bars and restaurants there. On your drive along the Ocean Road you'll see all the famous surf beaches but it's also a great area for walking. There are hundreds of tracks through the tropical rain forest. I think you'd really enjoy that, too.

Well, I'd better stop now. Give me a call as soon as you get in and we'll meet up somewhere. I might even join you on the Ocean Road trip.

> *Close your email or letter by mentioning the next time you will see or speak to the person you are writing to.*

All the best,

Alex

> *Use an appropriate informal phrase for closing your email or letter.*

EXAM HELP

- Use appropriate informal conventions to start/end your email/letter.
- Group ideas into paragraphs and link them with informal connectors.
- Use language that is appropriate for the person you're writing to.

OVER TO YOU

Now write your own answer to the task. Make sure that you include everything required in the task and use the Exam help to check your work.

USEFUL LANGUAGE

Beginning the email/letter

Thanks so much for your letter/email. It was really great to hear from you.

Sorry not to have written/been in touch for so long/such a long time. I've been really busy lately.

I thought I'd better drop you a line/write to let you know …

Ending the email/letter

I think that's all my news for the moment. Do write soon and let me know what you've been doing.

Can't wait to see you on the 24th/next week in Cambridge …

Don't forget to say hi to … from me.

Give my love to …

Apologising

I'm really/terribly/awfully sorry about what happened the other night.

Inviting

How about meeting up for a cup of coffee some time?

Why don't we try to get together soon?

I was wondering if you might like to get together next time you're in town.

Responding to an invitation

Thanks very much for inviting us to your party. We're really looking forward to it.

Making a request

I was wondering if you happen to know anywhere in Dublin we could stay.

If you've got a spare moment, do you think you could find out when the music festival is on this year?

Referring to a previous email/ letter

You said in your letter that you were thinking of applying for a scholarship.

You know that course I told you I had applied for? Well, …

WRITING FILE

Part 2 Formal email or letter

EXAMPLE QUESTION

▶ Unit 8 pp88–89

You see an announcement about a summer course at a university in a subject you are interested in. You must have a good level of English and some experience in your chosen subject area. You decide to apply for a place on the course. Write a letter of application outlining your reasons for applying, describing the relevant experience and qualifications you have and explaining how you expect to benefit from the course. Write your **letter**. Write **220–260** words.

> Think carefully about who you are writing to and how well you might know them. Make sure you adopt an appropriate tone for your reader.

EXAMPLE ANSWER

Dear Mr Cleary,

I am writing to you in response to your announcement about summer courses at your university. I would like to apply for a place on the Computer Coding course.

> Always start your letter by stating your reason for writing.

I would be very interested in this course because it is an opportunity to learn something that is essential for my future career. I note that the course is for beginners and there have not been many of these courses available recently. I have also heard that your university has a very good reputation for teaching and courses which increase employability.

I have been studying computer science for one year at school and have exams in this subject at the end of the academic year. My teacher feels that I have ability in this area and that I am likely to pass the exams with a good mark. Computer science has always been my area of interest. In fact, I also spend a lot of time at home exploring this and am currently developing an app with a fellow student.

> Give reasons for your point of view. Support your opinions with examples from what you are reviewing.

Although I have done some coding, I believe the course would give me a thorough grounding in coding language. With the acquisition of this skill, I would be better equipped to develop my own web design, apps and other software. I would also relish the opportunity to interact with other students, which I find especially important when working through ideas.

I hope you find my application of interest and I look forward to hearing from you.

> Use the final paragraph to describe the desired outcome from your letter.

Yours sincerely,

Cora Lynch

EXAM HELP

- You may be asked to write a letter of complaint, application, recommendation, etc. Make sure you understand the purpose of the letter (to complain, persuade, apply, etc.).
- If required to respond to someone else's letter or article, underline the key points so it's clear what you must comment on.
- If the letter is to complain or disagree, remember to modify any abrupt language, e.g. with modal verbs.
- Think carefully about whether you need to use formal or semi-formal language.

OVER TO YOU

Now write your own answer to the task. Make sure that you include everything required in the task and use the Exam help to check your work.

USEFUL LANGUAGE

Greetings

Dear Sir/Madam,

Dear Mr/Ms … ,

To whom it may concern,

Opening your email or letter, explaining why you're writing

I would like to complain / explain / apply for

I am writing to …

Thank you for your email/letter.

I have been asked to write to you concerning …

Making suggestions

You could think about …

It would be a good idea to …

I recommend …

Finishing your email or letter

I very much hope you will consider …

I look forward to hearing from you.

I hope my ideas are helpful.

Yours, / Best wishes,

Part 2 Proposal

EXAMPLE QUESTION

▶ Unit 4 pp44–45

Your college has raised some funds through various events and has now asked students to suggest what the money could be spent on. You decide to write a proposal to the principal. In your proposal, you should outline how you think the money should be spent, describe how this could be organised and explain what the benefits to the college or the students would be. Write your **proposal**. Write **220–260** words.

Think carefully about the purpose of your proposal and what you will need to do to persuade the reader.

EXAMPLE ANSWER

Introduction

The purpose of this proposal is to suggest how the money raised from the recent fundraising events could be spent to best benefit the school and its students. The proposal outlines a suggestion for purchasing new gym equipment.

The need for gym equipment

Most of the school gym equipment is very old, having been purchased over 15 years ago, and the equipment is very well used by the whole school. Advances in technology have prompted the development of new equipment, which has changed enormously in the last few years, and it would be much better for athletes and the wider school to have access to this newer apparatus.

Managing the equipment purchase

If new gym equipment is purchased, a decision would have to be made about what is prioritised and at what cost. Possibly the best way to approach this would be to ask students to vote or sign up for what they use most and, in collaboration with the coaches, draw up a list of priorities.

Use formal and objective language.

Benefits

If funds could be invested in new equipment, this would not only mean that students were working on more up-to-date equipment, which is probably safer and more efficient, but also it may enable performance to improve and for the students and school to compete more successfully.

Explain the benefits of adopting your idea or suggestions.

Summary

Create a strong summary and make your rationale clear to the reader.

All in all, I would urge you to seriously consider setting aside all or some of the funds to invest in new gym equipment. It would motivate more students to take up sports and would be an investment in the future of the school.

EXAM HELP

- Read the task carefully and think about who the target reader is.
- Plan an outline by using the task requirements to create sub-headings. Use a separate focus for each section.
- Make sure you give all the information asked for in the task.
- Make sure you give a clear outline of the current situation as a background to establish the need for your proposal.
- Be persuasive by giving evidence for the benefits of your suggestions. Do this with concrete reasons rather than using emotional appeals.
- Make sure the reader has enough information to make a decision about your proposal.

OVER TO YOU

Now write your own answer to the task. Make sure that you include everything required in the task and use the Exam help to check your work.

USEFUL LANGUAGE

Talking about change

It would improve …
It would be different from …
This progress towards …
The proposal to alter … would …
This modification involves …
It is time to transform …

Pointing out benefits

There is no doubt that …
The advantage is that …
It will give … the opportunity to …
There is no better way to …

Persuasive language

I would urge you to …
It is essential/critical that …
There is an urgent need …

Predicting outcomes

It may be the case that …
It could be that …
It might mean that …

WRITING FILE

Part 2 Report

EXAMPLE QUESTION

▶ Unit 5, pp56-57

The manager of a club that you attend regularly has asked members to write a report about their experiences of using the club. In your report you should underline what has been successful in the club, describe any improvements you would recommend and suggest how the club could attract new members. Write your **report**. Write **220-260** words.

> Underline the key points in the task and use these to organise your headings.

EXAMPLE ANSWER

Introduction

The purpose of this report is to evaluate how well the Chess Club is working, recommend any improvements that could be made and suggest how the club could attract new members.

Successes in the club

Over the last year, the club has offered a lot to members. There have been more competitions than in previous years and, as a consequence, more inter-club events. This has the added advantage of raising the quality of the games played. In addition, there has been more coaching by senior members, especially for younger members, and this appears to have been successful as numbers have increased.

> Be careful not to make your report too personal. Make your evaluations objective and not about your personal experiences.

Recommendations for improvements

If the club wishes to better its position in the local league table, it would be sensible to consider formal training from a professional expert. This could be funded through membership fees, but there could be a selection process for participants. In order to give members further practice, it might be an idea to run 'fast game' sessions on Saturday mornings, to allow as many people to play as possible.

> Give your opinion in the final sections.

Suggestions for attracting new members

The club still wishes to attract more members, especially young people. We could give a demonstration or coaching sessions at the local primary school, to spark interest in pupils. We could also offer reduced fees for a limited period.

Overall, the club has had a successful year but we can continue to progress, especially if these recommendations are implemented.

> Your conclusion or final section should link clearly to the rest of the report.

EXAM HELP

- Make sure you understand who the report is for and why they need it.
- Remember you will normally have to give some factual information, an evaluation and some suggestions. Make sure these are in clear paragraphs under the appropriate headings.
- Make sure your factual information connects with your recommendations and that the reader can see a clear need for the recommended actions.
- Use formal and objective language, e.g. passive structures, noun phrases, introductory *it*.
- Check that you don't repeat points.
- Use a range of more formal or academic vocabulary.
- Check that your report makes clear recommendations, presenting the expected outcomes/benefits of the recommendations.

OVER TO YOU

Now write your own answer to the task. Make sure that you include everything required in the task and use the Exam help to check your work.

USEFUL LANGUAGE

Openings

The purpose/aim of this report is to …

In this report …

This report gives a description …

This report is intended to …

Objective language

It needs (work) done because …

(Work) needs to be done because …

Closings

I would strongly recommend …

One suggestion would be to …

It may be advisable to …

If these changes are introduced, …

If these recommendations are implemented, …

In conclusion, …

Part 2 Review

EXAMPLE QUESTION

▶ Unit 2 pp22-23, Unit 7 pp78-79

Your college recently put on the annual student performance in order to raise money for a charity which the school supports. You have been asked to write a review of the show for your college magazine. In your review, you should evaluate the performance, say how far it was successful in achieving its objectives and outline any changes you would make for next year's performance. Write your **review**. Write **220–260** words.

> Underline key words in the task to make sure you understand which aspects must be included in your review.

EXAMPLE ANSWER

The annual performance of a well-known musical by the senior year is always exciting and also very well supported because the funds from the ticket sales go to the Children First charity, which the school supports.

There was a packed crowd to watch this year's offering of *West Side Story*. The school orchestra did a spectacular job of delivering the songs and music, which was much more of a challenge for them than last year. The action moved along at a cracking pace and the lead actors did a wonderful job making each part their own and really conveying the emotion of the story. Of course, it's a great plot – *Romeo and Juliet* set in the gangland of 1950s New York – and something all the students could relate to. Credit must also go to the directors and the team who managed the stage sets and lighting as this all added to an electric atmosphere.

> Use plenty of modifiers and adjectives to help the reader understand your experience.

All in all, this was the best performance ever by a senior year and the collection tins at the end reflected this as the audience were very generous with their contributions, so in the end we raised over 1,000 euros for the charity. A school record, so well done, all!

> Give reasons for your point of view. Support your opinions with examples from what you are reviewing.

> Remember to give a summary of your opinion, even if it is negative.

Now we will already be looking towards next year's performance and, if I were to advise the directors, I would suggest they think about how they can make the smaller roles more significant so that more of the students can play a fuller part in the play. It would also be nice to see the backstage staff come onstage at the end.

EXAM HELP

- Plan the outline of each paragraph so that each one has a clear focus.
- Remember to introduce your review by giving details about what you have seen/visited/done.
- Think carefully about the different features of the play/restaurant/book, etc. that you can review.
- Remember to compare aspects of the restaurant/music/film/game, etc. with others or with previous versions or performances.
- Reviews are normally written in informal or semi-formal language, to engage the reader.
- It may help to explain what you think the author/director, etc. was trying to achieve and how successful they were.

OVER TO YOU

Now write your own answer to the task. Make sure that you include everything required in the task and use the Exam help to check your work.

USEFUL LANGUAGE

Describing your experience
relaxed atmosphere
stunning special effects
incredibly good acting
uninteresting plot
surprisingly poor exhibits

Making comparisons
much better than
not nearly as good as
It was disappointing compared to …
One of the more exciting games this year …
Compared to his/her previous …

Making a recommendation
I would certainly recommend …
Definitely go to see/visit/buy it!
Although it raised money, it was not …
It's worth / It's not worth …
I strongly suggest …
You would be mad to miss this.
This … is a must-see.
I wouldn't bother …

Unit 1

🎧 1.1 (Opener)

It's now so familiar that it rolls off the tongue without thinking – Neil Armstrong's quote about walking on the Moon, that is. Yet some believe that he may have been misquoted ever since the first Moon landing in 1969. This includes Armstrong himself, who claims that the words he actually came out with were, 'That's one small step for a man, one giant leap for mankind.' But the version that has become associated with the event doesn't include the 'a' before man. As such, it doesn't carry the meaning that Armstrong intended, and instead implies that humans had only made a small amount of progress, yet had moved on a huge amount in the same breath!

🎧 1.2 (Opener)

Whether or not Armstrong was misquoted, was the Moon landing really the giant leap for mankind that he suggested? In many respects, yes. Many fascinating inventions have appeared as a result of preparations for space travel, with scientists devoting themselves to making astronauts' lives easier and more efficient.

Communication was key to relaying information from the Moon back to Earth on that first landing. While satellite imagery was already in existence by the 1960s, as space travel became more common scientists threw themselves into improving the technology, ultimately resulting in today's satellite TV. Then, in the 1990s, camera phones came into being: they were portable and could take high-quality images. This technology quickly caught on beyond space travel. Imagine not having a phone with a camera these days!

The health and comfort of astronauts was crucial to successful space missions, too, and led to useful applications here on Earth. In the 1960s, water-purification systems were used to filter astronauts' drinking water, and the idea was later put forward that the same process could be used to kill bacteria in swimming pools – it's still used today.

Of course, astronauts needed to eat as well as drink, and freeze-dried food – which already existed for coffee and crops – became much-improved. At only 20 percent of its normal weight but retaining 98 percent of its nutrients, it was the perfect solution for keeping astronauts full of energy without taking up vital room on the spacecraft.

There are countless other things that have sprung up as a result of problem-solving in space. Even the trainers on your feet today wouldn't exist if scientists hadn't created the materials for spacesuits!

🎧 1.3 (Opener)

See 1.1 and 1.2.

🎧 1.4 (Reading and Use of English Part 5)

OK, so to answer your question about travel companions – it's an interesting one, and I guess I would say yes, I go with different people to different places. It makes a lot of sense, doesn't it? I mean if you're off for a fun-filled break, somewhere like Ibiza, it's great to go in a group, isn't it? But you might not want to spend a week skiing with the same group of people! Your fun-loving friends might have the stamina to dance the night away, but not the fitness level to ski all day – and not everyone likes both the heat AND the cold like me. Oh, and can you imagine dragging someone round museums on a sightseeing city break, when all they want to do is lie on a beach somewhere to de-stress after months of hard work? No, definitely different companions. Oh, and while we're on the subject – I have to say there's no way I would ever spend longer than a weekend with my wonderful parents. I love them dearly but after a couple of days we'd drive each other up the wall. Far better to preserve a relationship than test it to its limits. And the same goes for friends!

🎧 1.5 and 1.6 (Reading and Use of English Part 1)

When I put myself forward for a TV talent competition, I didn't expect to get through the first round of auditions, let alone end up on the live shows. The competition consisted of a series of knock-out rounds over ten weeks – the public voted to eliminate one person each week. There was a fascinating range of acts – stuff like acrobatics and stand-up comedy – and I wasn't convinced my singing would capture the public's attention. But they kept me in week after week and before I knew it, it was the live final and I smashed it! I definitely exceeded my expectations!

I immediately started conjuring up fantasies of fame and fortune – I'd seen previous winners reap the rewards with highly paid recording contracts, advertising endorsements, the lot. I felt I deserved to do just as well after all my hard work!

The first year after winning the competition was awesome, and I was definitely suited to my new lifestyle! People recognised me everywhere I went – I could always get a table in a restaurant, I got a ton of free stuff from top fashion brands, and I went on to record my first album. The first time I heard someone humming one of my songs in the street it blew my mind – I really felt like I'd made it, regardless of the fact that my family kept warning me that people who shoot to fame overnight after winning this kind of contest tend to disappear from the limelight just as quickly.

They were right, unfortunately. The next series of the show aired a year later, and things started to go a bit cold. I'd released a new single but it didn't take off. I was dropped by my record label and it felt like my fans were abandoning me for the next big thing. I was incapable of doing anything about it, though, and got pretty down about it.

On reflection, I'm inclined to think that shows like that are more about creating short-term celebrities and making as much money from them as quickly as possible than they are about discovering real talent. It's just another form of reality TV.

All things considered, my fifteen minutes of fame was an incredible experience and I wouldn't change a thing. Not many people get to realise an ambition so young!

🎧 1.7 (Listening Part 1)

Only around ten percent of what we laugh at is something we actually find funny, but we laugh an average of seventeen times a day. So, if what we're hearing doesn't genuinely amuse us, why do we laugh so often?

Interestingly, studies have indicated that we tend to laugh more after our own sentences than someone else's. Do we really find ourselves that hilarious? In a word, no. But laughter's a social lubricant, and we most frequently laugh in order to strengthen our relationships and ease things along. Think about it: you probably don't laugh spontaneously when you're alone!

We sometimes laugh to show that what we've just said was intended to be amusing, but we also laugh when we're nervous or at inappropriate moments, such as when hearing about someone else's misfortunes. This might be seen as unkind or even cruel, but the fact is we're not knowingly in control of this kind of laughter – our subconscious is. And it also serves to release tension and allow us to relax, reducing the impact of stressful experiences.

There's no faking laughter, either. It's a completely subconscious reaction.

However, it can be very embarrassing if we don't understand a joke and have to force a laugh to save face – though perhaps we shouldn't pretend, as we're also great at spotting fake laughter!

Jokes also act like social glue, and they've been around for a very long time. Hundreds of years ago, wealthy households would employ an entertainer known as 'the fool'. Fools were not only proficient at making jokes for their audiences' enjoyment – much like stand-up comedians do today – but at storytelling, singing, acrobatics and magic tricks. They were considered not only funny, but smart, too.

Perhaps today's 'jokers' – we all know someone who loves a practical joke or makes light of awkward situations – take on the fool's role in modern society, creating harmony wherever they go. After all, as long as we're laughing, we feel OK.

🎧 1.1EB and 1.2EB (Listening Part 1 – Exam boost)

1 Don't you find it incredible how infectious laughter is? Even when you don't have a clue what someone's laughing at, if they're crying with laughter, we often join in.

2 If only I hadn't missed the plane, I'd be sunning myself on the beach by now. I really ought to plan my time better.

3 I've just been given an extension on the deadline, happily. That means I can make sure I do a decent job of my essay after being off college sick.

4 I've got mixed feelings about going to the party. A friend I fell out with is going to be there which could be awkward, but I'd love to see some other people I haven't seen for ages. I can't make my mind up.

5 Don't you think we should invite the whole class to the barbecue on Thursday? I'd hate for anyone to be upset because they've been left out.

🎧 1.8 (Listening Part 1)

Extract 1

A: I've just been reading an article about famous April Fools' Day jokes – there've been some funny ones. In the fifties, the BBC broadcast a report about a spaghetti harvest in Switzerland. They managed to convince viewers that spaghetti grew on trees. I hadn't come across the story before and I did wonder how people could've been deceived so easily. I reckon the broadcasters were simply playing on their ignorance – spaghetti was apparently a pretty exotic foodstuff in Britain back then. The BBC intended it as a light-hearted joke but not everyone took it that way, probably cos the segment aired on what was usually

a serious documentary programme and people objected to being taken in like that. But it was only a bit of fun.

B: Well, maybe they had a point but April Fool's Day's good for the soul – it gives you a day off from behaving properly and in modern society where everyone spends the majority of their time working and studying hard, it provides an outlet for stress, albeit a temporary one. Practical jokes can be hilarious and you can pay people back for jokes they've played on you in the past. Within reason, of course!

Extract 2

A: People say fake news is harmless. My take on it varies. There's information that's put out there with the intention of being misleading – and in many cases to make money. Then there's information that journalists – people like you and me – unwittingly circulate in the belief that it's the truth. The latter can be forgiven – and I'd rather call it 'false' news than fake – but the former's difficult, if not impossible, to justify. We all know of someone whose career's been finished by it, but you know, contrary to popular belief, this kind of stuff's been around for quite some time, though admittedly it's only been brought to our attention lately.

B: Right. Of course, we write stories, but we read them, too. I'm sceptical about what I read online – especially via social networking sites – and my reporter's instinct to dig out the truth has so far kept me from falling for nonsense, thankfully. But some of it's pretty credible and you can see why some people believe things that are published by what seem like reliable sources. As a journalist, I think I'd be pretty red-faced at being taken in by something and spreading it around as fact.

Extract 3

A: If you have an online bank account – and most of us do – you'll be aware of ensuring your money is protected at all times. Hackers use ever-more sophisticated techniques to try to get at your cash or personal details, and this poses a real threat not only to individuals but organisations, too. In the past, it was easier to identify a fraudster – they'd ring the doorbell and try to convince you to part with your hard-earned cash for a product or service that would fall short of expectations. Now, scammers hide behind technology, and their tricks are becoming increasingly difficult to spot. So, what should you do? Beth, fill us in.

B: Well, we're all aware that we shouldn't go round handing out passwords and pin codes. But it's the unsolicited emails and phone calls from companies we've heard

of and think we deal with on a regular basis that catch us out. A good rule of thumb is to take a deep breath and think 'Does this sound too good to be true?' Be suspicious, look out for spelling mistakes or inaccurate information, think rationally. I'd also like to stress that if you have been taken in, don't give yourself a hard time about it – today's scams are incredibly convincing.

🎧 1.9 and 1.10 (Reading and Use of English Part 2)

Everyone knows fingerprinting is a useful tool in determining who committed a crime, but personal identification isn't the reason we have fingerprints. So, what purpose do they serve? This is a question that scientists have long been pondering.

The patterns on our fingertips – which are formed months before we're born – might look like miniature grips, enabling us to prevent things quite literally slipping through our fingers. But scientists have dismissed this theory. This is because only the ridges really have much contact with a surface, and the 'valleys' between them have a lot less. This suggests grip might actually be minimised by fingerprints. Although it was something that had puzzled scientists for a long time, few had tried to find out how fingerprints are useful to us. That is, until scientists who were working in Paris conducted an experiment in which they compared different kinds of artificially made fingertips – some ridged, like our own, and some smooth. They had been working on their experiment for a while when they finally discovered that ridges increase skin sensitivity, vibrating as our fingertips glide over surfaces. This helps us sense what we're holding and allows us to detect texture.

And because fingerprints are made up of arches, loops and whorls, which point in different directions, they came to the conclusion that we can sense what we're touching whichever way we hold it.

🎧 1.11 (Speaking Part 1)

Examiner: Do you find it easy to talk to people when you meet them for the first time?

A: Actually, not all that easy. I sometimes get stuck for words and let the other person do all the talking. Sometimes it's OK. Like at a social event and we both know the host, then there's something we've got in common to talk about. Whereas at other times, like at a work interview I might get a bit tongue-tied. Not good!

B: Quite easy, I'd say. I like meeting new people.

1.3EB (Speaking Part 1 – Exam boost)

1

Examiner: Where are you from?

Candidate A: The south of Italy.

Candidate B: I was born and brought up in Italy but the family moved to Sweden because of my mum's job when I was two. They loved the way of life there so much that they stayed and I consider myself more Swedish than Italian now!

Candidate C: I'm from in France. Is a small village near of the capital city.

2

Examiner: What do you do here?

Candidate A: I am staying here for two weeks and then I'm going back to my home town.

Candidate B: At the moment I'm studying at Uppsala University. It's a course for interpreting, which I have to say I'm finding both challenging and enjoyable. I'm in the second year of a three-year course.

Candidate C: I work as a waiter in a restaurant.

3

Examiner: How long have you been studying English?

Candidate A: Oh – a long time – it must be eleven years now. I started learning quite young, at primary school and then continued at secondary.

Candidate B: I first started when I was six years old. I was in a small group of students and we all studied English and Italian. Then when I moved to secondary school, I dropped the Italian and concentrated on the English, because I thought it was a more important language. I regret dropping the Italian because it's also useful and I think I might take it up again when I have enough time. There are evening classes at my local college or I could take an online course. That might be …

Candidate C: About ten years, I think.

4

Examiner: What do you enjoy most about learning English?

Candidate A: I like the pronunciation. I think English is a very musical language that sounds very attractive! However, it's also tricky to pronounce correctly, but I try my best. I also enjoy being able to exchange emails in English with my friends in England.

Candidate B: It's a difficult language and I think the grammar is particularly hard. For example, I find the tenses very confusing and of course, the phrasal verbs, too!

Candidate C: I enjoy the vocabulary games we play in class.

1.12 (Speaking Part 1)

Examiner: Would you say that you lead a healthy lifestyle?

A: Yes, I do. My lifestyle is very healthy.

B: No, not really, I'm afraid.

Examiner: Do you feel that your week includes as much free time as you'd like?

A: Yes, I have a good work–life balance.

B: No, I don't have much free time during the week.

1.13 (Writing Part 1)

OK, so this game is called Room 101 and it's about imagining there's a room where you could lock away some of your pet hates forever! In case you're wondering where you've heard the name before, it's from the book *1984* by George Orwell and it was a room where people were sent where they confronted their worst nightmares! For Winston Smith in *1984* it was rats! Apparently, George Orwell based this on Room 101 at the then BBC offices where he had to suffer really long, boring meetings. So, since then – the phrase 'I'd love to put that in Room 101' refers to things we'd like to get rid of. Hence the game. For you today I'd like you to work in groups of four. Three of you need to choose a pet hate – it can be as quirky as you like. For example, mine might be soap operas, or chewing gum, or Maths! Then you talk for a couple of minutes about why this should go in Room 101. The others should say why they disagree. Finally, the fourth person decides which of the three items should go in. So, you need to be as persuasive as possible. OK? Right, first you have some time to think of a pet hate and why it should disappear forever …

1.1GF

See Ex 4 on page 99.

1.1VF

1 Those stripes really do help disguise the tiger in the long grasses don't they?

2 So, we balanced this packet of flour on top of the door and when Denzel came into the room he got covered in white powder!

3 I find jogging is actually a great way to let off steam and chill out.

4 Don't believe everything Michael says – he only does it to make everyone think he's super confident and not afraid of anything but it isn't true.

5 There's really no shame these days in going to the cinema alone but it used to be considered a bit sad if you had to go on your own.

6 Whether you like the idea or not, humans are classed in the same group of animals as monkeys.

7 The burglar must have been wearing gloves as there are no marks on anything that's been disturbed.

8 Look! He's about to launch himself off the cliff, into the air! I'd love to go paragliding!

1.2VF and 1.3VF

See Ex 7 on page 115.

Unit 2

2.1 (Opener)

Lecturer: K2, K2 - a mountain of mystery and the focus of many people's obsession! Today we'll be finding out more about this enigmatic natural feature. But first up I'd like some input from you. Most of the great mountains in the world have romantic or poetic names - think of Everest, The Matterhorn, Siula Grande … So, why should the second highest mountain of them all be so simply named? K2? It sounds more like a mathematical formula than one of the most beautiful mountains in the world. Any ideas why it's called that?

Student: Is it something to do with it being the second highest?

Lecturer: Good try - but no. It was back in 1856 when the mountains in the Karakoram Range - that's on the border between Pakistan and India - were being surveyed. This mountain just happened to be second on the list. The first mountain they checked out was K (for Karakoram) 1, the second K2, and so on. With other mountains the surveyors would return and get the local name for a mountain and that was generally how it came to be known - but K2 was so remote, there was no real local name, so K2 it remained!

And it's not only famous for its odd name. From the outset it gained the reputation of being a 'savage' mountain and continues to challenge the most daring climbers in the world. None of the eight thousanders (the 14 mountains over eight thousand metres) are a pushover for mountaineers but K2 presents particular challenges. Being nearly a perfect pyramid with steep ice slopes and hardly any relief on the way up to the summit, it was considered unclimbable for a very long time. Several attempts were foiled by outbreaks of disease and sickness but eventually the mountain was summited by an Italian team in 1954. Since then people have conquered K2 only 300 times. And surprisingly, most of those successes were achieved without the backup of additional oxygen, in order to reduce the weight of the climbers. There have been recent breakthroughs in how oxygen is carried, and this means that it is used more frequently these days. However, K2 still manages to defeat the best – it is a dangerous mountain, prone to avalanches, and setbacks caused by appalling weather conditions have prevented the mountain ever being climbed in the winter – the only one of the eight thousanders that hasn't. The outcome of many of those failed attempts can be found in the mass of literature about the mountain, and several films and documentaries. So, I recommend you check them out.

Now, I mentioned earlier that …

2.2 (Reading and Use of English Part 6)

Presenter: Anna, what's your view?

Anna: They say you shouldn't make decisions late at night, because your brain is tired, but quite honestly some of the best decisions I've made have been just before I've gone to bed. I guess maybe because I've cut straight to the chase and not wasted time going backwards and forwards through a lot of options!

Presenter: OK! What do you think Ben?

Ben: Yeah, Anna's got a point, but sometimes I'll decide something last thing at night and then in the morning think – oh no, what was I thinking? It does sometimes pay, in my book, to delay a decision until first thing, when your brain is fresh and can think through all the ramifications.

Presenter: And how about you, Jessie? What are your thoughts?

Jessie: Well, it surely depends on the type of decision, doesn't it? If it's a straight choice between chocolate ice-cream, or strawberry, then the consequences don't matter – and I could easily make that decision at any time! But if it's about where you want to study, or about extra work you're being asked to take on, then it's a completely different matter. Those kinds of decisions need a clear focus and a fresh mind – and for me that means mornings.

2.3 and 2.4 (Reading and Use of English Part 3)

Presenter: Today's phone-in is all about losing things! With me in the studio is Georgia Williams, memory expert, who's here to advise our listeners on how to avoid misplacing everyday items. We've got Karl on the line. Karl, tell us about your experiences of losing things.

Karl: Well, I'm always doing it! Whenever I'm about to leave the house, I spend a good few minutes trying to locate my car keys or wallet or phone. It drives me insane! I do come and go at irregular times cos I work varying shift patterns, and I was wondering whether that's anything to do with it? I'm not particularly disorganised – my house is generally pretty neat and tidy, and I'm punctual and everything. But I'll end up finding my door keys in the bathroom or my phone charger on top of the fridge. I seem to have this inability to keep track of the stuff I need every day. What's wrong with me?

Presenter: Georgia?

Georgia: So, finding your keys in the bathroom isn't as illogical as it might seem and you aren't an irresponsible person, so don't give yourself a hard time! These days, we're always trying to do two things at once. Undoubtedly, what's happening is you're coming in from work tired, and you go straight to the bathroom to freshen up, or to the fridge for a cold drink. The keys are still in your hand, unnoticed – you're thinking about what you're going to make for dinner, perhaps – and you just pop them down and dismiss them from mind. Now, you probably have a couple of places in your home where you think you always keep important things, so when you go to that place when you need them and they aren't there, you're impossibly confused – you always put them there, you think! But your mind's misleading you. You don't actually remember whether you put the keys down where they 'should' be or not – it's such an insignificant thing in your busy life.

Presenter: Karl?

Karl: Yeah, that makes sense – I'm just distracted, I guess. So, what's the answer?

Georgia: Well, this constant mislaying of things is obviously causing you some distress, so you need to reconsider what you do when you arrive home – make a conscious decision to be aware of how you interact with your surroundings. Pause at the front door, look at your hand with the key in it. Enter your house and put the keys down immediately in that special place – the little bowl or the hook in the cupboard. And keep that place free of other stuff – do a little reorganisation if need be.

Presenter: Karl, does that help?

Karl: Yes, I'll give that a go – thank you!

Presenter: Now, on to our next caller, who …

2.5 and 2.6 (Listening Part 2)

I set up my catering company a couple of years ago, and have two assistants. We specialise in Japanese food and recently won the silver award at our region's small business awards.

Our company was nominated by our customers. It was only when we were shortlisted to attend the ceremony that we actually looked into the aim of the awards, and determined that they not only celebrate small firms' achievements and contribution to the local community, but also aim to raise their profile. The founder of the awards believes that small companies like mine are an undervalued sector of the national economy.

We were super-excited to win and in my acceptance speech I was keen to extend my gratitude to everyone who supported us. Our company's built on values like integrity and loyalty. However, first and foremost in our approach is sustainability, which remains a buzzword for businesses – and that's what we were recognised for. We source ingredients locally, avoid waste wherever possible, and we take health and nutrition seriously, too.

I became a convert to Japanese food when I travelled in the country after catering college and I wanted to bring some of that 'deliciousness' back to my home town. We produce top-quality Japanese dishes from scratch. These include traditional favourites, like tempura, with innovative twists, and I like to class our food as a sensory feast – indeed, that's what we've got written on our promotional material! We think visual elements are equally as important as taste and smell.

Now that we've won silver, people keep asking us what's going to happen going forwards. Until now, we've put our energies into catering for small private functions, like dinner parties or birthday lunches in clients' homes. Weddings are unlikely as they're beyond our scope – though corporate hospitality is something that's very much on our radar. We've no plans to open a restaurant for the time being but we have every intention of forging ahead with the social events side of things.

You never know, maybe we'll win gold next time!

2.1EB (Listening Part 2 – Exam boost)

A: Psychologists believe that those who achieve bronze in a race are actually more satisfied with their position than those who got gold or silver. The person who comes last will be disappointed but probably aware that they were never likely to win, and is therefore probably relatively philosophical about it – at least they finished the race!

The winner understands that they have to try to maintain their position at the top, and although they feel overjoyed in the moment, they soon come down to earth with a bump. The runner-up can feel dissatisfied because they think that if only they'd done just a little better, they might have won, whereas the person who comes next is often grateful to have made it to the podium at all.

It's difficult to banish negativity when we don't win because we find it tricky to get out of what we might call a 'thought loop'. But with the aid of meditation and neurolinguistic programming, we might find a way to reframe our experiences.

B: My name's Petra and I recently completed my first five-kilometre run. On the day itself, we were all in the preparation area, warming up for the run. I wasn't even sure I'd have the strength to get to the finish line, and stood in awe of a lot of the runners who were dashing backwards and forwards in what looked like an attempt to deplete all their energy reserves before the race had even begun!

I'd done some training for the race but I didn't fancy my chances of winning. I'm not very tall and have a short stride which I knew meant I wouldn't be able to keep up with many people. I didn't really expect to be running alone on my own at the back – though that's pretty much what happened. But my positive attitude kept me going to the end.

When I got there, most runners had already packed up and gone home. I was indeed last, but I wasn't embarrassed – someone has to come last! And only a few weeks before, I hadn't been able to run to the end of my street and back. I actually felt powerful – I'd achieved my goal and am enthusiastic about starting to train for a marathon.

2.7 (Listening Part 2)

Some people say that when you come second, you don't win silver, you lose gold. As a sports psychologist, I'd argue against that. Let me tell you why.

The person who comes first in a major sports event will always come under a lot of scrutiny because the public upholds them as the ideal. Winners therefore place a lot of pressure on themselves to keep coming up with the goods – they believe that now they've got to the top, they have to stay there.

There's no such spotlight shone on the runner-up, but being 'almost best' means still benefitting from the perks – there's recognition of your achievements from the sporting community, if not the fame and fortune that goes with winning. Being second is no bad place to be.

In fact, some studies have shown that coming second is actually beneficial in some ways, not least of which is life expectancy – the difference between those who come first and those who come second is remarkable. And second-finishers are more likely to achieve financial success after their career in sport comes to an end.

Even though those who finish in first and second places are pretty identical physically and neurologically, it's thought that trying to win every competition is harmful to the health of those who pursue victory at all costs. But the motivation levels of those who fail to reach the top spot are usually high.

How does it feel to come second? Those who believe they've put up a good fight are likely to have mixed feelings. It's painful coming second after all your hard work and dedication, but while winners may feel momentarily elated, many second-finishers may feel optimistic, too, because there's always next time, whereas those used to winning feel let down when they don't get gold.

Wanting to be the best is an increasing trend. The expectation's not only enormous in sport but for young people making their way in life, too. They have to deal with fierce competition and there are a lot of demands placed on them – they're expected to get the best grades at school, a place at a top university and subsequently a great job.

But coming second – in sport at least – still means being one of the best, and from what I've seen, those still trying to reach first position are also still figuring out how to do it, relishing the opportunity for experimentation, whereas those who already have a few wins under their belt tend to be afraid to try anything new, sticking to tried and tested preparation for events.

Many highly respected sportspeople never get first place, but are, in my opinion, still heroes. They may never be champions, but are often influential in their field. My personal favourite is the racing driver Stirling Moss, who, when he could once have taken first place, defended his opponent against disqualification, and gracefully accepted second place. He'll forever be remembered as the greatest driver never to win the World Championship.

2.8 (Reading and Use of English Part 4)

I part-own a bicycle shop – no ordinary one, mind you! We're a social enterprise, and our primary objective is to achieve positive social impact rather than generate profit.

We offer quality second-hand bikes that are priced for any budget and provide a full repair and maintenance service, too. We also do charity work, and hundreds of bikes have been donated to overseas communities which had never been given access to them before. We support a local charity for young people with disabilities, providing work experience opportunities and aiding independence. We also have our own coffee shop where you can have a cuppa while your bike is being fixed. We'll try our hand at restoring bikes of any age and condition, and we've even written our own guide to local bike routes which is called 'Bike your way round Brighton' – the city where our shop is located. We've been operating for ten years now and people say we're the best bike shop in the area. I hope that will still be being said in another ten years.

I love messing about with bicycles but even more important to me personally is the time that's spent learning about those who come into our shop. They make me laugh with their biking anecdotes. I even heard about a tandem ride this way not long ago, that was being organised in order to raise money for a charity for visually impaired people. I decided to take part and got people to sponsor me like the other participants were doing. A lot of money was raised this way, which was great! It was fun, too.

As you can imagine, I'm a firm advocate of cycling and believe it's a skill that should be taught to everyone when they're young. Not enough is being done to ensure all school-age children are able to ride a bike, and recently, campaigns have been being held around the country to make cycling proficiency part of every school curriculum. It's been found that not only is cycling fun and great for physical fitness, but it promotes coordination and mental well-being, too. Life on two wheels is the best life!

2.9 (Speaking Part 2)

It's something we've probably heard many times. 'Hey – did you know you've got a double? I saw someone in town yesterday and she looked exactly like you!' It can be intriguing to think there's someone out there walking around with the same face as you. And the fascination with finding a doppelganger has even resulted in websites where you can enter your facial details and search for yours! The science behind doppelgangers is that the probability of finding a true doppelganger – that is someone whose face matches eight specific measurements – is one in a trillion. Extremely unlikely! However, the odds reduce to one in 135 when we talk about 'look-alikes'. These are people who an observer would identify as a 'double' because of a strong similarity of features. This is basically because our brains look at the whole of a face, and not the individual parts. They adjust what we see to fit an expected pattern. So, yes, your friend may well have seen someone who looks like your double, but it wouldn't be a true doppelganger! That really would make the headlines.

2.10 and 2.11 (Speaking Part 2)

Ah – interesting pictures! As you say, both pictures feature people who look similar to each other, but the focus of similarity is different in each picture. Whereas in the first picture the children have a strong physical resemblance, implying that they are probably brothers, and very likely twins – in the second picture the two people are connected by their uniforms, which identify them as police officers. A major difference between the pictures is clearly the location. The children are wearing seatbelts in the backseat of a car, whilst the police officers are in the open air and observing the crowd at some sort of sporting event. Both pairs of people are interacting with each other in different ways. While the twins are interacting physically – play-fighting – the police officers are working together and maybe they are even commenting on the event they are watching. I would say that the relationship between both pairs of people is good. The twins have a strong family bond which allows them to play-fight with each other, without getting really angry. The police, on the other hand, have respect and I would imagine, confidence and trust in each other. The way they're standing appears to show that they're relaxed in each other's company, whilst remaining professional. As for how they might be feeling, I would say that the twins are likely to be feeling a bit frustrated whereas the police are undoubtedly relaxed on the surface but are still probably on the alert for any problem occurring that might require them to step in.

2.12 (Writing Part 2)

A: Sequels? Me? I'm really in two minds about them. In my experience, if you've got a really favourite film and they bring out a sequel, it never, ever lives up to expectations. And that's usually because you're expecting something impossible. We want to get the same reaction as we did with the original, but sadly, that can't happen. Some sequels try but end up being just a weak version of what made the first so good. But that doesn't stop me, personally, from hoping each time that I'll be proved wrong.

B: I love sequels – because the original film introduces the characters and the storylines and then the next film develops it. You get to see what happens to the characters down the line. No one wants a good film to end, and having sequels means that it doesn't! Admittedly, sometimes if it develops into a series it just goes on and on, there are going to be spin-offs and the quality sometimes gets diluted – but in my view, they're still fun to watch!

2.1GF

See Ex 5 on page 101.

2.1VF

1   For me, the film was ridiculous. The plot was so …

2   Scientists have discovered a new way to treat colds and flu. Apparently, it's a real …

3   The new book I'm reading is excellent. I was so … in it that I forgot the time and missed my train.

4   My brother's … to sneezing a lot at this time of year.

5   Using the company car was the main … at my last job.

6   Although he didn't eventually win the award, Morgan was delighted to have been …

7   What the novelist said just doesn't make sense to me. Starting a book by writing the ending first just seems …

8   The new one-way system for traffic through the town centre simply isn't working. People have had doubts about it from the …

2.2VF

See Ex 6 on page 117.

Unit 3

3.1 and 3.2 (Opener)

A: You know how we had to research a useful app for our technology project?

B: Yeah – have you found something to write about?

A: Yep – the what3words app.

B: Oh. Isn't that just for use in an emergency? Don't we need to choose something with more functions?

A: Oh, it's got more. As you say, it's useful for, like, if you're out for a walk on a mountain somewhere and you fall and hurt your leg and need someone to come and assist you.

B: Right, so you use the app to provide your exact location to the rescue team. But how?

A: Well, every three-by-three-metre-square area in the world has a unique combination of three words that refer to it. You consult the app, tell the rescuers and they can get you out of wherever you are really quickly.

B: But you said that isn't all the app does.

A: Well, even if it was, about a hundred and seventy countries use it this way! Anyway, it's used by the United Nations, too, to deliver emergency aid, as well as for postal services in some countries – I think Mongolia was one. More and more companies and countries are adopting the app. Incredible, really – it's such a simple idea, yet so useful.

B: Cool! I wonder how it all came about, then? The app, I mean.

A: Well, I looked it up, and it was something to do with this guy who worked in the music industry and travelled all over the world – he spent loads of time trying to locate places and turning up at the wrong place, so he and his mate sat down and came up with the idea. So, it all stemmed from one guy repeatedly getting lost! Apparently, he once even did a sound check at the wrong wedding! Stuff like that can really set you back in terms of reputation.

B: Oh, that's hilarious! A lot of work must've gone into it, though. Impressive.

A: It is, and it's compatible with navigation apps as well. So, you can put in the three-word location, then use Google Maps, for example, to take you there.

B: Cool.

A: Yeah – and then businesses don't have to mess about with giving directions to suppliers or customers all the time. Like, 'Take the track between the library and the town hall and it's the yellow door partly hidden by a bush opposite the warehouse etcetera, etcetera. I read that there are vehicles which already incorporate the technology. You get in, say 'blah, blah, blah' and are navigated straight to that yellow door.

B: Brilliant. Hey, maybe they'll extend what3words to the universe if space tourism ever becomes a reality!

A: You never know. It'll be fascinating to see what future applications it might have. I think eventually we might do away with stuff like road maps altogether.

3.3 (Reading and Use of English Part 7)

Good morning everyone. It's good to see you've all come armed with notebooks, cups of coffee and – I hope – a lot of questions for me! As your schedules indicate, today's talk is about preparing to give effective presentations and we'll be looking at types of research, structuring your talk and the most effective ways of delivery. To start with, research – remember that whatever you find online needs to be checked, checked and checked again! You can't rely on one source. There are many ways to do this – there's reverse tracing of photographs or other visuals, checking out other reports containing similar information and also looking at the website itself and its history. And remember, …

3.4 and 3.5 (Reading and Use of English Part 1)

Had you asked people half a century ago what was visible from space, they'd undoubtedly have said with confidence, 'the Great Wall of China'. The idea that this is the only man-made structure you can see on Earth from space has been disproven time and again by astronauts, who confirm that it is exceptionally difficult to make it out with the naked eye, even from a low orbit. What's more, you definitely can't see it from as far away as the Moon.

So, what can astronauts see from space? Some of what I'm about to tell you may come as a surprise! As far as man-made structures are concerned, the Pyramids of Giza in Egypt, which are highly symmetrical, are easily identifiable, but the most distinctive features, say astronauts, are long roads and bridges, which dissect the landscape in straight lines. And when night falls on the third rock from the sun, cities light up and become astonishingly evident.

What about geographical features? The Great Barrier Reef in Australia, the delta of the Indian River Ganges, the Grand Canyon and the Himalayas are not only remarkably beautiful on Earth but also when seen from space, too. It's relatively unsurprising that such impressive aspects of the natural landscape would be visible, I guess, but would you expect to see humans? The likely response is 'No', and the accurate response is, 'Not individuals'. But very large congregations of people,

numbering millions, such as those which gather for the Kumbh Mela festival in various sites around India, have been picked up in images from space. Other visible signs of life include massive herds of migrating cattle, shifting across the landscape in black clouds.

And as we deepen our understanding of the planet we call home, and analyse photos taken by satellites, we now know that the gorgeous patterns in our oceans are phytoplankton blooms, the sandy-coloured swirls across the land are dust storms, and those huge smoking plumes reaching up into the sky are volcanic eruptions. We can even identify the changing seasons, with huge snow-covered patches and vast swathes of scorched earth.

For everything we can see, there are a million things we can't. It isn't that they're necessarily too small, but what complicates matters are the atmospheric conditions, height of orbit and how powerful the imaging technology is. And there are some unsolved mysteries out there regarding other planets and what we can see of them from Earth. But as we accumulate knowledge on these planets, perhaps we'll eventually be able to recognise all kinds of shapes and shadows even further afield.

3.6 (Listening Part 3)

Presenter: Psychology professor Michael Miller is with me on the programme today to have a chat about the concept of the 'third place'. For those unfamiliar with the term – what does it mean?

Michael: The third place is somewhere you regularly spend time that isn't work or home. You hang out and catch up with the people there.

Presenter: OK, so, I often go to a particular café during my lunch break – is that my third place?

Michael: It's the perfect example! And let me ask you, why that café, and not another?

Presenter: Well, they do excellent cheese toasties and coffees, for one thing! And I've struck up a kind of friendship with the owner now. We're both interested in motor racing, so we often have a chat about the latest races, and I sometimes get talking to other regulars. I actually feel like I know some of them quite well now, though I don't see them outside the café socially.

Michael: Great, so what you're actually doing by visiting the café is all about getting some social contact. You could probably just make your own cheese toastie, maybe even a better one!

Presenter: Right, that's interesting. It was actually the first café I went to after I moved here. And I almost didn't go in at first, cos I could see what appeared to be an established group of friends hanging out, laughing and chatting. It was a bit intimidating but I so wanted to be part of it. Maybe you're onto something!

Michael: You wanted to belong. Most likely you hadn't established firm connections yet if you'd only just moved to the area.

Presenter: Apart from a couple of good friends, not really. Anyway, I soon discovered that the people in the café weren't a bunch of mates but individuals who just call in on a regular basis. It's a dynamic group, too – new people arrive, others leave … I could be there three weeks in a row or not go for a while and the warm welcome's exactly the same when I turn up again.

Michael: Well, that's the very definition of a third place!

Presenter: So, Michael, do you think that the idea of the third place will …

3.7 (Listening Part 3)
Extract 1

A: I used to go to this local meetup where I'd chat about philosophy and stuff but it's been cancelled. I really enjoyed it as well. It's like people have moved on and I'm left with a hole I'm not sure how to fill.

B: It can be tough, change. I'm not saying you won't adapt but …

A: I know!

Extract 2

A: You know, I've actually been looking for something new to do, somewhere to go. I need a deeper connection with this place we live in. Something beyond my apartment, the factory where I work and all these massive skyscrapers I walk amongst on my way to and fro!

B: Something that gives meaning to the concrete jungle… I get it. They have members' events at the museum every week – you love museums, how about that?

Extract 3

A: Didn't you just say you walk around a lot? Maybe the city itself is your third place!

B: The streets? Well, there is a sense of belonging – I'm from here, after all … It's a fascinating idea, what you just said. I'll give it some thought. I do get into conversations with people when I'm out and about … I'm not entirely satisfied it could be called my third place, though.

3.1EB (Listening Part 3 – Exam boost)

See Ex 1 on page 32.

AUDIOSCRIPTS

🎧 **3.8 (Listening Part 3)**

Presenter: Today I'm with Julia Bernardi and Adam Spright to discuss the concept of the third place. Professor Oldenburg, the sociologist who first wrote about the idea, said that third places have common characteristics. Adam?

Adam: The third place, wherever it is – your book club, coffee shop, wherever – is unprejudiced. Everyone there is on the same level and social status is irrelevant. You can come and go without anyone taking exception to that. If you don't turn up for a few weeks, it's no big deal – when you return, you'll be greeted warmly. That's key to their success. And that's a stark contrast with work or home – imagine not turning up to work for a few days. Your unexplained absence would be a grave cause for concern, if not, get you fired! Similarly, your homelife might suffer if you went AWOL for a while.

Presenter: What does Oldenburg say are the most common third places and why? Julia?

Julia: Let me just set one thing straight. Many assume third places are the physical places themselves. On the contrary, it's their social aspect which matters. Generally, we consider the third place to be anywhere people gather that isn't the workplace or home – coffee shops, community centres, other places where people meet on a regular basis. You might pop in on your way past, or plan your visit in advance. The emphasis is on conversation, so, the gym, say, where you're working out hard and probably couldn't string a sentence together, doesn't meet the criteria. However, enjoying a coffee or energy drink in the leisure centre café with others after your workout, probably would.

Presenter: What do you both think is the most important function of third places?

Julia: One I find interesting is Oldenburg's concept of social capital – to put it simply, people from different backgrounds who get to know each other develop trust, which enables society to function effectively. There are economic advantages, too – money's generated in third places and you may gain personally by finding out about an employment opportunity, for example.

Adam: When we're at work or at home, we're in contact with people similar to us, whereas in the third place, we're more likely to encounter people from different walks of life. That's the perfect learning opportunity in terms of cultural awareness and sensitivity to people from different social groups.

Presenter: Some workplaces have embraced Oldenburg's concept. Julia, Adam, how does the third place work – at work?!

Julia: Companies, particularly ones occupying sizeable premises, are incorporating spaces where employees can take time out, chat in a relaxed environment away from their desks – for example, a separate café in the building. It's a far cry from the outdated belief that staff are more productive the longer they're at their desk. I must admit though, I'm unconvinced that a place within the work building offers the same freedoms as those elsewhere.

Adam: We now know it's nonsense that people should be at their desks in order to be productive. Flexibility creates innovation, talking's what allows companies to come up with the next big thing. Personally, I think you need to get away from the office altogether. Third places in the public domain are better for the individual's development.

Presenter: What about social media – is that a third place? Adam?

Adam: Oldenburg would insist that face-to-face interaction's what constitutes a third place. Virtual spaces don't meet this criterion. The word 'virtual' seems far from the essence of Oldenburg's concept. You can establish a rapport with someone online – I'd hesitate to call that a real relationship in the sense that you gain a deep understanding of someone in person, though. The screen creates a physical barrier, which doesn't exist at actual third places in the real world. That's not to devalue the people we meet in virtual spaces, and the opportunity to establish friendships worldwide is fantastic. Some argue there are similarities in terms of characteristics like interaction and approachability, which are crucial elements of the third place. That isn't enough in my opinion.

Presenter: Finally, some philosophers have argued there's a fourth place. Julia, Adam, what do you think about that?

Julia: My understanding of this is that elements of each place – first, second and third – combine in different ways, and they're no longer as separate as they once were. Many people round the world, though they're in a minority, live and work in the same place, and there are third places within second places – remember the chill-out spaces at work? Where elements of all three places combine, some philosophers call it a fourth place. I'm so far unconvinced about this but I might be persuaded, given time.

Adam: This hypothesis is in its early days and I've yet to come round to the idea. There might be something in it – I'll be looking into it. I get where the thinker who came up with the concept's coming from, but it does need further development.

🎧 **3.9 (Reading and Use of English Part 2)**

The Brontë family, who lived in the early to mid-1800s in England, consisted of six siblings, three of whom – the famous sisters Charlotte, Emily and Anne – remain some of the country's most celebrated authors. They each started writing stories at home at a young age, and all three went on to become published novelists, with varying degrees of professional success. While the eldest sister, Charlotte, wrote four novels, and had started a fifth before she died, only three were published during her lifetime. Anne wrote two novels, but Emily published only one. Not only did the sisters write books now considered classics, but they were also held in high regard for their poetry.

Today, I'd like to compare two of the sisters' most famous and widely read novels: *Jane Eyre* and *Wuthering Heights*, by Charlotte and Emily, respectively. Both are essentially love stories, but many believe *Jane Eyre* to have a more plausible storyline, whereas *Wuthering Heights* has a much more daring plot.

Jane Eyre – the main character in the book of the same name – is an isolated young girl at the beginning of the novel but gradually becomes a strong and intellectually capable young woman during the story. By the end of the book, she is powerful, independent and happily married to Rochester, the man she loves. Since she's an admirable and straightforward character, readers cannot help but identify with her. Cathy, the protagonist in *Wuthering Heights*, is an altogether different character. Although she is loyal and determined, she is also wild and has a stubborn streak which makes her more difficult to warm to.

Whatever your preference for the characters of Jane or Cathy, you'll certainly find plenty of people who agree with you. But readers tend to be split on the subject: either they're touched by Jane Eyre's honesty, dignity and triumph over adversity, or they prefer Cathy's darker, more passionate and complicated character. However, when it comes to the structure and style of the writing, many critics concur that *Jane Eyre* is the superior novel.

Why is this? Well, for much of *Jane Eyre*, it's as though the character is talking to her audience, and on occasion she does indeed directly address the reader. Charlotte draws on everyday experiences everyone can relate to. What's more, she'd already written one novel before *Jane Eyre*, and had an understanding of how to develop a storyline successfully. Emily's novel is considered a little disorganised in terms of structure and story-telling. Even so, Emily Brontë is upheld as an ambitious and brave writer, and indeed, both Charlotte and Emily are now celebrated as feminist writers.

Personally, I love both novels and as yet, have found it impossible to say which I prefer because, although they are so different in style, they are equally compelling. And both books must have been highly thought of throughout their history or they wouldn't have endured as favourites in the field of literature.

Before I finish, just a word about the youngest sibling, Anne Brontë, and her writing endeavours …

🎧 3.10 and 3.11 (Speaking Part 3)

A: OK, so for a successful launch like that the whole team would have had to really pull together, wouldn't they?

B: I couldn't agree more. Good teamwork is fundamental. There's no room for individual egos at all.

A: That's a great way of putting it! Although each team member has their own role and uses their own talents, it all has to come together in the end and that's where the real teamwork comes in, don't you think?

B: That's true, but don't you think the team members have to support each other all the way through a project like that, working together, not just in the final stages?

A: You've got a point, but I'd say that it's more a case of knowing the strengths of the individual team members and using them to everyone's advantage to contribute to the end result.

B: You're right, but I think you need to run ideas past people to get constant feedback and keep people in the loop as to how you're doing. Anyway, moving on, in addition to teamwork – another important factor in my view is motivation, don't you agree?

A: Absolutely! And that comes from the work environment, doesn't it? I mean, how your work is valued and appreciated by the management and what incentives there are.

B: That's it in a nutshell. If your work is undervalued, you won't go the extra mile for the company.

A: Although, having said that, in my experience, if you feel passionate about something, that can be motivation in itself, what others think doesn't necessarily make much difference.

B: I don't entirely agree with you there. I'd say that without encouragement, your passion may subside a little!

A: Oh – very nicely put! And an incentive like a bonus usually focuses people well …

🎧 3.12 (Writing Part 2)

Presenter: … and now Rob will answer some questions from listeners. Yes – hi there – what's your question?

Caller: Hi – my uncle is taking part in an Ironman challenge and what he tells us about the triathlon is fascinating. Firstly, I didn't realise the word came from Greek – even though, obviously, it wasn't an actual event at the original Olympic Games! But he was talking about the calories you can use up – Is it true that you can burn up to 10,000?

Rob: Well – Ironman is really tough, and well done your uncle for attempting it! But yes, generally speaking 10,000 is about right.

Caller: He's not doing the annual championships in Hawaii. He says it's pretty hard to qualify for that, and to be honest, he's not that young – although he is fit.

Rob: OK! Well, the oldest person to finish an Ironman challenge was eighty-five – and I'm guessing your uncle isn't that old yet!

Caller: Well, there's a chance for him then! I also wanted to ask you about going into triathlons myself. Is it hard for a beginner?

Rob: It's a great event – really. Obviously, it's an endurance race but since the first official triathlon was held in 1974, many different events with different distances have been open to competitors. As long as you can swim, cycle and run, you can enter. Swimming is possibly the most worrying for beginners because it's usually in open water and you have to jostle other people, deal with the waves and head in the right direction! So, getting some swimming training is vital. Then, transitioning to the bike takes practice. The final element – the run – can really test your stamina – but train hard and you can get there!

Caller: Thanks!

🎧 3.1GF

See Ex 5 on page 103.

🎧 3.1VF

1 I'll let you know what's going on with our travel arrangements as and when I get any news.

2 The election results were so nail-bitingly close that I couldn't tear my eyes away from the TV.

3 Hang on a minute! You said that you didn't want the promotion but you've accepted it? What changed your mind?

4 Travelling on your own means you get to meet a range of people from all nationalities and all kinds of backgrounds.

5 Matt was so nervous he kept falling over his words and pausing. It was difficult to understand what he was trying to say.

🎧 3.2VF

See Ex 7 on page 119.

Unit 4

🎧 4.1 and 4.2 (Opener)

Presenter: OK, so it's four o'clock. It seems an eternity since lunch time and your stomach is rumbling away – what do you do to stave off the hunger pangs until dinner time? In my case, it's reach for a packet of biscuits – with of course a mug of tea to wash them down. It's a habit I've been indulging in since my teens and apparently the Duchess of Bedford felt exactly the same way in the mid-19th century! Our British custom of afternoon tea dates back to 1840 when the lady in question asked for a plate of bread and butter, a pot of tea and some cake to tide her over until dinner. Afternoon tea became fashionable and has been part of our food culture ever since. These days you need to go to an upmarket hotel or tea room to get the full treatment – scones with jam and cream, small cakes and dainty sandwiches – often with cucumber – tea in china cups, and the experience will probably set you back rather a lot of money! It got me thinking. We assume that our daily food intake revolves around three meals a day – breakfast, lunch and dinner, in some shape or form – but in fact, if you look round the world, many countries or cultures actually favour four rather than three. So, earlier I asked listeners to phone in with their experiences of unusual mealtimes in countries they've visited and I have some callers on the line. Hi – is that Sara?

Sara: Yes, hi! We definitely need an extra meal – and when I went to France last year to stay with my French friend's family, I realised that the French also have an afternoon snack – in style! The family I stayed with observe the tradition of le goûter. Because the French tend to eat later than we do – more like 8 p.m. – everyone needs something mid-afternoon, having worked up an appetite during the day. It's expected that children after school will have le goûter, which can be quite substantial – and unlike our afternoon tea, in France it's usually sweet – cream cakes, pancakes, chocolate (the kids in my family actually had a baguette with a chocolate bar inside!) And it can be quite a social occasion for the parents, too. They invite people round and you're more or less expected to bring some homemade cakes and pastries.

Presenter: Ooh, baguette and chocolate – my mouth is watering! Gosh and yes, I remember now, my French friend used to ply me with slices of bread with thick butter and cocoa powder on it! Very decadent! Thanks, Sara – now, do we have Jason?

Jason: Hi there – my favourite fourth meal has got to be the Polish second breakfast! I was working in Poland and when I was offered a plate of sandwiches mid-morning, I passed on it, thinking that it would ruin my appetite for lunch. Big mistake – lunch didn't happen until mid-afternoon! I've heard since that in other parts of Europe, like Bavaria and Hungary, they have the same thing, and on occasions this can be quite big – like sausages and things.

Presenter: What a great idea. Sausages for elevenses. Nice one! Hope my boss is listening. Cathy – hi there. You studied in the USA, didn't you?

Cathy: I did and they have a great tradition during college finals week. It's something called a Midnight breakfast! The college kids stay up so late studying that a lot of colleges actually officially lay on a meal in the dining room called Midnight breakfast, to keep them going.

Presenter: That's such good thinking! I just remember lots and lots of black coffee and occasionally we'd rustle up something simple to keep our brains working! So, Cathy, what do they actually …

4.3 (Reading and Use of English Part 8)

If you live in the middle latitudes – that is north or south of the tropics – like Europe and most of North America – you'll be used to experiencing four distinct seasons during the year – spring, summer, autumn and winter, whereas the tropics, and the extreme northern and southern latitudes basically just get two; in the tropics – hot and dry and hot and rainy. In the far north or south – a long, cold, dark winter season and a short, light, warmer summer one. At least that's what has, more or less, been

the case, until more recently. And we may not realise it, but so much depends on the seasons for us – when we plant and harvest crops being just one of them. It's not just humans that are affected by the seasons – animals, plants, insects, the whole delicate balance maintained in nature is controlled by the seasons and any changes can have far-reaching consequences. What has been evident to scientists for many decades is now becoming clear to us all. The seasons are changing. According to some statistics in the middle latitudes, summers are on average 13 days longer, and winters 20 days shorter than they used to be, and some experts are now talking in terms of two main seasons, rather than four, with transitional months in April and October. The reason is pretty obvious – climate change. Just a couple of degrees' warmer weather affects the whole planet and the seasons no longer follow expected patterns. And climate change? Well, it's down to us – humans have really messed up, and the changing seasons are one very clear way the planet has of telling us.

4.4 and 4.5 (Reading and Use of English Part 3)

So, we were tasked with the project of researching a symbol of luck in our own culture to tell the class about, and I've looked into the history and significance of the four-leaved clover.

What is a clover, first of all? Well, it's a small plant, which produces leaves with three distinctive 'lobes' – three connected parts which look like single leaves in themselves. Very occasionally the plant produces leaves with four lobes, and the discovery of one like this is considered very lucky. In fact, you'd be remarkably fortunate to even come across one, as the probability of that happening is one in ten thousand!

So, how did this tiny plant become such a symbol of good fortune? Well, even as far back as the Ancient Egyptians, people were offering them to newlyweds to bless the marriage and wish the couple a life of happiness and prosperity. That was around five thousand years ago, but other early cultures also believed in the power of the four-leaved clover to repel bad luck. Some of our early ancestors believed the four-leaved clover to have healing powers, and used them in medicine.

What about today? Well, some say that the four leaves represent faith, love, hope and, of course, luck. Some say that four-leaved clovers help you find true love, and put clovers in their shoes to carry them to their soulmate!

So, let's say you're hunting amongst the grass for a four-leaved clover. Should you be lucky enough to find one, what ought you to do with it? This is dependent on which tradition you choose to adhere to: some say that in order to benefit from the luck, you should keep your four-leaved clover hidden, whereas others dictate that you ought to pass it on to someone else, so that your luck will double, and they'll receive some, too!

It's probable that because four-leaved clovers are not commonly seen in nature that the beliefs around them have perpetuated. The rarer something is, the more special it becomes, however far from rational any belief surrounding that may seem. But whether you profess to believe in the existence of luck or not, I suspect it would take a strong-minded person not to hang onto a four-leaved clover if it came their way – I'd certainly be thankful if someone gave one to me!

4.6 and 4.7 (Listening Part 4)

A: Would you say you had a good sense of direction?

B: You have actually experienced my driving, haven't you?! North, south, east, west – I haven't got a clue which of the four compass points I'm heading towards! I'm the sort of person who doesn't even realise they've walked in a circle and ended up in the place they started at ten minutes ago. I don't know whether it's poor observation skills, getting distracted, or what. Actually, you probably think I'm joking but it can be really frustrating when I'm driving from one side of the city to the other and have no idea how to get there, no matter how many times I might've done it before.

A: Well, apparently there's some science behind it. Having a good or bad sense of direction, I mean. Some people can go somewhere once and no matter how complicated the route, they'll remember it next time they go – weeks, months or even years later. I read about it in this article – that's why I asked you – and it mentioned poor observation skills, too. You're obviously not taking note of clues in your environment or retaining them. That's why you can do the same journey repeatedly and still not remember how you did it last time. You're dismissing the visual evidence.

B: That actually reminds me of a programme that was on not long ago about cultures that navigate without technology or maps. They have a better sense of direction than cultures that do rely on those. So, they use nature - sea currents, stars - to understand where they're heading.

A: Right. Probably cos they've been doing it since they were really young, whereas many of us haven't. And the lack of distracting technology could mean they're more in tune with their surroundings.

B: So, I should pay more attention to my surroundings, then. But it's not as if I go round with my eyes shut!

A: Well, you're clearly not a walking compass, but I think it's something to do with the brain, too.

4.8 (Listening Part 4)

Apparently, people's sense of direction is affected by something that happens in the frontal and temporal lobes – the ones responsible for things like memory and vision. The larger they are, the better awareness of direction you're likely to have. And also, some people need more environmental cues to help them determine which direction they're facing – so I guess if they're in a field, they need more trees or a house on the horizon or something? The article didn't elaborate on that. But it did confirm that there are links with personality. More open-minded people or those who are more attentive will be better at finding their way. Oh, and they also said that if you believe you've got a good or bad sense of direction, you're probably right cos we've got good insight into that!

4.1EB (Listening Part 4 – Exam boost)

1 I live in the Arctic Circle, in a village almost as far north as it's possible to live. The extreme cold means agriculture is virtually impossible, so everything has to be bought in, leading to hiked prices. You don't see much of the sun during winter months and, of course, much of life happens indoors at this time due to the harsh conditions. Having said that, the incredible phenomenon of the Northern Lights flickering colourfully in the night sky really is awesome, and if you love snow sports, then you can't get much better than this.

2 I'm from the far south of my country, a region which isn't particularly well-off. There's a lot of unemployment, too, which unfairly seems to suggest to the rest of our country that we're lazy. Well, there are stereotypes in every country, aren't there, for people who live in different areas? So, I refuse to pay too much attention to comments about that. I wouldn't change where I live for the world, though. I know everyone, and everyone helps each other out. You don't get that kind of thing happening as much in big cities.

3 The eastern region I live in has some spectacular scenery, and the people are some of the friendliest you'll meet. This means it makes it onto many a tourist to-do list, to be ticked off. Though I appreciate that you shouldn't think of a place as 'yours' and resent those who come, the yearly influx does have an impact on resources. It's driven prices up, too, in restaurants, for example. But I completely understand what draws people here, and the upside is getting to meet people from all over the country.

4 We're a kind of forgotten area, here in the west of the country. It isn't that people don't want to see the stunning landscapes, but it takes a day and a half from the nearest city to reach us. You could hardly say tourism's had a negative impact on the environment, that's for sure! It can feel isolated, so many young people tend to leave as soon as they're old enough. Not me. I can't think of anything better than sitting on top of a mountain watching the sun set over the pristine countryside. And this area has the highest density of rare species, too, largely due to the unspoiled habitats.

4.9 (Listening Part 4)

1 As a delivery driver, finding addresses isn't straightforward. Taxi drivers where I'm from have to complete a test proving they know the city like the back of their hand before they get a licence. It must save time in the long run. Other drivers waste time trying to get to places – the GPS signal always drops out when you need it! Timing can be crucial with deliveries – the fear of missing deadlines used to keep me awake at night. After getting lost down one backstreet too many, I decided to do something about it. Requesting the specifics of where I'm going in advance ensures I don't revisit those backstreets! I haven't had a sleepless night since.

2 I've never been one for following sat-navs. I'd rather work things out for myself, even though that's got me into difficulties. Like, I went to work abroad one year but hadn't bothered to look up a map of the city. Wandering around trying to locate my accommodation, I had a flashback – I'd spent my childhood somewhere with similar architecture – that brought a sense of nostalgia – I'd loved it there. Anyway, that didn't help me find my flat, but when I eventually turned up there, I resolved to take note of distinctive buildings and forks in the road so I didn't have to take an hour to do a five-minute journey from the bus stop!

3 I set off to a friend's party not long ago, driving. Being a non-driver, she hadn't thought to explain the complicated one-way system there was in the area, so the directions she gave me were useless. I hate going anywhere new alone and after I'd driven round the same block four times, I knew I'd just have to swallow my pride and approach someone for help – something I never fail to do now cos it avoids the frustration. Anyway, the person I got talking to was actually a friend of the person I was trying to locate, heading the same way. So, I gave her a lift and we've now become good mates.

4 People say I shouldn't go off hill-walking on my own but I know the hills back to front. So, I've no idea what happened one day when I realised I'd somehow wandered off the beaten track. There didn't seem any point worrying about it so I just carried on until I found something I knew – an ancient pine, its branches twisted from the wind. My lengthy walk gave me a bit of space to think and I came up with a solution to a work problem that had been bugging me – very helpful! I know where I went wrong on my walk now, and look out for particular landmarks that point me in the right direction.

5 I got lost inside a building! I was staying with a friend abroad when she was taken ill and I went to see her in hospital. I felt proud of myself getting there in the first place – I'd looked it up online and caught the right bus. Anyway, I grabbed a plan of the hospital from reception and headed to my friend's ward. There was a passage that seemed to cut out a lot of walking, so I followed that. It's a mistake I've never made again because I ended up completely disorientated, in a staff-only area. At least my newly acquired Spanish got a workout as I explained what'd happened to a confused-looking nurse!

4.10 (Reading and Use of English Part 4)

The fourth dimension, or 4-D as it is commonly known, is an area of physics which relates to adding a fourth spatial dimension to the three dimensions of length, breadth and depth. Let me explain. A dimension is just a direction in which you can go. The first dimension can be considered as a single point – think of a line on a page. Now imagine drawing a circle or a square on that piece of paper. The square has length, width and area, but not depth. You can't pick it up, or turn it round to see the other side. That square is

2-D. The paper itself is also 2-D – you can only go along it's X- or Y-axes – in other words, you can only travel in two directions on it.

I'm sure you'll be very familiar with the concept of 3-D. Real life is in 3-D. Virtually all the objects around us are 3-D – they have length, breadth and depth. They have height and volume. You can move them – or move around them – and view them from different angles – that's the chair you're sitting on, the apple you ate for lunch, your mobile phone. A square made three dimensional becomes a cube. To sum up quickly, then: 1-D is length; 2-D is length and breadth; and 3-D is length, breadth and depth.

So, now we've got that clear, let's think about what 4-D means. To do this, we can talk about what's known as a tesseract – or a 4-D cube. That is, a cube in four-dimensional space. It's a 4-D shape where every surface is a cube. Now, a tesseract doesn't exist in real life – it's a geometrical concept. But this is how it works: Take a 3-D cube and replace each face – which is a square – with a cube. That's a tesseract! Imagine what a cube looks like if you flatten it. It has six squares and if you fold the squares together, they make a cube. With a tesseract, we're folding cubes, rather than squares, into 3-D space. It's difficult to visualise because we can only see things in 3-D. You can't see a tesseract. We can't visualise the fourth dimension in space or make sense of it easily – but the concept exists and has been proven by mathematicians!

4.11 (Speaking Part 4)

Kate does a lot of challenges for different charities but this time she wanted to raise awareness of the smaller charities that do a lot of brilliant work, but which are often overlooked because people lead such busy lives these days. To that end, she challenged herself to complete the busiest day of her life – she set herself the task of doing twenty-four jobs in twenty-four hours! Can you believe it? And these weren't just your everyday type of tasks – she did a whole range of different jobs including cleaning out the shark tank at the Sea Life London Aquarium and warming up the studio audience for a TV show. She appeared onstage in a London musical and worked as a sous-chef in a restaurant. Other things she tackled were window cleaning, train platform announcing, shoe shining, being a receptionist and trying her hand as a barista. She must have been totally exhausted. Well done, Kate – I don't think many of us have got the guts or stamina to take on a challenge like that!

4.12 (Speaking Part 4)

Examiner: Some people say that we focus too much on getting a good study or work-life balance these days. What's your opinion?

A: Well, I personally don't agree, but I can't speak for everyone, obviously.

B: Yes, I see where they're coming from. It does seem to have become a bit of a thing. Everyone seems to be expected to get balance in their lives. You've only got to look at lifestyle websites and it's all about tips for this and that to make every twenty-four hours better! But speaking from experience, I have to say that I really love what I'm studying and I'm happy to spend a lot of time on it. For instance, I once spent about fifteen hours working on a project in my own time because I was so involved! I didn't feel my work-life balance had been compromised in any way!

C: Yes, we're always hearing about that these days. They say we need to strike a good balance between time we spend working or studying and our leisure time. They also say that because we are always available – due to having phones and being online – that we can't switch off.

4.2EB and 4.3EB (Speaking Part 4 – Exam boost)

It's an interesting question and I have to say that there's no one answer really. What makes a true friendship isn't always easy to identify. If you look at people around you, you'll find that some friends are very close but they have completely different characters and interests, and you wonder how on earth they became friends in the first place! I guess being different and doing different things gives people more to talk about, perhaps? However, for me personally, it's good to have things in common. My best friend and I are really similar. We like the same music, the same fashion, food … In fact, we are SO similar that the kids at school used to call us 'the twins'! But then, there's another couple of friends I see around sometimes, who are very, very different. One guy loves technology and is really into games whereas his friend is always out on the football pitch or training for marathons! Takes all sorts, I think.

4.4EB (Speaking Part 4 – Exam boost)

I would say that it really doesn't matter. A lot depends on what brought you together as friends initially. A case in point would be when you start a new school. You're feeling a bit lonely and scared, vulnerable too perhaps. And if someone befriends you and helps you settle in, there's a chance that they could go on to become a close friend. Look back, there was a time when I …

4.13 and 4.14 (Writing Part 2)

The USA certainly know how to celebrate in style! Our New Year's Eve fireworks set the bar pretty high, but fireworks in the USA are really something else. Last month I was staying over in Nashville, Tennessee, with some family friends and the day before I flew back was 4th July – Independence Day. Quite amazing! The celebrations finished with a gigantic fireworks' display along the river, which I've never seen the like of before. Apparently, it was even better than the New York display, which is saying something. In fact, the whole day was a load of fun. The family I was staying with did what a lot of Americans do – went out of town to have a picnic. The kids all dressed up in red, white and blue clothes and played exhausting games. Then we went into the city where there were flags, balloons everywhere and, being Nashville, of course there was live music every corner we turned. But the fireworks were just incredible – and what was so impressive was that they linked up with a live performance by the Nashville Symphony Orchestra. Wow again! I have to say I was so shattered that I spent the flight home the following day dead to the world.

4.1GF

See Ex 4 on page 105.

4.1VF

1   This decision is going to have consequences that we shall continue to be affected by long into the future.

2   When I'm talking on the phone I often doodle on a notepad and draw a whole range of weird triangles and squares.

3   My sister's teacher told our parents that she always listened really carefully to what was being taught. They were very impressed!

4   The committee made a ridiculous decision which I can see no reason for whatsoever.

5   The radio presenter speaks very deeply and I would know his voice anywhere.

6   Some operations seem very simple, but in fact it takes a long time for the body to recover.

7   Although some people are reluctant to believe it, the evidence for climate change is very strong indeed.

8   Using public transport instead of individual cars is a very good option for commuters in this city.

4.2VF

See Ex 6 on page 121.

Unit 5

5.1 and 5.2 (Opener)

Whether we think we do it or not, we all talk with our hands. Some people do it more than others – those who are in the public eye, such as politicians, gesture a lot when they're making a point – and they might be described as someone who waves their arms around a lot! But everyone uses their hands to some degree when they're talking.

So, why do we do this? Well, science shows that using gestures helps us to think more clearly and speak more expressively. Gestures also help listeners understand what we're talking about, such as drawing the shape of something in the air as you describe it. However, it isn't something we always do consciously: the part of the brain that controls speech is also active when we gesture, suggesting that they're linked.

Gesturing is something we learn to do at an early age, and psychologists say that the younger we are when we start to interpret and use gestures, the better we'll be at expressing ourselves as adults. As a rule of thumb, the more gestures an adult uses, the more communicative, agreeable and lively they're considered to be.

Hand gesturing tells people how we're feeling, too. You might raise your arms when cheering or even when you're furious! The more animated the gestures are, the more passionate or angry or excited we know the speaker is. Again, this may not be something we do knowingly – our body is simply responding to our emotions. So, if you want to know how someone really feels, observe their body language closely because speech and gesture go hand in hand to help us make our point.

Gesture adds to what we say, rather than representing the words in a straightforward way. A hand signal, such as raising your palm or a finger, may indicate to listeners that they should pay careful attention to what the speaker's saying right now, or even show they aren't sure what they're talking about! And when what someone says isn't matched by what they do, we consider them less trustworthy!

Another interesting observation we can make about gestures is …

5.3 (Reading and Use of English Part 5)

Paris is a wonderful city, but the first time I visited I got really confused by the way the districts are numbered! They're called arrondissements and they've all got a number, but somehow it just didn't feel logical! You might be at the Eiffel Tower, which is in the 7th arrondissement, walk south a few hundred metres and find yourself in the 15th! Why? There is actually a logic to it. As we all know, the French are famous for eating 'escargots' (snails to you and me) but the snail is also important when trying to get your head around the arrondissements. You see, the numbers curl out in a spiral – just like a snail shell. So, they start with the First, right in the centre – The Louvre etcetera and then 2nd, 3rd and 4th move east along the right bank of the River Seine. Then the numbers cross the Seine and work back on themselves. Interesting, isn't it? It's apparently all down to Napoleon (not Bonaparte but Napoleon III). In 1860, he redesigned the former districts so that there were twenty, in a spiral format. Each of these arrondissements is divided into quarters which are called 'quartier' – the most famous is probably the 'quartier Latin' or as we know it, the Latin Quarter – that very famous area on the left bank, which is part of the fifth arrondissement – home to students and artists, riverside stalls and a maze of narrow lanes where there are numerous multicultural student-priced restaurants and little shops …

5.4 and 5.5 (Reading and Use of English Part 1)

In the first modern Olympics, which took place in 1896, two hundred and forty-one participants competed in just nine different sports, including athletics, cycling, fencing, gymnastics, shooting, swimming, tennis, wrestling and weightlifting. Now, around thirty or so sports are usually lined up for inclusion in the Games each time, including all nine of the original sports and with the list extending to activities such as handball, karate and, for the first time, skateboarding.

Sports come and go at the Olympics, so how does the International Olympic Committee – or IOC – decide what will appear at each Games? They certainly can't rush into making a decision. Once an activity has been put forward by a sports organisation for consideration, the committee takes on the job of making sure it's recognised internationally as a sport. In order for this to be the case, the activity must already be overseen by an international, non-governmental organisation. If so, the sport moves to International Sports Federation status and must thereby comply with all rules drawn up in the Olympic Charter which specifies how the Games should be run.

Sometimes, a sport gains recognition from the IOC but doesn't get included at the Olympic Games – chess, for example. Why not? Well, an Olympic sport must be practised by men in over seventy-five countries on four continents and by women in at least forty countries on three continents. It should also be modern and have wide appeal. Surely chess falls into this category? Well, yes, it does. But another Olympic rule forbids sports which come under the heading of 'mind sports', so sports like chess can't be included.

What's more, the opportunity for a new sport to be admitted to the Games only comes up when the decision to drop something else is made. All sports are reviewed on occasion to decide whether or not they should be retained. Reasons why a sport may not make it to a particular Olympics include a lack of suitable venues in the host country, how interested the media and the public are in a sport in that country, and whether costs can be managed. It's also important that the sport fits in with the Games' values of excellence, respect and friendliness, and has a good image.

Some sports are dropped from the Olympics because they are deemed old-fashioned, such as rope pulling or tug-of-war, whereas others never make it onto the list because they are practised by so few people – a case in point would be Sumo wrestling, only practised at a professional level in Japan. Having said that, the IOC is keen to cater for young people in the sports it selects, so, although skateboarding and sport climbing may not generate a lot of cash or have been included at the Olympics before, their relevance as youth sports adds value to the Olympic Movement. Events that come off well will likely be included next time round.

5.6 (Listening Part 1)

Presenter: With me today is life coach Valentina Espinosa, who is interested in boosting productivity. Valentina, how does the working day differ around the world?

Valentina: Well, fairly widely, actually. The USA has long had a reputation for putting in the most hours, but newly gathered data suggests otherwise, with the average worker doing 34 hours a week, or six point eight hours a day. According to one source, it's people in Colombia and Turkey who work the longest days, each coming in at 48 hours a week, or just over nine and a half hours a day. The shortest working week is in the Netherlands, where workers do just twenty-nine hours weekly, a daily average of five point eight hours.

Presenter: Is there a difference between the kinds of jobs people do?

Valentina: Yes. Self-employed people and those running their own businesses work longest – often up to 50 hours a week or more. Eighty-four percent of the latter report having a mere one point five hours of highly productive time each day. And even if you officially work a 40-hour week, it doesn't mean you're productive for 40 hours a week.

Presenter: So, how can any of us be more productive?

Valentina: We all have natural peaks and troughs of energy throughout the day, so it stands to reason that there'll be times when we might well simply be sitting and staring into space. Our peak productivity times are precisely when we should be solving problems, making plans and being creative. Then, during our troughs, we can get the more mundane tasks done, the stuff we don't need to think too hard about.

During peak productivity periods – you'll know when you're naturally more alert – try to ensure there are as few interruptions as possible and avoid distractions. Working in blocks of ninety to a hundred and twenty minutes seems to work best for most people and fits in with natural rhythms.

Presenter: But you can't always avoid being interrupted. How do you deal with that?

Valentina: Well, of course, you don't have much control over what everyone else does: people will still call you, appear at your desk to ask a question, or call you into a meeting. There isn't much you can do about that other than avoiding wasting time looking at cats on the internet when you know you could be making progress with that report instead! The thing to bear in mind is that you're simply striving to be more productive during your higher energy periods, not aiming to increase your output in general.

Presenter: OK, thanks!

🎧 5.1EB (Listening Part 1 – Exam boost)

1 While we're on the subject of day-dreaming, you have to understand that when someone appears to be looking out of the window at work, they aren't necessarily watching shoppers in the street below or thinking about what they're going to cook for dinner, but are actually thinking deeply about what they're working on.

2 Although what you've just said goes against my initial instincts, I appreciate that the evidence you've provided in support of your argument does hold up.

3 Oh, I really am exasperated with this project. No matter which approach I take, it just isn't coming together in the way I'd hoped.

4 The greater your input, the greater your output. That's what they say, and there's little reason to dispute that. Basically, as long as you keep putting in the effort, no matter whether that's while you're completing a university assignment, practising a sport or preparing a presentation, the results will show that.

5 There's a widespread belief that in order to be good at something, you just have to work hard. If this were the case – and there really was no such thing as natural aptitude – then wouldn't we all be top musicians or business leaders? I think not.

🎧 5.2EB (Listening Part 1 – Exam boost)

1 So, what is productivity? Well, it's a measure of the efficiency of a person or machine, factory or system and so on. So, it converts inputs into outputs. It's calculated by dividing the average output per, say, quarter of the year, by the total costs incurred or resources used in that period.

2 Right, so what the chart appears to suggest is that there is little point in expecting workers to do overtime. If you look at the figures, we can see that productivity slows the later workers continue into the evening.

3 I feel I've already addressed the argument that the typical eight-hour work day – that stereotypical 'nine-to-five' pattern – does not, in fact, ensure that workers get more done. Evidence shows the average worker only spends between two and four hours every day actually working. Research indicates that in companies where this has been promoted as a good idea, and ultimately implemented, productivity has increased, provided that rates of pay aren't similarly reduced. So, let me reiterate the idea of introducing shorter working days.

🎧 5.7 (Listening Part 1)

Extract 1

A: I've just been reading this article about the Ford Motor Company. Apparently, they were one of the first American companies to introduce a five-day, 40-hour working week, down from six nine-hour days, in 1926. And Henry Ford – who ran the company – nearly doubled his workers' wages, which was unheard of. The results were apparently very positive, though – reports suggested that productivity went through the roof. Ford believed that workers needed more than one day off a week – and this became the industry standard. Impressive, if that's the truth of it. People do even fewer hours now on average – in the UK at least. And there's even talk of going down to a four-day week. Before we know it, we'll be off more than we're at work!

B: I can't see that benefiting productivity. To my mind, reducing hours would only work if people continued to receive the same salary. Whether that's sustainable or not, though … You've got to strike a balance between what you earn and how much free time you get. You can't live on fresh air. More time off sounds great but if you can't afford to do anything with it … You really couldn't create the same output with so much less input.

Extract 2

A: How are you getting on with checking the new version of 'Day Again' for bugs?

B: Not too bad. I didn't work on the first version, so I can't compare ease of use or anything.

A: Well, if you had been involved, you'd realise how impressive this new version is in comparison. It was along the same lines as this in plot and progression and so on.

B: I haven't seen it actually.

A: Well anyway, the earlier version got stuck at one stage of development for ages. We just couldn't iron out the glitches. And it already looks outdated even though it was only released a couple of years ago. The sequel, on the other hand, is far superior in graphics and everything.

B: That's what I heard – hence my request to join this team. I'd got a bit bored where I was and was desperate for a new challenge, something to get my teeth into. I like what I've seen of the game so far. It raises a smile and the characters seem well rounded. I'm not convinced it's as brilliant as I'd been led to believe, but time will tell.

A: It will!

Extract 3

A: It's Monday again tomorrow! Why do we hate them so much? I mean, we both either work or study over the weekends, anyway, so it's hardly like we've got that Sunday gloom!

B: Well, we don't work flat out like we do during the week. It's still an anti-climax.

A: Like the day after your birthday. How can anything live up to the fun you've just had? I suppose if we weren't to have Mondays, we wouldn't enjoy Saturday and Sunday so much!

B: Well, that's one way to look at it. But I happen to know that there's some science behind feeling bad before the first day of the working week. Coincidentally, we were talking about it in a psychology seminar last week.

A: Oh?

B: Yeah. It's called an 'emotional shift'. One minute you're sky high with happiness, doing something you love – even if that's just lounging on the sofa – and the next you're back to earth with a bump – back to doing something you don't like as much. Try as you might, carrying that warm glow of the weekend into Monday morning just doesn't happen. And, if we changed the weekend around, had different days off, we'd still feel the same.

🎧 5.8 and 5.9 (Reading and Use of English Part 2)

It's the trend of the 2020s, but if you haven't yet embraced a plant-based diet, perhaps you'll have come round to the idea by the end of this brief talk.

Vegans omit all meat, fish, dairy, eggs and honey from their diet, and refuse to wear leather, wool or silk. But the reasons for going vegan don't just come back to concerns about animal welfare. Put simply, veganism is good for you.

If we were all to go vegan, the environment would be better off than if we continued to munch through meat. Plant-based foods are sustainable and have a positive impact on the environment, because rearing animals uses many more resources in terms of land, water and energy. In other words, if everyone went vegan, greenhouse gas emissions related to food production would decrease by 70 percent. Vegetables are cheaper to produce, too.

It goes without saying that fruit and vegetables are full of essential vitamins, minerals and fibre. But if you're one of the people who believes vegans don't get enough calcium or protein, you might want to think again. Seeds, beans, lentils and nuts are packed with protein, and leafy greens, tofu and some fruit contain all the calcium you need.

If that hasn't convinced you, what about this – vegans live longer! Several scientific studies have proven that should you stick to a vegan diet for long enough, your risk of getting diabetes, heart disease or other serious conditions will drop. If you had only been fed vegan food from birth, you might even be healthier now.

If we all switched to a plant-based diet, we would smell better, too. Yes, you heard me correctly! Another study has shown that vegans have sweeter-smelling sweat. That seems like a pretty good reason to ditch the beef to me.

And finally, as for the argument that vegan food is tasteless, well if you should happen to see a vegan dish on the menu one day, give it a go – the myth will soon be dispelled. There's no reason why vegan meals can't be just as appetising as those containing meat or cheese. You might have to learn to cook in a different way but there's plenty of delicious recipes out there for you to have a go at. And lots of vegan foods are superfoods, too.

So, if you haven't already, why not go vegan? Not only will you help save the planet but you'll save yourself, too!

🎧 5.10 (Speaking Part 2)

OK, I'm a coin nerd – and I'm proud of it! I just love coins and what they show. I think it's amazing that we carry round little pieces of history with us every day without thinking about it. Some coins I collect are really special. One is called a crown and it's really big and chunky. A new one is made every year to celebrate different events in our history. That's like – say, a famous author or a significant royal birthday. Since 1990 they've been called Five Pound coins. These aren't actually in circulation – that is, you can't spend them like all the others. Think about it – they're way too big and heavy. No, you buy them specially from the Royal Mint – that's who produces all the UK coins. They used to be considered an investment and that later they'd go up in value and you could cash them in. But apparently not. Banks now say they won't accept them. So, you can't even get face value – unless you sell to a special collector. But another great coin in the UK is the 50p piece. This has been in circulation since 1969 and was the first coin in the world to have an equilateral curve heptagon! To you and me that's seven-sided, but curved. This celebrates events, too, but it's not just for show – it's a working coin. I really love this coin because it celebrates so many weird and wonderful things – like the Olympics, Women getting the vote, etcetera. Some can be worth a lot of money – like one version with a character from a children's story on it, Peter Rabbit, is rare and worth one and a half thousand pounds. See – there can be money in being a coin nerd!

🎧 5.11 (Speaking Part 2)

So, I'd like to talk about these two pictures – and the main similarity between the two of them is that the people are handling coins. The first picture is of someone outside. I would imagine he's been busking, that is, playing his guitar in the street, with his guitar case in front of him for passers-by to put money in to show their appreciation. Generally speaking, people use coins in this situation because it's easy – it's loose change that they carry in their pockets. In all probability the guy has an official space and it may well be that his time is up and he's counting the money he's been given. So, the money for him is like a reward. The other picture, on the other hand, shows a coin in a boy's palm and there's no way that that is payment of any kind! It looks as if they're about to start a game – football, because I can see one child holding a multi-coloured ball in his hands. I would assume that they're about to toss the coin to see which team starts the game. This often happens in sports. As for how they're feeling – I guess the children are feeling pretty excited and probably hoping their side wins the toss, whereas the man might well be feeling tired. How happy he is, would depend on how many coins he's been given.

🎧 5.12 (Writing Part 2)

This trend – I'm talking about rating products and leaving reviews – has the possibility of revolutionising the way we choose what products and services we buy. In fact, it's changing habits already. With some industries in particular – like electronic goods, travel and hospitality – restaurants and so on, more and more people are sharing their experiences online and this is having a considerable knock-on effect on other consumers and the companies involved themselves. It seems like everyone is looking – or aiming – for that five-star rating! According to a recent survey, more than 70 percent of us are happy to leave feedback, both good and bad, and about 50 percent will check out reviews before they buy something. That's extremely interesting from a marketing point of view. It shows that consumers are being influenced more by ratings and reviews than by brand loyalty or advertising! This trend is good all round. Companies have to step up and deal with complaints or problems. Consumer power – this trend can only grow and become even more significant.

🎧 5.1GF

See Ex 4 on page 107.

5.1VF

1 I really wanted to go backpacking in Spain on holiday but my mate wanted to go to France. I said why don't we do a few days in each, and he agreed.

2 The plan of this building just hasn't been well thought out. Maybe we need to contact an architect and see if they can help us improve the spaces.

3 You're always trying to pass on stuff you don't need anymore to me – give it to someone else for a change!

4 Look at the sunlight dancing on the water like that. It reflects all the different colours around it in pretty little spots.

5.2VF

See Ex 8 on page 123.

Unit 6

6.1 (Opener)

It's a familiar little piece of wood or maybe plastic, isn't it? Rectangular, black, with two sets of dots on it. Most of us know the name – dominoes – but I wonder just how many of us have actually played a game with them. Today there are plenty of board games to play with the family when you're at a loose end and, of course, there are the video games where we try, often in vain, to outdo ourselves or opponents, racing through imagined worlds at breakneck speed.

I'm by no means anti-computer games, and I'll often end up playing them by default. However, I'm really in my element when I'm researching traditional games. They fascinate me. My current interest is in finding out all I can about the humble domino!

At first glance dominoes appears to be a simple game where you just lay the pieces to match the numbered dots, but there are people who take the game very seriously. Also, you can play dominoes with different size dominoes and different sets. The most common set of dominoes is called a double-six set, because double six is the highest number on a tile but at a stretch it's just possible to play with a set of double fifteens, but beyond that the tiles get unmanageable!

By all accounts, the use of dominoes goes back nearly a thousand years, originating – as did many old board games – in China. It then moved to Europe where it got its name from the black and white Venetian carnival masks. These were called 'domini' which, in turn, came from the 'Dominican' monks who wore black and white hoods. Interesting, isn't it? In no time, the domino trend spread to France and then into Britain. Today, all over the world people lay out the little black tiles to engage in friendly rivalry or in organised competitions.

And the little black tiles have also given us a linguistic term – 'domino effect'. It's the idea that one small event can lead to other events which eventually lead to a catastrophe. That comes from placing upright dominoes in a line and pushing the first one over, so that it topples the next, which topples the next and so on … People can create amazing visual effects by arranging different lines and patterns of dominoes to knock over. You can watch videos of these achievements in action online – sometimes involving thousands and thousands of dominoes. The people behind these complex creations, domino artists, can take days to set up the dominoes, and it's by no means certain that things will go according to plan. Recently, in a world record attempt in Germany, long hours of preparation were ruined by a fly. Apparently, it flew into the dominoes, starting the toppling sequence before the judges were there to see it! Imagine the frustration!

6.2 (Reading and Use of English Part 6)

A: Yeah, well, there's that thing, you know, when you can feel that someone's watching you – but you can't see anyone? I get that a lot. Sometimes I turn round and yeah, there's someone doing just that.

B: Animals definitely have an extra sense! Our dog always knows when my dad's coming home from work – and he works irregular hours. She goes and sits by the front door! And animals usually know if there's going to be an extreme weather event and take shelter or move to higher ground.

C: Sixth sense? OK – yes, I think it's like, when you've just got a feeling – you don't know where it comes from, that something's going to happen – or not happen, and it turns out to be right? And you think – how did I know that?

D: In my opinion, what many people cite as examples of someone having a sixth sense, after investigation, usually turns out to be either coincidental or a heightened awareness related to one of the existing five senses.

6.3 (Reading and Use of English Part 3)

1 There's one thing I'd like to address first – blind people don't have a better sense of touch or better hearing than sighted people. We simply use these senses more to make up for lack of sight. We have to work hard at braille, in the same way people who can see have to work at their reading, writing and spelling, too, and use the same memorisation techniques. I don't use braille to read for pleasure – I might as well listen to e-books and save myself the hassle! But braille has a huge significance for me when it comes to certain situations that require 'pen and paper', or for me, braille. Unfortunately, braille literacy is on the decline, as younger blind people have a high dependence on note-takers and mobiles to get by. That's a real shame as the skill and its usefulness is being lost.

2 When people who know little about being blind see me holding one of my technological gadgets, they invariably want to know how it works. I don't mind their curiosity – it's the perfect opportunity to educate people about what life's like for blind or visually impaired people, and that promotes understanding and tolerance. The technology's cool – we can use refreshable braille displays, where screen-reader software gathers information from a computer screen and converts it to braille which is then sent to the display. Then, a series of pins pops up on the display to represent braille dots, and blind people can read what's on a computer screen. New technology's currently in development, where a kind of braille wheel will rotate at a selected speed so that people like me can read continuously with a stationary finger – can't wait!

6.4 (Listening Part 2)

You will almost certainly have heard of Route 66 in the USA. Also known as the Mother Road, it was one of the first highways in the States. It was established on November 11th, 1926, although road signs for the route weren't erected until the following year, in 1927. Stretching an incredible 3,940 kilometres from Chicago in the Midwest to Santa Monica on the west coast of California, the road served as the main – and what's more, crucial – route for migrants to the west during the 1930s. This was needed when long-lasting drought damaged agriculture and ecology and people needed to go elsewhere for work. Dust storms and strong winds swept away much of the topsoil, eroding it beyond recovery.

The highway became increasingly popular and, understandably, businesses sprang up along it to cater for travellers: motels, diners and gas stations abounded and profited from visitors who stopped along the way. It was the first road in the USA to be completely paved, and numerous roadside attractions were built, such as museums, animal farms and drive-in movie theatres.

When the new Interstate Highway System came into effect in 1956, the popularity of the road began to decline. Travellers abandoned Route 66 in favour of the newer faster roads which bypassed the old one. Although many sections of the new roads followed alongside the old route, it was eventually replaced in its entirety, and although those who operated business along the old route fought for its survival, it ultimately fell into disrepair, and sadly, multiple businesses died with it.

The road was officially decommissioned from the U.S. Highways System in 1985. Road signs were removed and it no longer appeared on official U.S. road maps, though some of the new sections of road which closely follow the old route were named State Route 66 in its honour. Those who wanted to travel the old Route 66 for nostalgic reasons found it frustratingly difficult to navigate, with no sat-nav coordinates, and a road that in places seemed to suddenly disappear.

However, Route 66 had become too popular to be forgotten altogether, especially as it had appeared in songs, TV programmes and novels, and it is currently undergoing a revival. Today, remaining sections of the old road have been renamed Historic Route 66, and these sections are once again included on maps, along with a new bicycle route known as U.S. Bicycle Route 66.

🎧 6.1EB and 6.2EB (Listening Part 2 – Exam boost)

Last summer, I travelled the Trans-Siberian railway, the longest railway in the world at around 8,000 kilometres long.

You might think there isn't much planning to do for a journey like this. After all, you're just sitting on a seat for the duration, right? Wrong! There are tons of cities to stop at and sights to take in, all to be researched in advance so you don't miss out on anything interesting. In addition to this, we needed to make sure we'd organised all the relevant documents in advance of travelling. Oh, and there can be quite a change in weather between the Moscow starting point and the last station in Vladivostok, so it's a good idea to be properly kitted out, with jackets, gloves and even sun cream!

You don't have to learn any Russian, but it does help to acquire a few useful phrases. What's more crucial, is learning to read the alphabet. Russian is written in the Cyrillic alphabet, of course, which you may or may not be familiar with – I wasn't! Luckily, it's a phonetic language, so once I'd worked out what each letter sounded like, I could start to recognise things on menus. I found place names a but trickier, though – some of them are really long!

As you travel along through the vast spaces of the Russian landscape, passengers come and go. If you can manage to find a language you both speak, you can have fascinating conversations with those sharing a compartment with you. Lots of people shared their food and drink with me and chatting with them provided a great opportunity to find out more about where I should get off and look around. Local knowledge is worth so much more than what the guidebooks tell you.

One of the most interesting places I stopped at was the city of Tomsk, where I coincided with the wood-carving festival. It was amazing. The material seems to play an important part in the city's architecture and there are some very old and beautiful buildings to admire. I then made a mental note to look up other festivals or special days that I could make stops for later in the journey, as I found it provided me with a real insight into local culture.

There were, of course, long stretches of time where the landscape remained unchanged and there was nothing to do but sit back and relax. During moments of boredom it helps to have a few good books tucked away in your luggage, or, as became my own preferred way of passing the time, chess. It was a great way to engage with people even when there was a language barrier.

🎧 6.5 (Listening Part 2)

During our last summer break, I drove the length of the old Route 66 with a friend. We'd prepared in advance, painstakingly researching directions, knowing that at times it would be difficult to find our way, especially if we were to make any diversions to some of the fascinating-sounding sights away from the road itself.

As we rolled out of Chicago, we'd barely got going when I spotted an iconic Route 66 diner and we had to stop. Expecting juicy steaks and ribs on the menu – and there was no shortage of those – it came

as a pleasant surprise to note some dishes I'd never heard of, too. I opted for fried pastries I couldn't pronounce the name of – they were superb – and a drink called root beer – a soft drink, and not quite as pleasant!

Back on the road the first day passed unremarkably. As night fell, we headed for a flashing neon light – an old 1950s motel. As we approached, I could hardly contain my excitement. I was thrilled by its Art Deco appearance and its inclusion on the National Register of Historic Places, which meant we were in for a truly authentic experience. It really was.

Waking early, we got back onto the road again, this time in search of a museum we wanted to visit. The Hall of Fame Museum not only included interesting exhibits from the town in which it was located, but memorabilia from the early days of Route 66. Those were what really captured my attention and I could've spent all day there.

It was inevitable that we'd get lost at some point, but if we hadn't gone off track, we'd never have come across what we've since nicknamed the 'deserted village' – an isolated trading post that had once been a bustling tourist trap. It had ghostly crumbling ruins, rotting wooden walkways and a graffitied gas station. We got some brilliant photos but were happy to get out of there, too!

For those of you with an interest in the construction of the route, you might be fascinated, as I was, by one town's solution to not being able to afford to pave the section of the route that ran through it. Known as the 'sidewalk highway', or perhaps more frequently the 'Ribbon Road', engineers built one perfect lane instead of two, bordering it with gravel sections that allowed cars to pass. Cool!

We travelled through every kind of landscape on our trip, from farmland to forests, and made stops at some of the funnier tourist landmarks – a giant blue whale, the world's largest rocking chair … And there was the natural scenery, too, of course. What made the greatest impression on me was the Painted Desert, which really did look as though an artist had taken his brush to it.

When we finally arrived in Santa Monica, we were both thrilled and relieved – the former because we'd survived a month on the road and the latter because the driving was, at times, monotonous. But we had countless tales to tell about our adventures, and it really was an ambition fulfilled.

🎧 6.6 (Reading and Use of English Part 4)

If I said the word 'nature' to you, how many of you would think of straight-sided shapes such as rectangles or hexagons? Probably not many. Yet hexagons are found everywhere in the natural world.

There's a reason why six sides are useful. Hexagons are strong and efficient, symmetrical and simple. They also tessellate, which means they can fit together without any gaps, much like tiling on a floor.

So, where on earth are all these hexagons? Well, think about honeycomb, which provides storage for honey, for example. Honeycomb hexagons actually start out as little round tubes of wax, which soften into interlocking hexagonal shapes as the bees go about their business.

Plants and fruits, including the Swiss cheese plant and the breadfruit, each have distinctive hexagonal markings. And in the animal kingdom, hexagons are all over the place. Now extinct, the Cyathophyllum hexagonum was made up of hexagons, as are the eyes of the still very much thriving dragonfly, made up of 30,000 miniscule hexagon shapes. Because of this, these beautiful insects experience colour in a far superior way to any other known creature.

Even humans are made of hexagons! Without carbon atoms, which we're all built of, we'd probably just be a shapeless mass on the floor! You've guessed it – those atoms join to form hexagonal rings, and these structures literally hold us together.

That's living things covered. But it's in inorganic structures that we might expect to find hexagons more frequently. Crystals are often hexagonal in nature; snowflakes, none of which are identical, only ever come in a six-sided shape! And water molecules form hexagons when they're arranged just right, joining up to create frozen sheets of ice.

Perhaps the largest hexagon of all is a cloud pattern which sits at Saturn's north pole. Twice as big as the Earth in diameter, this hexagon shape is an unchanging feature of that planet, but how it is sustained is as yet unknown.

Has anyone got any questions?

🎧 6.7 (Speaking Part 3)

Oscar: I have got to be the most disorganised person I know. I sometimes look at my desk in despair – It's as if someone's dumped a waste-paper bin on it. And it really frustrates me. I'm looking for a vital piece of information that I know I've put somewhere, but can I find it? Then I end up wasting valuable time because I know it's there and I'm not going to give up because that would be defeatist! And it's not just my workspace – if I invite people round for dinner, I try to organise things but usually get carried away by something else, forget the time and with only five minutes before they're supposed to be arriving, I'm at sixes and sevens rushing round getting the table set, peeling vegetables, stressing over the still uncooked chicken, not knowing whether I'm coming or going … one day I'll learn, take my time and be organised but currently I would say that I'm your classic case of someone suffering from chronic disorganisation.

Psychologist: Hi Oscar! Be reassured, you are not alone! And you may be surprised to learn that your chronic disorganisation could well be a sign that you are, in fact, highly intelligent and creative! Research shows that being disorganised can indicate high energy and the need to always be learning, experiencing new things, multitasking and coming up with wonderfully creative new ideas that excite you. People like you just don't have time for the less important stuff, like planning and tidying. You're too busy!

Oscar: Thanks! Now that's something to tell my family and friends who criticise my mess all the time. Brilliant!

🎧 6.8 and 6.9 (Speaking Part 3)

Examiner: Now you have a minute to decide which of these problems you think would be hardest to deal with.

Candidate A: So, now we need to think about which of these problems would be hardest to deal with. OK, as you mentioned previously if they've got their own room, then leaving their bed in a mess, and clothes all over the floor isn't going to be a problem for others – they'll be in charge of cleaning up after themselves.

Candidate B: On second thoughts – that's fine unless they keep stale food in there and it starts to smell!

Candidate A: Ah. Good point! Umm, and I appreciate that we said buying food and cooking might be a problem – you know, them not doing their fair share, but on reflection, I think a timetable – or like, taking turns, could help that.

Candidate B: True. OK, if I remember rightly, we also agreed one thing that would irritate us might be leaving the bathroom messy and dirty. I wouldn't want to have to pick up clothes in the bathroom! And also, we mentioned security, if this person lost their keys or forgot to lock up and things like that.

Candidate A: Yes, well, taking everything into consideration, I'd go for being messy around the house as the hardest to deal with. That's awful if you're sharing. You'd worry about inviting friends round for a start.

Candidate B: Personally, I'd be more concerned about keys and security! The place could end up getting burgled!

Candidate A: You're right. Good point. I'd go along with that.

🎧 6.10 (Writing Part 1)

In my day, learning history at school was all about dates and wars and kings, queens and prime ministers! As a subject it was dry, and I certainly didn't see any reason why we should be learning about stuff that happened before I was born. And as for dates – well, I had a complete mental block when it came to remembering any! But today, when I visit primary schools to give readings from my history books, I can see how dramatically this has all changed. The teachers use their creativity to make the subject come alive and the kids dress up, do projects, watch films, make food from the period … some schools are even introducing VR sessions. For me, history is about a lot more than dates. For one thing, it's full of great stories – and kids love a good story. My job is to be a story-teller and what better place to find good stories than in the past? So, my new series is specifically for primary age children. I write about the gory side of history – the battles, the conspiracies – and admittedly, I tend to exaggerate to bring in a lot of comedy. If reading or listening to any of my stories gets even a few kids interested enough to study history seriously when they're older, then I've succeeded!

🎧 6.1GF

See Ex 4 on page 109.

🎧 6.1VF

1   Need any help with anything? I've got nothing to do.

2   I'm never happier than when I'm dancing.

3   We didn't do the project alone. We worked with another class on it.

4   I've been trying to contact him for several days, but I haven't managed to.

5   When I saw the questions in the exam, I thought they were impossible, but when I read them carefully, they weren't so bad.

6   I've got so many different things to do this afternoon I don't know where to start!

🎧 6.2VF

See Ex 7 on page 125.

🎧 6.3VF

1   The meeting was in an uproar when the government announcement to cut funding was made. Everyone started shouting at the same time.

2   I was going to book the taxi for 8.30 but on second thoughts that might be too late, so I'll book for 8.00.

3   After the accident in the town centre, the traffic was at a standstill for half an hour.

4   I wasn't intending to buy a new laptop, but the price was so good I bought it on impulse.

5   The boots in my size that I want to get are out of stock, so I'll have to check out some other stores.

6   My brother doesn't usually remember family birthdays but to his credit he did remember mine this year and got me a great present.

7   It's important to be on good terms with your neighbours as you can often help each other out when there are problems.

8   In line with government policy, there is going to be an increase in the number of CCTV cameras in city centres.

Unit 7

🎧 7.1 and 7.2 (Opener)

Today we're going to take a look at nitrogen, a particularly fascinating chemical element which can be used in various states, including gas and liquid. It's interesting because it's in every living thing on the planet. That's me, you, your pet cat and even the plant in that pot over there!

Although nitrogen forms part of us and it makes up most of the air we breathe, it can have a devastating effect on the body in certain circumstances. You can't breathe pure nitrogen, for example, because it's poisonous and causes asphyxiation. Therefore, when nitrogen's being used in an enclosed space, the room must be ventilated.

Has anyone heard of decompression sickness? It's what scuba divers can get if they rise to the surface too quickly. The rapidly changing pressure of water releases nitrogen bubbles into the body and decompression sickness kicks in. This has a serious effect on organs and blood and can be life-threatening. Fortunately, this is now no longer a common occurrence because of increased knowledge and better equipment.

There are many uses and applications of nitrogen, including its use in pharmacological drugs. Nitrogen becomes a liquid at minus a hundred and ninety-five point five degrees and below. A lot of effort goes into conserving blood and other biological specimens and in its liquid state, nitrogen is perfectly suited to do this. It's used in anaesthesia and cryogenics – medical freezing – too.

Nitrogen's ability to cool means it's also used to prevent large computer systems and things like X-ray machines from overheating. Electrical components use it, and it's used in military aircraft systems and high-voltage equipment to combat fire hazards. Although nitrogen itself can be a pollutant, it is also used to control worse pollutants, by disposing of toxic liquids and vapours from industrial tools.

In the food industry, food needs to be kept fresh long enough for it to be in near-perfect condition when it reaches us. Nitrogen's used in packaging to ensure a stable atmosphere within it. This keeps the food – er, fruit, say – from oxidising, which would lead to it going off. Mixed with carbon dioxide, it ensures food stays fresh. You'll also see chefs using liquid nitrogen, too, to create spectacular effects when serving fancy dishes!

Motorsports engineers also draw on nitrogen's properties. It's used to inflate tyres in motorsports. This is because it has no moisture in it, so it does not cause fluctuations in pressure like air does, so the tyre pressure remains constant whatever the climatic conditions, thus avoiding complications while driving.

🎧 7.3 (Reading and Use of English Part 7)

In Christopher Booker's extremely long publication 'Seven Basic Plots', he asserts that all stories adhere to one of seven types. These narrative structures apply to stories told and written over the centuries from Greek myths to modern-day films. In the course of 738 pages he takes us through plots that he gives interesting labels: 'Overcoming the monster' apparently applies to beating physical entities such as the shark in 'Jaws', as well as triumphing in other battles such as fighting illness. Another that he calls 'Rags to riches' brings together the classic 'Jane Eyre' and the more modern 'Brewster's Millions' type of tale. Following these we have 'The Quest' where we follow people like Ulysses or the Hobbits in pursuit of a goal, and then 'Voyage and Return' where our protagonists go off to a strange land, returning successfully, having profited from the experience – think 'Alice in Wonderland'. Another type, 'Rebirth' outlines inner journeys from ignorance to wisdom – such as 'The Frog Prince'. The final two types of plot are 'Comedy', not necessarily referring to humour but to confusions which are smoothed out resulting in clarification and happiness – most romance stories fall into this category, and finally 'Tragedy', where, unlike all the others, a fatal flaw prevents the hero from reaching his desire and precipitates his fall. The book is definitely interesting but for me, there is a great deal of overlap and his categorisation doesn't seem to be applicable to some very modern types of novel. But worth a read, certainly.

🎧 7.4 (Reading and Use of English Part 1)

At the age of 73, Deke Duncan was finally offered a DJ slot on his local BBC radio station. For the previous 44 years, Deke had been broadcasting his own radio station via a speaker to an audience of one – his wife!

Deke set up his station – Radio 77 – from his garden shed back in 1974, naming it after an American station he'd bought some jingles from to use in his shows. His interest in radio stemmed from listening to Radio Caroline, a pirate radio station broadcast from boats off the coast of the UK during the 1960s. However, he was fully aware that, much as he'd have liked to, he would never make it as a professional DJ.

Without a broadcasting licence, Deke could only be on air in his own living room where his wife was listening in. From his shed, Deke played his and his wife's favourite pop songs, recording non-stop, dawn-to-midnight weekend shows with friends Richard and Clive and then playing them back.

A lack of budget meant he couldn't keep everything they'd recorded, and they would reuse the tapes by recording new shows over old ones. While he was 'on air', Deke frequently referred to the fact that he was broadcasting to and from his own home. He sometimes suggested that he'd lost his whole audience when his wife had popped out.

This wasn't the first time Deke had appeared in the news. Coverage of his story was broadcast in 1974 when he'd not long been in operation. When the footage was recently rediscovered in the BBC archive, they tweeted about Radio 77 online, prompting BBC Three Counties – Deke's regional radio station – to track him down and offer him a one-off slot, where he could play whatever he wanted for a whole hour. Deke was overwhelmed at the chance to realise his 'ultimate ambition'.

🎧 7.5 (Listening Part 3)

A: Have you finished looking into the causes of so-called overpopulation for our research project?

B: Yes, and you've researched the effects, right?

A: Yes. Great, let's compare notes then. Why don't you go first and tell me about the causes, and then I'll summarise what I've found out about the effects.

B: Sounds good. So, firstly, I tried to redefine 'overpopulation'. There are differing views about whether it's really a thing, as far as I can tell. Like, some people say there are too many people in the world which creates problems, and others don't believe so.

A: But the basic concept for those who believe in overpopulation is that there are more humans on the planet than it can sustain, right?

B: Right. One source said the world can sustain somewhere between 4 and 16 billion – so we've either exceeded the number of people the planet can sustain, or we're still some way off.

A: Interesting. So, what causes did you come across in your reading?

B: Well, the first is a decline in mortality rates. People are living longer than ever, partly due to better medical facilities.

A: So, as life expectancy increases, so does the population?

B: That's the idea. When the rate of deaths and births is equal, the population remains stable. But that's not what's happening at the moment. Advancements in science and technology have led to easier food production as well as medical progress.

A: Ah, OK, so because there's more food and less illness, people are living longer. That makes sense.

B: Now, there was something else. In the past, infant mortality rates were higher so people had a lot of children to ensure that enough would survive to support the family – more hands for agricultural work, say, and better provision for the family. And another source I read made the assumption that some people have loads of children because they're less aware, under-educated even, of the impact of overpopulation. Now, I'm just quoting what I've read, remember!

A: Hmmm, that's totally patronising! I wish people didn't say that sort of stuff. And in any case, many people are having fewer children than they did in the past, and also doing it later in life, so it must balance out. Sounds like a weak argument to me. Forgive me for being sceptical.

B: Well, like I said, we don't have to agree with everything we read. These are opinions.

A: Was there anything else? Other causes?

B: That's it for now. So how about the effects?

🎧 7.6 (Listening Part 3)

So, I read about the effects of overpopulation and came across a few arguments. The first was depletion of resources – there's only so much water and food to go round. And we've also been damaging the environment through pollution, by overusing natural resources like coal, oil and gas, as well as through industry and of course, the massive number of vehicles on roads. Along with deforestation to make way for more agricultural land, this has led to damaged air quality and increased CO2 emissions, which in turn has led to global warming and climate change – and we all know the effects of melting ice caps and rising sea levels.

Other effects of overpopulation include a potential rise in conflict, such as 'war over water'. Lack of clean drinking water leads to uncontrolled disease and starvation. And overpopulated areas can have higher unemployment, exacerbating poverty and other social issues which may lead to an increase in crime. The cost of living also increases – as more people compete for limited resources, the price of commodities, including food and shelter, goes up, meaning people have to pay more in order to feed themselves and keep a roof over their heads.

But before you despair too much, I did come across a positive – further advances in technology will occur in order to find solutions to overcrowding and overpopulation.

🎧 7.1EB (Listening Part 3 – Exam boost)

1 Just leave me alone, will you? I'm not in the mood to chat. I'd rather be on my own.

2 What a terrible way to treat a customer! I couldn't believe that the sales assistant was so rude to me!

3 Oh, wow! I can't believe you've all travelled so far just to celebrate my birthday with me. I'm lost for words!

4 What?! There's another flood warning? We'd better move the furniture upstairs – quick!

5 I've never had particularly good self-esteem. I cringe when I have to address a group of people, even if they're my friends.

🎧 7.7 (Listening Part 3)

Presenter: Good morning and welcome. Joining me in the studio today are Hugo Silva and Bethany Wright, who are here to discuss the concept of overpopulation. Hugo – is overpopulation actually a problem?

Hugo: Well, I know for a start that Bethany, among others, is going to disagree with me here but no, it isn't. Now, I can almost hear listeners shouting at the radio – 'we're wasting our resources!' they'll be crying. I'm not deterred by that. I know my ideas are unpopular in some circles, but that doesn't mean they aren't credible. People do challenge me when I attempt to put my arguments forward on this matter, but I'm prepared for the onslaught! Whether they choose to really hear what I'm saying is up to them.

Presenter: So, tell us. Why isn't overpopulation a problem?

Hugo: People say we're rapidly depleting the world's natural resources and the Earth can't carry on carrying us all. This simply isn't true. The ecology of human systems doesn't work in that way. Humanity is not sustained naturally, and never has been. People have made use of technologies and engineering – from as far back as the earliest stone tools – to manage ecosystems and sustain populations. It's taken thousands of generations to become as sophisticated as we are today, but that's what's happened all along.

Presenter: Bethany. You believe overpopulation *is* something to worry about.

Bethany: Yes. The first problem is the displacement and extinction of species, caused by humans. There are too many of us for people and animals to share the planet harmoniously. We've ruined ecosystems and destroyed habitats by building all over them and using the land for industry and agriculture.

Presenter: Hugo – what about the matter of extinction?

Hugo: All species die out eventually. In the past, when an animal that humans hunted became rare, they learnt to extract more nutrients from what they hunted, or they would move onto other species. They started to burn woodland, too, and create spaces for animals to graze, and be used for food. So, they learnt to sustain not only themselves but other species, too. We're still doing that.

Bethany: Well, I'll concede that species do naturally die out – we're accelerating that too quickly, though.

Presenter: Bethany, tell us about overcrowding.

Bethany: People living in overcrowded places are becoming more and more vulnerable and that's a terrible state of affairs. They lack fresh water, safe housing, they live in polluted environments. In today's megacities, some kids have never even seen a garden, let alone countryside, such is the lack of green spaces. And would climate change have occurred if we'd kept our population down to, say, half what it is today? Tens of millions of people are hungry and there's likely to be even more insecurity about where the next meal's coming from in future. That's an unacceptable fact for too many people, while the rest of us over-consume. We need to stop consuming and slow down population growth. Then the future would look rosier.

Presenter: Hugo – anything you'd like to say about food and hunger?

Hugo: Yes. Some commentators say there won't be enough food in future – or that there isn't enough food now. Population doesn't outrun the food supply as some would have you believe. We can make and have always made the same land productive. We *are* able to sustain ourselves. It isn't to do with environmental limits, but our own. The only threats to our survival are social and technological systems which need to improve. There's no need for people to be hungry – either now or in future and it's nonsense to suggest otherwise. We don't need more land; we need better ways of using it.

Presenter: Do we all need to become vegan? Bethany?

Bethany: Good question. I think that our food choices do have an impact on nature. We have a lack of diversity in our diets. It may not seem like it but we tend to eat the same few things. Most of what we eat comes from about twelve crops – though there are thousands available – and we eat far more meat than we actually need nutritionally.

Presenter: Hugo?

Hugo: We overfish, too. Not enough of what we do protects water, soil or animals, making current practices unsustainable for the large part. I'm not necessarily convinced that veganism would work for everybody though, or an insect-based diet, as some have suggested.

🎧 7.8 and 7.9 (Reading and Use of English Part 2)

I came across a company called Seventh Generation recently. They inspired me to become more sustainable in my life. I mean, I already do my bit – I take my reusable shopping bags to the supermarket, I buy shampoo bars instead of shampoo in plastic bottles, and I walk everywhere I can. But these guys inspired me to push myself even further.

Seventh Generation is an American company which sells cleaning products, paper and personal care products – like hand wash and nappies for babies. They distribute products to natural food stores and supermarkets, amongst others. 'What's so special about that?' you might be asking. Well, they develop their products sustainably, conserving natural resources. They use ingredients in their products that are bio-degradable, plant-based and chlorine-free, and they consider the impact of every decision they make on the next seven generations and beyond. They've got lots of goals for the future and in the next few years, they're hoping to become a zero-waste company. They'll be doing a lot of things to achieve that goal. These will include reducing the amounts of products and packaging that still end up in landfill despite their best efforts. By 2025, they say that one hundred percent of their products and ingredients will be bio-based – made from plants or renewable materials. By then, they'll also have been working hard to reduce the amount of palm oil they use, and will have replaced 30 percent of it with bio-based oil.

In addition, they're going to ensure that all their packaging will not only be reusable but reused, recyclable, recycled or biodegradable. In other words, they aren't leaving rubbish behind for other people to deal with. What's more, they plan to reduce their greenhouse gas emissions and are promising that the water cycle will not be contaminated during a product's life cycle.

I wonder how many other companies will be following in Seventh Generation's footsteps by 2025, and ensuring a cleaner, greener planet for the future? Many, many more, I hope.

🎧 7.10 (Speaking Part 4)

Examiner: Marius, do you think a child's family and friends have less influence on them as the child grows older? Why?

Marius: That's a fascinating question. The whole thing about influence, as we said before, is very complex. For me, I'd say that as a child grows older a parent or sibling's influence becomes less and the balance shifts towards friends, their opinions of friends becomes more significant. And to be honest, I think that's the right way for things to go. As we get older, gain more experience and change as our lives develop, our friends are more in touch with how best to advise us on important matters. For example, if you think about decisions on whether to …

Jeanne: Oh no, I don't agree. For me, the family always knows a person better than anyone else. And what do you mean 'more significant?' I don't understand that at all.

Marius: OK, basically, I'm saying that friends' advice is more relevant, more important than a family member – that is unless you have a particularly close relationship such as …

Jeanne: In my country, family is always important. Your family can help you with any decision.

Marius: I appreciate that. I'm just not sure that a family can necessarily keep track of an individual's development and they may not be best placed to advise on …

Jeanne: What's that 'best placed'? Explain please.

Marius: Well, what I meant was …

🎧 7.11 (Speaking Part 4)

Examiner: Marta, do you think a child's family and friends have less influence on them as the child grows older? Why?

Marta: OK, I think, me, that it depends on the family, you know? Sometimes families stay very close and can help advise you all through your life. Perhaps their influence is not so strong because as you get older you have more experience yourself, and you meet new people who can influence you in different ways. And if, for example, you don't stay very close to your family for whatever reason, then their influence is not strong. They don't know you that well as you grow older.

Hans: If I could just come in here?

Marta: Sure – what do you think, Hans?

Hans: I would completely agree with you, Marta. And to expand a little, I would say that if your family has given you good role models when you're young and helped you with useful advice throughout your formative years, then this will have taught you to be independent and choose the right paths when you're older, don't you think?

Marta: You've made a great point there. Could you give an example perhaps of choosing the right path?

Hans: Of course, I was thinking of something like being offered promotion at work maybe, and balancing the extra money against increased workload and pressure. An important decision but one that only you can make!

Marta: Thanks – I see what you mean!

🎧 7.12 (Writing Part 2)

Spying, or espionage to give it its proper name, is an intriguing and highly popular topic for both those who create and those who are entertained by fiction. It presents the opportunity to enter a fascinating world of secrets and lies, violence and intelligence, daring, courage, betrayal and patriotism, and the endless surprises at reveals of agents, double-agents, double-double-agents, and so on. Because of this trend we are nearly all now well versed in the nature of espionage and words such as infiltration, defection, counter-intelligence and clandestine operations roll off our tongues easily. The spying profession has a very definite public face in the 21st century.

Interest in fictional espionage was triggered for many by the works of 20th-century writers such as John Le Carré, Somerset Maugham, Frederick Forsyth and Ian Fleming, authors who were informed by their own experiences of working for the secret services. We learnt about spy activity during the two world wars and also during the period of the Cold War when espionage became ever more active and discussed, with regular news revelations about double agents, defectors and exchanges.

What is fascinating is how far back the job of a real spy actually goes. It is one of the oldest professions in the world. As long as there have been wars there have been those sent to discover secrets to be used against the enemy. The methods have developed, the sophistication of the networks and the systems have been refined, but spies still basically do the same work as they did back in ancient China when General Sun Tzu wrote 'The Art of War' in the fifth century BCE. For the British, the art of spying took a great leap forward in Elizabethan times as a result of threats to the Queen, when systems were set up, coding and decoding became sought-after skills and well-organised networks of spies ranged across countries and even continents. To learn more about this really intriguing topic check out my new book which will be …

🎧 7.1GF

See Ex 4 on page 111.

🎧 7.1VF

1 This is a mass of very small drops of liquid which float in the air, for example, because of evaporation.

2 This is something that makes air, water or soil dangerously dirty.

3 Divers can get this when they come up from deep in the sea too quickly.

4 This is what happens when you combine something with oxygen, making it bad.

5 This is a small amount or piece that is taken from something so that it can be tested or examined.

6 A room or building is this when you let fresh air into it.

7 This is a chemical substance, such as carbon or oxygen, that consists of atoms of only one kind.

8 This means related to the scientific study of drugs and medicines.

🎧 7.2VF

See Ex 8 on page 127.

Unit 8

🎧 8.1 and 8.2 (Opener)

OK, so, my collection – which I think is totally fascinating – but there again most collectors would say the same – is collecting umbrellas. I'm what is universally known as a 'brolliologist' – there, I bet you've never heard that one before! I guess it comes from the word 'brolly', which is an affectionate name for an umbrella in the UK. I have to admit that it's a bit of an obsession with me. For me, the object is one big contradiction. Just think, a small tube that can be held in a hand magically opens up into something enormous! And the design is endlessly versatile. There are tiny umbrellas (I have a mini collection of cocktail umbrellas) or enormous ones, beach parasols for example. And their traditional eight-panel canopies can carry a range of pictures and messages from artistic designs to advertising slogans.

Another fascinating thing for me is that the design of modern umbrellas is still strikingly similar to that of the very first parasols that were used – it's widely believed – over four thousand years ago in ancient Egypt, China and Greece. In those days, they were used to protect noble women's pale skin when it was blisteringly hot. These early parasols were exquisite. They were painstakingly decorated by craftsmen and symbolised wealth and rank. It was the Chinese who developed a form of waterproofing and they became popular in rainy northern Europe from the sixteenth century onwards. At first, parasols and umbrellas were exclusively used by women, who found that using an umbrella was infinitely preferable to getting drenched. For a while, men considered it too unmanly until the middle of the eighteenth century when a man called Jonas Hanway started to carry an umbrella in public in England, and the trend finally caught on.

Brolliologists like myself are fiercely competitive when it comes to auctions. Some old umbrellas are notoriously difficult to get your hands on. However, I've been lucky and my collection includes examples of most types of umbrellas through their various stages of development. I have umbrellas with intricately carved handles which could also carry items like small bottles or even types of swords; transparent bubble umbrellas, heavy-duty storm umbrellas and a recently designed 16-panel umbrella that is able to go back to its original shape after blowing inside out! I think we've all experienced the frustration of how easily the standard eight-panel umbrella breaks!

I guess I'm weird, but I feel a bit sad for lost and broken brollies. We do tend to take these amazing objects for granted. On the London Underground more than a hundred thousand umbrellas are found every year! However, this does keep the umbrella industry busy. By the way – did you know that most umbrellas are produced in China? And that one city – Shaoxing – has more than a thousand umbrella factories? Amazing!

🎧 8.3 (Reading and Use of English Part 8)

Just met someone with a weird phobia. It's a phobia of the number eight, so I thought I'd check it out. I've got a bit of a thing about the number 13 myself – I KNOW it sounds odd, but I've had it since I was young – and I'm definitely not the only one. For example, I try to avoid travelling on a Friday 13th if possible or visiting someone at a number 13! So, I checked out phobias about number eight and apparently there are quite a few people with this, too! It's called octophobia and it's all to do with the way the shape of the number circles in two loops and people get panicked by the idea that you get trapped in it – you can't escape – a bit like an ice skater skating in a figure of eight forever. So, it's got me thinking – are there any people who have phobias about other numbers and why? Let me know! I'm fascinated!

🎧 8.4 (Reading and Use of English Part 3)

The concept of infinity is represented by a symbol which looks like the figure eight on its side. The word itself is derived from Latin and means 'without end'. Perhaps infinity is best explained by numbers, which can go on forever. Whatever number you think of, you can always add another to it. In mathematics there are three kinds of infinity – I won't go into that now as it's pretty complex, so I'll just give you a brief overview of infinity in other fields.

Let's start with physics. Some people think that space is infinite, that it just goes on without end. Cosmologists – those who study the physical universe – say that instead, it is curved and finite, but unlimited. They make a comparison with a sphere, like the Earth. It's finite in that you could keep walking in a straight line and you would eventually come back to where you started. But you could also do this forever. Cosmologists think that the universe could be similar. While the universe itself is thought to be finite, the viewpoint of some astrophysicists is that there may even be an infinite number of universes.

In art, the concept of infinity can be seen in perspective. On a painting, you might see a road stretching off along a straight line into the distance, for example. At some point, it will disappear completely, at a point on the horizon. This is known as the vanishing point, an artistic concept related to infinity. The road disappears at an infinite distance from the observer. Use of perspective in art makes space, form and distance look realistic.

Where else do we find the concept of infinity? Well, there's an interesting variation of chess – called infinite chess – in which the game is played on an unbounded board – there are no borders! Then there's the 'infinite loop' in computer programming, a piece of coding which repeats indefinitely. And the infinity symbol itself is used to represent eternal love, and as such is sometimes used in jewellery. Let me now tell you a little more about …

🎧 8.5 and 8.6 (Listening Part 4)

We all know that at a certain time of the evening our bodies start winding down for sleep. We also know that sleep is crucial for health and well-being. We certainly feel more alert after a few hours' shut-eye, with increased energy and better mood. Without enough rest, we can feel sleepy and down.

Scientists have proposed various theories as to why we spend about a third of every day asleep.

One theory is the inactivity, or evolutionary, theory. This suggests that way back in the past, animals which stayed quiet during the hours of darkness were less likely to be attacked by predators or have accidents. Natural selection ensured species that did this survived and this period of rest evolved to become sleep.

The energy-conservation theory encompasses the idea that animals that compete for resources benefit from

sleeping in order to conserve energy for times when hunting's most efficient. You can see this in big cats such as lions, for example, which don't move around much unless they are hunting for food, and they rest after eating, too. This allows for effective energy use as sleep reduces the amount of energy we need and use.

A third theory is the restorative theory, which proposes that we need sleep for our bodies to repair and rejuvenate overnight, such as muscle growth and tissue repair. Studies show the detrimental effect on the immune system of sleep deprivation – we couldn't survive without sleep. It improves our cognitive function, too – with a less than optimal amount of sleep, you'll find it harder to perform work or study tasks.

Finally, we come to the brain plasticity theory. Sleep is correlated to changes in the brain in terms of structure and organisation, known as brain plasticity. The brains of babies and young children – who spend 13 to 14 hours asleep every day – develop during sleep.

Although scientists aren't sure yet about which of these theories, or combination of theories, answers the question 'Why do we sleep?', we're on the road to finding out.

🎧 8.1EB and 8.2EB (Listening Part 4 – Exam boost)

I suffer from excessive daytime sleepiness, which is known as hypersomnia. I struggle to stay awake when I should be studying or doing other daily tasks, and feel sleepy whatever I'm doing. I have to take frequent naps during the day or I simply wouldn't get through it without dropping off during a meal or even in the middle of a sentence. I sleep for longer than most people during the night as well, and when I wake, it's almost like I haven't slept at all. I'm rarely fully alert, which can be incredibly frustrating when I'm trying to get things done. It does affect my quality of life, though I've made significant lifestyle changes to reduce the condition's impact on me.

🎧 8.3EB and 8.4EB (Listening Part 4 – Exam boost)

1   I have narcolepsy, which is a brain condition that causes me to fall asleep at inappropriate times. My brain doesn't regulate sleeping and waking patterns normally, which results in me feeling very drowsy during the day – sometimes I fall asleep suddenly without being able to prevent it. It sometimes happens when I laugh a lot or get angry – I guess it's a kind of response to that. That does make it difficult to have an ordinary life and at

present, there's no cure. I find ways round it, though, like scheduling in nap times and rigidly sticking to a regular bedtime. There are tablets you can take, too, but my narcolepsy's well controlled at the moment.

2   Narcolepsy can make life challenging. It makes you drop off without a moment's notice. It can happen anywhere, which can be a bit weird for those around you. The thing I find particularly difficult to deal with is the sleep paralysis – that means my muscles sort of freeze when I'm falling asleep or waking up. I don't drive because of the condition, which isn't too much of an inconvenience as I live in the city centre. In fact, I made the choice to move here for that reason. I also work freelance from home, which means if I really need to go and have a sleep, I can do so without it being problematic. So, I've found ways round it without resorting to medical treatment – I'd take it if I needed to, of course.

🎧 8.7 (Listening Part 4)
Speaker 1
People say I could fall asleep on a washing line and that's probably true! It can be tricky waking me up in the morning at times. I certainly sleep more than the average person, and it's difficult to grasp the idea that others suffer from things like insomnia. I simply can't imagine being anxious about going to bed in case it strikes. I did start suffering from headaches at one point, and the doctor said maybe I was sleeping too much. I now go to bed a bit later and wake a little earlier and so far, so good. The headaches haven't returned, which is a relief, though I guess they could come back at some point.

Speaker 2
Now that I've started writing stuff down when I wake up, I know I'll be able to fill the next chapter. I have to get one a day done or I won't meet my self-imposed weekly target – you have to have discipline as a writer. Anyway, if I suffer from block, I turn to my notes and they often spark an idea which gets me going again. Thank goodness I remember my dreams – and weirdly, sometimes even nightmares help, though they've never bothered me in the same way they do other people – I'm fascinated by it all. I'm no sleep expert, though. All I know is that I love tucking myself up at night!

Speaker 3
Apparently, I quote lines from films when I'm asleep. I've woken up hearing myself saying stuff! I'm not a film buff, so who

knows what's going through my mind at the time – I've never got to the bottom of the whole thing. Anyway, my partner thinks it's hilarious to engage me in conversation when I start speaking… But it does interrupt my sleep, leaving me a bit foggy-headed next day. I thought it might help to keep myself cooler – so tried what's known as the Egyptian method – sleeping between slightly damp sheets. There must be something in it cos I've never been so alert on waking and I just get on with the day ahead.

Speaker 4

I have a tendency to sleepwalk! It doesn't bother me cos I don't remember it the next day, though I know my sister's often on high alert because of it, waiting for sounds from the kitchen. I've tried to cook while I'm asleep and she's concerned about me injuring myself, though there are no detrimental physical effects to sleepwalking itself. Now, I ensure I'm not hungry before bed – that seems to make me less likely to sleepwalk! I've realised the constant pressure of my workload might've been having an effect on my sleep too, though. I've been sticking to my new routine and I seem to be managing things better at work for the time being.

Speaker 5

For years I was blissfully unaware of my snoring. As I got older, my big snorts started waking me up! And on occasion I noticed I had a sore throat. I still get that after a particularly heavy snoring session! At least I don't share a bedroom – I'd hate to keep people up because of it. The doctor said there was no underlying medical issue. But it could've created difficulties further down the line. I took his advice about exercising more and sleeping on my side. Reports from flatmates are that it works. I still snore if I'm exhausted, much to their amusement, though problems shouldn't reoccur if I carry on as I have been.

8.8 and 8.9 (Reading and Use of English Part 4)

How often do you take notice of the sky above you? You probably notice particularly impressive sunsets or anvil-shaped storm clouds. The rest of the time you probably barely look up at the grey and white fluffy things floating overhead. If studied more closely, however, the clouds would tell us all kinds of things about the atmosphere.

Meteorologists like me are, of course, very interested in cloud patterns and we do the best we can to use them to interpret the approaching weather. Clouds are classified into ten main groups, first described in 1803 by amateur weather watcher Luke Howard. We still use the terms he invented today. There are rain-bearing clouds, thread-like clouds, high clouds and sheet clouds, amongst others, many of which are instantly recognisable. Some, though, are rather rarer and we may never spot them in a lifetime because they rely on certain conditions that may never occur in our part of the world. Spot one of these beautiful formations, though, and you'll want to see them all!

Many of us dread a darkening sky and thick cloud cover and welcome what we interpret as fine-weather cloud. Meteorologists are interested in all kinds of cloud, of course, and, based on something known as the oktas chart, they can tell us what percentage of the sky is covered. This scale is divided into eighths, so a sky completely covered in cloud is reported as eight oktas, whereas a cloudless sky is zero oktas. Should there be mist or fog around, making it impossible to see the sky, then it is not possible to apply the scale. In some places, such as the UK, a report of eight oktas is not an unusual occurrence, while zero is much less likely – even on sunny days there's often very thin cloud at high altitudes.

Not having a great understanding of weather as a youngster, I, like many other people, believed that the vapour trails left by planes were also a kind of cloud. Known as contrails, they are the result of water vapour leaving jet engines at high speed but they aren't actually clouds. However, if you've ever watched a contrail as its shape shifts, you'll notice that it hangs about for a while, and sometimes eventually turns into a real cloud due to the particles that are left hanging in the sky.

8.10 and 8.11 (Speaking Part 2)

When we think of musical instruments, we tend to talk about violins, guitars, flutes, etcetera but one of the most incredible instruments is actually the human voice. We use all manner of complex sounds and pitches daily to express a whole range of emotions and functions from showing sympathetic concern to giving an instruction, from whispering a secret to barking orders. It reflects our joy and anger, and of course, we use it to sing. The average human singing voice is about one and a half octaves. With professionals that rises to two or above, and that's what we'll be looking at today. There are ways that training can extend your vocal range,

in some cases quite significantly. Before we start, a quick question – what do you think the record is for the widest octave range for a singer? No takers? Well, there's a music teacher from China who can sing across six octaves! The record for the lowest note ever produced was only detectable by some audio equipment – much lower than the human ear could pick up. And there's also a guy who claimed to be able to go up 12.5 octaves, imitating bird calls! Still only a claim though! Now, on a practical note (ha!) let's look at our voices and …

8.12 and 8.13 (Speaking Part 2)

I really like this pair of pictures. They both show people using their voices, as you say, but the way they're using their voices is very different, for different reasons. So, starting with a comparison, clearly voice is important in both pictures, but where and why they're using voices is very different. In one, a mother is reading a bedtime story in the intimacy of a bedroom, whereas in the other, a professional singer is entertaining an audience in an auditorium. As to HOW they're using their voices, going back to the first picture, the mum who's telling the bedtime story needs her voice to be soft and interesting, she may well need to impersonate the voices of different characters to bring it alive for her daughter. The professional singer on the other hand, needs a strong, powerful voice that can project into a big space. But there again, she needs to be soft and loud to create the right emotions in the people who are listening. Moving on to the effect on the audiences, I imagine that the child is mesmerised by her mother's voice, and she definitely looks caught up in the story. She's quite possibly feeling sleepy, too – ready for bed. Whereas, the audience listening to the singer could well be feeling emotional, either sad or happy, depending on the song and the singer's expertise. They certainly shouldn't be feeling sleepy!

8.14 (Writing Part 2)

You're looking at a picture of a very famous group of people in the fight for votes for women in the UK at the beginning of the twentieth century – the Suffragettes. Women had started campaigning to be given the same rights to vote as men as far back as 1832, but despite their efforts nothing happened. So, in 1897 the National Union of Women's Suffrage was formed. Their campaign was not successful and in 1903 another group – the Women's Social and Political Union – was created by the now famous Emmeline Pankhurst and her daughters. They believed that more dramatic action was required to bring their cause to the attention of parliament. Their campaign involved protest rallies and marches, as you can see in the picture. Their action often led to arrests and many ended up in prison, where another tactic they used was going on hunger strike. Some famously chained themselves to railings at a big rally in Hyde Park. However, it wasn't until one campaigner, Emily Davison, was killed by a horse at the Derby racecourse that the women's cause started to have an impact. In 1918 women were finally given the right to vote, but only those over 30. It was another ten years before men and women had equal rights. It hardly seems possible now, does it? The woman in the centre of the picture is probably …

🎧 8.1GF

See Ex 4 on page 113.

🎧 8.1VF

1 This article looks … to one I read on another website. Perhaps it's the same writer?

2 I was watching a programme about decorating last night and it … about what to do in my room. Can I run it past you and see what you think?

3 I meant to audition for the concert, but I got nervous and couldn't … to go!

4 As soon as I respond to my emails, others arrive. The list is … !

5 They want to build new houses on the field, but the … of the land is being questioned so there will be a delay in the planning.

6 I won't be … to vote in a general election until next year when I'm eighteen.

7 We have to stay … about the project in spite of the poor results so far.

8 All these ideas sound really good but on a … , who is actually going to pay to implement them?

🎧 8.2VF

See Ex 5 on page 129.

🎧 8.3VF

See Ex 6 on page 129.

CONTENTS

Exam boost

These pages provide practice exercises for specific language and skills for each exam paper and part. You are referred to the exercise sections from the main lessons when you should complete them.

Exam reference

EXAM BOOST

SECTION A
Fixed phrases

You may be required to choose a word or words to complete a phrase, or select the most appropriate phrase. It's helpful to think carefully about the meaning of the text, and the sentence you have to complete.

1 Complete the fixed phrases with words from the box.

> event   light   matter   question

1 a _____ of course
2 in any _____
3 in _____ of
4 be a _____ of

2 Match the fixed phrases in Ex 1 with their definitions (A–D).

A considering something, or taking something into account
B used to say that something will definitely happen or be true in spite of anything else that may happen
C the correct and usual thing to do in a particular situation
D used to say what the most important fact, part, or feature of something is

SECTION B
Collocations

You may have to choose the word which collocates with a word in the text. The other three options will have similar meanings, but will not fit the meaning of the sentence.

3 Choose the word that does NOT collocate with the adverb in each case.

1 **highly**   controversial / efficient / held / sophisticated
2 **widely**   available / held / similar / understood
3 **deeply**   crafted / offended / regretful / upset
4 **broadly**   accepted / attached / interpreted / similar
5 **strongly**   attached / available / implied / opposed
6 **heavily**   built / guarded / involved / offended
7 **finely**   balanced / crafted / controversial / tuned

SECTION C
Phrasal verbs

You need to choose the answer which fits the context. All four options may be similar in meaning, so think carefully about the exact meaning of each word.

4 Match the phrasal verbs 1–6, with their definitions, A–F.

1 come across   A start
2 come on   B become conscious again
3 come over   C experience something unpleasant
4 come round   D move from one place to another
5 come under   E happen
6 come up   F seem to have particular qualities

5 Complete the sentences with the correct form of the phrasal verbs from Ex 4.

1 I've got a cold _____ . I don't think I'll come out this evening after all.
2 When I _____ after the operation, I felt a bit sick.
3 Has your family _____ from the USA for your brother's wedding?
4 The same problems have been _____ again and again with this programme.
5 Jenna _____ as a warm and genuine kind of person.
6 I've _____ a lot of pressure at work recently. It's been a stressful period.

SECTION D
Easily confused words

You may have to choose between words which are similar in meaning but not the same.

6 Complete the sentences with each pair of words. Use each word once only.

1 sympathy / empathy
_____ is when you're able to imagine what it must be like to be in someone's situation, whereas _____ is understanding and caring about someone's problems.
2 discrete / discreet
_____ means separate or different, whereas _____ means being careful not to cause embarrassment or attract too much attention.
3 illicit / elicit
To _____ something is to ask the right questions to get the information you want, whereas _____ means something that is illegal or disapproved of.
4 alternately / alternatively
_____ means one out of every two (e.g. days, weeks, months), whereas _____ is used to give a second possibility.

NUMBER OF QUESTIONS
8 (with 4 options to choose from)

TASK
Short reading text

SCORING
1 mark per question

ABOUT THE TASK

- You will read a short text with eight questions.
- You choose the word or phrase that best fits each gap from four multiple-choice questions.
- Only one of the options will fit each gap.

What is being tested?

This part of the exam focuses on your knowledge of vocabulary.
The questions may test your knowledge of:

- collocations, e.g. vitally important
- fixed phrases, e.g. do your utmost
- phrasal verbs, e.g. read up on
- precise meaning, e.g. Humans have evolved from ape-like ancestors.
- linking words, e.g. Alternatively,

Grammatical knowledge may be involved, too:

- what preposition follows a verb, e.g. be impressed by

How do you do it?

___ BEFORE THE TASK ___

- Read the title and whole text quickly to get a general understanding of the content and how the text is organised.
- Don't look at the options at this point.
- Look at the example given and think about why the answer is correct.

___ DURING THE TASK ___

- Read the text again carefully, stopping at each gap and reading the four options.
- If you think you know the answer, check your idea against the four options and choose the one that is closest.
- Check the words before and after each gap. You are looking for clues such as words that are followed by a particular preposition, or words that form part of a fixed phrase.
- If the gap includes linking words, make sure you read all the sentences around the gap.
- If you're not sure of an answer, cross out the options that are definitely wrong.
- If you are still not sure, choose the one that seems the most likely answer. You should always put an answer, as your guess may be right!
- Choose ONLY one of the four options: do not write your own word, even if it may fit the sentence.

___ AFTER THE TASK ___

- Read through the text again quickly with the words in place. Does it make sense? Can you see any mistakes?
- Make sure you have chosen an answer for each gap. No marks are lost for incorrect answers, so make a sensible guess.

Are you exam-ready?

Did you …

… read the text through quickly to get a general understanding? .... ☐

… stop at each gap and think about what word might be missing? .... ☐

… check your idea against the four options? .... ☐

… cross out the options that are definitely wrong if you are not sure? .... ☐

… choose the most likely answer if you are still not sure? .... ☐

… answer every question? .... ☐

… remember to read the text again at the end, to make sure it makes sense? .... ☐

Are you ready for Reading and Use of English Part 1? Identify an area to improve.

3

EXAM REFERENCE

EXAM BOOST

SECTION A
Perfect and continuous tenses

You may need to complete a verb form, such as an auxiliary verb used to form a particular tense. Think carefully about the time references in the text as a whole, which will help you determine which word you need.

1 Complete the sentences with an appropriate auxiliary verb or verbs.

1 I _____ expecting a phone call any minute now. Can I get back to you later?

2 Jodie _____ never met anyone quite like Stephanie before and was intrigued to find out more.

3 They _____ just put the finishing touches to the decorations, so the room will be ready shortly.

4 José _____ working on his assignment all afternoon and hopes to finish it by the end of the day.

5 Sara _____ waiting in the queue for two hours before she decided to give up and go home.

SECTION B
Conjunctions

You may have to use a conjunction to link clauses or sentences. It's important to understand how the different conjunctions are used, so you can choose one that fits the meaning of the sentence.

2 Complete the sentences with a word or phrase from the box. There is one word or phrase that you do not need to use.

> as though   as yet   not only   since
> whatever   whereas   while

1 _____ do triplets look alike, they have identical brain wave patterns, too.

2 _____ some non-identical triplets look very different from each other, other non-identical sets can look remarkably similar.

3 Identical triplets have the same blood type and eye colour, _____ their teeth marks and fingerprints are different.

4 It seems _____ the DNA of triplets may not be 100 percent identical.

5 _____ only 150 sets of triplets are born in the UK each year, this means that only 1 in 5,000 births results in triplets.

6 _____ the gender, it's fairly common to find that one triplet writes with a different hand to the others.

SECTION C
Conditional forms

You have to decide which grammatical word fits in each of the gaps. This may include conditional forms.

3 Complete the conditionals with a suitable word. You may need to use a contracted form.

1 If Joe _____ studied harder, he might have a better job now.

2 Had I learnt to cook professionally, I _____ been able to make you a restaurant-standard dinner.

3 If I _____ have to go to the dentist tomorrow, I wouldn't be so worried today.

4 If Jenny were here, she'd _____ shown us how to play this game.

5 If I had more free time, I _____ definitely go to more gigs with you.

6 If I _____ going to visit my grandma at the weekend, I'd have planned to go shopping with Bernie.

7 Had Danny _____ going to the conference, he'd be packing his bags right now.

8 If you'd recorded that programme about veganism, we _____ put it on.

SECTION D
Future tenses

You may have to complete tenses. You will usually be tested on the auxiliary elements of the tense, rather than the main verb.

4 Complete the sustainability plan using an appropriate auxiliary verb or verbs.

How I plan to be more sustainable

I'm [1]_____ to buy one of those reusable coffee cups made of bamboo.

I [2]_____ mend all my clothes instead of buying new ones.

By this time next year, I [3]_____ got rid of my car and [4]_____ riding a bicycle.

I [5]_____ already reducing household energy use by installing energy-efficient appliances.

I [6]_____ using far more Fairtrade™ products in the future.

In a year's time, I [7]_____ planted several more trees in my garden.

ABOUT THE TASK

- You will read a short text with eight gaps.
- You have to think of the word that best fits each gap. There are no options to choose from.
- The answer is ALWAYS a single word.
- The word you write must be spelled correctly, and must fit the grammar and meaning of the sentence.
- Very occasionally, there may be more than one correct answer.

NUMBER OF QUESTIONS
8

TASK
Short reading text

SCORING
1 mark per question

What is being tested?

This part of the exam focuses on your knowledge of grammar and your understanding of how a text is organised. The questions may test your knowledge of, for example:

- prepositions, e.g. within, towards
- pronouns, e.g. its, oneself
- auxiliary and modal verbs, e.g. have, can, must
- articles, e.g. a/an, the

- determiners, e.g. some, much
- relatives, e.g. what, which, who, how
- conjunctions, e.g. or, although
- phrasal verb particles, e.g. come over, do away with, draw on

How do you do it?

BEFORE THE TASK

- Read the title and whole text quickly to get a general understanding of the content and how the text is organised.
- Don't focus on the gaps at this point.
- Look at the example given and think about why the answer is correct.

DURING THE TASK

- Read the text again carefully, stopping at each gap.
- Think about what type of word is missing, e.g. is it a pronoun, a preposition, an article?
- Read the whole sentence containing the gap. Is the missing word part of a verb, and is it singular or plural, passive or active, an auxiliary verb?
- Check the words before and after the gap. The missing word may be a dependent preposition or part of a fixed phrase.
- Read the sentences before and after the one with the gap. The missing word may be linking to ideas in the same sentence, or in different sentences.

AFTER THE TASK

- Read through the text again quickly with the words in place. Does it make sense? Can you see any mistakes?
- If you still don't know the answer, make a sensible guess. No marks are lost for incorrect answers, so don't leave any empty gaps.

Are you exam-ready?

Did you …

… read the text through quickly to get a general understanding? .... ☐

… stop at each gap and think about what type of word might be missing? .... ☐

… check the words before and after the gap carefully? .... ☐

… read the sentence before and after the gap if the missing word is a linking word? .... ☐

… answer every question? .... ☐

… remember to read the text again at the end, to make sure it makes sense? .... ☐

SECTION A
Prefixes

1 Match the words 1–8 with their definitions A–G.

1 perfection
2 adjust
3 reasonably
4 adequate
5 regularity
6 inform
7 advantaged

A good enough but not very good
B give information
C change something slightly
D the state of happening at uniform intervals
E having a favourable position
F in a fair way, showing good judgement
G when something is without fault

2 Now add a prefix from the box to the words in Ex 1 to make another word. Which words become opposites? What do the other words mean?

dis- im- in- inter- ir- mis- re- un-

SECTION B
Suffixes

3 Replace the words in bold with words from the box. One of the words means the opposite of the word in the sentence: which word is it?

constructive   courageous
lengthy   pointless   priceless

1 Oh, this is **hopeless**! I'm wasting my time and yours trying to get a straight answer!
2 I've had some **supportive** feedback about that project I've been working on. It's made me feel a whole lot better about it.
3 We're offering you a **worthless** opportunity to work in our subsidiary company abroad.
4 I'm not as **audacious** as you. There's no way I'd stand up to someone who holds such power and authority.
5 This is a rather **wordy** report. Can you cut it down and make it easier for the readers to digest?

SECTION C
Internal word changes

You may need to make more than one change to the root word, which might include internal changes. This means making changes to the spelling of the root word, as well as adding a prefix and/or suffix.

4 Decide which suffix to add, '-able' or '-ible', to the root words below. Make any other necessary changes.

1	NOTICE	3	JUSTIFY	5	PROFIT
	_____		_____		_____
2	DEBATE	4	EAT	6	DEFEND
	_____		_____		_____

5 Change the form of the word to match the definition.

1 ALTERNATE _____
otherwise (adv)
2 ASSUME _____
the thought that something is true without proof (n)
3 BENEFIT _____
helpful or useful (adj)
4 ENDURE _____
ability to keep doing something difficult/unpleasant for a long time (n)
5 IMPLY _____
result or effect that seems likely in the future (n)
6 MOVE _____
the act of taking something away (n)

SECTION D
Compounding

You may need to form compounds. The word in capital letters at the end of the line may be the first word in the compound or the second, so think carefully about the meaning of the sentence.

6 Choose one word from box A and one from box B to make compounds. Then match the compounds with their definitions, 1–5.

A   break   counter   guide   spokes   work

B   down   line   part   person   shop

1 someone with the same position as someone but in another place or organisation
2 advice about how to do something
3 someone chosen to speak officially for a group or organisation
4 when a group of people meet to learn about something through discussion and practical exercises
5 failure, such as with communication

NUMBER OF QUESTIONS
8

TASK
Short reading text

SCORING
1 mark per question

ABOUT THE TASK

- You will read a short text with eight gaps.
- The base forms of the missing words are at the end of the line containing the gap.
- You have to change the form of the word so it fits the gap.

What is being tested?

This part of the exam focuses on your ability to form new words from a base form. The questions may test your knowledge of, for example:

- prefixes, e.g. prerequisite, biannual
- suffixes, e.g. captivate, elusiveness
- internal spelling changes, e.g. long → length, rely → reliance
- compound words, e.g. sun → sunshine, draw → drawback

How do you do it?

___ **BEFORE THE TASK** _____

- Read the title and whole text quickly to get a general understanding of the content and how the text is organised.
- Don't focus on the gaps at this point.
- Look at the example given and think about why the answer is correct.

___ **DURING THE TASK** _____

- Read the text again carefully, stopping at each gap.
- Think about what type of word is missing, e.g. is it a noun, a verb, an adjective or an adverb?
- Is the missing word singular or plural, countable or uncountable, positive or negative?
- Look at the base word. Think about how you need to change it to the form you need.
- Think about prefixes or suffixes you may need to add, and think about other spelling changes.

___ **AFTER THE TASK** _____

- Read through the text again quickly with the words in place. Does it make sense? Can you see any mistakes?
- Make sure you have completed all the gaps. No marks are lost for incorrect answers, so make a sensible guess if you are still not sure.

Are you exam-ready?

Did you …

… read the text through quickly to get a general understanding? .... ☐

… stop at each gap and think about what type of word might be missing? .... ☐

… look at the base word and think about how to change it? .... ☐

… remember to think about prefixes and suffixes, and other spelling changes? .... ☐

… answer every question? .... ☐

… remember to read the text again at the end, to make sure it makes sense? .... ☐

EXAM REFERENCE

Are you ready for Reading and Use of English Part 3? Identify an area to improve.

7

SECTION A
Passive forms

You must use the word given in bold without changing its form. You may need to change the verb forms, such as active to passive, and you may need to make other changes as well.

1 Complete the sentences with an appropriate form of the verb in brackets.

1 The fastest speed reached on a bicycle _____ (record) as 268.7 kilometres per hour.

2 Over the years, 479 bicycle records _____ (include) as Guinness World Records.

3 One of the most expensive bikes in the world _____ (estimate) to cost around £25,000 and _____ (make) by Aston Martin.

4 You can _____ (prosecute) for cycling too fast in the UK, though speed limits do not apply to bikes.

2 Complete the second sentence so that it has a similar meaning to the first, using the word given.

1 They didn't take the car away because we didn't leave it parked on the pavement.
WOULD
The car _____ if we'd left it parked on the pavement.

2 The mechanic says he will repair the car by Thursday.
BE
The car _____ Thursday, the mechanic says.

SECTION B
Reported speech

3 Match the reporting verbs with the sentences.

> acknowledge   deny   dismiss   remind
> threaten   warn

1 'Don't you dare keep splashing me or I'll splash you back more!'

2 'I shouldn't really have to tell you again but you fasten the window like this.'

3 'I wasn't even in the area at the time of the burglary, never mind actually breaking in.'

4 'There's some flooding on the perimeter road and three lorries have already got stuck.'

5 'I know equations are tricky to get your head round but it is worth the effort.'

6 'The theory just doesn't hold up so you'll have to abandon it.'

SECTION C
Verb and noun phrases

You may have to transform a noun phrase to a verb phrase and vice versa.

4 Complete the second sentence so that it has a similar meaning to the first, using the word given.

1 No one explained why the lecture had started so late.
WAS
No _____ to why the lecture had started so late.

2 Rectangles are used in space planning because of their efficiency.
TERMS
Rectangles are efficient
_____ space and are therefore used in planning.

3 There is a mistaken belief that diamonds are valuable.
THAT
People _____ diamonds are valuable.

4 Symmetry refers to a sense of harmonious proportion and balance.
IS
There _____ of proportion and balance in symmetry.

SECTION D
Clause patterns

You may have to transform one kind of clause to another.

5 Rewrite the sentences using the clause types in the box and the words given.

> 'if' + past participle
> 'should there' + infinitive without 'to'
> 'the best' + pronoun + 'can' or 'could'

1 If there's a halo around the sun or moon, you can be sure it's going to rain.
BE
You can be sure it's going to rain
_____ a halo around the sun or moon.

2 The frequency of cricket chirps can tell you the temperature when you listen to it carefully.
TO
The frequency of cricket chirps will tell you the temperature _____ carefully.

3 Daisies try their hardest to protect themselves from rain by closing their petals soon before it's due.
THE
Daisies _____ to protect themselves from rain by closing their petals soon before it's due.

ABOUT THE TASK

NUMBER OF QUESTIONS
6
TASK
Six pairs of sentences
SCORING
2 up to 2 marks per question

- You will read six pairs of sentences.
- The sentences in each pair have a similar meaning, but they are expressed in different ways.
- There is a gap in the second sentence which you have to complete.
- You must use between three and six words to fill the gap.
- Contractions (e.g. don't, can't, needn't, etc.) count as two words.
- You are given one of the words (called the key word). You MUST include this word in your answer.
- You must not make any changes to the key word.

What is being tested?

This part of the exam tests your knowledge of both grammar and vocabulary. You need to show that you can express a sentence in a different way, using different grammar patterns or different vocabulary, but without changing the meaning. The questions may test your knowledge of:

- clause patterns, such as conditional, comparative, relative, etc.
- active and passive forms
- reported speech
- collocation and fixed phrases
- synonymous phrases
- phrasal verbs
- verb phrases transformed to noun or adjectival phrases and vice versa

How do you do it?

BEFORE THE TASK

- Read the example to make sure you know exactly what to do.
- Read the instructions carefully, and make sure you know how many words you must use to fill the gap.

DURING THE TASK

- Read each first sentence carefully and think about what it means.
- Look at the key word. Is it a noun, verb, pronoun?
- Think about whether there is a particular structure that usually follows this key word, e.g. 'have' + 'something' + 'done', 'allow' + 'someone' + 'to do something'.
- Read the second sentence in each pair. Think about the information that is missing from the second sentence.
- Think about how you can complete the second sentence using between three and six words, including the key word.
- Remember, you can change other words from the first sentence, and add different words, but you must not change the key word.
- If you are not sure what the correct answer is, make a sensible guess using the key word. No marks are lost for incorrect answers.

AFTER THE TASK

- Read through both sentences in each pair again to check that they have the same meaning.
- Check that you have used the correct number of words to complete each gap.

Are you exam-ready?

Did you …
… read the first sentence and think about the meaning carefully? ☐
… think about structures that are used with the key word? ☐
… complete the second sentence, using between three and six words? ☐
… leave the key word unchanged? ☐
… answer all the questions? ☐
… read the two sentences again to check they have the same meaning? ☐

SECTION A
Understanding inference and implication

The multiple-choice questions and options usually target implied but not stated meaning in the text.

1 Read the paragraph and answer the questions. Find clues in the text for your answers.

A

The following morning the ground was damp underfoot and Joe needed to wear boots to collect water from the stream. The clouds were hurtling across the sky and he nearly got hit by a broken branch as he stumbled in his hand-me-down boots that were too big for him along the track back up to the tent, clutching his thin jacket to his chest with one hand and swinging the bucket of water in the other. He hoped the weather forecast of torrential rain later that morning would prove to be wrong, as his parents had promised him a trip to the local fairground and the attraction of riding the big wheel had kept him awake through much of the noisy night.

1 What is implied about
a the weather when Joe went to the stream?
_____
_____

b the weather the previous night?
_____
_____

2 What can we infer about the financial status of Joe's family?
_____
_____

3 What is implied about Joe's age and interests?
_____
_____

SECTION B
Understanding purpose and attitude

You may need to answer questions relating to the writer's intention; how they want the reader to be affected by a piece of writing, or a paragraph or extract. You will often need to read beyond one or two sentences to decide what this is.

2 Choose from the writer's intentions, 1–6, regarding extracts A and B. The writer wants to

1 reassure people about the efforts to eliminate phone scamming.
2 familiarise people with how to detect phone scammers.
3 correct an assumption related to phone scamming.
4 look at phone scamming from a humorous angle.
5 warn people about falling for phone scams.
6 explain why some people are more likely to be targeted than others.

A

It is often thought that elderly people are the main targets for phone scammers as they have less experience of dealing with the tricks that are used by these criminals, unaware of the number and type of scams being perpetrated these days. This is, however, a generalisation and a misconception. Many older people, quite the opposite, are extremely unwilling to interact with unknown callers and distrust anyone purporting to be a random computer engineer or bank official.

B

Hannah looked across at Josh as his fingers flew over the keyboard. 'You appear to be inspired.'

'Yes,' Josh muttered, not wanting his flow to be interrupted. 'It's the article on scamming. I just want to get the right balance between informing and panicking. No point in scaring people half to death, is there? And I don't want to come across as critical of how some people believe anything they're told.'

'Even though that's what it comes down to, isn't it – gullibility?' The phone started to ring, and Hannah answered it. 'Hannah Barnes speaking.' She frowned and passed it to Josh. 'I don't believe it!' she whispered. 'Apparently there's a problem with our internet connection. The guy wants to talk you through …'

Josh disconnected the phone and smiled. 'What were you saying about gullibility?'

NUMBER OF QUESTIONS
6 (with 4 options to choose from)

TASK
One long text

SCORING
2 marks per question

ABOUT THE TASK

- You will read a long text which is followed by six multiple-choice questions.
- Each question has four options to choose from.
- The questions come in the same order as the information in the text.
- Some questions focus on a sentence or phrase in the text.
- Other questions ask about a longer section of text.
- It is always clear which part of the text the question refers to. You should not bring information from other parts of the text into your answers.

What is being tested?

In this part of the exam, the multiple-choice questions focus on different aspects of reading. They may ask about:

- the writer's attitude or opinion, or the writer's message or purpose in writing.
- your detailed understanding of one part of the text.
- the writer's use of a particular expression or phrase, or its meaning in context.
- the writer's purpose in part or all of the text.
- something that is implied in the text rather than stated.
- some features of text organisation, such as reference or comparison.

How do you do it?

BEFORE THE TASK

- Read the context sentence, as this tells you what type of text it is and what it's about.
- Read the title and whole text quickly to get a general understanding of the content and how the text is organised.
- Read the questions to identify what you're looking for. Underline key words. Find the paragraphs in the text that each question refers to.
- Read the paragraphs you have identified again to see if you can find the answer before necessarily looking at the options.

DURING THE TASK

- Read the options for each question and underline key words.
- Read each relevant paragraph again and choose the option that is closest to answering the question. Remember that you may not see the same words in the text and the options, as they may be paraphrased.
- Check that the other options are definitely wrong.
- If a question asks about the meaning of a particular vocabulary item or a reference, make sure that you read the sentences before and after it carefully, as these will help you find the answer.
- If you're not sure of an answer, leave it and move on – you can go back to it later. If you are still not sure, identify the options that are definitely wrong and choose from the others the one that seems most likely.

AFTER THE TASK

- Check your answers quickly to make sure you are happy with them.
- Make sure you have answered all the questions, even if you are not sure of the answers.

Are you exam-ready?

Did you …

… read the first whole text to get a general understanding? .... ☐
… read the questions and identify the paragraph where each answer will be? .... ☐
… underline key words in the questions to help you find the correct information? .... ☐
… read the relevant paragraph carefully to find the information you need? .... ☐
… choose the option that is closest to the meaning? .... ☐
… answer all the questions, even if you are unsure of the answers? .... ☐

Are you ready for Reading and Use of English Part 5? Identify an area to improve.

11

SECTION A
Identifying contrasting opinions

You have to compare the different writers' opinions or attitudes towards aspects of the topic they are writing about. Their opinion may be expressed in different ways, and sometimes may not be immediately clear.

1 Which writers A–F share the same opinions about applying for planning permission with the current designs for the new community centre?

A While a new community centre is desperately needed by the town, I consider the current plans unsuitable for the location, and it is pointless putting forward a planning application at this time.

B I have read about the designs for the new centre and by all accounts, although on the surface appearing to meet the needs of the community, they require further work to be acceptable by the planning authorities.

C Some people argue that the new centre will look out of place in the location and that not enough thought has gone into the design. I would take issue with that.

D It was originally thought that the new plans for the centre met all the planning requirements. However, this is now being questioned and I tend to concur with the general feeling that more work needs to be done before permission can be given.

E It is hoped that the planning officers will look favourably on the designs for the new centre, as the people involved in their development have spent a long time getting them right, and they are impressive.

2 Read the extracts again and highlight the words or phrases that indicate the writers' opinions.

SECTION B
Identifying similar opinions

You will need to identify similar opinions in texts. Read carefully, as the writer may mention other points of view before or after giving their own.

3 Read the text about subjects on the school curriculum. Which two opinions 1–5 does the writer agree with? Highlight the phrases that helped you decide.

School curriculums need to cover a wealth of different topics and can sometimes squeeze out certain subjects which may be felt to be no longer vital for a student's education. Disciplines such as drama, art and music could be considered by some as extras which can be taken up as interests in after-school clubs or societies. This is an extremely short-sighted approach and one that should be reversed. What is to be admired is the time given to helping students develop life skills such as presentations or debating abilities. Whereas many might consider this a waste of time, they should realise the value of these skills when students leave the protected school life and need to survive in the real adult world.

1 Students today do not need to study arts subjects like drama as they can do them outside school.

2 Decisions to cut some minority subjects are wrong, and the decision makers are not looking at the importance of an overall education for life.

3 It is not worth spending time in class learning how to debate, as other subjects are more important.

4 People who teach life skills are talented and deserve our respect.

5 School education should prepare students for life beyond school and include lessons on the different skills they will need to use in their future lives.

4 Read the text about subjects on the school curriculum in Ex 3 again and think about what you highlighted. What types of words did you highlight?

5 Check your answers to Ex 3. How do you know that the writer does not agree with the other three opinions?

ABOUT THE TASK

- You will read four short texts which are related to the same theme or topic.
- You will answer four questions in which you have to identify one of the texts or writers.
- You need to compare information in each of the texts to find the correct answers.

NUMBER OF QUESTIONS

4

TASK
Four short texts on a related topic

SCORING

2 marks per question

EXAM REFERENCE

What is being tested?

In this part of the exam, you will need to read across several texts to compare and identify different viewpoints and information about a particular topic. You need to:

- understand the writers' attitudes and opinions, which is often inferred.
- decide which writers agree or disagree with each other.
- identify distraction to avoid mistakes.

How do you do it?

___ BEFORE THE TASK _____

- Read the context sentence as this will help identify the topic the texts relate to.
- Read all four texts to get a general idea of how the writers have reacted to the topic.
- Read the questions and underline the information you are going to look for to answer the questions.

___ DURING THE TASK _____

- Take each question in turn and identify whether you are looking for agreement or disagreement between writers.
- You may be given a writer and asked which other writer agrees or disagrees with them about a certain point. First read the text chosen and locate the point referred to.
- Read the other texts and highlight any references to the point, whether they indicate agreement or disagreement.
- Be aware that you may need to look beyond one reference in each text to get the full picture.
- The wording in the texts will often be a paraphrase of what you are looking for, or an opinion may be implied but not stated. Look for synonyms and ways in which similar and contrasting opinions can be expressed.
- Choose the writer whose opinion matches the section(s) of text you originally highlighted.
- One question may ask you to find a writer who has a different opinion from the others on a topic. Do this question last and read all four texts again and highlight references to identify the correct writer.

___ AFTER THE TASK _____

- Read the texts again to check you are happy with your answers.
- If you are unable to answer one question, do not leave it blank, but make an educated guess.

Are you exam-ready?

Did you …

… read the instructions carefully? .... ☐

… read all texts first to get general understanding? .... ☐

… highlight words in the questions and relevant phrases in the texts? .... ☐

… look for implied meaning and synonyms? .... ☐

… look for different ways of expressing similar or contrasting opinions? .... ☐

… check your answers? .... ☐

SECTION A
Using content clues

The first sentence in each paragraph is very important, as this often (although not always) provides the main link with the previous one. The sentence will always have some relevance or reference to the previous paragraph and develop a theme.

1 Choose which sentences 1–3 fit the gaps in the paragraphs A–C.

1 I sometimes recognise a character from a drama I've watched or a room from a place I've visited and wonder why these appear in a dream.

2 I have been plagued with such restless nights since my childhood and have accepted that my nightly sleep adventures are part of who I am.

3 Many people maintain, including several of my acquaintants, that they never dream, often with an insistence that goes completely against everything we are told by sleep experts who have been investigating the nature of sleep for years and years.

A
_____ It simply is not true. It is just that not everyone has a recollection. I sometimes wish that I counted myself in that number and could awake, refreshed, not mentally exhausted after a nightmare or a lucid dream.

B
_____ Despite dream explanations involving symbolism and various forms of interpretation, I remain convinced that my dreams are informed by events and fragments of information my brain has settled on during the previous day or days.

C
_____ Is it meaningful in some way? Does it perhaps reflect something I've been subconsciously concerned about? Or is it merely a jumbled meaningless mix?

SECTION B
Understanding the structure of a text
Using reference to establish links across paragraphs is important.

2 Put the paragraphs in the correct order and highlight the references that helped you to do this.

1 _____   3 _____
2 _____   4 _____

A
As a result of this, a project has been started to try to ensure that there are places of solitude for those who really want it. Silent Space hopes to introduce areas in public parks and gardens where people turn off phones and stop talking for certain periods each day.

B
Today many people visit parks and gardens to relax and get away from busy streets and offices. However, all too often they are finding that the parks they visit are busy and noisy places themselves, and the opportunity to find peace and quiet is getting progressively more and more difficult.

C
It is believed that this can benefit us in many ways. It can contribute significantly to our well-being and general health. Apparently, just five minutes sitting quietly looking at nature can have an effect and help us to relax. It is hoped that this idea will be implemented more widely in public spaces in the coming years.

D
Some places have already made the move, an example of which is at the University of East Anglia. Students who want to get away from their labs and study rooms are encouraged to spend time in an area called 'The Dutch Garden' where they can sit in complete silence and appreciate the natural beauty.

ABOUT THE TASK

- You will read a long text with six gaps where paragraphs have been removed.
- The missing paragraphs that fit these gaps are written below the text, in a jumbled order.
- There is also a seventh paragraph which does not fit any of the gaps in the text.
- You have to decide which of the seven paragraphs fits each of the six gaps.

NUMBER OF QUESTIONS

6

TASK
One long text with six gaps (with seven options)

SCORING

2 marks per question

What is being tested?

In this part of the exam, you need to:

- show global understanding of a text.
- understand the way that text is structured and develops.
- be aware of how paragraphs link together, both to a previous paragraph and the following one.

How do you do it?

___ BEFORE THE TASK _____

- Read the context sentence, as this tells you what type of text it is and what it's about.
- Read the title and whole text quickly, ignoring the gaps, to get a general understanding of the content and how the text is organised.
- Read the seven paragraphs.
- Decide if you can immediately choose any paragraphs to fit the gaps.

___ DURING THE TASK _____

- Read the base text again, stopping at each gap. Read the text before and after each gap and think about what kind of information might be missing.
- Read the extra paragraphs again and check for topic links with the base text.
- Look also for language links. These could be references to people, places, events or time.
- Discourse markers or sequencers can sometimes help you, e.g. 'Some time later …'
- Choose the best option to fit each gap.

___ AFTER THE TASK _____

- When you have completed all the gaps, check that the extra paragraph does not fit into any gap.
- Read the whole text again, with the missing paragraphs in place. Make sure that it makes sense and the ideas follow each other in a logical way. If you have any doubts, check your answers again.
- Make sure you choose an answer for each gap – no marks are lost for incorrect answers, so make a sensible guess if you are not sure.

Are you exam-ready?

> **Did you …**
>
> … first read the whole text to get a general understanding? .... ☐
>
> … read the seven paragraphs carefully? .... ☐
>
> … focus on each gap and think about the flow of the text? .... ☐
>
> … choose the best paragraph for each gap and check that it fits with the previous and following paragraphs? ☐
>
> … check that the extra paragraph does not fit into any gap? .... ☐
>
> … check that the overall text makes sense with the sentences in place? .... ☐

Are you ready for Reading and Use of English Part 7? Identify an area to improve.

15

SECTION A
Identifying paraphrase

You will often need to identify paraphrasing. The questions will usually use different wording to the relevant parts of the text. Sometimes the introductory verb summarises an attitude expressed in the text.

1 Choose the correct introductory verbs for the questions relating to these extracts.

> compares   compliments   criticises   questions

1

> Many people move to the city from the countryside because of their job, but for several reasons I am not convinced this is a good idea.

Question: The writer _____ the advisability of relocating to the city for work purposes.

2

> How people are expected to live comfortably in such tiny spaces is beyond me. The way the houses were planned leaves a lot to be desired.

Question: The writer _____ the architects for not considering the impact of their designs on the residents.

3

> In my opinion, the council are to be thanked for introducing a congestion charge for through-traffic as it is contributing to the reduction of pollution in the town centre.

Question: The writer _____ the authorities on their traffic-control initiative.

4

> Whereas it is really pricey to stay at city-centre chain hotels, it is always possible to find cheaper bed and breakfast places nearby.

Question: The writer _____ the costs of accommodation in the same location.

2 Compare the extracts and the questions again and find other examples of paraphrasing.

SECTION B
Avoiding distraction

There will be distraction that you must avoid when choosing your answers.

3 Read two sets of extracts from posts about people's attitudes towards job interviews. Highlight the key words in the questions and then choose the correct extracts to answer the questions. Highlight the distraction in the incorrect extracts.

Which interviewee

1 has a tendency to be overconfident?

A

> It's important to present a good image during the interview and I hope I manage to give the impression that I'm self-assured and that I know what I'm talking about, although usually I'm shaking inside.

B

> Most interviewers are looking for someone who can deal with whatever questions they're asked. I find I can usually talk my way through nearly anything and sometimes I guess I might come across as a bit of a know-it-all.

2 is unsure of the importance of appearance in an interview?

A

> The morning before I'm a mess in terms of my nerves, and for me one way of overcoming them is to look good. If I can see a smart-looking guy in the mirror, I can trick myself into thinking that this guy is not only smart looking but smart enough to get the job, too. The interviewers are probably oblivious to my new suit and shiny shoes, but it makes me feel good.

B

> The self-help books on how to get through an interview talk about keeping calm, doing your research, getting there on time but I don't remember them making much mention of what to wear. I guess it depends what the job is, but as far as I'm concerned, looking as good as you can helps make that first impression, and smart clothes and clean shoes are a must.

NUMBER OF QUESTIONS
10

TASK
One long text or up to six shorter texts

SCORING
1 mark per question

ABOUT THE TASK

- You will read one long text which may be continuous and divided into sections, or several shorter texts on a similar topic.
- You will have ten questions to answer which ask you to locate information in a correct section of the text.
- The questions will contain information or statements that you need to match to the information you find in the sections.

What is being tested?

This part of the exam tests your ability to skim or scan a text quickly to find the information you need. You need to:

- read quickly without worrying about the meaning of every word.
- read carefully to match the exact meaning of the question or statement to the relevant part of the text.
- understand the detail, specific information, attitude or opinion in the question, and find the part of the text where those ideas are stated or implied.
- recognise that there may be ideas in other sections which appear to be similar, but which don't match the question accurately.

How do you do it?

BEFORE THE TASK

- Read the context sentence, as this tells you what type of text it is and what it's about. It will also tell you the overall topic if you are given several short texts.
- Scan the text or texts quickly to get the general ideas and information expressed.
- Read through all the questions. You may be able to match some already after your first scan.
- Read the questions again and think about what each one means.
- Underline key words in the questions. You won't see these words in the text – they will be paraphrased, but identifying the key information you need will help you.

DURING THE TASK

- Focus on each question in turn.
- Skim or scan the part of the text where you think the answer is. Avoid distraction.
- Check carefully to make sure that it matches the question completely. Sometimes there are two parts to a question and a text might match one but not both points.
- If you have difficulty with one of the questions, don't spend time worrying about it. Move on to another question and then come back to it.

AFTER THE TASK

- Quickly check your answers to make sure you are happy with them.
- Make sure you have answered all the questions – don't leave any questions unanswered.

Are you exam-ready?

Did you …

… read the instructions and questions carefully? .... ☐

… focus on each question in turn and skim or scan the text to find the information that matches? .... ☐

… read the relevant part of the text very carefully to make sure the meaning matches exactly? .... ☐

… check that you answered all the questions? .... ☐

Are you ready for Reading and Use of English Part 8? Identify an area to improve.

17

EXAM REFERENCE

SECTION A
Structuring an essay

You are required to address certain points.

1 **Discuss the essay task below and say which sentences A–D would be relevant when writing it. Why are the other sentences irrelevant?**

A 'I train at least twice a week at my tennis club and am looking forward to taking part in their annual competition at the end of June.'

B 'The cost of using the swimming pool has doubled over the last year.'

C 'It can be alarming to find out what is actually in much of the ready meals sold in supermarkets.'

D 'Another useful thing could be to introduce cookery classes at secondary schools so that students can cook cheap meals when they leave home.'

You have had a class discussion on what could be done by the council in your area to help improve people's health and fitness levels. You have made the notes below.

How to help improve local people's health and fitness levels.

- Subsidise membership of leisure centre
- Distribute nutrition leaflets through the local surgery
- Organise fun runs and outdoor group exercise sessions in local park

Some opinions expressed in the discussion?

'A lot of people would like to use the centre but the fees are too high.'

'Many people aren't really aware of the nutrition values of different foods.'

'People often enjoy exercising with other people rather than on their own.'

Write an essay discussing **two** of the points in your notes. You should **explain which idea would be more effective, giving reasons** in support of your answer.

You may, if you wish, make use of the opinions expressed in the discussion, but you should use your own words as far as possible.

2 **Plan your essay. Decide how many paragraphs and what each will contain.**

SECTION B
Complex sentences

In addition to ensuring your essay has a clear structure and appropriate tone, it is important to use a range of vocabulary and grammatical forms. One way to achieve this is to use complex sentences to communicate your ideas clearly and effectively.

3 **Read two extracts from candidates' essays about ways to keep fit. Which is more appropriate, A or B? Why?**

A

Kids need to learn how to keep fit. Lots of them just hang out with their mates after school and don't work out at all, so they don't get into the habit. Once you get into something and you get hooked on it, like skateboarding, which is pretty cool after all, then you're going to keep at it, aren't you? I vote for building a skateboarding park in the park.

B

What is really important is for adults to be role models for their children, and if they eat healthily and use sporting facilities, their children will follow suit and feel that a healthy lifestyle is normal. However, the leisure centre, although offering a wide range of facilities for both families and individuals, is relatively expensive. Therefore, I believe that providing cheaper access to the leisure centre is definitely the way forward, and would be welcomed by the community.

4 **Read the more appropriate extract again and highlight examples of how the writer has created complex sentences.**

ABOUT THE TASK

- This task is compulsory.
- An essay is usually written for a teacher, and uses formal or semi-formal language.
- In this task you read an input text which gives a discussion situation, a question, three points to consider and three opinions expressed in the discussion.
- You are required to write a discursive essay based on two of the points given, explaining which of the points are more important and why.
- You can use some of the opinions expressed in the discussion.

TIMING
Approximately 45 minutes

TASK
Write a discursive essay in 220–260 words.

SCORING
Half the available marks in the Writing paper

EXAM REFERENCE

What is being tested?

The main purpose of the essay is to write about relevant issues related to the stated topic and to support an argument with reasons and examples. You are marked on a scale of 1–5 in the following areas:

- **Content**: This must be relevant, and use the ideas given. Address all parts of the task.
- **Communicative achievement**: Your essay must have a clear structure leading to a logical conclusion, and deal effectively with straightforward and complex ideas. The reader must be able to understand the argument.
- **Organisation**: Organise your ideas into clear paragraphs including an introduction and conclusion, and use linking words to connect your ideas.
- **Language**: Use formal or semi-formal language in your essay. Use a range of vocabulary and grammatical forms.

How do you do it?

BEFORE THE TASK

- Read the task carefully so that you know what you need to include.
- Think about your own opinions about the topic.
- Decide which two points you will consider.
- Plan how you will divide your ideas into paragraphs. Think about what will go in the introduction, main body and the conclusion.

DURING THE TASK

- It is sometimes a good idea to note down points in a rough plan before starting to write the final version.
- Make the introduction engaging for the reader and present some background to the issues.
- Develop your main points with reasons and examples.
- Write a conclusion that reviews and summarises what you have written and clarifies your point of view.

AFTER THE TASK

Read through the essay again and make sure that:

- it is coherent and logical, uses formal or semi-formal language, and check for any mistakes.
- you have done everything the task requires and rephrased any information from the input text in your own words.

Are you exam-ready?

Did you …

... spend enough time planning? .... ☐

... include all the information required? .... ☐

... use the right tone? .... ☐

... check for mistakes in grammar, spelling and punctuation? .... ☐

... write the correct number of words? .... ☐

SECTION A
Using correct register

In this exam task, you need to use the appropriate register.

1 Find formal equivalents for the following in the email extract.

1 get in touch with
2 put up on / posted
3 if you need
4 just to let you know
5 fun
6 bought
7 lots of
8 don't need to buy

We would like to inform you that the awards ceremony for the young sportsperson of the South West will be held at the West Bank Hotel, London, on 28th September. Those on the shortlists for the different categories will automatically receive tickets for the event. The cost of attending the event for family and other guests will be £35 and tickets can be purchased through the website. It will be an entertaining evening, with dinner followed by the many presentations to successful young sportspeople. The shortlists will be announced on the website on 5th August. Should you require wheelchair access to the event, please contact Lucy Dobson on the number below.

2 Imagine you are a coach writing to young sportspeople in your club to tell them about the awards ceremony. Rewrite the email using the informal phrases from Ex 1 and making any other changes you think are necessary.

3 Decide which phrase in each pair would be appropriate for an informal email (I) and which for a more formal one (F).

1 a It was a pleasure to meet you …
  b It was so good to see you …
  … at the conference yesterday.

2 a What I'd do is …
  b I would suggest you …
  … rewrite the essay from the beginning.

3 a I'm a bit worried about …
  b I am slightly concerned about …
  … remembering everything for the exam.

4 a That's really good news.
  b I am glad that you have decided to visit.
  I can't believe you're coming at last!

5 a If you've got a spare moment, could you possibly …
  b I would be grateful if you could spare the time to …
  … help me solve this problem on my tablet?

SECTION B
Writing a formal email or letter

You may choose to write an email or letter. This could require a formal register.

4 Rewrite these sentences so that they would be appropriate for a formal email or letter.

1 Good to hear from you.
  _____

2 This is to let you know that I got your letter.
  _____

3 About the suggestions for a new play area in the park – sorry, but I think it's a bad idea.
  _____
  _____

4 I'm with you on the need for a shorter school day.
  _____
  _____

5 Rewrite these sentences in a more informal style.

1 I would be grateful if you could offer me some advice regarding improving my fitness for the competition.
  _____
  _____

2 It is my honest opinion that such a job would be unsuitable for you.
  _____
  _____

3 On consideration of all the factors presented in your letter, I would favour the latter suggestion.
  _____
  _____

4 On reflection, I would say that it might be preferable for you to arrive earlier in the evening.
  _____
  _____

TIMING
Approximately 45 minutes

TASK
Write an email or letter in 220–260 words.

SCORING
Half the marks available in the Writing paper

ABOUT THE TASK

- An email or letter is written in response to a given situation, or to an email or letter from another person.
- In the task, you are given the context telling you who you are writing the email or letter to, why and what to include.
- The style will depend on whether you're writing to a friend (informal) or whether the situation is more formal (a potential employer, colleagues, a magazine editor, etc.).
- You should address any questions or points given in the task.

What is being tested?

The main purpose of an email or letter is to respond to a given situation and to inform the reader. The email or letter should be structured in paragraphs with suitable ideas grouped together. You are marked on a scale of 1–5 in the following areas:

- **Content**: This must all be relevant. You should engage the reader, and write in an interesting way, e.g. by including anecdotes or amusing examples in an email to a friend.
- **Communicative achievement**: Use a semi-formal or informal style, depending on the situation. Your email or letter must have a clear structure, communicate complex ideas effectively, and inform the reader.
- **Organisation**: Organise your email clearly and coherently in paragraphs, using a good range of cohesive devices.
- **Language**: Use a variety of vocabulary and structures (including complex structures) accurately. If your email or letter is to a friend, then you can use idioms and information phrases.

How do you do it?

___ BEFORE THE TASK ___

Read the instructions and the question carefully. Think about:

- who you're writing to. This will tell you the style of language to use.
- what you need to include in the email or letter. Are there any questions requiring answers, or points you are asked to mention?
- any functional exponents you need to use, e.g. for giving advice / making suggestions / reminding, etc.
- how to group your points and organise your email in paragraphs.

___ DURING THE TASK ___

- Write appropriate opening and closing sentences and paragraphs.
- Make your points and give reasons and examples.
- Use a range of vocabulary and grammatical forms, including some more complex forms if you can.
- Use linking expressions to create complex sentences and use discourse markers to guide the reader through the email or letter.

___ AFTER THE TASK ___

- Read through your email or letter again to check that it is coherent and logical, and that there are no grammar or spelling mistakes.
- Make sure you have included all the information required and that you have written the right number of words.

Are you exam-ready?

Did you …	
… spend enough time planning? .... ☐	… link your sentences and paragraphs clearly? .... ☐
… include all the information required? .... ☐	… check for mistakes in grammar or spelling? .... ☐
… respond to any questions? .... ☐	… write the right number of words? .... ☐
… start and end using appropriate language? .... ☐	

EXAM BOOST

You need to write to a peer, or someone in authority, making suggestions for a project or in response to a particular need. You are usually writing on behalf of other people which could be a small group or the wider community. You must address each point given in the task.

1 Read some different types of proposal tasks and highlight what must be included in the proposal.

1
> Your local town council is planning to sell the site of a disused factory for development as a retail park. You feel the land could be used for purposes that would better benefit the community. Write a proposal to the council explaining why the retail park is not a good use of the site and offering alternative suggestions, saying how they could benefit the community.

2
> Your college is planning its yearly budget and asked students to submit proposals for which departments require additional funding. Write a proposal on behalf of the students in your Media department, requesting funding and outlining why extra money is important and what it could be used for. Mention the benefits for both students and teachers in the department.

3
> Your manager is looking for ideas for a team-building weekend. He has asked for proposals for the weekend, offering a choice of two ideas which you are to evaluate, saying which would most benefit the employees and why.

4
> You live in a small village with very narrow winding roads. Heavy trucks regularly drive through the village and you are concerned about the congestion they cause and dangers to pedestrians. Write a proposal to the town council outlining a way of stopping trucks from travelling through the village, giving your reasons and explaining why it needs to be given priority.

2 Look again at the tasks. Which of the alternatives below are likely to be unsuitable? Why?

Task 1

A   Build another factory that would employ a lot of people

B   Build an upmarket hotel with spa

C   Relocate the current bus station to a more central position

D   Develop land into a park or garden

Task 2

A   Use money to invite media celebrities in to give motivational talks

B   Use money to send a small group of top students to a film festival

C   Use money to finance a short film for an international competition

Task 3

A   Having a weekend away at a seaside resort

B   Going on a team assault course

C   Giving two teams a challenge to complete in two days

Task 4

A   Put a ban on lorries over certain size and weight

B   Build a road round the village

C   Ban the village to all traffic

3 Tick which of the following a proposal should contain.

1   Division into sections.

2   Headings for sections to guide the reader.

3   Formal or semi-formal language

4   A balance of points for the proposal and those against.

5   Reference to statistics where appropriate.

6   Inclusion of comments from the people involved.

7   Some surprising or fascinating information to engage the reader.

8   Impersonal and objective language.

9   Anecdotes to illustrate different points.

10   A conclusion that summarises the proposal in different words.

There are many possible headings that can be used in a proposal. They will depend on the topic. You will need an introduction and a conclusion, but the other two or three headings should be linked to the points you are asked to consider in the task.

4 Look again at the tasks in Ex 1 and note down what headings you would use.

1 _____   3 _____

2 _____   4 _____

5 Choose one of the proposal tasks in Ex 1 and plan and then write your proposal in 220–260 words.

ABOUT THE TASK

- A proposal is written for a peer or superior, outlining a course of action which the writer would like to see implemented.
- The task will detail a situation that requires a solution, or suggestions for alternative action. It will indicate who the proposal is for.
- The desired outcome of the proposal is that your ideas will be accepted, therefore you need to use a persuasive argument, and persuasive language.
- Your proposal needs to be backed up by valid and clear reasons and some factual information.

TIMING
Approximately 45 minutes

TASK
Write a proposal in 220–260 words.

SCORING
Half the marks available in the Writing paper

What is being tested?

The reader needs to have a clear understanding of what you are proposing and why, and give a favourable response. The proposal is marked on a scale of 1-5 in the following areas:

- **Content**: This must all be relevant and cover all points requested in the task.
- **Communicative achievement**: Use an appropriate formal style to outline your ideas. The reader must understand your suggestions and reasons easily and clearly, and be persuaded to adopt them.
- **Organisation**: Organise your proposal clearly in sections. You may use headings to guide the reader more clearly. The introduction should set out what your proposal is and the conclusion summarise and express a hope that the proposal will be accepted.
- **Language**: Use a variety of vocabulary and structures (including complex structures) accurately. Use formal language without contractions or idioms.

How do you do it?

BEFORE THE TASK

- Make sure you know what to include and think about topics of the different paragraphs.
- List headings for the different sections.
- Note down reasons for your proposal and the benefits.

DURING THE TASK

- Give your proposal a title.
- Give a brief introduction where you say what the proposal is for.
- Keep your points clear and easy to follow.
- Give headings to the sections.
- Use formal language throughout.
- Use persuasive language and expressions.
- Finish by saying what you hope will happen.

AFTER THE TASK

- Read through the proposal again and check that it is clear and coherent.
- Check for mistakes in grammar, spelling and punctuation.
- Check the number of words and edit as necessary.

Are you exam-ready?

Did you …	
… spend enough time planning? .... ☐	… use persuasive language? .... ☐
… include all the points required? .... ☐	… link your sentences and paragraphs clearly? .... ☐
… use formal language? .... ☐	… check for mistakes in grammar or spelling? .... ☐
… use headings and sections? .... ☐	… write the correct number of words? .... ☐

Are you ready for Writing Part 2? Identify an area to improve.

23

You will need to avoid idiomatic language and write in a formal or semi-formal style.

1 Rewrite these extracts from a report in a more formal style.

1 Everyone on the course really loved it and didn't think they were too stressed out by the workload.

2 One thing I'd say is that it would've been great to have done a bit more practical stuff.

3 The training manuals were a bit pricey, but we got a load of free handouts, too.

4 They could maybe make the lessons a bit longer as we'd just get into something interesting and the bell would ring!

5 To sum up, I'd say that going on the course was a great idea of the management, and it would be good to do it again for another group of workers.

6 The rooms were OK, but the wi-fi didn't work terribly well, which was a pain.

When writing a report, you need to divide it into sections including an introduction, main points, recommendations and conclusion, to make it clear for the reader.

2 In which sections of a report about a weekend training course would you find these phrases: Introduction (I), Training (T), Accommodation (A), Recommendations (R) or Conclusion (C)?

1 The consensus of opinion was that every participant profited from the course.

2 Attendees would appreciate more information about the course before the weekend.

3 The principal aim of this report is to evaluate the course attended by a group …

4 Overall, the course proved both interesting and valuable for all those who attended.

5 The lighting in the bedrooms was not particularly strong, which is important when working in our own time.

6 The course would benefit from having longer individual lessons as …

7 In this report I plan to comment on the training course …

8 Taking into account these recommendations, my suggestion would be for the company to organise future training weekends of a similar nature.

9 This report will provide an assessment of the training course …

10 The rooms were well furnished and comfortable …

11 I would suggest that introduction of a new wi-fi system would be advantageous to anyone staying at the venue in the future.

12 The hard work of the trainers was greatly appreciated.

3 Put your rewritten phrases from Ex 1 into the correct section of the report in Ex 2.

1 _____

2 _____

3 _____

4 _____

5 _____

6 _____

You may sometimes be asked to write a report which includes reference to research or background information.

4 Complete the phrases with the words from the box.

according   conducted   considerable
indicate   majority   stated

1 The vast _____ of people surveyed …

2 A _____ number of people responded to the questionnaire.

3 A minority _____ that …

4 _____ to a small percentage of the respondents …

5 Interviews were _____ with all those concerned

6 The results of the survey appear to _____ that …

ABOUT THE TASK

- A report may be written for a club or group or a superior.
- It should review a situation and make suggestions or recommendations based on certain facts or requirements given in the task.
- It uses formal language, sections and headings.
- The task will give the context for the report, outlining what needs to be covered.
- It should inform the target reader of the current situation, your recommendations and the reasoning behind them.

TIMING
Approximately 45 minutes

TASK
Write a report in 220–260 words.

SCORING
Half the marks available in the Writing paper

What is being tested?

The reader of your report should understand the situation, your recommendations and why you are making them. They should have enough information to make an informed decision about the situation. Your report is marked on a scale of 1–5 in the following areas:

- **Content**: This must all be relevant. You should inform the reader, assess a situation and make recommendations.
- **Communicative achievement**: You should use a semi-formal or formal style. The reader must understand the situation, the reasons for your recommendations and be able to assess what to do.
- **Organisation**: You should write clear paragraphs with appropriate headings and possible bullet points for recommendations. Your report should include a brief introduction and conclusion.
- **Language**: You should use a variety of vocabulary and structures (including complex structures) as accurately as you can. Idiomatic and dramatic language are not appropriate. In a report, your priority is to be clear.

How do you do it?

BEFORE THE TASK

Read the instructions and the question carefully. Think about:

- the purpose of the report and what you need to include.
- the number of sections and how you will organise them.
- the target reader and appropriate style.

- the functions you will need to use, e.g. evaluating, recommending, suggesting, etc.
- how best to present your points – possible use of bullet points.
- note down points in a rough plan before you start writing.

DURING THE TASK

- Write an introduction that sets out the aim of the report.
- Give clear headings to the sections.
- Use a range of vocabulary and grammatical structures (including some complex forms).

- Use an appropriate style, usually formal.
- Finish with a conclusion that summarises your points and gives recommendations.

AFTER THE TASK

- Read through the report. Check that it is clear and coherent, and that you have included everything in the task.

- Check for mistakes in grammar, spelling and punctuation.
- Check the number of words and edit as necessary.

Are you exam-ready?

Did you …

… spend enough time planning? .... ☐	… make recommendations? .... ☐
… include all the information required? .... ☐	… use formal language? .... ☐
… use clear and suitable headings? .... ☐	… check for mistakes in grammar or spelling? .... ☐
… write a brief introduction and conclusion? .... ☐	… write the right number of words? .... ☐
… link your ideas clearly? .... ☐	

SECTION A
Using descriptive and dramatic language

You should structure your review by dividing it clearly into:

1 an introduction.
   - what you are reviewing, why and your general reaction
2 main sections (one or two paragraphs) about the film or book and your reactions.
   - positive and/or negative reactions with examples
   - comments on different aspects of the film, with examples
3 a summary and recommendation.
   - balancing reactions and impression (not repeating the same points)
   - advising whether to see or read it, etc., or to avoid

1 In which parts of a review (1–3) would you expect to find the following extracts?

A An additional reason for my very positive reaction to the series is the quite brilliant casting.

B I was lucky enough to be given the book for my birthday and read it in one sitting.

C People might be wondering whether the latest offering by the author … is on a par with the previous three novels.

D It would definitely be a shame to miss the chance of seeing quite a unique theatrical event.

E The most tender moment in the play for me comes after the scene with Katharine's father.

F On balance, I must say that I feel the film is far better than the original in both concept and execution.

G I would give this book a miss, unfortunately, and if you haven't already read them, check out some of the earlier books in the series.

H Having said that, there are some points in the script that I feel could well have been improved on. For example, …

2 Add a sentence of your own to extend each extract.

SECTION B
Engaging the reader

A review needs to engage the reader.

3 Which extracts, A or B, would suit a review better? Why?

1

A Dracula is one of my favourite books and I'm going to set out my reasons for this.

B It's night-time. Something's knocking against the window panes, making them rattle. You sit up in the darkness, heart beating. Perhaps you've fallen asleep while reading my favourite book. Dracula.

2

A Would you really want to continue reading a story after such a boring and depressing beginning? Unfortunately, I had to.

B The opening paragraphs of the book are sadly quite long and uninteresting and I found it hard to continue.

3

A The book follows four characters' lives in a series of twists and turns which I, however, found rather complicated and confusing, leading to an eventual misunderstanding about who had, in fact, been at college with whom and who were part of the extended families.

B Some of the directions the plot takes us in are not always clear. Perhaps the author was taking himself a bit too seriously? I certainly didn't get which characters were supposed to have studied with each other, or who were just distant cousins!

4

A Whether a week trapped with friends in an isolated hotel will always lead to a closer relationship is interesting to consider!

B I enjoyed the way the developing friendships are described and have no hesitation in recommending this book to someone looking for an interesting read this weekend.

ABOUT THE TASK

- In the task there is a context sentence, explaining the reason for writing the review and asking for certain points to be included.
- The review may be about a book, film, magazine, concert or website. It could also be for a product or experience, e.g. something you've bought, or a holiday you've been on.
- A review should engage and inform the reader.
- You will need to give information, explain your own reactions, and make recommendations.

TIMING
Approximately 45 minutes

TASK
Write a review in 220-260 words.

SCORING
Half the marks available in the Writing paper

What is being tested?

The reader should be informed about certain aspects of your experience and your opinion. They should be able to decide whether or not they would be interested in seeing, reading, attending or buying what you have reviewed. The review is marked on a scale of 1-5 in the following areas:

- **Content**: All points mentioned in the task should be addressed. There should be an evaluation of what is being reviewed rather than a detailed description.
- **Communicative achievement**: The reader should immediately be engaged by the review, understand your opinion and recommendations, and have enough information to assess what action they might take as a result.
- **Organisation**: The review should be organised in clear paragraphs so that the reader can follow your line of thought clearly. The first paragraph should introduce the review and the conclusion give a summary and recommendation.
- **Language**: Use a range of vocabulary and grammatical forms, including some complex structures. Use language that is appropriate for the reader – usually quite lively and idiomatic.

How do you do it?

BEFORE THE TASK
- Read the task carefully and think of something you have experienced (a book, a product, etc.) that you can write about.
- Note down the most important points you want to mention regarding information, interesting features, your reaction and reasons and a recommendation. Consider both pros and cons.
- Group your points into paragraphs.

DURING THE TASK
- Use appropriate language, e.g. if the review is of a film or book, you may wish to use dramatic adjectives.
- Vary the sentence length for dramatic effect.
- Engage the reader with direct and indirect questions.
- If possible, finish the review memorably with a surprising fact or amusing comment.

AFTER THE TASK
- Read through the review again and make sure that it is clear and coherent.
- Check for mistakes in spelling, grammar and punctuation.
- Check the question again to make sure you've covered everything.

Are you exam-ready?

Did you …

… spend enough time planning? ☐	… make it interesting for the reader? ☐
… include all the information required? ☐	… give a recommendation? ☐
… respond to any questions? ☐	… check for mistakes in grammar or spelling? ☐
… use a variety of vocab and grammar forms? ☐	… write the right number of words? ☐
… link your sentences and paragraphs clearly? ☐	

Are you ready for Writing Part 2? Identify an area to improve.

EXAM BOOST

SECTION A
Understanding attitude and opinion
You may have to work out what someone's attitude towards something is, or understand the opinion they're giving. They may not use the same words that you read in the question, so you should listen carefully for meaning, synonyms and paraphrases.

1a 🎧 **1.1EB** Listen to five people. What is each person expressing? Choose from the box.

> annoyance   disapproval   distress   fascination   gratitude   nervousness
> regret   sensitivity   uncertainty   unwillingness

Speaker 1 _____
Speaker 2 _____
Speaker 3 _____
Speaker 4 _____
Speaker 5 _____

1b 🎧 **1.2EB** Listen again and check your answers.

SECTION B
Identifying purpose or function
You may need to answer questions about the speaker's purpose, or what they are doing during the conversation (function). You should listen to the whole dialogue carefully before choosing your answer.

2 Match the verbs below to the situations.

> acknowledge   convey   determine   dismiss   exemplify   generalise   illustrate   reinforce

a   you want to express your opinion or feeling in a stronger way.
b   you say something basic that's often true, though not always.
c   you wish to communicate your feelings to others.
d   you want to provide an example of something.
e   you give more information about something.
f   you refuse to consider an idea or opinion.
g   you want to show you accept an idea.
h   you decide what to do next.

3 🎧 **5.1EB** Listen to five short recordings. What are the speakers doing? Choose some of the verbs in Ex 2 to explain.

1 _____   4 _____
2 _____   5 _____
3 _____

4 🎧 **5.2EB** Listen to three speakers. Use a verb from the box to say what each speaker is doing. Then say what it is that they are defining, determining and so on.

> defining   determining   evaluating   exemplifying   interpreting   reflecting   reinforcing

1 _____
2 _____
3 _____

ABOUT THE TASK

- You will hear three short extracts. These will be dialogues and are unrelated to each other.
- There are two multiple-choice questions for each extract, each with three options to choose from.
- Each question has a different focus.
- You have time to read the questions before you listen to the recording, and you hear each extract twice.

NUMBER OF QUESTIONS
6 (with three options to choose from)

TASK
3 short extracts lasting around 60 seconds

SCORING
1 mark per question

EXAM REFERENCE

What is being tested?

This part of the exam focuses on different aspects of what the speakers say. The questions may ask about:

- the speaker's attitude or feeling, e.g. whether they're irritated or enthusiastic, etc.
- their opinion, e.g. whether they approve, like, etc.
- their purpose or what they're doing, e.g. to advise, to persuade, etc.
- what they're doing, e.g. warning, encouraging, etc.
- a detail about a point they are making.
- the gist or general meaning of what they are saying.
- whether the two speakers agree.
- what the listener should do next.

How do you do it?

BEFORE THE TASK

- Look at the context sentence for each question so you know what the situation is and who is speaking.
- Read the question to identify what you are listening for, underlining any key words, e.g. what the man believes or how the woman feels.
- Read the options and underline any key words.
- Remember that you'll usually hear a paraphrase rather than the same words used in the question.

DURING THE TASK

- The first time you listen, try to answer the question yourself. Put a small mark against the option in each question that you think is correct. When you listen the second time, confirm your answer.
- If the question asks about the speaker's feelings or attitude, listen for phrases to express these, e.g. 'I really wish I hadn't said that' (regret), 'I'm absolutely furious' (anger).
- Listen to everything the speakers say. Some questions test your understanding of their main point, which will not be just one phrase or sentence.
- Check that the other options are definitely wrong. For example, they may be mentioned in the recording but not answer the question.
- If you miss an answer, don't worry. Just choose an option and move on. No marks are lost for incorrect answers, so don't leave any question unanswered.
- Remember that you must answer both questions as you listen. These will be in the same order as what you hear, or test the whole of the extract.

AFTER THE TASK

- Quickly check your answers to make sure you are happy with them.
- You have time at the end of the Listening paper to transfer your answers to the answer sheet.

Are you exam-ready?

Did you …

… read the context sentence to determine the situation and speaker? ☐
… read the question and identify what to listen for? ☐
… underline key words in the options? ☐
… listen to everything the speakers said? ☐
… identify which options are definitely wrong? ☐
… answer every question? ☐

SECTION A
Identifying cues

You have to complete the sentences with a word or short phrase. Read the sentences carefully before you listen to help you understand what kind of information is missing (e.g. noun, verb, adjective). The sentences contain information to help you follow the recording and decide what to write in each space.

1 You will hear two short recordings. Read the sentences and highlight the words which you think will help you follow the text when you listen to it.

A

1 It is said that coming _____ in a race can be more rewarding than winning.

2 Those who finish in this position usually feel _____ to have achieved something.

3 We sometimes get stuck in a '_____' which perpetuates negative feelings.

B

4 Petra wondered why many runners were using valuable _____ during the warm-up period.

5 Petra expected not to win the race because of her _____ and lack of height.

6 Petra says that she did not feel _____ about coming last in the run.

2 Read the sentences again and decide what kind of information is missing from each gap.

3 🎧 2.1EB Now listen and complete the sentences.

SECTION B
Understanding specific information and stated opinion

You have to listen for key pieces of information. The sentences are in the same order as the information in the recording and you have to write exactly the word or phrase which fits in each gap.

4a 🎧 6.1EB Listen to a man called Kelvin who is talking about a long journey he has been on across Russia, on the Trans-Siberian railway. Complete the sentences with a word or short phrase.

Kelvin says that he arranged the required **(1)** _____ before he travelled.

Kelvin says that once he could recognise the Russian alphabet, he was able to use **(2)** _____ fairly well.

Kelvin enjoyed the **(3)** _____ and meals he had with fellow passengers.

Kelvin was particularly interested in a **(4)** _____ he came across in Tomsk.

Kelvin particularly enjoyed occupying himself with **(5)** _____ when he became bored.

4b 🎧 6.2EB Listen again and check your answers.

ABOUT THE TASK

- You will hear one long monologue, which may be a presentation or a talk.
- There are eight sentences about what the speaker says. These may focus on the speaker's opinion, how he/she feels about something, or a detail about something he/she mentions.
- There is one gap in each sentence, which you complete with a word or short phrase.
- You have time to read the questions before you listen to the recording, and you hear the recording twice.

NUMBER OF QUESTIONS

8 gaps to complete with a word or short phrase

TASK

1 long monologue

SCORING

1 mark per question

What is being tested?

This part of the exam focuses on listening for specific information, detail and stated opinion.

- The sentences are paraphrases of what you hear in the recording.
- The sentences are in the same order as the information you hear, and form a kind of summary of the talk.
- You mustn't change the form of the word(s) you write in the gap. You hear the exact word(s) you need to write.
- The word(s) you write in each gap should be spelled correctly, and must fit grammatically in the sentence.

How do you do it?

BEFORE THE TASK

- Look at the context sentence. Think about the topic you're going to hear about and who the speaker is.
- Read all the sentences. This will give you an idea of how the talk is organised.
- Think about any function words in the sentences. Is the speaker surprised, happy or annoyed about anything? This will help you identify the kind of information to listen out for.
- Think about the kind of word missing in each sentence. Is it a noun or an adjective? The structure of the sentence helps you identify this, e.g.
  - Stefan felt _____ about missing the boat. (adjective)
  - Julia says that the _____ is an important part of the activity of fencing. (noun)

DURING THE TASK

- The first time you listen, write the word(s) you think is/are correct in pencil.
- Don't write more than a word or short phrase.
- Make sure you're not writing any unnecessary information that is already in the sentence.
- If you miss an answer, don't worry. Leave it for the second time you listen and move on to the next question.
- The second time you listen, complete any missing gaps and confirm those you have already filled in.

AFTER THE TASK

- Quickly read through each sentence to check that everything makes sense.
- Check the word(s) you have written are spelled correctly and fit grammatically.
- You have time at the end of the Listening paper to transfer your answers to the answer sheet.

Are you exam-ready?

Did you …

… read the context sentence so that you know what the situation is? .... ☐

… read each sentence and identify what kind of word(s) to listen for? .... ☐

… remember to avoid including unnecessary information? .... ☐

… check your spelling and grammar? .... ☐

… complete every gap? .... ☐

EXAM REFERENCE

EXAM BOOST

SECTION A
Identifying agreement and disagreement

You may have to decide whether the speakers agree or disagree. They may not use direct phrases such as 'I agree' or 'I'm not sure', so you need to listen carefully to what each person says.

1 🎧 **3.1EB** Listen to the short dialogues. Are the people agreeing or disagreeing?

1

I'm struggling to appreciate the benefits of a third place that aren't already available from friends, colleagues and family.

That's one way of looking at things. The input we receive from those we wouldn't normally cross paths with could be invaluable, though.

2

Trends are always shifting in terms of the workplace and encouraging workers to get creative.

One minute it's bean bags to sit on and think, the next it's a separate room where you can have a nap and wake up feeling refreshed.

3

Wanting to belong is a very strong instinct. Humans need to be needed.

Even those who say they enjoy their own company.

SECTION B
Understanding feeling

You may need to understand how the speakers are feeling. They will not always state their emotions directly, but what they say will help you to determine how they feel.

2 Match the adjectives with their definitions.

1 alarmed
2 appalled
3 grumpy
4 insecure
5 overwhelmed

a very shocked and upset by something
b a feeling of something being too much
c bad-tempered and annoyed
d worried or frightened
e not confident

3 🎧 **7.1EB** Listen to five short extracts. How does each person feel? Choose one of the adjectives from Ex 2.

1 Just leave me alone, will you? I'm not in the mood to chat. I'd rather be on my own.

_____

2 What a terrible way to treat a customer! I couldn't believe that the sales assistant was so rude to me!

_____

3 Oh, wow! I can't believe you've all travelled so far just to celebrate my birthday with me. I'm lost for words!

_____

4 What?! There's another flood warning? We'd better move the furniture upstairs – quick!

_____

5 I've never had particularly good self-esteem. I cringe when I have to address a group of people, even if they're my friends.

_____

ABOUT THE TASK

- You will hear one long text which is usually an interview or discussion between two people. There may be a third person who conducts the interview or discussion.
- Each question has a different focus, including what speakers think or feel.
- Sometimes both speakers will address the same point with a single question for you to answer.
- You have time to read the questions before you listen to the recording, and you hear the recording twice.

NUMBER OF QUESTIONS
6 (with 4 options to choose from)

TASK
One long text lasting around 4 minutes

SCORING
1 mark per question

What is being tested?

This part of the exam focuses on your ability to show a detailed understanding of an interview or discussion which involves detailed arguments. The questions may ask about:

- the speakers' attitudes, feelings or opinions.
- a detail about a point they are making.
- the gist or general meaning of what they are saying.
- whether they agree or both say the same thing.

How do you do it?

BEFORE THE TASK

- Read the context sentence. This will tell you what the interview or discussion will be about.
- Read questions and options, and identify what you are listening for.
- Underline any key words in the question and options, e.g. 'How does the woman feel?' (annoyed/frustrated/angry). Remember you won't hear the same words as you read in the question or options: you will hear a paraphrase.
- The information you hear is in the same order as the questions.

DURING THE TASK

- Each question is introduced by the interviewer or third person so you know when to move on to the next one. This person does not express their views and there are no questions about this person.
- The first time you listen, try to answer the question based on what you hear. Then check the options and choose the one closest in meaning.
- If the question asks about the speaker's feelings or attitude, listen for phrases which express these, e.g. 'Thank goodness I managed to get that work in on time.' (relief)
- If both speakers answer the same question, try to keep in mind what the first speaker says, so you can decide whether the second speaker agrees or says the same thing.
- Don't be distracted if you do hear the same word you see in an option as it may not be the correct answer.
- Check that the other options are definitely wrong. For example, they may be mentioned in the recording but not answer the question.
- If you miss an answer, don't spend time thinking about it but move on to the next question. You will hear it again.
- The second time you listen, confirm your ideas and complete any answers that you did not get the first time.

AFTER THE TASK

- Quickly check through your answers to make sure you are happy with them.
- If you have missed an answer, make a sensible guess. No marks are lost for incorrect answer.

Are you exam-ready?

Did you …	
… read the context sentence? .... ☐	… identify which options are definitely wrong? .... ☐
… identify what to listen for? .... ☐	… answer every question? .... ☐
… underline key words in each question? .... ☐	

Are you ready for Listening Part 3? Identify an area to improve.

33

SECTION A
Understanding the main point
You have to choose the option which corresponds with what each speaker says. Each correct answer reflects the speaker's main point.

1 🎧 **4.1EB** Listen to four people talking about where they live. What point do they each make about where they live? Choose from A-E. There is one option which you do not need to use.

A This place attracts a lot of visitors for good reason.
B Life's hard here sometimes but it has its compensations.
C Visitors tend to avoid spending too much time here.
D People from here have a reputation which isn't founded on fact.
E Lack of easy access preserves this place's wilderness.

Speaker 1 _____
Speaker 2 _____
Speaker 3 _____
Speaker 4 _____

SECTION B
Understanding gist
You need to understand the gist of what the person says rather than picking out details. Listen to the whole section before choosing your answer, as there may be distraction for other options. You should read the question before listening.

2a 🎧 **8.1EB** Listen to someone talking about a sleep disorder called hypersomnia. What is the gist of what the speaker says?
a I feel as though I sleep too much.
b I never feel properly refreshed.
c I am unable to take part in certain activities.

2b 🎧 **8.2EB** Listen again and check your answers.

3a 🎧 **8.3EB** Listen to two people talking about a sleep disorder called narcolepsy and choose the correct option for the two questions.

1 What does each speaker say they find most challenging about the condition?
   A the way it is sparked by strong emotions
   B the way it strikes without warning
   C the way it interferes with movement
2 How does each speaker manage their condition?
   A by adopting a strict daily routine
   B by making adaptations to living arrangements
   C by taking appropriate medication

3b 🎧 **8.4EB** Listen again and check your answers.

EXAM REFERENCE

ABOUT THE TASK

- You will hear five short monologues. Each one has a different speaker talking about the same topic, e.g. work or free time.
- There are two tasks relating to the topic, each with a different focus and eight options to choose from. You match one option from each task to one of the speakers as you listen.
- In each task, there are three options that you do not need to use, and you can use an option only once.
- You have time to read the questions before you listen to the recording.
- You will hear all five extracts first, and then you will hear them a second time.

NUMBER OF QUESTIONS

10

TASK

5 short texts lasting around 35 seconds each

SCORING

1 mark per question

What is being tested?

This part of the exam focuses on understanding the gist or main point of what each speaker is saying.

- The options in the two tasks may focus on how speakers feel, what they think or what their purpose is.
- Whilst speakers may say similar things, their main point will only match one option from each task.
- You need to be able to eliminate the incorrect options in each task.
- You need to listen to the whole extract and choose an option for each of the tasks.

How do you do it?

___ BEFORE THE TASK ___

- Look at the context sentence. This gives you the topic that all the speakers will talk about.
- Read both tasks and their options and think about what they mean. Their focuses will be different, for example, one might ask about the speakers' feelings, and the other might ask about their intended course of action.
- Underline any key words in the options.
- Make sure you understand exactly what you are listening for in each task.

___ DURING THE TASK ___

- The first time you listen, concentrate on understanding the speakers' main points.
- Listen to everything the speaker says. Don't worry if you don't understand every word.
- Mark the option in each task which you think is closest to the speaker's main point. If you're not sure, mark all those you think are possible.
- Remember that you may hear the answer to the second task before you hear the answer for the first task, so make sure you keep looking at both tasks and all the options as you listen.
- There is enough time for you to look at both tasks and choose the correct options as you listen.
- The second time you listen, eliminate any incorrect possibilities and confirm your answers.
- Check that the three options you do not use are definitely wrong.

___ AFTER THE TASK ___

- Check that you have chosen an answer for every question and have not used an option more than once.
- If you are still not sure of an answer, make a sensible guess.

Are you exam-ready?

Did you …	
… read the context sentence? .... ☐	… use each option only once? .... ☐
… read both tasks and all the options and think about what they meant? .... ☐	… make sure the options you did not choose are definitely incorrect? .... ☐
… underline any key words in the tasks? .... ☐	… answer every question? .... ☐

EXAM BOOST

The first questions you will be asked will be about where you're from, and then perhaps about your work or studies and/or your experience of learning English.

1 🎧 **1.3EB** Look at the following Part 1 questions and listen to three alternative answers for each. For each question, decide which of the answers (A–C) is good, and identify what is wrong with the others.

1 Where are you from?
2 What do you do here/there?
3 How long have you been studying English?
4 What do you enjoy most about learning English?

2 Read through the Useful language and a set of Part 1 questions. Then complete the example answer for question 1 with the correct words.

Adding	**Recounting**	**The future**
It's just occurred to me that …	A standout experience was when …	It's hard to imagine, but I guess I'll probably be …
As well as that, I …	It's hard to choose just one event, but if I had to, I'd say that …	Nothing's definite yet, but I'm considering …
In addition to that, I …	Well, that's got to be when I …	If everything goes according to plan, I'll …
Balancing	**Hypothesising**	
You could say … but there again …	If I had the chance, I'd definitely / I'd jump at …	
There are times when I … but at other times I …	Given the opportunity, I'd …	
I suppose most people would consider me … but people who know me well …	That would be my idea of the perfect …	
Having said that, I …		

1 Are there a lot of foods that you refuse to eat? (Why?)
2 Do you prefer to have very active weekends or would you rather relax and chill out at home? (Why / Why not?)
3 What stands out in your memory about your first school? (Why?)
4 What is the most interesting TV series or film you've seen recently? (Why?)
5 What would be a perfect job for you? (Why?)
6 What are you looking forward to doing over the next couple of weeks? (Why?)

Example answer for question 1

I suppose you ¹_____ say that I'm a 'selective' eater in that I certainly don't eat everything but there ²_____ I would say that I'm a healthy eater, as I'm trying to cut down on meat in favour of vegetables. ³_____ said that, I must admit that there are some things, like carrots, that I've hated since I was young – so in my mum's opinion, yes, I'm fussy!

3 Write a sentence using an appropriate phrase from the box for each of the remaining questions in Ex 2.

2 _____
_____
3 _____
_____
4 _____
_____
5 _____
_____
6 _____
_____

ABOUT THE TASK

- There are two examiners. One speaks to you, and the other one just listens.
- You and your partner answer personal questions in turn from the examiner.
- These questions are on everyday topics such as your friends and family, leisure time, work plans, etc.
- You may need to talk about the present, past or future.
- You shouldn't talk to your partner in this part. It's a chance for you each to give personal information, and feel comfortable at the start of the test.

TIMING
about 2 minutes

TASK
answering personal questions

SCORING
marking takes place throughout the test

EXAM REFERENCE

What is being tested?

This part of the exam focuses on your ability to use social language and to give basic information about yourself. The examiners mark you all through the test on your use of:

- **Grammar and vocabulary.** Try to use a range of structures and words and don't worry about making mistakes.
- **Discourse management.** This means organising what you say clearly, using linking words.
- **Pronunciation.** This includes individual sounds and word stress, but the important thing is that you can be understood easily.
- **Interactive communication.** This means responding to and interacting with another person. In Part 1, this means interacting with the examiner and answering their questions appropriately.

How do you do it?

BEFORE THE TASK

- Prepare to answer questions about yourself, and your interests, but don't practise full answers.
- Practise using a range of vocabulary and structures.
- Think about reasons you can give to support your answers, which will make what you say more interesting.
- When you enter the exam room, greet both examiners with a smile.

DURING THE TASK

- Listen carefully to each question. If you don't understand, you can ask the examiner to repeat it, although they can't explain meanings of unknown words or rephrase a question. If you really don't understand, you should say so and a different question can be asked.
- You should answer as naturally as possible, giving relevant information, but not a long, detailed answer.
- Listen to your partner's answers. Although you won't be asked to interact with your partner, it can help you settle down at the start of the test.
- There's no 'right' answer to any question. For example, if you're asked about your favourite television programme but you don't have one, you can say so and explain why.
- Don't worry about being nervous or making mistakes – speak clearly and confidently so that both examiners can hear you.

Are you exam-ready?

Did you …	
… listen to the examiner's question carefully?	☐
… answer the question you are asked, giving reasons for what you say?	☐
… use a range of language?	☐
… speak clearly and confidently?	☐
… feel confident about answering the questions?	☐

EXAM BOOST

SECTION A
Comparing

You will need to choose two out of three pictures to talk about, and while you speak you may need to refer to different pictures.

1 Complete the extracts A–D with the words from the box.

> middle   on   one   the   these   top   underneath

Selecting pictures

A
> OK, I'd like to talk about ¹_____ two pictures. [indicates with a gesture]

B
> Yes, I'm going to talk about ²_____ picture with the two boys, and the ³_____ of the family on the beach.

C
> Right, I'm going for the ⁴_____-left one and the one ⁵_____ .

D
> I'll choose the one ⁶_____ the right and the ⁷_____ one.

2 Choose the correct words to complete the extracts A–C.

Referring to pictures

A
> The boys in the ¹**left-hand** / **left** picture look dressed for going running, whereas the family are clearly getting ready for a picnic.

B
> The people in ²**a** / **the** restaurant are possibly waiting for the waiter, who is hovering behind them, to take their order. The ³**other** / **another** picture, of the café, shows people who have already eaten.

C
> In both ⁴**these** / **those** pictures the people look as if they're frustrated, waiting for someone or something, but in the ⁵**first** / **one** picture they're at a station, so it's probably a train they're waiting for, whereas in the ⁶**second** / **next**, someone is obviously late for a party or for dinner.

SECTION B
Speculating

You will probably need to speculate about the pictures you are comparing. There will be assumptions you may need to make regarding the situation, the people and likely related events.

3 Choose the correct alternatives to complete the extracts from a candidate's answer.

1   Looking at the state of their clothes I'd say there's a **strong** / **firm** chance they've been caught in a heavy shower.

2   In **every** / **all** likelihood the team have been playing for ages – they're looking totally exhausted and I **get** / **feel** the impression that they can't wait for the final whistle.

3   You know, it **could** / **must** be that they've just arrived on the platform – or that they've been there for a while. But whatever, **it's** / **there's** no indication that a train is coming any time soon.

4   From the expressions on the girls' faces I'd **throw** / **hazard** a guess that something exciting has just happened. Some good news, an invitation maybe …

SECTION C
Structuring a long turn

You will need to talk for a minute without hesitation. This involves sequencing and linking the sections of your answers logically.

4 Complete the phrases with the words from the box.

> back   finish   firstly   question
> regarding   should   spite   which

1   _____ , **when looking at** both pictures, it's clear that …

2   **In** _____ of these similarities the people are …

3   _____ **why** they might have chosen to …

4   **The** _____ **of how** they might be feeling is tricky, as …

5   **To go** _____ **to** the reason for … , I'd like to add that …

6   **I** _____ **have mentioned** that …

7   _____ **brings us to** how memorable these moments might be …

8   **So, to** _____ , I'd have to say that …

ABOUT THE TASK

TIMING
about 4 minutes
in total

TASK
talking about two
photographs

SCORING
marking takes place
throughout the test

- You have the chance to speak on your own for one minute.
- The examiner gives you three photographs, and asks you a question in two parts about them.
- You have to choose two of the photographs to compare, and answer the two-part question. You will need to speculate about certain things.
- The questions are also written on the paper above the two photographs.
- Once you have finished speaking about your photographs, the examiner will ask your partner a short follow-up question about them.
- Your partner is then given their photographs to talk about, and you are asked a short follow-up question about these photographs when your partner has finished speaking.

What is being tested?

This part of the test focuses on your ability to organise a longer piece of speech, give your opinions and make speculations relevant to the questions. The examiners mark you all through the test on your use of:

- **Grammar and vocabulary**. Use a range of structures and words and don't worry about making mistakes.
- **Discourse management**. Organise what you say clearly, using linking words.
- **Pronunciation**. This includes individual sounds and word stress, but the important thing is that you can be understood easily.

How do you do it?

——— BEFORE THE TASK ———

- Listen carefully to what the examiner says, as they will tell you what you'll see in your photographs. This prepares you for what you have to talk about.
- When the examiner gives you your photographs, you have to start speaking immediately.

——— DURING THE TASK ———

- Indicate which two photographs you will talk about.
- Remember there are always two parts in the task – comparing the photographs and answering the questions. You should balance your time to address both parts in your talk.
- Avoid simply describing what you can see in the photographs. You should compare and speculate.
- Try to organise your short talk logically. Refer to the written questions if you forget.
- Use markers and linking words to help the examiner follow your talk, e.g. 'firstly', 'moving on to', etc.
- Listen to your partner's talk as you will have to answer a follow-up question, and you might wish to refer to one of your partner's points, e.g. 'As … said, … '.
- The follow-up question about your partner's photographs will ask you to make a choice. Remember to give a short reason for the choice you make.

Are you exam-ready?

Did you …	
… listen to the examiner's question carefully?	☐
… answer all parts of the task?	☐
… use linking words to organise your talk?	☐
… use expressions for comparing and speculation?	☐
… answer the follow-up question with a short reason?	☐

Are you ready for Speaking Part 2? Identify an area to improve.

39

EXAM BOOST

SECTION A
Interacting in a two-way conversation

You need to give opinions, sometimes revise your opinion and refer to your partner's comments.

1 Complete the phrases with the words from the box.

> along coming concerned convinced
> raised reasonable said spot
> think view ways with

1 Having _____ that, I think maybe
2 Now that I _____ about it …
3 What you're saying is _____ on.
4 I see where you're _____ from …
5 Looking at this from a different point of _____ , I think …
6 You've _____ an interesting point.
7 I'd say that was a _____ assumption.
8 I'm _____ you on that, it's an important point …
9 Yes, I'd definitely go _____ with that.
10 There are two _____ of looking at this.
11 You've _____ me …
12 As far as I'm _____ , what we need to consider is …

2 Put the phrases 1–12 in Ex 1 into the correct categories.

A Giving your own opinion
_____ , _____

B Revising your opinion
_____ , _____ ,
_____ , _____

C Commenting on your partner's opinion
_____ , _____ ,
_____ , _____ ,
_____

3 Write a short dialogue between two candidates discussing the following task. Use as many of the phrases in Ex 1 as you can.

How can these things affect where we choose to live?

> amount of traffic   closeness to our family
> leisure facilities   location of our work
> neighbourhood

SECTION B
Evaluating, referring, reassessing

You will need to answer a decision question related to the previous discussion you had in Part 3. You will need to look again at the prompts and perhaps consider them from a different angle or revisit your original discussion and make a choice.

4 Complete the extract from a discussion with the words from the box.

> appreciate being compare far
> go looking previously reflection
> taking talked

So, [1]_____ again at these people, we have to think about which person might have the greatest influence on a person's career choice.

Well, I know we [2]_____ about parents and teachers both [3]_____ important for different reasons, but if we [4]_____ these two in the light of which has the greatest influence, I'd probably [5]_____ for teachers. How about you?

Hmm. It's tricky. I [6]_____ that we said parents are important, but on [7]_____ , that's only to a certain extent. [8]_____ everything that we mentioned [9]_____ into account – like the teacher's knowledge of the students' abilities and their experience of dealing with different personalities over the years, I think I'd agree. Teachers have by [10]_____ the greatest influence on …

ABOUT THE TASK

- This part of the exam has two parts. In both parts you discuss questions on a given topic with your partner.
- The examiner reads a question aloud, then gives you the same question to read. There are 5 ideas (called prompts) around the question as a mind map.
- You have 15 seconds to read the question and the prompts before you are asked to start speaking.
- The examiner stops your discussion after 2 minutes. You don't need to talk about all the prompts.
- The examiner asks you a second question about the topic which involves making a decision.
- The examiner stops this discussion after a minute.

TIMING
about 4 minutes in total

TASK
discussing a question and working towards a decision

SCORING
marking takes place throughout the test

What is being tested?

This part of the test focuses on your ability to maintain a discussion by exchanging ideas, making suggestions, agreeing/disagreeing, expressing and justifying opinions, etc. The examiners mark you all through the test on your use of:

- **Grammar and vocabulary**. Use a range of structures and words and don't worry about making mistakes.
- **Discourse management**. Organise what you say clearly, using linking words.
- **Pronunciation**. This includes individual sounds and word stress, but the important thing is that you can be understood easily.
- **Interactive communication**. You should respond to and interact with another person. In Part 3 this means interacting with your partner.

How do you do it?

BEFORE THE TASK

- Listen carefully to the examiner as he/she gives you the task.
- Use this time to make sure you understand the question – you can check with your partner if you're not sure.
- Think about how the prompts relate to the question and what you could say about them.

DURING THE TASK

- You don't have to talk about the prompts in any particular order. Start with the one you have most ideas about.
- Say as much as you can about each prompt before you move on. You don't need to discuss them all.
- Don't always give your opinion first – invite your partner to say what they think and share talking time with them.
- Listen carefully to your partner's ideas and refer back to them.
- Try to give a reason for your opinion, but remember there are no right answers.
- It doesn't matter if you and your partner disagree or don't have time to reach a decision for the second question.

Are you exam-ready?

Did you …	
… read the question and prompts carefully?	☐
… talk about the prompts in depth?	☐
… interact well with your partner?	☐
… use a range of structures and vocabulary?	☐
… discuss the decision question fully?	☐

EXAM BOOST

SECTION A
Justifying your opinions

You need to answer individual questions as fully as possible. This includes justifying your answers and adding examples.

1 Read the Part 4 question below and make some notes for 1–5.

How important is it for close friends to share the same interests and lead similar lifestyles? Why?

1 How important do you think it is?

2 Why do you think this?

3 Give a general example.

4 Give an example from your own experience.

5 Give a short anecdote about something you've seen or heard related to the question.

2 🎧 4.2EB Listen to a student answering the question. Does she mention anything similar to what you noted in Ex 1?

3 🎧 4.3EB Listen again and complete the phrases in the sentences with the correct words.

1 I have to say that **there's no** _____ **answer** really.

2 **If you** _____ **at** people around you, …

3 However, **for me** _____ , it's good to have **things in** _____ .

4 **But** _____ , there's another couple …

5 Takes all _____ I think …

4 🎧 4.4EB Choose the correct alternatives to complete another answer to the same question. Listen and check.

I would say that it really doesn't ¹**care / matter**. A lot ²**depends / relies** on what brought you together as friends initially. A ³**case / situation** in point would be when you start a new school. You're feeling a bit lonely and scared, vulnerable too perhaps. And if someone befriends you and helps you settle in, there's ⁴**a chance / the luck** that they could go on to become a close friend. ⁵**Remembering / Looking back**, there was a ⁶**time / memory** when I …

SECTION B
Developing the discussion

You may need to interrupt politely, add your opinion, ask for clarification and/or encourage a reticent partner to contribute.

5 Read an extract from a Part 4 discussion question and complete the conversation with the phrases from the box.

> Before you go on   Could you give an example
> I guess I'm talking about
> If I could expand on that a little
> So, when you say   This is something

Examiner: Jacques and Helena, do you think it's possible to do too much sport or physical exercise?

Jacques: OK, so yes, it's an interesting question. Is it possible to do too much sport or physical exercise? In my opinion there needs to be a good balance. It's clearly important for everyone to get exercise because it contributes to a healthy lifestyle. However, I think it's also quite easy to get a little obsessed and do too much.

Helena: ¹_____ I've also thought about a fair amount. One example might be when someone starts going to the gym every day for hours and hours. There's a danger that they can't live without it!

Jacques: Yes. I would completely agree with you. It can mean their social life suffers.

Helena: ²_____ perhaps?

Jacques: Well, if they're at the gym all the time, they're not out with friends, so they miss out on maintaining relationships, and just relaxing.

Helena: ³_____ , in my opinion it can also have a detrimental effect on their health, both physical and mental.

Jacques: Interesting you should say that. ⁴_____ both physical and mental, what are you thinking of?

Helena: ⁵_____ the physical stress on the body of working out excessively and also the mental stress of trying to maintain strength and fitness, and also, I know a lot of people who go to gyms actually compete with each other to see who can lift the most weights or develop the biggest muscles. One of my friends …

Jacques: ⁶_____ , I'd like to say that in my opinion, athletes who train hard to reach certain standards are usually advised by their coaches and trainers how to exercise properly, without harming their bodies. I'm not sure that individuals have that discipline?

ABOUT THE TASK

TIMING
about 4 minutes
in total

TASK
answering and
discussing questions

SCORING
marking takes place
throughout the test

- In this part of the exam, you answer questions from the examiner related to the same general topic as you discussed in Part 3. These questions develop the topic into more abstract areas.
- The examiner may ask you and your partner individual questions, or ask you to discuss a question together.
- You may be asked several questions, or only one or two.
- The examiner doesn't take part in the discussion, but starts it off by asking the questions. You and your partner then take over.

What is being tested?

This part of the test focuses on your ability to express and justify your opinions, agree/disagree and speculate on different aspects of the topic. The examiners mark you all through the test on your use of:

- **Grammar and vocabulary**. Use a range of structures and words and don't worry about making mistakes.
- **Discourse management**. Organise what you say clearly, using linking words.
- **Pronunciation**. This includes individual sounds and word stress, but the important thing is that you can be understood easily.
- **Interactive communication**. This means responding to and interacting with another person. In Part 4 this means interacting with your partner.

How do you do it?

BEFORE THE TASK

- The questions you will be asked are related to the topic you have just discussed in Part 3. Be ready to give your opinions and expand your answers.

DURING THE TASK

- Listen carefully to the examiner's questions. If you don't understand, you can ask them to repeat it, or ask your partner what they think.
- It's important to listen to your partner's answers. The examiner may ask you what you think about their opinion.
- You can agree or disagree with your partner, or add more details to something they've said. However, you shouldn't interrupt them.
- Remember that the questions are only asking for your opinion, and that there are no right answers. Express your opinions clearly, and give reasons for what you think. Invite your partner to contribute to the discussion.
- As this is the last part of the test, you can relax and really show what you can do!
- Don't forget to thank the examiners at the end of the test.

Are you exam-ready?

Did you …	
… listen to the questions carefully?	☐
… give detailed answers, with reasons for your opinions?	☐
… interact with your partner?	☐
… use a range of structures and vocabulary?	☐

Are you ready for Speaking Part 4? Identify an area to improve.

43

The **Cambridge English Assessment: C1 Advanced**, is set at Level C1 on the CEFR (Common European Framework of Reference) scale. The exam is made up of **four papers**, each testing a different area of ability in English. If a candidate achieves an A grade, they will receive a Certificate in Advanced English stating that they demonstrated ability at Level C2. If a candidate achieves a grade B or C, they will receive the Certificate in Advanced English at Level C1. If a candidate only achieves a B2 level, they may receive a Cambridge English Certificate stating that they demonstrated ability at Level B2.

Reading and Use of English: 1 hour 30 minutes
Writing: 1 hour 30 minutes
Listening: 40 minutes (approximately)
Speaking: 15 minutes for each pair (approximately)

All the questions are task-based. Rubrics (instructions) are important and should be read carefully. They set the context and give important information about the tasks.There is a separate answer sheet for recording answers for the Reading and Use of English and Listening papers.

Paper	Format	Task focus
Reading and Use of English Eight parts 56 questions	**Part 1:** multiple-choice cloze. A text with eight gaps, and four options to choose from for each gap.	**Part 1:** use of vocabulary including idioms, fixed phrases, complementation, phrasal verbs.
	Part 2: open cloze. A text with eight gaps. Candidates write the correct word in each gap.	**Part 2:** use of grammar, vocabulary and expressions.
	Part 3: word formation. A text with eight gaps and a word at the end of the line in which the gap appears. Candidates write the correct form of this word in the gap.	**Part 3:** vocabulary, particularly prefixes and suffixes, changes in form and compound words.
	Part 4: key-word transformations. Candidates rewrite six sentences using a given word, so that they mean the same as the original sentences.	**Part 4:** use of grammatical and lexical structure.
	Part 5: multiple choice. A text with six four-option, multiple-choice questions.	**Part 5:** identify details, such as opinion, attitude, tone, purpose, main idea, text organisation and features.
	Part 6: cross-text multiple matching. Four short texts followed by four multiple-matching questions	**Part 6:** comparing and contrasting opinions and attitudes across four different texts.
	Part 7: gapped text. One long text with six paragraphs missing. Candidates replace paragraphs from a choice of seven.	**Part 7:** reading to understand cohesion, coherence, organisation and text structure.
	Part 8: multiple matching. A text or several short texts with ten multiple-matching questions.	**Part 8:** reading to locate specific information, detail, opinion and attitude.
Writing Two tasks, carrying equal marks.	**Part 1:** compulsory task. Using given information to write an essay of 220–260 words.	**Part 1:** writing an essay with a discursive focus based on two points given in the task.
	Part 2: Producing one piece of writing of 220–260 words, from a letter/email, proposal, review or report.	**Part 2:** writing for a specific target reader and context, using appropriate layout and register.
Listening Four tasks 30 questions	**Part 1:** multiple-choice questions.Three short dialogues with interacting speakers, with two multiple-choice questions (three options) per extract.	**Part 1:** understanding gist, detail, function, agreement, speaker purpose, feelings, attitude, etc.
	Part 2: sentence completion. One monologue with eight sentences to complete with a word or short phrase.	**Part 2:** locating and recording specific information and stated opinions.
	Part 3: multiple-choice questions. A conversation between two or more speakers, with six four-option multiple- choice questions.	**Part 3:** understanding attitude and opinion.
	Part 4: multiple matching. A set of five short monologues on a theme.There are two tasks. In both tasks candidates match each monologue to one of eight prompts.	**Part 4:** identifying main points, gist, attitude and opinion.
Speaking Four tasks	**Part 1:** examiner-led conversation.	**Part 1:** general social and interactional language
	Part 2: individual long turn with visual and written prompts. Candidates talk about two pictures from a choice of three.	**Part 2:** organising discourse, speculating, comparing, giving opinions.
	Part 3: two-way collaborative task. Candidates discuss a question with 5 written prompts and then answer a second question on the topic.	**Part 3:** sustaining interaction, expressing and justifying opinions, evaluating and speculating, negotiating towards a decision, etc.
	Part 4: The examiner asks questions related to the Part 3 topic.	**Part 4:** expressing and justifying ideas and opinions, agreeing and disagreeing, speculating.